ADVANCES IN PUBLIC ECONOMICS: UTILITY, CHOICE AND WELFARE

THEORY AND DECISION LIBRARY

General Editors: W. Leinfellner (*Vienna*) and G. Eberlein (*Munich*)

Series A: Philosophy and Methodology of the Social Sciences

Series B: Mathematical and Statistical Methods

Series C: Game Theory, Mathematical Programming and Operations Research

Series D: System Theory, Knowledge Engineering an Problem Solving

SERIES C: GAME THEORY, MATHEMATICAL PROGRAMMING AND OPERATIONS RESEARCH

VOLUME 38

Scope: Particular attention is paid in this series to game theory and operations research, their formal aspects and their applications to economic, political and social sciences as well as to socio-biology. It will encourage high standards in the application of game-theoretical methods to individual and social decision making.

The titles published in this series are listed at the end of this volume.

ADVANCES IN PUBLIC ECONOMICS: UTILITY, CHOICE AND WELFARE

A Festschrift for Christian Seidl

Edited by

ULRICH SCHMIDT
University of Hannover, Germany

and

STEFAN TRAUB
University of Kiel, Germany

Springer

A C.I.P. Catalogue record for this book is available from the Library of Congress.

ISBN-13 978-1-4419-3820-6 (PB)
ISBN-13 978-0-387-25706-8 (e-book)

Published by Springer,
P.O. Box 17, 3300 AA Dordrecht, The Netherlands.
www.springeronline.com

Printed on acid-free paper

Contents

PREFACE

This *Festschrift* in honor of Christian Seidl combines a group of prominent authors who are experts in areas like public economics, welfare economic, decision theory, and experimental economics in a unique volume. Christian Seidl who has edited together with Salvador Barberà and Peter Hammond the *Handbook of Utility Theory* (appearing at Kluwer Academic Publishers/Springer Economics), has dedicated most of his research to utility and decision theory, social choice theory, welfare economics, and public economics. During the last decade, he has turned part of his attention to a research tool that is increasingly gaining in importance in economics: the laboratory experiment. This volume is an attempt to illuminate all facets of Christian Seidl's ambitious research agenda by presenting a collection of both theoretical and experimental papers on *Utility, Choice, and Welfare* written by his closest friends, former students, and much valued colleagues.

Christian Seidl was born on August 5, 1940, in Vienna, Austria. Beginning Winter term 1962/63, he studied Economics and Business Administration at the Vienna School of Economics (then "Hochschule für Welthandel"). 1966 he was awarded an MBA by the Vienna School of Economics and 1969 a doctoral degree in Economics. In October 1968 Christian became a research assistant at the Institute of Economics at the University of Vienna. 1973 he acquired his habilitation (right to teach) in Economics — supervised by Wilhelm Weber — from the Department of Law and Economics of the University of Vienna. He was awarded the Dr. Theodor-Körner Preis in 1970 and 1975 and the Leopold-Kunschak-Preis in 1974.

In July 1975 he was appointed a professorship in Economics at the University of Graz, Austria. He held the position as Director of the Institute of Public Economics there since its foundation in 1976. With effect of October 1986 he accepted a position as a Professor of Economics at the University of Kiel, Germany. Since then he has held the position as Director of the Institute of Public Finance and Social Policy (now merged with other institutes to the department of economics) at the University of Kiel. In addition he was elected as a Director of the Lorenz-von-Stein Institute for Administrative Sciences at the University of Kiel in 1998.

Since 1970 he has given lectures in public economics, social policy, and other fields at the Universities of Vienna, Linz, Graz, and Kiel. In 1983 he was elected as a corresponding member to the Austrian Academy of Sciences. He is a member of the Verein für Socialpolitik, of the American Economic Association, of the Econometric

Society, of the Royal Economic Society and of the European Economic Association. Christian Seidl has been a co-editor of the Journal of Economics/Zeitschrift für Nationalökonomie since 1980, of Economic Systems since 1988, and of History of Economic Ideas since 1992. He served as a member of the editorial board of the European Journal of Political Economy between 1983 and 1998. He was a visiting scholar at the Universities of Oxford, Stanford (several times), and British Columbia (Vancouver), at Queen's University (Kingston), and at Beer Sheva (Israel).

Between 1979 and 1985 he served as a member of the Austrian Tax Reform Commission, and between 1982 and 1986 he was a member of the extended managing committee of the Verein für Socialpolitik. He has acted as an expert for the Österreichischer Forschungsföderungsfonds, the Jubiläumsfonds der Österreichischen Nationalbank, the Deutsche Forschungsgemeinschaft, the Stiftung Volkswagenwerk, and the Fritz-Thyssen Stiftung.

Christian Seidl has published more than 120 articles in learned journals, proceedings volumes, and lexicographical works. He is the author of three books and has edited or co-edited 10 books in various fields of Economics. He regularly attends the congresses of the European Economic Association, the Econometric Society, the Verein für Socialpolitik, the Society for Social Choice and Welfare, the FUR Conferences, and other related meetings.

Christian Seidl has been our academic teacher since the early 90's. He not only supervised our dissertations and habilitations, but he also always lend a ready ear to our questions and concerns. Right from the start, he paid much attention to an international orientation of his students. Besides all his professional support, we are very grateful for the excellent work atmosphere we enjoyed at Christian Seidl's chair. We will never forget many enjoyable evenings (and hope for more) at the Seidls' home with excellent food and tons of good (red Bordeaux) wine. In particular, we would like to express our thanks to Christine Seidl, Christian's wife, who has been very effective in creating a familiar atmosphere.

Finally, we would like to thank all people who made this volume possible. First and foremost, we have to mention "our" authors Michael Ahlheim, Otwin Becker, Michele Bernasconi, the late Dieter Bös, Hans Wolfgang Brachinger, Valentino Dardanoni, Dirk Engelmann, Oliver Frör, Susanne Fuchs-Seliger, Ana Guerrero, Carmen Herrero, Veronika Grimm, Peter Hammond, John Hey, Martin Kolmar, Christos Koulovatianos, Johannes Leitner, Ulrike Leopold-Wildburger, Robin Pope, Carsten Schröder, Kotaro Suzumura, Walter Trockel, and John Weymark. We thank Herma Drees, Cathelijne van Herwaarden, and Elseliene van der Klooster from Springer Economics for their superb support. Philip Kornrumpf assisted us with some LaTex figures. Last but not least, we would like to thank our sponsors.

Kiel, March 2005

Ulrich Schmidt and Stefan Traub

COMPETITION, WELFARE, AND COMPETITION POLICY

KOTARO SUZUMURA
Hitotsubashi University & Fair Trade Commission of Japan

1. Introduction

The antimonopoly law and competition policy in Japan are currently under careful public scrutiny, and some parts of the law, as well as the procedures for its implementation, are in the process of careful redesign and deliberate social choice. As an economist in charge of the Competition Policy Research Center within the Fair Trade Commission of Japan, I would like to engage in the Confucian exercise of learning a lesson from the past in the controversial arena of welfare and competition in order to orient our future research on the theory of competition policy. In view of the rapid and drastic changes which are recently taking place in the global arena of competition, as well as the unprecedented progress in information technology which seems to be exerting a strong influence on the types and extents of sustainable competition, another maxim, to the effect that you can't put new wine in old bottles, may appear to be more appealing than the ancient Confucian maxim. Whether or not the accumulated wisdom in the past on welfare and competition may still be able to generate new revelation, or they cannot but fade out in the face of dazzlingly novel realities, can be determined only by the end of the day.

It was Harold Demsetz who began his lectures on economic, legal, and political dimensions of competition with the following thoughtful remark: "Competition occupies so important a position in economics that it is difficult to imagine economics as a social discipline without it. Stripped of competition, economics would consist largely of the maximizing calculus of an isolated Robinson Crusoe economy. Few economists complete a major work without referring to competition, and the classical economists found in competition a source of regularity and scientific propositions" (Demsetz, 1982, p. 1). Not many economists would dare to disagree with Demsetz on the central place he assigned to competition, yet there may remain a broad spectrum of disagreements among economists and, a *fortiori*, the public at large concerning the precise meaning of competition, the exact role competition plays as a decentralized resource allocation mechanism, and the social values attainable through the unconstrained working of competition. At one polar extreme of this broad spectrum lies the first conventional belief on the relationship between welfare and competition, which

U. Schmidt and S. Traub (eds.), Advances in Public Economics: Utility, Choice and Welfare, 1-15.

originates in Adam Smith's invisible hand thesis. It is held by many, if not all, orthodox economists. At the other polar extreme of the spectrum lies the second conventional belief, which is widely held among the public in general, and the government officials in charge of industrial policies in particular. It regards competition as a kind of necessary evil to be kept under deliberate public control for it to be at all socially useful. Let us begin our discourse with these two conventional beliefs on welfare and competition.

2. Conventional Belief among Economists: Invisible Hand Thesis

It was Adam Smith who praised the role of competition in Book 1, Chapter 2 of *The Wealth of Nations* by saying that producers as well as consumers, pursuing their own private incentives, are guided, as if by an invisible hand, to accomplish what is socially desirable in terms of the common good. Most, if not all, orthodox economists accepted Smith's invisible hand thesis, and applauded competition as a decentralized mechanism for socially good allocation of resources. For modern economists in the late 20th century, however, Smith's invisible hand thesis seemed to be too mythical to be left unvindicated. Thus, a modern vindication of Smith's invisible hand thesis was established in the mathematically sophisticated form of the fundamental theorems of welfare economics: with perfectly competitive and universal markets and provided that some environmental conditions including the non-existence of externalities, increasing returns, and public goods are satisfied, those resource allocations attainable at competitive equilibria are Pareto efficient, whereas any Pareto efficient resource allocation can be attained through the appropriate redistribution of initial resources and the use of perfectly competitive market mechanism.

A strong criticism against this interpretation of Smith's invisible hand thesis was raised by the Austrian school of economics, however, which is forcefully put forward by Friedrich von Hayek (1948, p. 92) as follows:

> It appears to be generally held that the so-called theory of "perfect competition" provides the appropriate model for judging the effectiveness of competition in real life and that, to the extent that real competition differs from that model, it is undesirable and even harmful.
>
> For this attitude there seems to me to exist very little justification. ... [W]hat the theory of perfect competition discusses has little claim to be called "competition" at all and that its conclusions are of little use as guides to policy. The reason for this seems to me to be that this theory throughout assumes that state of affairs already to exist which, according to the truer view of the older theory, the process of competition tends to bring about (or to approximate) and that, if the state of affairs assumed by the theory of perfect competition ever existed, it would not only deprive of their scope all the activities which the verb "to compete" describes but would make them virtually impossible.

It is against this background that the following restatement of the conventional belief among orthodox economists on the welfare effect of increasing competition due to William Baumol (1982, p. 2), one of the creators of the theory of contestable markets, is of particular relevance:

> [T]he standard analysis [of industrial organization] leaves us with the impression that there is a rough continuum, in terms of desirability of industry performance, ranging from unregulated pure monopoly as the pessimal [sic] arrangement to perfect competition as the ideal, with relative efficiency in resource allocation increasing monotonically as the number of firms expands.

This restatement of the first conventional belief can be theoretically tested in terms of a standard model of oligopolistic competition, which will enable us to check the sustainability of this conventional belief widely held among orthodox economists. Before actually engaging in such an exercise, however, let us turn to the second and opposite conventional belief which is widely held by the public in general, and the government officials in charge of industrial policies in particular.

3. Conventional Belief among the Public in General: Necessary Evil

The enthusiasm among orthodox economists in support of the invisible hand thesis, or its modern vindication in the form of the fundamental theorems of welfare economics, does not seem to be widely shared by the public in general. This disconsent seems to reflect itself in such expressions as "excessive competition" or "destructive competition." This expression sounds almost like a self-contradiction in terms to those who hold the first conventional belief. Nevertheless, it has been extensively used throughout Japan's modern economic history. Indeed, there is the second conventional belief, according to which a Confucian maxim to the effect that "to go beyond is as wrong as to fall short" applies above all to the use and value of competition as a resource allocation mechanism. An interesting testimony to the ubiquity of this belief is provided by Yukichi Fukuzawa, one of the most important and influential intellectuals at the dawn of modern Japan. He wrote vividly in his autobiography of his experience with an official in the Tokugawa Government before the Meiji Restoration of 1868 in these terms (Fukuzawa, 1899/1960, p. 190):

> I was reading Chambers's book on economics. When I spoke of the book to a certain high official in the treasury bureau one day, he became much interested and wanted me to show him the translation. ... I began translating it ... when I came upon the word "competition" for which there was no equivalent in Japanese, and I was obliged to use an invention of my own, *kyoso*, literally, "race-fight."
>
> When the official saw my translation, he appeared much impressed. Then he said suddenly, "Here is the word, 'fight.' What does it mean? It is such an unpeaceful word."
>
> "That is nothing new," I replied. "That is exactly what all Japanese merchants are doing. For instance, if one merchant begins to sell things cheap, his neighbor will try to sell them even cheaper. Or if one merchant improves his merchandise to attract more buyers, another will try to take the trade from him by offering goods of still better quality. Thus all merchants 'race and fight' and this is the way money values are fixed. This process is termed *kyoso* in the science of economics."
>
> "I understand. But don't you think there is too much effort in Western affairs?"
>
> "It isn't too much effort. It is the fundamentals of the world of commerce."
>
> "Yes, perhaps," went on the official. "I understand the idea, but that word, 'fight' is not conducive to peace. I could not take the paper with that word to the chancellor."

It is obvious that the government official could understand the instrumental value of competition at least to some extent, but he could not dare to confer the sacred status of the economic principle for managing a nation to the unpeaceful idea of competition.

The second conventional belief on the use and value of competition as a resource allocation mechanism persisted ever since. Indeed, there are numerous instances in which references were made to such expression as excessive competition or destructive competition in the public writings on the management of Japan's market economy. Suffice it to quote just one example. During the rapid growth period of the 1960s, one of the major concerns of MITI (the Ministry of International Trade and Industry) was the avoidance of "excessive competition in investment" in some class of manufacturing industries. It was alleged that excessive competition in investment tends to develop in industries characterized by heavy overhead capital, homogeneous products, and oligopoly, typical examples thereof being iron and steel, petroleum refining, petrochemicals, certain other chemicals, cement, paper and pulp, and sugar refining.

It may deserve recollection that the dictionary meanings of "excessive," viz., "extreme," "unreasonable," and "too much," connote in common "overshooting one or the other 'optimal' or 'reasonable' standard." Thus, the logical coherence of the second conventional belief can be properly examined only if we specify "one or the other 'optimal' or 'reasonable' standard." Before doing this logical exercise in the next section, however, it may not be out of place to cite a thoughtful observation made by Ryutaro Komiya (1975, p. 214) on the "excessive competition in investment" in the 1960s.

> The "excessive competition in investment" in an industry appears to me to depend on the following three factors: (i) the products of the industry are homogeneous, not differentiated; (ii) the size of productive capacity can be expressed readily by a single index such as monthly output in standard tons, daily refining capacity in barrels, number of spindles, etc; and (iii) such an index of productive capacity is used by the supervising *genkyoku* [viz. the government office having the primary responsibility for the industry in question] or by the industry association for administrative or allocative purposes. If, for example, import quotas for crude oil are allocated on the basis of refining capacity at a certain time, this encourages oil companies to expand their refining capacity beyond the limit justified by market conditions, in the hope of gaining both market shares and profits. That productive capacity has actually been used or referred to for administrative or allocative purposes in direct controls, administrative guidance, or cartelization, and the companies rightly or wrongly expect this to be repeated in the future, seems to be the real cause of the "excessive competition in investment." In industries where products are differentiated or made to order, so that marketing efforts are the determining factor in gaining market shares, or where it is difficult to express the size of productive capacity because of a wide variety of products (e.g., pharmaceuticals, machine tools), excessive investment has rarely been observed.

Thus, in Komiya's perception, the "excessive competition in investment," which is often cited as a reason why competition must be harnessed by deliberate public control, is in fact what triggered the "excessive competition in investment." Whether or not this paradoxical explanation can also apply to other instances of excessive competition should be carefully checked, but Komiya's observation seems to be rather widely supported by those who studied the Japanese experiences in the 1960s.

4. Competition and Welfare: Can Competition Ever be Excessive?

The first conventional belief on welfare and competition, which may be crystallized into "a widespread belief that increasing competition will increase welfare" (Stiglitz,

1981, p. 184), goes squarely counter to the second conventional belief, according to which competition may turn out to be socially excessive and/or destructive. A natural question, then, suggests itself. Can competition ever be excessive in a wide class of economies? Paying due attention to Komiya's empirical observation to the effect that the "excessive competition in investment" tends to develop in industries characterized by heavy overhead capital, homogeneous products, and oligopoly, consider an oligopolistic industry in which firms produce a single homogeneous product with large fixed cost. Suppose that the incumbent firms are currently earning higher-than-normal profits in the short-run Cournot–Nash equilibrium. If the first conventional belief, to the effect that "the relative efficiency in resource allocation increases monotonically as the number of firms expands," is indeed correct, the profit-induced new entry of firms into this profitable industry must improve economic welfare. By carefully examining whether or not this conjecture is valid, we can check if competition can ever be excessive.

With this theoretical scenario in mind, consider Figure 1 which describes the long-run Cournot–Nash equilibrium among identical firms. MM is the market demand curve for this industry and $R^N R^N$ is the residual demand curve for the individual firm. Individual firm's output and industry output, both in the long-run Cournot-Nash equilibrium are denoted, respectively, by $q^N(n_e)$ and $Q^N(n_e)$, where n_e denotes the number of firms in the long-run Cournot–Nash equilibrium. It is clear that $Q^N(n_e) = n_e q^N(n_e)$. To verify these facts, we have only to notice that the marginal cost curve crosses the marginal revenue curve, derived from the residual demand curve $R^N R^N$, at $q^N(n_e)$ and profits at $q^N(n_e)$ are exactly zero.

Suppose that the number of competing firms is lowered marginally from n_e to n. Since fewer firms are now sharing the same market demand curve, the residual demand curve for an individual firm must shift up ro $R^S R^S$, so that the new Cournot–Nash equilibrium, denoted by $q^N(n)$ and $Q^N(n) := nq^N(n)$, must satisfy $q^N(n_e) < q^N(n)$ and $Q^N(n_e) > Q^N(n)$. It is clear that this decrease in the number of firms from n_e to n must exert two conflicting effects on social welfare, which is measured in terms of the net market surplus, viz. the sum of consumer's surplus and producer's surplus. The first is its effect on the allocative efficiency due to the concomitant decrease in consumer's surplus, which results from the increase in equilibrium price from $p^N(n_e)$ to $p^N(n)$. In Figure 1, this negative effect is measured by the area $Ap^N(n)p^N(n_e)B$. The second is its effect on the production efficiency due to the further exploitation of residual scale economies, which results from the induced increase in individual equilibrium output from $q^N(n_e)$ to $q^N(n)$. In Figure 1, this positive effect is measured by the area $Ap^N(n)c^N(n)D$. The net effect on social welfare is given by the difference between these two effects, viz., the area $Cp^N(n_e)c^N(n)D$ less the area ABC. Because the latter area must be a higher order infinitesimal than the former area, the net effect turns out to be positive, vindicating that a marginal decrease in the number of firms increases welfare. In other words, the long-run Cournot–Nash equilibrium number of firms, n_e, is socially excessive at the margin. Although this theorem is verified in this paper by means of a simple geometric device, a full analytical proof is available, e.g., in Kotaro Suzumura and Kazuharu Kiyono (1987), whereas several generalizations

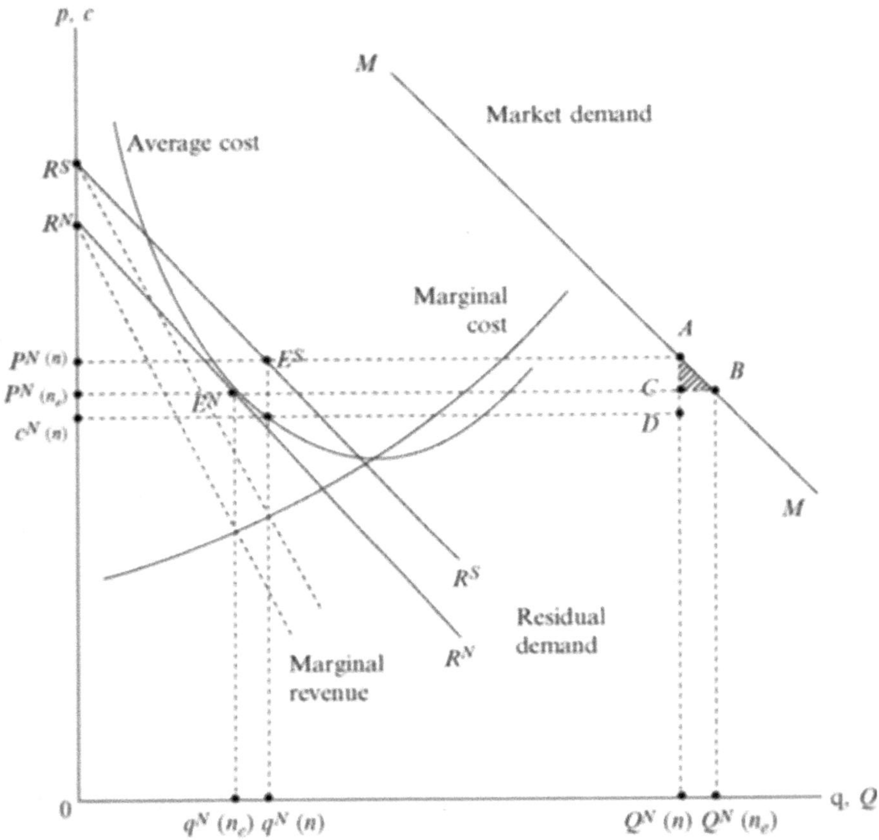

Figure 1. Excess entry theorem at the margin.

of the excess entry theorem are presented in Masahiro Okuno–Fujiwara and Kotaro Suzumura (1993), and Kotaro Suzumura (1995).

Contrary to the first conventional belief widely held among orthodox economists, we have thus demonstrated that there is a clear welfare-theoretic sense in which competition can be socially excessive. As a corollary to this proposition, we must be ready to admit in principle that the "regulation by enlightened, but not omnipotent, regulators could in principle achieve greater efficiency than deregulation" (Panzer, 1980, p. 313). Note, however, that this observation, which is valid in itself, does not offhandedly justify that the second conventional belief should be supported in rejection of the first conventional belief. In other words, the excess entry theorem at the margin does not necessarily provide a rationalization of the actual intervention by the down-to-earth regulators into the industrial organization of specific sectors. The reason for this verdict is worthwhile to spell out in some detail. In the first place, restricting competition to control excessive competition in the sense we have identified boils down to the protection of producer's benefits at the expense of consumer's benefits. Unless there is a clear social agreement that the producer's benefits should be given priority over the consumer's benefits, it seems hard to justify such a lopsided treatment between the two components of social welfare, viz., net social surplus. Nevertheless, there is a regrettable tendency towards the implementation of producer-oriented regulation for the reason which Vilfredo Pareto (1927, p. 379) uncovered well ahead of his own time: "A protectionist measure provides large benefits to a small number of people, and causes a very great number of consumers a slight loss. This circumstance makes it easier to put a protectionist measure into practice."

Although the argument in support of the meaningful sense in which we can talk about the "social excessiveness of competition" is useful and revealing, we should be carefully on guard so as not to be exploited by those who have too much vested interest to leave matters to be determined by free and impersonal force of competition. The following acute warning by Avinash Dixit (1984, p. 15) seems to be worthwhile to keep always in mind:

> Vested interests want protection, and relaxation of antitrust activity, for their own selfish reasons. They will be eager to seize upon any theoretical arguments that advance such policies in the general interest. Distortion and misuse of the arguments is likely, and may result in the emergence of policies that cause aggregate welfare loss while providing private gains to powerful special groups.

To conclude this section on the possible excessiveness of competition from the welfare-theoretic viewpoint, let us remind ourselves that the validity of excess entry theorem as well as its various variants hinge squarely on the three basic assumptions: single homogeneous product, large fixed cost, and oligopolistic competition. If any one of these assumptions fails to be true, the excess entry theorem, or the variant thereof, is easily invalidated. For example, if the industry is producing a wide spectrum of differentiated commodities, the entry of a new firm, more often than not, accompanies a further widening of the product spectrum, which results in the expansion of the freedom of choice on the part of consumers. With the addition of this new channel through which firm entry can exert influence on social welfare, the excess entry theorem may well fail to apply to the industry in question. The important moral is that the theoretical verdicts on the welfare effects of competition hinge squarely on the specification of industry characteristics and types of competition, so that there exists no universally applicable conventional wisdom in this slippery arena of welfare and competition.

Thus, the general moral of our exploration on welfare and competition seems to be as follows. Just as "[d]emocracy is the worst form of government except all those other forms that have been tried from time to time [Winston Churchill's speech in the House of Commons (November 1947)]," competition may be the worst form of economic mechanism except all those other forms that have been tried from time to time. We should add that the task of competition policy is precisely to make the functioning of this imperfect mechanism better than otherwise.

5. Consequential Value versus Procedural Value of Competition

There is one more aspect of our theoretical analysis of excessive competition which is in fact quite insidious. As Kenneth Arrow (1987, p. 124) once observed, "[e]conomic or any other social policy has consequences for the many and diverse individuals who make up the society or economy. It has been taken for granted in virtually all economic policy discussions since the time of Adam Smith, if not before, that alternative policies should be judged on the basis of their consequences for individuals." There is no way of denying that almost all, if not literally all, economists are consequentialist in the sense of Arrow, viz., they are ready to judge the goodness of economic mechanisms and/or economic policies on the informational basis of their consequences. As a matter of fact, their evaluative perspective is even narrower than *consequentialism* as such. This is because, more often than not, they are willing to judge the goodness of consequences of an economic mechanism and/or economic policy vis-à-vis another mechanism and/or policy exclusively in terms of the welfare which accrues to "the many and diverse individuals who make up the society or economy." As a matter of fact, *welfarist-consequentialism*, so-called, or *welfarism* for short, permeates through the mainstream of contemporary welfare economics and social choice theory. It is clear that the excess entry theorem in the previous section is no exception to this general observation.

Recent years have witnessed an upsurge of criticisms against welfarism by some of the leading moral and/or political philosophers such as John Rawls (1971) and Ronald Dworkin (2001), as well as the leading scholar in welfare economics and social choice theory such as Amartya Sen (1985, 1999). They commonly emphasized the importance of non-welfaristic features of consequences, or even the non-consequentialist features, of economic mechanisms and/or economic policies in their evaluative exercises. Those alternative viewpoints which are emphasized along with the welfaristic viewpoint include procedural fairness, richness of opportunities, responsibility and compensation, and liberty and rights. In our present context of welfare and competition, however, there is even more classic criticism against welfarism than these recent criticisms by moral and/or political philosophers and normative economists. It was in fact voiced by one of the most celebrated neoclassical economists, viz., John Richard Hicks (1981, pp. 137–140):

> Why is it ... that anti-monopoly legislation (and litigation) get so little help, as they evidently do, from the textbook [economic] theory? Surely the answer is that the main issues of principle — security on the one hand, freedom and equity on the other, the issues that lawyers, and law-makers, can understand — have got left right out. They cannot be adequately translated, even into terms of surpluses. ... To put the same point another way. The liberal, or non-interference, principles of the classical ... economics were not, in the first place, economic principles; they were an application to economics of principles that were thought to apply over a much wider field. ... As the nineteenth century wore on, the increasing specialization of economics led to an increasing emphasis on the economic argument. Then it was discovered — it was rightly discovered — that the economic case for non-interference is riddled with exceptions: exceptions which may well have become more important in fact in the course of technological progress, and which certainly became of greater importance as the demands which were made on the economic system, in the direction of stability as well as of growth, became more exacting. Accordingly, since the other side of the case which had at one time been the more important side, had been so largely forgotten, what had begun as an economic argument for non-interference became an

> economic argument for the opposite. I do not question that on its own assumptions that argument ... was very largely right.
>
> What I do question is whether we are justified in forgetting, as completely as most of us have done, the other side of the argument. Not that I wish to regard that 'non-economic' side as overriding; all that I claim for it is a place, and a regular place. I do not suppose that if we gave it this due attention, we should find ourselves subscribing ... to all the liberal principles of a century ago. ... Neither side should give way to the other; but there is no reason why there should not be scope for marginal adjustments, in great things as well as small. ...
>
> I have accordingly no intention, in abandoning Economic Welfarism, of falling into the 'fiat libertas, ruat caelum' which some latter-day liberals seem to see as the only alternative. What I do maintain is that the liberal goods are goods; that they are values which, however, must be weighed up against other values.

To illuminate the Hicksian proposal of non-welfaristic value of economic mechanism and/or economic policy in concrete terms, it may be worthwhile to cite a salient example of the non-welfaristic or procedural evaluation of the competitive resource allocation mechanism. It was Milton Friedman (1962, p. 21) who emphasized the intrinsic value of competitive market mechanism as follows:

> No one who buys bread knows whether the wheat from which it is made was grown by a Communist or a Republican, by a constitutionist or a Facist, or, for that matter, by a Negro or a white. This illustrates how an impersonal market separates economic activities from political views and protects men from being discriminated against in their economic activities for reasons that are irrelevant to their productivity — whether these reasons are associated with their views or their color.

To bring this important point into clearer relief, Friedman (1962, pp. 109–110) recapitulated it in more general terms as follows:

> [A] free market separates economic efficiency from irrelevant characteristics. ... In consequence, the producer of wheat is in a position to use resources as effectively as he can, regardless of what the attitudes of the community may be toward the color, the religion, or other characteristics of the people he hires. Furthermore, ... there is an economic incentive in a free market to separate economic efficiency from other characteristics of the individual. A businessman or an entrepreneur who expresses preferences in his business activities that are not related to productive efficiency is at a disadvantage compared to other individuals who do not. Such an individual is in effect imposing higher costs on himself than are other individuals who do not have such preferences. Hence, in a free market they will tend to drive him out.

It may deserve emphasis that Friedman's argument in favor of competitive market mechanism is non-welfaristic in nature, as his praise for it is based on the procedural fairness it confers to the market participants. However, this is not to deny the fact that his argument does not neglect consequences altogether, as he also invokes the fact that those producers who discriminate individuals for any reason other than their productivity would have to face dire consequences.

A general moral seems to be the following. In evaluating the social value of competition, and in designing and implementing competition policy in search for the better functioning of competitive market mechanism, we should pay due attention to procedural considerations as well as to consequential considerations. People seem prepared to accept this extended viewpoint and make regularly the following type of reasoning. Let x and y be the consequences of economic mechanisms m^1 and m^2, respectively. According to Mr. A's judgements, having x through m^1 is better than having y through m^2, but Ms. B may judge otherwise. Indeed, one is making such judgements when one says that it is better to obtain whatever commodity bundle which the free market enables one to choose than to be assigned another commodity bundle by the central planning board, even when the latter bundle contains more of all commodities than the former. One is also making such judgements when one asks for more bread, more wine and more whatnot, irrespective of how these commodities are made available to him. In the former case, the resource allocation mechanisms have clear lexicographic priority over the consequences emerging from these mechanisms, whereas, in the latter case, the consequences are given lexicographic priority over the mechanisms. Although such extreme lexicographic judgements are not at all inconceivable, it is presumably more realistic to think that people care not only about the intrinsic values of resource allocation mechanisms, but also about their instrumental values in bringing about desirable consequences, and they are prepared to strike a balance between these two rival considerations. This point should not be forgotten in the design, implementation, and evaluation of competition policies.

6. Boundary between Private Sphere and Public Sphere

Let us proceed from the analysis of competition to the analysis of competition policy. According to our perception, the economic analysis of competition policy should consist of the following three parts: (1) Drawing the boundary line between the private sphere and the public sphere; (2) Designing and implementing the fair market game; and (3) Coordinating domestic market games in the globalized world economy through the design and implementation of an interface mechanism. In the following two sections, let us list some of the basic agendas for the economic analysis of competition policy along this scenario.

How to distinguish the private sphere, over which private agents should be basically free to compete with each other for the promotion of their own private objectives, from the public sphere, over which the government authority is within its jurisdiction to take public actions by itself, or regulate the actions of private agents in accordance with the socially agreed public objectives, is a deep and old issue; it can be traced back at least to John Locke and John Stuart Mill in England, and Benjamin Constant and Alexis de Tocqueville in France. Although the recognition that "a frontier must be drawn between the area of private life and that of public authority" (Berlin, 1969, p. 124) is certainly not new, many attempts to provide a principle for drawing a frontier to this effect proved to be rather futile. Such an attempt goes all the way back to Mill's *On Liberty* (Mill, 1859/1977, p. 276), where he posed this issue in his idiosyncratic manner: "What ... is the rightful limit to the sovereignty of the individual over himself? Where does the authority of society begin? How much of human life should be assigned to individuality, and how much to society?" Mill's own answer to this crucial problem was a famous, but deceptively simple, principle: "Each will receive its proper share, if each has that which more particularly concerns it. To individuality should belong the part of life in which it is chiefly the individual that is interested; to society, the part which chiefly interests society." Unfortunately, Mill's "simple principle" to this effect seems to have posed more problems than it settled, as "[m]en are largely interdependent, and no man's activity is so completely private as never to obstruct the lives of others in any way. 'Freedom for the pike is death for the minnows'; the liberty of some must depend on the restraint of others (Berlin, 1969, p. 124)." These difficulties become all the more serious when our focus is shifted to the freedom of competition for private enterprises. It is no wonder that the design and implementation of the fair game of competition have been the subject of harsh dispute.

Suppose, for the sake of argument, that a proper boundary line between the private sphere and the public sphere could be somehow drawn. Even then, it does not follow that the government authority in charge of competition policy could relax and be indifferent to what private agents — individuals and private enterprises — would do within their respective private spheres for at least two reasons.

In the first place, the government authority has the major task of designing the fair market game, which private agents are entitled to participate and play on their own initiatives, and seeing to it that all the participants faithfully observe their obligation of fair play. If there are infringements on the obligation of fair play, the government authority in charge of competition policy should rectify this divergence from the proper play of the game. It is to cope with this major task efficiently and effectively that the competition policy authority must legislate the competition laws, monitor the performance of market participants and, if need be, enforce the fair play of the competitive market game.

In the second place, drawing the boundary line between the private sphere and the public sphere, as well as the design of the fair market game, cannot be done once and for all. Quite to the contrary, depending on the state of technology, the boundary between the private sphere and the public sphere, as well as the structure of fair market game, must be subject to incessant review, and constant effort must be made for further improvement on the mechanism design for the promotion of public welfare. To lend concreteness to what we are discussing, let us cite a couple of examples. (1) There are many cases of regulatory reforms in Japan and elsewhere, which transformed the traditional state monopoly of, say, telecommunications industry by a public corporation into the mixture of liberalized competitive segments, where one of the competitors is the privatized ex-public corporation, on the one hand, and regulated segments with residual natural monopoly elements, on the other. With the further development of technology, however, even the regulated segments with residual natural monopoly factors elements might be subject to gradual transfer to the competitive segments. The design and implementation of the fair market game must also adjust themselves to the need of this gradual process of regulatory reforms. (2) Friedman's emphasis on the procedural fairness of competitive market mechanism may be under serious threat by the rapidly developing devices of electric money. It should be recalled that the Friedmanian protection of individuals from being discriminated against for reasons unrelated to their productivity is closely connected with the so-called "anonymity of money"; it is because no one can be traced back after the completion of market exchange of commodities and/or services for money that individuals are warranted to be free from being discriminated against in the competitive market mechanism. Electric money, which is expected to be effective against such unlawful acts as money laundering and fraudulent product quality, may undermine one of the important procedural merits of the competitive market mechanism. In order to maintain the procedural fairness of the competitive market mechanism in the face of otherwise beneficial technological development, those who are in charge of designing and implementing the fair market game may have to confront a totally different ball game.

Thus, the story of competition policy is not like a fairy tale in which prince and princes marry, and then live happily forever; it is more like Alice's *Through the Looking-Glass* (Lewis Carroll, 1939, p. 152), where "it takes all the running *you* can do, to keep in the same place. If you want to get somewhere else, you must run at least twice as fast as that!"

7. Interface Mechanism among Domestic Competition Policies

An important fact about competition policy is that there are not many countries which have competition laws rooted deeply in the spontaneous evolution of domestic rules and conventions. In the case of Japan, which has the second longest history in the world and next only to the USA in this arena, for example, the original antimonopoly law was transplanted from the American soil during the post World War II occupation period as an integral part of the economic democratization of Japan. It is true that several rounds of revisions, which took place after the end of the occupation period in 1952, were intended to strike a balance between the rules transplanted from the American soil and the indigenous sense of "fair" competition. Nevertheless, it remains to be the case that the formal contents of Japan's antimonopoly law is not that different from the American prototype law and, for that matter, the EU model. The difference, if any, lies mostly in the administrative methods of implementation. There are room as well as reason for talking about harmonization of domestic competition policies in this arena.

Recollect that international harmonization of domestic rules — including domestic competition laws and policies — requires that the domestic rules of the game prevailing in the country A must be in basic harmony with those prevailing in the country B. Certainly, it has no root in the two basic principles of the GATT/WTO regime, viz. the *principle of most favored nation treatment* and the *principle of national treatment*. The former principle requires the member countries to accord the most favorable tariff and regulatory treatment, given to the product of any one of the trading partners, to all other member countries at the time of import or export of like products; the latter principle requires the member countries not to accord any discriminatory treatment between imports and like domestic products. As far as the same domestic rules are applied undiscriminatingly by each member country to domestic and foreign agents, and to domestic and foreign products, there is no infringement on the two basic principles of the GATT/WTO regime. Why, then, don't we retain the domestic rules of the game, and leave matters to be settled by international competition among alternative economic mechanisms? What is wrong with this mutual recognition approach? This question is worth asking, as it seems to be rooted in the classical dictum: "When in Rome, do as the Romans do."

The answer seems to depend crucially on the type of harmonization we choose for examination. It is certainly irrational and unreasonable to require the convergence of domestic rules of other countries to those domestic rules prevailing in the hegemonic country. However, this seems to be more a straw man model of harmonization, whose sole function is to be ridiculed and shot down, than a real model to be seriously discussed. More sensible approach to harmonization is to coordinate domestic rules of the member countries by means of a cleverly designed and implemented interface mechanism, which allows idiosyncratic domestic rules to function side by side harmoniously. Just as computers of the different make can collaborate harmoniously if only they are coordinated by an appropriate interface mechanism, the domestic rules of different countries can collaborate at least in principle.

This may be easier said than done, but there seems to be essentially no real alternative to this piecemeal approach to international harmonization with a deliberately designed and collectively adopted interface mechanism.

8. Concluding Remarks

Instead of summarizing the whole contents of this paper, let us conclude with a brief recapitulation of its main messages.

1. There are two conventional beliefs concerning the relationship between social welfare and market competition. According to the first conventional belief, the more competition will there be, the better will be the welfare performance of market competition. According to the second conventional belief, the Confucian maxim to the effect that "to go beyond is as wrong as to fall short" applies to the welfare effect of market competition too. We have argued that either one of these two conventional beliefs, widely though they are respectively held, may turn out to be wrong upon careful scrutiny, depending on the types of market competition and the conditions under which the industry is operated. The design and implementation of competition policy should pay due attention to this subtle relationship which holds between social welfare and market competition.
2. Even when it is theoretically verifiable that "[r]egulation by enlightened, but not omnipotent, regulators could in principle achieve greater efficiency than deregulation," this does not in itself justify the intervention by the down-to-earth government. The social cost of regulation should be carefully gauged and weighed against the social benefit of regulation. In doing so, it is also of crucial importance to pay due attention to the distributional implications of regulation.
3. In evaluating the social performance of regulation versus competition, we should pay due attention not only to the welfaristic effects and/or the non-welfaristic effects on consequences, but also to the non-consequentialist effects thereof as exemplified by the procedural fairness of regulation versus market competition, the

richness of opportunities thereby opened, and the liberty and rights of individuals and private enterprises under these social contrivances.

4. The main functions of competition policy consists of (i) drawing the separating line between the private sphere and the public sphere, (ii) designing and implementing the fair market game, and (iii) coordinating the domestic market games through the clever design and implementation of international interface mechanisms. Although harsh disputes occurred on the international harmonization of domestic rules and conventions, the shift of focus from the unrealistic convergence of domestic rules of many countries to those rules prevailing in the hegemonic country to the coordination of domestic rules by means of a cleverly designed international interface mechanism, thereby allowing idiosyncratic domestic rules to function together harmoniously, seems to be not only workable but also sensible.

Acknowledgements

An earlier version of this paper was delivered as the Keynote Speech at the International Symposium on Competition Policy, November 20, 2003, which was organized by the Competition Policy Research Center within the Fair Trade Commission of Japan. Thanks are due to Professors Kenneth Arrow, Timothy Besley, Akira Goto, Kazunori Ishiguro, Motoshige Itoh, Ryutaro Komiya, Masahiro Okuno–Fujiwara, Amartya Sen, Paul Samuelson, and John Vickers, with whom I had several discussions on the topics related to this paper. Needless to say, they should not be held responsible for any opinion expressed in this paper.

References

Arrow, K. J. 1987. "Arrow's Theorem", in: J. Eatwell, M. Milgate, and P. Newman (eds.): *The New Palgrave: A Dictionary of Economics*, Vol. 1, London: Macmillan, 124–126.

Baumol, W. J. 1982. "Contestable Markets: An Uprising in the Theory of Industrial Structure," *American Economic Review* 72, 1–15.

Berlin, I. 1969. *Four Essays on Liberty*, Oxford: Clarendon Press.

Carroll, L. 1939. *The Complete Works of Lewis Carroll*, London: The Nonesuch Press.

Demsetz, H. 1982. *Economic, Legal, and Political Dimensions of Competition*, Amsterdam: North–Holland.

Dixit, A. 1984. "International Trade Policy for Oligopolistic Industries," Supplement to *Economic Journal* 94, 1–16.

Dworkin, R. 2000. *Sovereign Virtue: The Theory and Practice of Equality*, Cambridge, Mass.: Harvard University Press.

Friedman, M. 1962. *Capitalism and Freedom*, Chicago: The University of Chicago Press.

Fukuzawa, Y. 1960. *The Autobiography of Fukuzawa Yukichi*, translated by E. Kiyooka with an Introduction by S. Koizumi, Tokyo: The Hokuseido Press.

Hayek. F. A. 1948. "The Meaning of Competition," in his *Individualism and Economic Order*, Chicago: The University of Chicago Press, 92–106.

Hicks, J. R. 1981. "A Manifest", in his *Wealth and Welfare*, Vol. I of *Collected Essays on Economic Theory*, Oxford: Basil Blackwell, 135–141.

Komiya, R. 1975. "Planning in Japan", in M. Bornstein (ed.): *Economic Planning: East and West*, Cambridge: Ballinger, 189–227.

Mill, J. S. 1859/1977. *On Liberty*, London: Parker. Reprinted in: *The Collected Works of John Stuart Mill XVIII*, ed. by J. M. Robson, Toronto: University of Toronto Press.
Okuno–Fujiwara, M., and K. Suzumura. 1993. "Symmetric Cournot Oligopoly and Economic Welfare: A Synthesis", *Economic Theory* 3, 43–59.
Panzer, J. C. 1980. "Regulation, Deregulation and Economic Efficiency: The Case of CAB", *American Economic Review: Papers and Proceedings* 70, 311–315.
Pareto, V. 1927. *Manual of Political Economy*, New York: A. M. Kelley.
Rawls, J. 1971. *A Theory of Justice*, Cambridge, Massachusetts: Harvard University Press.
Sen, A. K. 1985. *Commodities and Capabilities*, Amsterdam: North–Holland.
Sen, A. K. 1999. *Development as Freedom*, New York: Alfred A. Knopf.
Stiglitz, J. E. 1981. "Potential Competition May Reduce Welfare", *American Economic Review: Papers and Proceedings* 71, 184–189.
Suzumura, K. 1995. *Competition, Commitment, and Welfare* Oxford: Clarendon Press.
Suzumura, K., and K. Kiyono. 1987. "Entry Barriers and Economic Welfare", *Review of Economic Studies* 54, 157–167.

Kotaro Suzumura
Institute of Economic Research
Hitotsubashi University
Naka 2–1, Kunitachi
Tokyo 186
Japan
suzumura@ier.hit-u.ac.jp

IN WHAT SENSE IS THE NASH SOLUTION FAIR?

WALTER TROCKEL*
Universität Bielefeld

1. Introduction

An abstract two-person bargaining problem is a pair (T, d) where $T \subset \mathbb{R}^2$ and $d \in T$ with the following properties:

- T closed, convex, comprehensive (i.e. $x \in T \Longrightarrow \{x\} - \mathbb{R}^2_+ \subset T$)
- $T \cap \mathbb{R}^2_{++} \neq \emptyset$
- $d \in int(T \cap \mathbb{R}^2_+)$.

The interpretation is that two players have to agree on a joint payoff vector in T, the ith coordinate for the ith player, $i = 1, 2$ in order to receive these payoffs or, else, to fall back to the status quo point d.

Assuming, that this scenario results as the image under the two players' concave von Neumann-Morgenstern utility functions on an underlying economic or social scenario, this model is determined only up to affine transformations of both players' payoffs. Accordingly, d is sometimes assumed to be $0 \in \mathbb{R}^2$ (0-normalization), sometimes in addition it is assumed that $max_{x \in T}\ x_i = 1, i = 1, 2$ $(0-1-1$-normalization). Moreover, every part of T not in $\mathbb{R}^2_+$ is skipped representing the fact that the interest focusses only on individually rational payoff vectors. The resulting $S \subset \mathbb{R}^2_+$ is then a $0 - 1 - 1$-normalized bargaining situation, whose boundary is often assumed to be smooth.

The Nash bargaining solution has been introduced by John F. Nash (1953) as a solution for two person bargaining games. Nash already presented three approaches to the solution that are methodologically and in spirit quite different. One is the definition of the Nash solution as the maximizer of the Nash product, i.e. the product of the two players' payoffs. This might be seen as maximizing some social planners' preference relation on the set of players' utility allocations. So whatever fairness is represented by the Nash solution it should be hidden in this planners' preferences.

---

* I am happy to be able to contribute with this article to the honoring of Christian Seidl, a highly esteemed colleague.

U. Schmidt and S. Traub (eds.), Advances in Public Economics: Utility, Choice and Welfare, 17-30.

The second approach of Nash is the one via axioms for the bargaining solution. This approach became quite popular later on in the literature on cooperative games and, in particular bargaining games. It turned out that several important alternative bargaining solutions, like the Nash, Kalai-Smorodinsky, Perles-Maschler or Raiffa solution, coincide on hyperplane bargaining games where they may be characterized by the three axioms of cardinal invariance, Pareto-efficiency and symmetry (or anonymity) but differ by specific fourth axioms on general bargaining games. Nash's fourth axiom, the *Independence of Irrelevant Alternatives (IIA)* may be replaced by *consistency* due to Lensberg (1988). So any fairness specific to the Nash solution might be hidden in these alternative axioms.

The third approach of Nash was via his simple demand game and built the first attempt in the Nash program. The Nash Program is a research agenda whose goal it is to provide a non-cooperative equilibrium foundation for axiomatically defined solutions of cooperative games. This program was initiated by John Nash in his seminal papers *Non-cooperative Games* in the *Annals of Mathematics*, 1951, and *Two-Person Cooperative Games* in *Econometrica*, 1953. The term *Nash Program* was introduced by Binmore (1987). The original passages due to Nash that built the basis for this terming are in fact quite short.

The Nash program tries to link two different ways of solving games. The first one is non-cooperative. No agreements on outcomes are enforceable. Hence players are totally dependent on their own strategic actions. They try to find out what is best given, the other players are rational and do the same. In this context the Nash equilibrium describes a stable strategy profile where nobody would have an interest to unilaterally deviate. Nevertheless there is an implicit institutional context. The strategy sets define implicitly what choices are not allowed, those outside the strategy sets. The payoff functions reflect which strategies in the interplay with others' strategies are better or worse. It is not said explicitly who grants payoffs and how the physical process of paying them out is organized. But there is some juridical context with some enforcement power taken for granted. There is no interpersonal comparison of payoffs involved in the determination of good strategies. Each player only compares his different strategies contingent on the other players' different strategy choices. As applications in oligopoly show, institutional restrictions of social or economic scenarios are mapped into strategy sets and payoff functions, thereby lending them an institutional interpretation. Yet, totally different scenarios may considerably be modelled by the same non-cooperative game, say in strategic form. This demonstrates clearly the purely payoff based evaluation of games. Payoffs usually are interpreted as reflecting monetary or utility payments. Associated physical states or allocations occur only in applications and may be different in distinct applications of the same game.

The second way to solve a game is the cooperative one via axioms as first advocated by Nash (1953). Again the legal framework is only implicit. Yet, now not only obedience to the rules is assumed to be enforceable but even contracts. Mutual gains are in reach now as it becomes possible by signing a contract to commit himself to certain behavior. In this context it is the specific payoff configuration which is of interest rather than the strategy profile that would generate it. In this framework it is reasonable, therefore, to neglect the strategic options and concentrate on the feasible payoff configurations or utility allocations on which the players possibly could agree by signing a contract. Again the formal model does not specify the process by which physical execution of a contract is performed. Again it is the payoff space rather than some underlying social scenario on which the interest rests except in applications of game theory.

In contrast to the non-cooperative approach now players *are* interested in what other players receive. Although utilities or payoff units for different players are in general not considered comparable typically there are tradeoffs that count. The axioms that are fundamental in this context reflect ideas of fairness, equity, justness that do not play a role in the non-cooperative model. But a process of negotiation with the goal to find an agreement makes it necessary for each player to somehow judge the coplayers' payoffs. But the axioms are in a purely welfaristic context. If very different underlying models lead to the same cooperative game in coalitional form it is only the solution in terms of payoff vectors that is relevant. And this determines in any application what underlying social or physical state is distinguished. It becomes irrelevant in the axiomatic cooperative approach which are the institutional details. Important are only the feasible utility allocations.

Now, why could it be interesting to have a non-cooperative strategic game and a cooperative game in coalitional form distinguishing via its equilibrium or solution, respectively, the same payoff vector? According to Nash the answer is that each approach *"helps to justify and clarify the other"*.

The equality of payoffs in both approaches seems to indicate that the institutional specifities represented by the strategic model are not so restrictive as to prevent the cooperative solution. Also the payoff function appears then to reflect in an adequate way the different axioms. On the other hand payoff combinations not adequate under the solution concept cannot be strategically stable. So the equivalence of both approaches seems to indicate that the strategic model from the point of view of social desirability is restrictive enough but not too restrictive. This abstract relation has different consequences if one is in one of the two different enforceability contexts. If we cannot enforce contracts the equivalence of two approaches means that this is not a real drawback, as we can reach the same via rational strategic interaction (at least in situations of games with a unique equilibrium). If, on the other hand, we are in a world where contracts are enforceable, we may use the equivalence of a suitable strategic approach as additional arguments for the payoff vectors distinguished by the solution. Therefore, results in the Nash program give players valuable insights into the interrelation between institutionally determined non-cooperative strategic interaction and social desirability based on welfaristic evaluation.

There is not, however, any focus on *decentralization* in the context of the Nash program simply because there is no entity like a center or planner. There are just players.

Nash's own first contribution to the Nash Program (1953) consists in his analysis of a game, the *demand game* and the so called *smoothed demand game* where he looked at the limiting behavior of non-cooperative equilibria of a sequence of smoothed versions of the demand game. Here the amount of smoothing approaches zero, and, hence the sequence approximates the demand game. While the original "simple" demand game has a continuum of equilibria, a fact which makes it useless for a non-cooperative foundation of the Nash solution, Nash argued that the Nash solution was the only necessary limit of equilibria of the smoothed games. Rigorous analyzes for his procedure have been provided much later by Binmore (1987), van Damme (1986) and Osborne and Rubinstein (1990).

A second quite different approximate non-cooperative support for the Nash solution is provided by Rubinstein's (1982) model of sequential alternate offers bargaining. Binmore, Rubinstein and Wolinsky (1986) showed in two different models with discounted time that the weaker the discounting is the more closely approximates the subgame perfect Nash equilibrium an asymmetric Nash bargaining solution. Only if subjective probabilities of breakdown of negotiations or the lengths of reaction times to the opponents' proposals are symmetric it is the symmetric Nash solution which is approximately supported. Again, in the frictionless limit model one does not get support of the Nash solution by a unique equilibrium. Rather every individually rational payoff vector corresponds to some subgame perfect equilibrium.

An exact support rather than only an approximate one of the Nash solution is due to Howard (1992). He proposes a fairly complex 10 stages extensive form game whose unique subgame perfect equilibrium payoff vector coincides with the bargaining solution.

Like in Rubinstein's model and in contrast to Nash framework Howard's game is based on underlying outcome space. Here this is a set of lotteries over some finite set on which players have utility functions. Although the analysis of the game can be performed without explicit consideration of the outcome space it is this underlying structure that allows it to look at the outcome associated with a subgame perfect equilibrium and thereby interpret Howard's support result as a mechanism theoretic implementation of some Nash social choice rule in subgame perfect equilibrium. Whatever non-cooperative support for the Nash solution we take, according to Nash himself it should provide to our understanding of the Nash solution, and, so we may hope, of its inherent fairness.

In what follows I shall try to relate Nash's three approaches to inherent fairness properties of the Nash solution. I will start with the axiomatic approach, continue with a related market approach and will derive from the latter one a further non-cooperative foundation, that allows a conclusion as to specific fairness. In the last part I shall discuss the fairness hidden in the Nash product.

2. The Axiomatic Approach

Nash's axiom IIA asserts that if one bargaining problem is contained in another one and contains the other one's solution as a feasible point its own solution should coincide with that point. The IIA is formally closely related to rationality axioms like the weak or strong axiom of revealed preferences. As such it does not hint to any underlying fairness concept. One may however weaken IIA in such a way that together with the other axioms it still characterizes the Nash solution. This is done by restricting in the IIA the larger bargaining problem to be always a hyperplane game, whose boundary, the intersection of $\mathbb{R}^2_+$ with a hyperplane, is tangent to the boundary of the game it contains. In such hyperplane games all bargaining solutions pick the barycenter, i.e. every player gets the same share of his utopia point or, put differently, makes the same concession measured in his specific personal utility units. This also represents a solution of the smaller NTU-game without making use of transfers offered by the containing hyperplane game. So in this weakened version IIA has the spirit of a no-trade equilibrium in general equilibrium theory. Once a Walrasian relation is considered possible one finds immediately that Lensberg's consistency, the alternative to IIA, that characterizes the Nash solution is formally almost identical to the consistency of Walrasian equilibrium (cf. Young, 1994, p.153). The inherent fairness of the Walrasian equilibrium is known to go beyond its Pareto efficiency guaranteed by the First Welfare Theorem. It is represented by the Equivalence Principle, a group of results assuring the near or exact equality of Walrasian allocations and those allocations determined by various game theoretical solutions in large pure exchange economies. The most famous equivalence results, those for the Shapley value, the Core and the Mas-Colell Bargaining set, guarantee that in large competitive environments any kind of strategic arbitrage is prevented by the power of perfect competition. True, this context of pure exchange economies is totally different from our purely welfaristic bargaining situations. Nevertheless, there are more indications in the axiomatic approach that underlying fairness of the Nash solution is a "Walrasian" one.

Shapley (1969) showed that the simultaneous requirements of efficiency (maximal sum of utilities) and equity (equal amounts of utility) that are in general incompatible become compatible for a suitable affine transformation of the original bargaining situation. The preimage under this affine transformation of the efficient and equitable utility allocation in the transformed problem turns out to be the Nash solution of the original problem. For the status quo point being zero the affine transformation becomes linear and is uniquely described by the normal vector λ at the Nash solution. This λ, that may be interpreted as an efficiency price system, defines endogenously local rates of utility transfer. Shubik (1985) speculates that this λ reminds very much of a competitive price system. In fact, this conjecture has been proved in Trockel (1996), where the bargaining problem has been interpreted as an artificial Arrow-Debreu economy, whose unique Walrasian equilibrium allocation coincides with the Nash solution, while the normal vector λ is an equilibrium price system.

So the fairness of the Nash solution seems to be the immunity against undue exploitation by the opponent as guaranteed by perfect competition.

Interestingly enough, a similar message can be read off Rubinstein's approximate foundation of the Nash solution in his alternating offer game. The approximation is the better the less Rubinstein's cake shrinks when time passes. That means almost no shrinking creates arbitrary many future alternative options for finding an adequate bargaining outcome. These future alternative options correspond to "the many outside options" represented in a stylized way by the concept of a Walrasian equilibrium. That the equivalence principle holds also for our special construct of a bargaining economy is shown in the next section.

3. An Edgeworth-Debreu-Scarf Type Characterization of the Nash Solution

In the present section that is based on Trockel (2005) we relate the Nash solution with the Edgeworthian rather than the Walrasian version of perfect competition. To do so, we define an artificial coalition production economy (cf. Hildenbrand, 1974) representing a two person bargaining game.

In a similar way the Nash solution has been applied in Mayberry et al. (1953) to define a specific solution for a duopoly situation and comparing it with other solutions, among them the Edgeworth contract curve. The relation between these two solutions will be the object of our investigation in this paper.

Though it would not be necessary to be so restrictive we define a two person bargaining game as the closed subgraph of a continuously differentiable strictly decreasing concave function $f : [0, 1] \longrightarrow [0, 1]$ with $f(0) = 1$ and $f(1) = 0$.

$$S := subgraph f := \{(x_1, x_2) \in [0, 1]^2 | x_2 \leq f(x_1)\}$$

The normalization reflects the fact that bargaining games are usually considered to be given only up to positive affine transformations. Smoothness makes life easier by admitting unique tangents.

The model S is general enough for our purpose of representation by a coalition production economy. In particular, S is the intersection of some strictly convex comprehensive set with the positive orthant of $\mathbb{R}^2$.

Define for any S as described above a two person coalition production economy $\mathcal{E}^S$ as follows:

$$\mathcal{E}^S := ((e_i, \succsim_i, Y_i)_{i=1,2}, (\vartheta_{ij})_{i,j=1,2})$$

such that

$$e_i = (0, 0), x = (x_1, x_2) \succsim_i x' = (x'_1, x'_2) \Leftrightarrow x_i \geq x'_i, i = 1, 2 ,$$
$$\vartheta_{11} = \vartheta_{22} = 1, \vartheta_{12} = \vartheta_{21} = 0, Y_1 = Y_2 = (\frac{1}{2})S .$$

The zero initial endowments reflect the idea that all available income in this economy comes from shares in production profits. Each agent owns fully a production possibility set that is able to produce for any $x \in S$ the bundle $(\frac{1}{2})x$ without any input. Both agents are interested in only one of the two goods called "agent $i's$ utility", $i = 1, 2$. Without any exchange agent i would maximize his preference by producing and consuming one half unit of commodity i and zero units of commodity $3 - i, i = 1, 2$. However, the agents would recognize immediately that they left some joint utility unused on the table.

Given exchange possibilities for the two commodities they would see that improvement would require exchange or, to put it differently, coordinated production

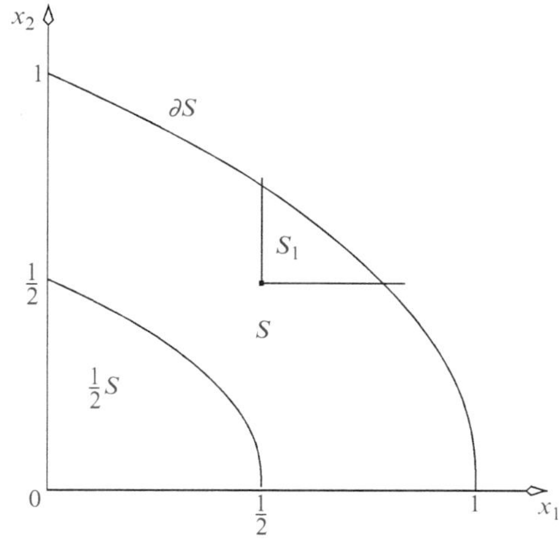

Figure 1.

(see Figure 1). The point $(\frac{1}{2}, \frac{1}{2})$ corresponds to the vector of initial endowments, the set $S_1 := S \cap (\{(\frac{1}{2}, \frac{1}{2})\} + \mathbb{R}^2_+)$ to the famous lens and the intersection of S_1 with the efficient boundary of S, i.e. $S_1 \cap \partial S$, to the core in the Edgeworth Box. This is exactly what Mayberry and al. (1953, p. 144) call the *Edgeworth contract curve* in their similar setting.

The according notions of improvement and of the core are analogous to the ones used for *Coalitional Production Economies* by Hildenbrand (1974, p. 211). $\tilde{Y} : \{\{1\}, \{2\}, \{1,2\}\} \Longrightarrow \mathbb{R}^2$ with $\tilde{Y}(\{1\}) = Y_1, \tilde{Y}(\{2\}) = Y_2, \tilde{Y}(\{1,2\}) = S$, is the production correspondence, which is additive, as $Y(\{1\} \cup \{2\}) = Y_1 + Y_2 = S$. An allocation $x^i = ((x^i_1, x^i_2))_{i=1,2}$ for $\mathcal{E}^S$ is *T-attainable* for $T \in \{\{1\}, \{2\}, \{1,2\}\}$ if $\sum_{i \in T} x^i \in \tilde{Y}(T)$; it is called *attainable* if it is $\{1,2\}$-attainable.

An allocation (x^1, x^2) can be *improved upon* by a coalition $T \in \{\{1\}, \{2\}, \{1,2\}\}$ if there is a *T-attainable* allocation (y^1, y^2) such that $\forall i \in T : y^i \succ_i x^i$. The *core* of $\mathcal{E}^S$ is the set of $\{1,2\}$-attainable allocations that cannot be improved upon. The analogous definitions hold for all n-replicas $\mathcal{E}^S_n$ of $\mathcal{E}^S$, $n \in \mathbb{N}$.

Notice that our choice of $Y_i = (\frac{1}{2})S, i = 1,2$ ensures the utility allocation $(\frac{1}{2}, \frac{1}{2})$ for the two players in case of non-agreement. This differs from Nash's status quo or threat point $(0,0)$.

Formalizing an n-replica economy $\mathcal{E}^S_n$ is standard. All characteristics are replaced by n-tupels of identical copies of these characteristics. In particular $\mathcal{E}^S_n$ has $2n$ agents, n of each of the two types 1 and 2. And the total production possibility set for the grand coalition of all $2n$ agents is nS.

Although the use of strict convex preferences as in Debreu and Scarf (1963) is not available here a short moment of reflection shows that a major part of their arguments can be used in our case as well.

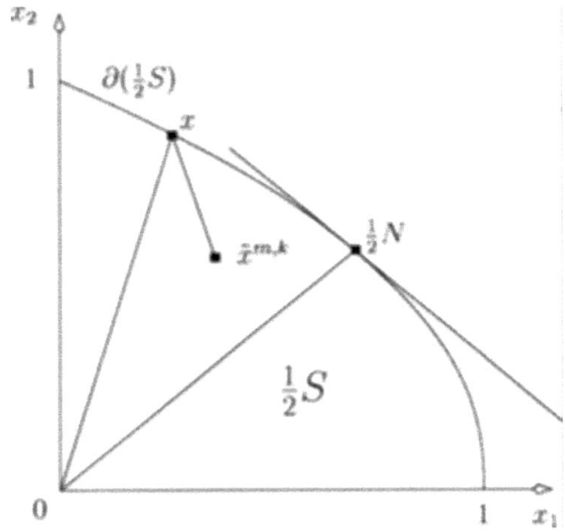

Figure 2.

Next we are looking at the core of n-replicas $\mathcal{E}_n^S$ of the economy $\mathcal{E}^S$. It suffices to look at S. Notice that it does not make any difference whether in an n-replica economy every agent has the technology $Y = \frac{1}{2n}S$ and the total production set is S or wether each agent has $Y = (\frac{1}{2})S$ and total production is nS. We will assume that each agent in $\mathcal{E}_n^S$ owns a production possibility set $Y := \frac{1}{2}S$ as illustrated in Figure 2.

We assume w.l.o.g. that $x \in \partial(\frac{1}{2}S)$ and $x_1 < \frac{1}{2}N_1, x_2 > \frac{1}{2}N_2$. By choosing $n, m, k \in \mathbb{N}, k < m \leq n$ sufficiently large we can make the vector $\frac{m-k}{m+k}(x_1, -x_2)$ arbitrarily small and, thereby, position the point $\tilde{x}^{m,k} := (x_1, x_2) + \frac{m-k}{m+k}(x_1, -x_2)$ in $int(\frac{1}{2}S)$.

A coalition C_n^x in the n-replica economy $\mathcal{E}_n^S$ of $\mathcal{E}^S$ consisting of m agents of type 1 and k agents of type 2 can realize the allocation $(m+k)\tilde{x}^{m,k} = ((m+k)x_1 + (m-k)x_1, (m+k)x_2 - (m-k)x_2) = (2mx_1, 2kx_2)$.

This bundle can be reallocated to the members of C_n^x by giving to each of the m type 1 agents $(2x_1, 0)$ and to each of the k type 2 agents $(0, 2x_2)$. Clearly, everybody gets thereby the same as he received in the beginning when everybody produced x. Therefore, nobody improves! However, for $\eta > 0$ sufficiently small $\tilde{x}^{m,k} \in int\ \frac{1}{2}S$ implies that $\tilde{x}^{m,k} + \eta N \in int\frac{1}{2}S$. Now reallocation of that bundle among the members of C_n^x can be performed in such a way that each type 1 agent receives $(2x_1 + \frac{m+k}{m}\eta N_1, 0)$ and each type 2 agent gets $(0, 2x_2 + \frac{m+k}{k}\eta N_2)$. Therefore x for every agent can be improved upon by C_n^x via production of $\tilde{x}^{m,k} + \eta N$ by each of its members. Again, the only element of $\partial(\frac{1}{2}S)$ remaining in the core for all $n-$replications of $\mathcal{E}^S$ is the point $\frac{1}{2}N$, i.e. the Nash solution for $\frac{1}{2}S$.

Notice that any point $y \in \partial(\frac{1}{2}S)$ with $y_1 < x_1 < N_1$ can be improved upon by the

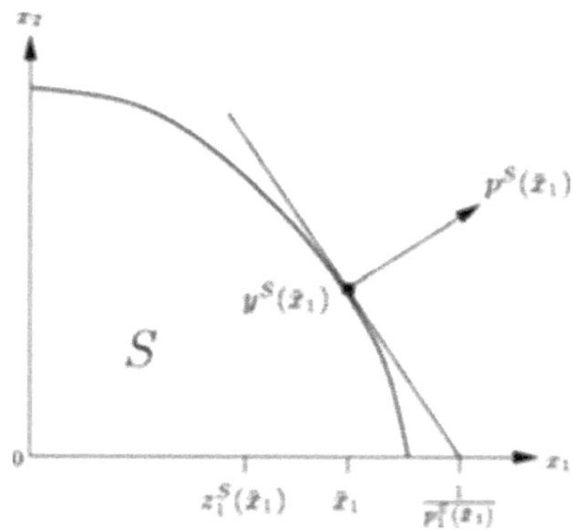

Figure 3.

same coalition C_n^x via $\tilde{y}^{m,n} + \eta N$ with the same η by a totally identical construction of $\tilde{y}^{m,n}$ from y. The same is not true for $z \in \partial(\frac{1}{2}S)$ with $x_1 < z_1 < N_1$. Here the $\frac{m-k}{m+k}(z_1, -z_2)$ may require a larger m and k to make $\frac{m-k}{m+k}(z_1, -z_2)$ small enough. We may for any $x \in \partial(\frac{1}{2}S), x_1 < N_1$ choose the m, k in the construction of $\tilde{x}^{m,k}$ in such a way that $\tilde{x}^{m,k}$ is on or arbitrary close to the segment $[0, \frac{1}{2}N]$.

This section continues the idea of Trockel (1996) to approach cooperative games with methods from microeconomic theory. Considering sets of feasible utility allocations as production possibility sets representing the possible jointly "producable" utility allocations and transformation rates as prices goes back to Shapley (cf. Shapley, 1969). See also Mayberry et al. (1953). The identity of the Walrasian equilibrium of a finite bargaining economy $\mathcal{E}^S$ with the Nash solution of its underlying bargaining game S stresses the competitive feature of the Nash solution.

Moreover the Nash solution's coincidence with the Core of a large bargaining coalitional production economy with equal production possibilities for all agents reflects a different fairness aspect in addition to those represented by the axioms.

4. A Walrasian Demand Game

Consider a two person bargaining situation S as illustrated in Figure 3. The compact strictly convex set $S \subset \mathbb{R}^2$ represents all feasible utility allocations for two players. For simplicity assume that the efficient boundary ∂S of S is the graph of some smooth decreasing concave function from $[0, 1]$ to $[0, 1]$. Such a bargaining situation can be looked at as a two-person NTU-game, where S is the set of payoff vectors feasible for the grand coalition $\{1, 2\}$, while $\{0\}$ represents the payoffs for the one player coalitions. The normalization to $(0; 1, 1)$ is standard and reflects the idea that S arose as the image under the two players' cardinal utility functions of some underlying set of outcomes or allocations. Cardinality determines utility functions only up to positive affine transformations and therefore justifies our normalization. Now, consider the following modification of Nash's simple demand game due to Trockel (2000)

$$\Gamma^S = (\Sigma_1, \Sigma_2; \pi_1^S, \pi_2^S) \; .$$

$\Sigma_1 = \Sigma_2 = [0,1]$ are the players' sets of (pure) strategies. The payoff functions are defined by $\pi_i^S(x_1,x_2) := x_i \mathbf{1}_S(x_1,x_2) + z_i^S(x_i)\mathbf{1}_{S^C}(x_1,x_2)$. Here S^C is the complement of S in $[0,1]^2$ and $\mathbf{1}_S$ is the indicator function for the set S. Finally $z_i^S(x_i)$ is defined as follows: For each $x_i \in [0,1]$ the point $y^S(x_i)$ is the unique point on ∂S with $y_i^S(x_i) = x_i$. By $p^S(x_i)$ we denote the normal vector to ∂S at $y^S(x_i)$ normalized by $p^S(x_i) \cdot y^S(x_i) = 1$. Now $z_i^S(x_i)$ is defined by $z_i^S(x_i) = min(x_i, \frac{1}{2p_i^S(x_i)})$, $i = 1, 2$.

This game has a unique Nash equilibrium (x_1^*, x_2^*) that is strict, has the maxmin-property and coincides with the Nash solution of S, i.e. $\{(x_1^*, x_2^*)\} = N(S)$. The idea behind the payoff functions is it to consider for any efficient utility allocation y its value under the efficiency price vector $p(y)$. If the utility allocation could be sold at $p(y)$ on a hypothetical market and the revenue would be split equally among the players there is only *one* utility allocation such that both players could buy back their own utility with their incomes without the need of any transfer of revenue. This equal split of revenue in the payoff function corresponds to *equity* in Shapley's (1969) cooperative characterization of the λ-transfer value via equity and efficiency. As for our two-person bargaining games the λ-transfer value just singles out the Nash solution this result does not come as a big surprise. By supplementing efficiency, which characterizes the infinitely many equilibria in Nash's demand game, by the additional equity, embodied in the payoff functions $\pi_i^S, i = 1, 2$, one gets the Nash solution as the unique equilibrium of the modified demand game. This result provides obviously a non-cooperative foundation of the Nash solution in the sense of the Nash program.

The fairness concept behind the rules of this game is the equity coming from the Walrasian approach in Trockel (1996) mentioned above, where "equity" means equal shares in the production possibility set used to produce utility allocations.

5. On the Meaning of the Nash Product

One possible way to try to find out any fairness concept behind the Nash product is it to derive the Nash product as a social planner's welfare function based on certain axioms on his preference relation on the set of feasible utility allocations. This route had been followed by Trockel (1999). For 0-normalized two-person bargaining situations it is shown that a preference relation on S is representable by the Nash product if it is a binary relation on S that satisfies the following properties: lower continuity, neutrality, monotonicity, unit-invariance and indifference-invariance. Continuity is a technical assumption, monotonicity reflects the planner's benevolence by liking higher utilities of the player's move. Neutrality is certainly a fairness property. What about the remaining two properties? *Indifference-invariance* is defined by:

$$x \succ y, x' \sim x, y' \sim y \Longrightarrow x' \succ y' \qquad \forall\, x, y, x', y' \in S \, .$$

It says that equivalent utility allocations for the planner are perfectly substitutable for each other in any strict preference. It is a weak consistency property.

Unit invariance is defined by:

$$x \succ y \Longleftrightarrow z * x \succ z * y \qquad \forall\, x, y, z \in S, * \text{ denoting pairwise multiplication.}$$

This property reflects the fact that the planner's preference is not influenced by the choices of units of the players.

Interestingly enough these properties not containing the standard rationality properties of transitivity and completeness suffice to yield a complete, transitive, continuous preordering on S representable by the Nash product. The only obvious fairness property is neutrality.

The Nash product itself is not seen in the literature as an easily interpretable function, not to speak of one reflecting any kind of fairness. This approach to the Nash solution is based on Trockel (2003). Concerning its direct interpretation the situation is best described by the quotation of Osborne and Rubinstein (1994, p. 303):

> Although the maximization of a product of utilities is a simple mathematical operation it lacks a straightforward interpretation; we view it simply as a technical device.

It is the purpose of the remaining part of this section to provide one straightforward, in fact surprising interpretation. Maximizing the Nash product is equivalent to finding maximal elements of one natural completion of the Pareto ordering. The maximal elements for the other natural completion are just the Pareto optimal points.

We shall look at the vector ordering and complete preorderings on compact subsets of $\mathbb{R}^n$ but restrict the analysis without loss of generality to the case $n = 2$. A complete preordering $\succsim$ on a compact set S is a complete, transitive (hence reflexive) binary relation on S. The weak vector ordering $\geq$ in contrast fails to be complete. It is, however, transitive, too. To make things simple assume $\succsim$ on S to be continuous, hence representable by a continuous utility function $u : S \longrightarrow \mathbb{R}$. The $\succsim$-maximal elements are given by the set of maximizers of u on S, i.e. $argmax_{x\in\, S}\, u(x)$.

Let $B_{\succsim}(x)$ be the set $\{x' \in S | x' \succsim x\}$ and $W_{\succsim}(x)$ the set $\{x' \in S | x \succsim x'\}$. For any $x', x \in S$ we obviously have:

$$x' \sim x \Leftrightarrow \lambda(B_{\succsim}(x)) = \lambda(B_{\succsim}(x')) \Leftrightarrow \lambda(W_{\succsim}(x)) = \lambda(W_{\succsim}(x'))\ .$$

Deviating from earlier notation λ now denotes the Lebesgue measure on $\mathbb{R}^2$ the extension of the natural measure of area in $\mathbb{R}^2$ to all Lebesgue measurable sets.

The correspondences $B_{\succsim} : S \Longrightarrow S$ and $W_{\succsim} : S \Longrightarrow S$ composed with the Lebesgue measure define alternative utility functions $\lambda \circ B_{\succsim}$ and $\lambda \circ W_{\succsim}$ representing $\succsim$ as well as u.

Now consider for the vector ordering $\geq$ the analogous sets $B_{\geq}(x)$, $W_{\geq}(x)$ for arbitrary $x \in S$:

$$B_{\geq}(x) = \{x' \in S | x' \geq x\},\ W_{\geq}(x) = \{x' \in S | x \geq x'\}\ .$$

Next, introduce the mappings $\lambda \circ B_{\geq}$ and $\lambda \circ W_{\geq}$ defined by:

$$\lambda \circ B_{\geq}(x) := \lambda(B_{\geq}(x)) \quad \text{and} \quad \lambda \circ W_{\geq}(x) := \lambda(W_{\geq}(x)) \, .$$

Both are mappings from S to $\mathbb{R}$ and define therefore preference relations that are completions of $\geq$.

We have $x \geq x' \implies \lambda(B_{\geq}(x)) \leq \lambda(B_{\geq}(x'))$ and $x \geq x' \implies \lambda(W_{\geq}(x)) \geq \lambda(W_{\geq}(x'))$. The two dual completions of $\geq$ are different in general:

$$x \succsim_1 x' :\iff \lambda(B_{\geq}(x)) \leq \lambda(B_{\geq}(x')) \, ,$$
$$x \succsim_2 x' :\iff \lambda(W_{\geq}(x)) \geq \lambda(W_{\geq}(x')) \, .$$

They only coincide when the binary relation one starts with is already a complete preordering. Notice, that $B_{\geq}(x)$ and $W_{\geq}(x)$ are in general proper subsets of $B_{\succsim_1}(x)$ and $W_{\succsim_2}(x)$, respectively.

Now we apply our gained insight to bargaining games. To keep things simple we define again a normalized two-person bargaining game S as the subgraph of a concave strictly decreasing function f from $[0,1]$ onto $[0,1]$. The two axes represent the players' utilities, S the feasible set of utility allocations. The vector ordering on S represents in this framework the Pareto ordering. The efficient boundary $graph f$ of S is the set of Pareto optimal points or vector maxima. Obviously each point x in $graph f$ minimizes the value of $\lambda \circ B_{\geq}$. In fact, for $x \in graph f$ we have $\lambda(B_{\geq}(x)) = 0$ Notice that $\lambda(W_{\geq}(x))$ takes different values when x varies in $graph f$.

Now, consider the set $argmax_{x \in S} \; \lambda(W_{\geq}(x))$ of maximizers of $\lambda \circ W_{\geq}$. This set is exactly the set $\{N(S)\}$ where $N(S)$ is the Nash solution of S. Maximizing the Nash product $x_1 x_2$ for $x \in S$ means maximizing the measure of points in S *Pareto dominated* by x'. Hence the two completions $\succsim_1, \succsim_2$ of the Pareto ordering $\geq$ on S have as their sets of maximizers the Pareto efficient boundary and the Nash solution, respectively. Thus we have shown that two different methods of representing complete preorderings via the measure of better sets versus worse sets may be applied as well to incomplete binary relations. Here they lead to two different functions inducing two different complete preorderings.

Applied to the non-complete Pareto ordering on a compact set S representing a bargaining situation the two completions have as their respective sets of maximizers the Pareto efficient boundary and the Nash solution of S. This result provides a straightforward interesting interpretation of the Nash solution as a dual version of Pareto optimality. In contrast to the latter it has the advantage to single out a unique point in the efficient boundary.

The idea of defining rankings by counting the less preferred alternatives has an old tradition in social choice theory as the famous Borda Count (cf. Borda, 1781) shows. In our context with a continuum of social alternatives counting is replaced by measuring. The level sets of the Nash product collect those utility allocations Pareto dominating equally large (in terms of Lebesgue measure) sets of alternatives.

6. Concluding Remarks

The Nash solution is the most popular and most frequently used bargaining solution in the economic and game theoretic literature. Authors working on efficient bargaining on labour markets predominantly use the Nash solution. Experiments on bargaining have been numerous and in various frameworks. Altogether they do not provide unanimous support for the Nash solution. But Binmore et al. (1993) provide empirical evidence for the Nash solution in laboratory experiments. Young (1993) presents an evolutionary model of bargaining supporting the Nash solution. And Skyrms (1996, p.107) writes:

> The evolutionary dynamics of distributive justice in discrete bargaining games is evidently more complicated than any one axiomatic bargaining theory. But our results reveal the considerable robustness of the Nash solution.

Despite the popularity of the Nash solution in the economic literature mentioned above Skyrms continues:

> Perhaps philosophers who have spent so much time discussing the utilitarian and Kalai-Smorodinsky schemes should pay a little more attention to the Nash bargaining solution.

Even if not a philosopher, in the present article I followed this advice by trying to find traces of fairness in different representations of the Nash solution available in the literature.

References

Binmore, K. 1987. "Nash Bargaining Theory I, II", in: K. Binmore and P. Dasgupta (eds.): *The Economics of Bargaining*, Cambridge: Basic Blackwell.

Binmore, K. 1997. "Introduction", in: J.F. Nash (ed.): *Essays on Game Theory*, Cheltenham: Edward Elgar.

Binmore, K., A. Rubinstein, and A. Wolinsky. 1986. "The Nash Bargaining Solution in Economic Modelling", *Rand Journal of Economics* 17, 176–188.

Binmore, K., J. Swierzbinski, S. Hsu, and C. Proulx. 1993. "Focal Points and Bargaining", *International Journal of Game Theory* 22, 381–409.

Borda, J.C. 1781. *Mémoire sur les élections au scrutin*, Paris: Histoire de L'Académie Royale des Sciences.

Debreu, G., and H. Scarf. 1963. "A Limit Theorem on the Core", *International Economic Review* 4, 235–246.

Hildenrand, W. 1974. *Core and Equilibria of a Large Economy*, Princeton: Princeton University Press.

Howard, J.V. 1992. "A Social Choice Rule and Its Implementation in Perfect Equilibrium", *Journal of Economic Theory* 56, 142–159.

Lensberg, T. 1988. "Stability and Collective Rationality", *Journal of Economic Theory* 45, 330–341.

Mayberry, J.P., J.F. Nash, and M. Shubik. 1953. "A Comparison of Treatments of a Duopoly Situation", *Econometrica* 21, 128–140.

Nash, J.F. 1951. "Non-cooperative Games", *Annals of Mathematica* 54(2), 286–295.

Nash, J.F. 1953. "Two-person Cooperative Games", *Econometrica* 21, 128–140.

Osborne, M.J., and A. Rubinstein. 1990. *Bargaining and Markets*, Academic Press, New York.

Osborne, M.J., and A. Rubinstein. 1994. *A Course in Game Theory*, Cambridge: MIT Press.

Rubinstein, A. 1982. "Perfect Equilibrium in a Bargaining Model", *Econometrica* 50, 97–109.

Shapley, L. S. 1969. "Utility Comparison and the Theory of Games", in: *La decision: aggregation et dynamique des ordres de preference*, Paris, 251–263.

Shubik, M. 1985. *Game Theory in the Social Sciences*, Cambridge: MIT Press.

Skyrms, B. 1996. *Evolution of the Social Contract*, Cambridge: Cambridge University Press.
Trockel, W. 1996. "A Walrasian Approach to Bargaining Games", *Economics Letters* 51, 295–301.
Trockel, W. 1999. "Rationalizability of the Nash Bargaining Solution", *Journal of Economics* 8, 159–165.
Trockel, W. 2000. "Implementation of the Nash Solution Based on Its Walrasian Characterization", *Economic Theory* 16, 277–294.
Trockel, W. 2003. *On the Meaning of the Nash Product*, Bielefed: IMW-working paper Nr. 354.
Trockel, W. 2005. "Core-Equivalence for the Nash Bargaining Solution", *Economic Theory* 25, 255–263.
Van Damme, E. 1986. "The Nash Bargaining Solution Is Optimal", *Journal of Economic Theory* 38, 78–100.
Young, H.P. 1993. "An Evolutionary Model of Bargaining", *Journal of Economic Theory* 59, 145–168.
Young, H.P. 1994. *Equity in Theory and Practice*, Princeton: Princeton University Press.

Walter Trockel
Institut für Mathematische Wirtschaftsforschung
Universität Bielefeld
D-33501 Bielefeld
Germany
wtrockel@uni-bielefeld.de

UTILITY INVARIANCE IN NON–COOPERATIVE GAMES

PETER J. HAMMOND
Stanford University

1. Introduction

Individual behaviour that maximizes utility is invariant under strictly increasing transformations of the utility function. In this sense, utility is ordinal. Similarly, behaviour under risk that maximizes expected utility is invariant under strictly increasing affine transformations of the utility function. In this sense, expected utility is cardinal. Following Sen (1976), a standard way to describe social choice with (or without) interpersonal comparisons is by means of a social welfare functional that maps each profile of individual utility functions to a social ordering. Different forms of interpersonal comparison, and different degrees of interpersonal comparability, are then represented by invariance under different classes of transformation applied to the whole profile of individual utility functions.[1]

This paper reports some results from applying a similar idea to non-cooperative games. That is, one asks what transformations of individual utility profiles have no effect on the relevant equilibrium set, or other appropriate solution concept.[2] So far, only a small literature has addressed this question, and largely in the context of cooperative or coalitional games.[3] For the sake of simplicity and brevity, this paper will focus on simple sufficient conditions for transformations to preserve some particular non-cooperative solution concepts.[4]

---

[1] See, for example, Sen (1974, 1977, 1979), d'Aspremont and Gevers (1977, 2002), Roberts (1980), Mongin and d'Aspremont (1998), Bossert and Weymark (2004).

[2] Of course, the usual definition of a game has each player's objective function described by a *payoff* rather than a utility function. Sometimes, this is the case of numerical utility described below. More often, it simply repeats the methodological error that was common in economics before Fisher (1892) and Pareto (1896) pointed out that an arbitrary increasing transformation of a consumer's utility function has no effect on demand.

[3] See especially Nash (1950), Shapley (1969), Roth (1979), Aumann (1985), Dagan and Serrano (1998), as well as particular parts of the surveys by Thomson (1994, pp. 1254–6), McLean (2002), and Kaneko and Wooders (2004). Recent contributions on "ordinal" bargaining theory include Kıbrıs (2004a, b) and Samet and Safra (2005).

[4] For a much more thorough discussion, especially of conditions that are both necessary and sufficient for transformations to preserve best or better responses, see Morris and Ui (2004).

U. Schmidt and S. Traub (eds.), Advances in Public Economics: Utility, Choice and Welfare, 31-50.

Before embarking on game theory, Section 2 begins with a brief review of relevant concepts in single person utility theory. Next, Section 3 describes the main invariance concepts that arise in social choice theory.

The discussion of games begins in Section 4 with a brief consideration of games with numerical utilities, when invariance is not an issue. Section 5 then considers concepts that apply only to pure strategies. Next, Section 6 moves on to mixed strategies. Thereafter, Sections 7 and 8 offer brief discussions of quantal responses and evolutionary dynamics.

Section 9 asks a different but related question: what kinds of transformation preserve equilibrium not just in a single game, but an entire class of game forms with outcomes in a particular consequence domain? In the end, this extended form of invariance seems much more natural than invariance for a single game. In particular, most of game theory can be divided into one part that considers only pure strategies, in which case it is natural to regard individuals' utilities as ordinal, and a second part that considers mixed strategies, in which case it is natural to regard individuals' utilities as cardinal. Neither case relies on any form of interpersonal comparison.

A few concluding remarks make up Section 10.

2. Single Person Decision Theory

2.1. INDIVIDUAL CHOICE AND UTILITY

Let X be a fixed consequence domain. Let $\mathcal{F}(X)$ denote the family of non-empty subsets of X. Let R be any (complete and transitive) preference ordering on X. A *utility function representing* R is any mapping $u : X \to \mathbb{R}$ satisfying $u(x) \geq u(y)$ iff $x \; R \; y$, for every pair $x, y \in X$. Given any utility function $u : X \to \mathbb{R}$, for each *feasible set* $F \in \mathcal{F}(X)$, let

$$C(F, u) := \arg\max_x \{ u(x) \mid x \in F \} := \{ x^* \in F \mid x \in F \Longrightarrow u(x^*) \geq u(x) \}$$

denote the *choice set* of utility maximizing members of F. The mapping $F \mapsto\!\!\!\to C(F, u)$ is called the *choice correspondence* that is generated by maximizing u over each possible feasible set.[5]

A *transformation* of the utility function u is a mapping $\phi : \mathbb{R} \to \mathbb{R}$ that is used to generate an alternative utility function $\tilde{u} = \phi \circ u$ defined by $\tilde{u}(x) = (\phi \circ u)(x) := \phi[u(x)]$ for all $x \in X$.

[5] The decision theory literature usually refers to the mapping as a "choice function". The term "choice correspondence" accords better, however, with the terms "social choice correspondence" and "equilibrium correspondence" that are widespread in social choice theory and game theory, respectively. Also, it is often assumed that each choice set is non-empty, but this requirement will not be important in this paper.

2.2. ORDINAL UTILITY

Two utility functions $u, \tilde{u} : X \to \mathbb{R}$ are said to be *ordinally equivalent* if and only if each of the following three equivalent conditions is satisfied:

(i) $u(x) \geq u(y)$ iff $\tilde{u}(x) \geq \tilde{u}(y)$, for all pairs $x, y \in X$;
(ii) $\tilde{u} = \phi \circ u$ for some strictly increasing transformation $\phi : \mathbb{R} \to \mathbb{R}$;
(iii) $C(F, u) = C(F, \tilde{u})$ for all $F \in \mathcal{F}(X)$.

Item (iii) expresses the fact that the *choice correspondence* defined by the mapping $F \mapsto\!\!\!\to C(F, u)$ on the domain $\mathcal{F}(X)$ must be invariant under strictly increasing transformations of the utility function u. Such transformations replace u by any member of the same ordinal equivalence class.

2.3. LOTTERIES AND CARDINAL UTILITY

A (simple) *lottery* on X is any mapping $\lambda : X \to \mathbb{R}_+$ such that:

(i) $\lambda(x) > 0$ iff $x \in S$, where S is the *finite support* of λ;
(ii) $\sum_{x \in X} \lambda(x) = \sum_{x \in S} \lambda(x) = 1$.

Thus $\lambda(x)$ is the probability that x is the outcome of the lottery. Let $\Delta(X)$ denote the set of all such simple lotteries.

Say that the preference ordering R on X is *von Neumann–Morgenstern* (or NM) if and only if there is a *von Neumann–Morgenstern* (or NM) *utility function* $v : X \to \mathbb{R}$ whose *expected value* $\mathbb{E}_\lambda v := \sum_{x \in X} \lambda(x) v(x) = \sum_{x \in S} \lambda(x) v(x)$ *represents* R on $\Delta(X)$. That is, $\mathbb{E}_\lambda v \geq \mathbb{E}_\mu v$ iff $\lambda \; R \; \mu$, for every pair $\lambda, \mu \in \Delta(X)$.

Let $\mathcal{F}_L(X) = \mathcal{F}(\Delta(X))$ denote the family of non-empty subsets of $\Delta(X)$. Given any $F \in \mathcal{F}_L(X)$ and any NM utility function $v : X \to \mathbb{R}$, let

$$C_L(F, u) := \arg\max_\lambda \{ \mathbb{E}_\lambda v \mid \lambda \in F \} := \{ \lambda^* \in F \mid \lambda \in F \Longrightarrow \mathbb{E}_{\lambda^*} v \geq \mathbb{E}_\lambda v \}$$

denote the *choice set* of expected utility maximizing members of F.

The mapping $\phi : \mathbb{R} \to \mathbb{R}$ is said to be a *strictly increasing affine transformation* if there exist an additive constant $\alpha \in \mathbb{R}$ and a positive multiplicative constant $\delta \in \mathbb{R}$ such that $\phi(r) \equiv \alpha + \delta r$. Two NM utility functions $v, \tilde{v} : X \to \mathbb{R}$ are said to be *cardinally equivalent* if and only if each of the following three equivalent conditions are satisfied:

(i) $\mathbb{E}_\lambda v \geq \mathbb{E}_\mu v$ iff $\mathbb{E}_\lambda \tilde{v} \geq \mathbb{E}_\mu \tilde{v}$, for all pairs $\lambda, \mu \in \Delta(X)$;
(ii) $\tilde{v} = \phi \circ v$ for some strictly increasing affine transformation $\phi : \mathbb{R} \to \mathbb{R}$;
(iii) $C_L(F, v) = C_L(F, \tilde{v})$ for all $F \in \mathcal{F}_L(X)$.

Item (iii) expresses the fact that the *lottery choice correspondence* defined by the mapping $F \mapsto\!\!\!\to C_L(F, v)$ on the lottery domain $\mathcal{F}_L(X)$ must be invariant under strictly increasing affine transformations of the utility function v. Such transformations replace v by any member of the same cardinal equivalence class.

3. Social Choice Correspondences

3.1. ARROW SOCIAL WELFARE FUNCTIONS

Let $\mathcal{R}(X)$ denote the set of preference orderings on X. A *preference profile* is a mapping $i \mapsto R_i$ from N to $\mathcal{R}(X)$ specifying the preference ordering of each individual $i \in N$. Let $R^N = \langle R_i \rangle_{i \in N}$ denote such a preference profile, and $\mathcal{R}^N(X)$ the set of all possible preference profiles.

Let $\mathcal{D} \subset \mathcal{R}^N(X)$ denote a *domain* of permissible preference profiles. A *social choice correspondence* (or SCC) can be represented as a mapping $(F, R^N) \mapsto\!\!\!\rightarrow C(F, R^N) \subset F$ from pairs in $\mathcal{F}(X) \times \mathcal{D}$ consisting of feasible sets and preference profiles to social choice sets. In the usual special case when $C(F, R^N)$ consists of those elements in F which maximize some social ordering R that depends on R^N, this SCC can be represented by an *Arrow social welfare function* (or ASWF) $f : \mathcal{D} \to \mathcal{R}(X)$ which maps each permissible profile $R^N \in \mathcal{D}$ to a social ordering $f(R^N)$ on X.

3.2. SOCIAL WELFARE FUNCTIONALS

Sen (1970) proposed extending the concept of an Arrow social welfare function by refining the domain to profiles of individual utility functions rather than preference orderings. This extension offers a way to represent different degrees of interpersonal comparability that might be embedded in the social ordering.

Formally, let $\mathcal{U}(X)$ denote the set of utility functions on X. A *utility function profile* is a mapping $i \mapsto u_i$ from N to $\mathcal{U}(X)$. Let $u^N = \langle u_i \rangle_{i \in N}$ denote such a profile, and $\mathcal{U}^N(X)$ the set of all possible utility function profiles.

Given a domain $\mathcal{D} \subset \mathcal{U}^N(X)$ of permissible utility function profiles, an SCC is a mapping $(F, u^N) \mapsto\!\!\!\rightarrow C(F, u^N) \subset F$ defined on $\mathcal{F}(X) \times \mathcal{D}$. When each choice set $C(F, u^N)$ consists of elements $x \in F$ that maximize a social ordering R, there is a *social welfare functional* (or SWFL) $G : \mathcal{D} \to \mathcal{R}(X)$ mapping $\mathcal{D} \subset \mathcal{U}^N(X)$ to the set of possible social orderings.

3.3. UTILITY INVARIANCE IN SOCIAL CHOICE

Given a specific SCC $(F, u^N) \mapsto\!\!\!\rightarrow C(F, u^N)$, one can define an equivalence relation $\sim$ on the space of utility function profiles $\mathcal{U}^N(X)$ by specifying that $u^N \sim \tilde{u}^N$ if and only if $C(F, u^N) = C(F, \tilde{u}^N)$ for all $F \in \mathcal{F}(X)$.

An *invariance transformation* of the utility function profiles is a profile $\phi^N = \langle \phi_i \rangle_{i \in N}$ of individual utility transformations $\phi_i : \mathbb{R} \to \mathbb{R}$ having the property that $u^N \sim \tilde{u}^N$ whenever $\tilde{u}^N = \phi^N(u^N)$ — i.e., $\tilde{u}_i = \phi_i(u_i)$ for all $i \in N$. Thus, invariance transformations result in equivalent utility function profiles, for which the SCC generates the same choice set. In the following, let Φ denote the class of invariance transformations.

3.3.1. *Ordinal Non-comparability*

The first specific concept of utility invariance for SCCs arises when Φ consists of mappings $\phi^N = \langle \phi_i \rangle_{i \in N}$ from $\mathbb{R}^N$ into itself with the property that each $\phi_i : \mathbb{R} \to \mathbb{R}$ is strictly increasing. So $u^N \sim \tilde{u}^N$ if and only if the two profiles $u^N, \tilde{u}^N$ have the property that the utility functions $u_i, \tilde{u}_i$ of each individual $i \in N$ are ordinally equivalent. The SCC $C(F, u^N)$ is said to satisfy *ordinal non-comparability* (or ONC) if $C(F, u^N) = C(F, \tilde{u}^N)$ for all $F \in \mathcal{F}(X)$ whenever u^N and $\tilde{u}^N$ are ordinally equivalent in this way.

Obviously, in this case each equivalence class of an individual's utility functions is represented by one corresponding preference ordering, and each equivalence class of utility function profiles is represented by one corresponding preference profile. So the SCC can be expressed in the form $C^*(F, R^N)$. In particular, if each social choice set $C(F, u^N)$ maximizes a social ordering, implying that there is a SWFL, then that SWFL takes the form of an Arrow social welfare function.

3.3.2. *Cardinal Non-comparability*

The second specific concept of utility invariance arises when Φ consists of mappings $\phi^N = \langle \phi_i \rangle_{i \in N}$ from $\mathbb{R}^N$ into itself with the property that each $\phi_i : \mathbb{R} \to \mathbb{R}$ is strictly increasing and affine. That is, there must exist additive constants α_i and positive multiplicative constants δ_i such that $\phi_i(r) = \alpha_i + \delta_i r$ for each $i \in N$ and all $r \in \mathbb{R}$. The SCC $C(F, u^N)$ is said to satisfy *cardinal non-comparability* (or CNC) when it meets this invariance requirement.

3.3.3. *Ordinal Level Comparability*

Interpersonal comparisons of utility levels take the form $u_i(x) > u_j(y)$ or $u_i(x) < u_j(y)$ or $u_i(x) = u_j(y)$ for a pair of individuals $i, j \in N$ and a pair of social consequences $x, y \in N$. Such comparisons will not be preserved when different increasing transformations ϕ_i and ϕ_j are applied to i's and j's utilities. Indeed, level comparisons are preserved, in general, only if the same transformation is applied to all individuals' utilities.

Accordingly, in this case the invariance class Φ consists of those mappings $\phi^N = \langle \phi_i \rangle_{i \in N}$ for which there exists a strictly increasing transformation $\phi : \mathbb{R} \to \mathbb{R}$ such that $\phi_i = \phi$ for all $i \in N$. An SCC with this invariance class is said to satisfy *ordinal level comparability* (or OLC).

3.3.4. *Cardinal Unit Comparability*

Comparisons of utility sums take the form $\sum_{i \in N} u_i(x) > \sum_{i \in N} u_i(y)$ or $\sum_{i \in N} u_i(x) < \sum_{i \in N} u_i(y)$ or $\sum_{i \in N} u_i(x) = \sum_{i \in N} u_i(y)$ for a pair of social consequences $x, y \in N$. Such comparisons rely on being able to compare different individuals' utility differences, so one can say that one person's gain outweighs another person's loss. Such comparisons are only preserved, in general, if and only if the increasing *co-affine* transformations are applied to all individuals' utilities. That is, the mappings ϕ_i $(i \in N)$ must take the form $\phi_i(r) = \alpha_i + \delta r$ for suitable additive constants α_i $(i \in N)$, and a positive multiplicative constant δ that is independent of i. An SCC with this invariance class is said to satisfy *cardinal unit comparability* (or CUC).

3.3.5. *Cardinal Full Comparability*
Some welfare economists, following a suggestion of Sen (1973), have looked for income distributions that equalize utility levels while also maximizing a utility sum. In order that comparisons of both utility sums and utility levels should be invariant, the mappings ϕ_i $(i \in N)$ must take the form $\phi_i(r) = \alpha + \delta r$ for a suitable additive constant α and a positive multiplicative constant δ that are both independent of i. An SCC with this invariance class is said to satisfy *cardinal full comparability* (or CFC).

3.3.6. *Cardinal Ratio Scales*
In discussions of optimal population, the utility sum $\sum_{i \in N} u_i(x)$ may get replaced by $\sum_{i \in M} u_i(x)$ for a subset $M \subset N$ of "relevant" individuals. Presumably, the individuals $i \in N \setminus M$ never come into existence, and so have their utilities set to zero by a convenient normalization. This form of welfare sum, with the set of individuals M itself subject to choice, allows comparisons of extended social states (M, x) and (M', x') depending on which of the two sums $\sum_{i \in M} u_i(x)$ and $\sum_{i \in M'} u_i(x')$ is greater. These comparisons are preserved when the mappings ϕ_i $(i \in N)$ take the form $\phi_i(r) = \rho r$ for a positive multiplicative constant ρ that is independent of i. An SCC with this invariance class is said to satisfy *cardinal ratio scale comparability* (or CRSC).

4. Games with Numerical Utility

4.1. GAMES IN NORMAL FORM

A *game in normal form* is a triple $G = \langle N, S^N, u^N \rangle$ where:

(i) N is a finite set of *players*;
(ii) each player $i \in N$ has a *strategy set* S_i, and $S^N = \prod_{i \in N} S_i$ is the set of *strategy profiles*;
(iii) each player $i \in N$ has a *utility function* $u_i : S^N \to \mathbb{R}$ defined on the domain of strategy profiles, and $u^N = \langle u_i \rangle_{i \in N}$ is the *utility profile*.

Of course game theorists usually refer to "payoff functions" instead of utility functions. But the whole point of this paper is to see what properties such functions share with the utility functions that ordinarily arise in single person decision theory. To emphasize this comparison, the term "utility functions" will be used in games just as it is in decision theory and in social choice theory.

4.2. NUMERICAL UTILITY

Before moving on to various forms of ordinal and cardinal utility in games, let us first readily concede that sometimes players in a game do have objectives that can be described simply by real numbers. For example, the players may be firms seeking to maximize profit, measured in a particular currency unit such as dollars, euros, yen, pounds, crowns, ... Or, as suggested by the title of von Neumann's (1928) classic paper, they may be people playing *Gesellschaftsspiele* (or "parlour games") for small stakes. The fact that players' objectives are then straightforward to describe is one reason why it is easier to teach undergraduate students producer theory before facing them with the additional conceptual challenges posed by consumer theory.

Even in these special settings, however, numerical utility should be seen as a convenient simplification that abstracts from many important aspects of reality. For example, most decisions by firms generate profits at different times and in different uncertain events. Standard decision theory requires that these profits be aggregated into a single objective. Finding the expected present discounted value might seem one way to do this, but it may not be obvious what are the appropriate discount factors or the probabilities of different events. As for any parlour game, the fact that people choose to play at all reveals either an optimistic assessment of their chances of winning, or probably more realistically, an enjoyment of the game that is not simply represented by monetary winnings, even if the game is played for money.

4.3. SOME SPECIAL GAMES

4.3.1. *Zero-Sum and Constant Sum Games*

Much of the analysis in von Neumann (1928) and in von Neumann and Morgenstern (1944) is devoted to *two-person zero sum* games, in which the set of players is $N = \{1, 2\}$, and $u_1(s_1, s_2) + u_2(s_1, s_2) = 0$ for all $(s_1, s_2) \in S_1 \times S_2$. Von Neumann and Morgenstern (1944) also consider *n-person zero sum games* in which N remains a general finite set, and $\sum_{i \in N} u_i(s^N) \equiv 0$. They also argue that such games are equivalent to *constant sum games* in which $\sum_{i \in N} u_i(s^N) \equiv C$ for a suitable constant $C \in \mathbb{R}$.

4.3.2. *Team Games*

Following Marschak and Radner (1972), the game $G = \langle N, S^N, u^N \rangle$ is said to be a *team game* if there exists a single utility function $u^* : S^N \to \mathbb{R}$ with the property that $u_i \equiv u^*$ for all $i \in N$.

4.4. BEYOND NUMERICAL UTILITY

All of the definitions in this section are clear and familiar when players have numerical utilities. One of our tasks in later sections will be to investigate extensions of these concepts which apply to different kinds of ordinal or cardinal utility.

5. Games with Ordinal Utility

5.1. ORDINAL NON-COMPARABILITY

A game $G = \langle N, S^N, u^N \rangle$ will be described as having *ordinal utility* if it is equivalent to each alternative game $\tilde{G} = \langle N, S^N, \tilde{u}^N \rangle$ with the same sets of players and strategies, but with transformed utility functions $\tilde{u}_i$ having the property that u_i and $\tilde{u}_i$ are ordinally equivalent for each $i \in N$. Thus, the players' utility functions are ordinally non-comparable. This section shows that most familiar concepts concerning pure strategies in non-cooperative games not only satisfy ordinal non-comparability because they are invariant under increasing transformations of individuals' utility functions, but are actually invariant under a much broader class of utility transformations.

5.1.1. *Two-Person Strictly Competitive Games*

A two-person game with $N = \{1, 2\}$ is said to be *strictly competitive* provided that for all $(s_1, s_2), (s_1', s_2') \in S_1 \times S_2$, one has $u_1(s_1, s_2) \geq u_1(s_1', s_2')$ iff $u_2(s_1, s_2) \leq u_2(s_1', s_2')$. Alternatively, the two players are said to have *opposing interests.*

Note that a two-person game is strictly competitive if and only if the utility function u_2 is ordinally equivalent to $-u_1$ — which is true iff u_1 is ordinally equivalent to $-u_2$. Thus, strict competitiveness is necessary and sufficient for a two-person game to be ordinally equivalent to a zero-sum game.

5.1.2. *Ordinal Team Games*

The game $G = \langle N, S^N, u^N \rangle$ is said to be an *ordinal team game* if there exists a single ordering R^* on S^N with the property that, for all $s^N, \tilde{s}^N \in S^N$, one has $s^N \; R^* \; \tilde{s}^N$ iff $u_i(s^N) \geq u_i(\tilde{s}^N)$ for all $i \in N$. Thus, all the players have ordinally equivalent utility functions. Often game theorists have preferred alternative terms such as "pure coordination game", or games with "common" or "identical interests".

The players all agree how to order different strategy profiles. So all agree what is the set of optimal strategy profiles, which are the only Pareto efficient profiles. Any Pareto efficient profile is a Nash equilibrium, but there can be multiple Nash equilibria. These multiple equilibria may be "Pareto ranked", in the sense that some equilibria are Pareto superior to others.

5.2. PURE STRATEGY DOMINANCE AND BEST REPLIES

5.2.1. *Strategy Contingent Preferences*

Suppose player i faces known strategies s_j $(j \in N \setminus \{i\})$ chosen by the other players. Let $s_{-i} = \langle s_j \rangle_{j \in N \setminus \{i\}}$ denote the profile of these other players' strategies, and let $S_{-i} = \prod_{j \in N \setminus \{i\}} S_j$ be the set of all such profiles.

Given the utility function u_i on S^N, player i has a (strategy contingent) preference ordering $R_i(s_{-i})$ on S_i defined by

$$s_i \; R_i(s_{-i}) \; s_i' \iff u_i(s_i, s_{-i}) \geq u_i(s_i', s_{-i})$$

Let $P_i(s_{-i})$ denote the corresponding strict preference relation, which satisfies $s_i \; P_i(s_{-i}) \; s'_i$ iff $u_i(s_i, s_{-i}) > u_i(s'_i, s_{-i})$.

5.2.2. *Domination by Pure Strategies*
Player i's strategy $s_i \in S_i$ is *strictly dominated* by $s'_i \in S_i$ iff $s'_i \; P_i(\bar{s}_{-i}) \; s_i$ for all strategy profiles $\bar{s}_{-i} \in S_{-i}$ of the other players. Similarly, player i's strategy $s_i \in S_i$ is *weakly dominated* by $s'_i \in S_i$ iff $s'_i \; R_i(\bar{s}_{-i}) \; s_i$ for all strategy profiles $\bar{s}_{-i} \in S_{-i}$ of the other players, with $s_i \; P_i(s_{-i}) \; s'_i$ for at least one $s_{-i} \in S_{-i}$.

5.2.3. *Best Replies*
Given the utility function u_i on S^N, player i's set of *best replies* to s_{-i} is given by

$$\begin{aligned} B_i(s_{-i}; u_i) &:= \arg\max_{s_i \in S_i} u_i(s_i, s_{-i}) \\ &= \{ s_i^* \in S_i \mid s_i \in S_i \Longrightarrow s_i^* \; R_i(s_{-i}) \; s_i \} \end{aligned}$$

The mapping $s_{-i} \mapsto\!\!\!\rightarrow B_i(s_{-i}; u_i)$ from S_{-i} to S_i is called player i's *best reply correspondence* $B_i(\cdot; u_i)$ given the utility function u_i.

5.2.4. *Pure Strategy Solution Concepts*
Evidently, each player i's family of preference orderings $R_i(s_{-i})$ $(s_{-i} \in S_{-i})$ determines which pure strategies dominate other pure strategies either weakly or strictly, as well as the best responses. It follows that the same orderings determine any solution concept which depends on dominance relations or best responses, such as Nash equilibrium, and strategies that survive iterated deletion of strategies which are dominated by other pure strategies.

5.3. BEYOND ORDINAL NON-COMPARABILITY

Each player i's family of preference orderings $R_i(s_{-i})$ $(s_{-i} \in S_{-i})$ over S_i is obviously invariant under utility transformations of the form $\tilde{u}_i(s^N) \equiv \psi_i(u_i(s^N); s_{-i})$ where for each fixed $\bar{s}_{-i} \in S_{-i}$ the mapping $r \mapsto \psi_i(r; \bar{s}_{-i})$ from $\mathbb{R}$ into itself is strictly increasing. This form of utility invariance is like the social choice property of ONC invariance for a society in which the set of individuals expands from N to the new set

$$N^* := \{ (i, s_{-i}) \mid i \in N, \; s_{-i} \in S_{-i} \} = \bigcup_{i \in N} [\{i\} \times S_{-i}]$$

The elements of this expanded set are "strategy contingent" versions of each player $i \in N$, whose existence depends on which strategy profile s_{-i} the other players choose. The best reply and equilibrium correspondences will accordingly be described as satisfying *strategy contingent ordinal non-comparability* (or SCONC).

5.4. SOME SPECIAL ORDINAL GAMES

5.4.1. *Generalized Strictly Competitive Games*

The two-person game $G = \langle N, S^N, u^N \rangle$ with $N = \{1, 2\}$ is said to be a *generalized strictly competitive game* if there exist strictly increasing strategy contingent transformations $r \mapsto \psi_1(r; \bar{s}_2)$ and $r \mapsto \psi_2(r; \bar{s}_1)$ of the two players' utility functions such that the transformed game $\tilde{G} = \langle N, S^N, \tilde{u}^N \rangle$ with $\tilde{u}_1(s_1, s_2) \equiv \phi_i(u_1(s_1, s_2), s_2)$ and $\tilde{u}_2(s_1, s_2) \equiv \phi_i(u_2(s_1, s_2), s_1)$ is a two-person zero-sum game. A necessary and sufficient condition for this property to hold is that the binary relation $\hat{R}$ on $S_1 \times S_2$ defined by

$$(s_1, s_2)\ \hat{R}\ (s_1', s_2') \iff \begin{array}{l} s_2 = s_2' \text{ and } u_1(s_1, s_2) \geq u_1(s_1', s_2') \\ \text{or } s_1 = s_1' \text{ and } u_2(s_1, s_2) \leq u_2(s_1', s_2') \end{array}$$

should admit a transitive extension.

5.4.2. *Generalized Ordinal Team Games*

The game $G = \langle N, S^N, v^N \rangle$ is said to be a *generalized ordinal team game* if there exists a single ordering R^* on S^N with the property that, for all $i \in N$, all $s_i, s_i' \in S_i$ and all $\bar{s}_{-i} \in S_{-i}$, one has $s_i\ R_i(\bar{s}_{-i})\ s_i'$ iff $(s_i, \bar{s}_{-i})\ R^*\ (s_i', \bar{s}_{-i})$. In any such game, the best reply correspondences and Nash equilibrium set will be identical to those in an ordinal team game.

6. Games with Cardinal Utility

6.1. CARDINAL NON-COMPARABILITY

A game $G = \langle N, S^N, v^N \rangle$ will be described as having *cardinal utility* if it is equivalent to each alternative game $\tilde{G} = \langle N, S^N, \tilde{v}^N \rangle$ with the same sets of players and strategies, but with transformed utility functions $\tilde{v}_i$ having the property that v_i and $\tilde{v}_i$ are cardinally equivalent for each $i \in N$. That is, there must exist additive constants α_i and positive multiplicative constants δ_i such that $\tilde{v}_i(s^N) \equiv \alpha_i + \delta_i v_i(s^N)$ for all $i \in N$.

6.1.1. *Zero and Constant Sum Games*

A game $G = \langle N, S^N, v^N \rangle$ is said to be *zero sum* provided that $\sum_{i \in N} v_i(s^N) \equiv 0$. This property is preserved under increasing affine transformations $v_i \mapsto \alpha_i + \delta v_i$ where the multiplicative constant δ is independent of i, and the additive constants α_i satisfy $\sum_{i \in N} \alpha_i = 0$. Thus, the zero sum property relies on a strengthened form of the CUC invariance property described in Section 3.3.4.

The *constant sum property* is satisfied when there exists a constant $C \in \mathbb{R}$ such that $\sum_{i \in N} v_i(s^N) \equiv C$. This property is preserved under increasing affine transformations $v_i \mapsto \alpha_i + \delta v_i$ where the multiplicative constant δ is independent of i, and the additive constants α_i are arbitrary. Thus, the constant sum property is preserved under precisely the class of transformations allowed by the CUC invariance property. In this sense, the constant sum property relies on interpersonal comparisons of utility.

6.1.2. *Constant Weighted Sum Games*
Rather more interesting is the *constant weighted sum property*, which holds when there exist multiplicative weights ω_i $(i \in N)$ and a constant $C \in \mathbb{R}$ such that $\sum_{i \in N} \omega_i v_i(s^N) \equiv C$. This property is preserved under all increasing affine transformations $v_i \mapsto \tilde{v}_i = \alpha_i + \delta_i v_i$ because, if $\sum_{i \in N} \omega_i v_i(s^N) \equiv C$, then $\sum_{i \in N} \tilde{\omega}_i \tilde{v}_i(s^N) \equiv \tilde{C}$ where $\tilde{\omega}_i = \omega_i / \delta_i$ and $\tilde{C} = C + \sum_{i \in N} \omega_i \alpha_i / \delta_i$. Thus, we are back in the case of CNC invariance, without interpersonal comparisons.

A two-person game with cardinal utilities is said to be *strictly competitive* if and only if the utility function u_2 is cardinally equivalent to $-u_1$. That is, there must exist a constant α and a positive constant δ such that $u_2(s_1, s_2) \equiv \alpha - \delta u_1(s_1, s_2)$. This form of strict competitiveness is therefore satisfied if and only if the two-person game with cardinal utilities has a constant weighted sum. The same condition is also necessary and sufficient for a two-person game to be cardinally equivalent to a zero-sum game.

6.1.3. *Cardinal Team Games*
The game $G = \langle N, S^N, v^N \rangle$ is said to be an *cardinal team game* if there exists a single utility function v^* on S^N which is cardinally equivalent to each player's utility function v_i. Thus, all the players must have cardinally equivalent utility functions, and so identical preferences over the space of lotteries $\Delta(S^N)$.

6.2. DOMINATED STRATEGIES AND BEST RESPONSES

6.2.1. *Belief Contingent Preferences*
Suppose player i attaches a probability $\pi_i(s_{-i})$ to each profile $s_{-i} \in S_{-i}$ of other players' strategies. That is, player i has *probabilistic beliefs* specified by π_i in the set $\Delta(S_{-i})$ of all probability distributions on the (finite) set S_{-i}.

Given any NM utility function v_i for player i defined on S^N, and given beliefs $\pi_i \in \Delta(S_{-i})$, let

$$V_i(s_i; \pi_i) := \sum_{s_{-i} \in S_{-i}} \pi_i(s_{-i}) v_i(s_i, s_{-i})$$

denote the expected value of v_i when player i chooses the pure strategy s_i. Then

$$\mathbb{E}_{\sigma_i} V_i(\cdot; \pi_i) := \sum_{s_i \in S_i} \sigma_i(s_i) V_i(s_i; \pi_i)$$

is the expected value of v_i when player i chooses the mixed strategy $\sigma_i \in \Delta(S_i)$. There is a corresponding (belief contingent) preference ordering $R_i(\pi_i)$ on $\Delta(S_i)$ for player i defined by

$$\sigma_i \; R_i(\pi_i) \; \sigma_i' \iff \mathbb{E}_{\sigma_i} V_i(\cdot; \pi_i) \geq \mathbb{E}_{\sigma_i'} V_i(\cdot; \pi_i).$$

6.2.2. *Dominated Strategies*
Player i's strategy $s_i \in S_i$ is *strictly dominated* iff there exists an alternative mixed strategy $\sigma_i \in \Delta(S_i)$ such that $\sum_{\tilde{s}_i \in S_i} \sigma_i(\tilde{s}_i) v_i(\tilde{s}_i, \bar{s}_{-i}) > v_i(s_i, \bar{s}_{-i})$ for all strategy

profiles $\bar{s}_{-i} \in S_{-i}$ of the other players. As is well known, a strategy may be strictly dominated even if there is no alternative pure strategy that dominates it. So the definition is less stringent than the one used for pure strategies.

Similarly, player i's strategy $s_i \in S_i$ is *weakly dominated* iff there exists an alternative mixed strategy $\sigma_i \in \Delta(S_i)$ such that $\sum_{\tilde{s}_i \in S_i} \sigma_i(\tilde{s}_i) v_i(\tilde{s}_i, \bar{s}_{-i}) \geq v_i(s_i, \bar{s}_{-i})$ for all strategy profiles $\bar{s}_{-i} \in S_{-i}$ of the other players, with strict inequality for at least one such strategy profile.

6.2.3. *Best Replies*

Given the NM utility function v_i, player i's set of *best replies* to π_i is

$$B_i(\pi_i; v_i) := \arg\max_{s_i \in S_i} V_i(s_i; \pi_i)$$

The mapping $\pi_i \mapsto\!\!\!\!\to B_i(\pi_i; v_i)$ from $\Delta(S_{-i})$ to S_i is called player i's *best reply correspondence* $B_i(\cdot; v_i)$ given the NM utility function v_i. It is easy to see that the set

$$\{ \sigma_i^* \in \Delta(S_i) \mid \sigma_i \in \Delta(S_i) \Longrightarrow \sigma_i^* \; R_i(\pi_i) \; \sigma_i \}$$

of *mixed strategy best replies* to π_i is equal to $\Delta(B_i(\pi_i; v_i))$, the subset of those $\sigma_i \in \Delta(S_i)$ that satisfy $\sum_{s_i \in B_i(\pi_i; v_i)} \sigma_i(s_i) = 1$.

6.3. BEYOND CARDINAL NON-COMPARABILITY

The definitions above evidently imply that the preferences $R_i(\pi_i)$ and the set of player i's dominated strategies are invariant under increasing affine transformations of the form

$$\tilde{v}_i(s^N) \equiv \alpha_i(s_{-i}) + \delta_i v_i(s^N)$$

where, for each $i \in N$, the multiplicative constant δ_i is positive. So, of course, are each player's best reply correspondence $B_i(\cdot; v_i)$, as well as the sets of Nash equilibria, correlated equilibria, and rationalizable strategies.[6] This property will be called *strategy contingent cardinal non-comparability* — or SCCNC invariance.

As in the case of SCONC invariance discussed in Section 5.3, consider the expanded set

$$N^* := \{ (i, s_{-i}) \mid i \in N, \; s_{-i} \in S_{-i} \} = \bigcup_{i \in N} [\{i\} \times S_{-i}]$$

of strategy contingent versions of each player $i \in N$. Then SCCNC invariance amounts to CUC invariance between members of the set $N_i^* := \{ (i, s_{-i}) \mid s_{-i} \in S_{-i} \}$, for each $i \in N$, combined with CNC invariance between members of different sets N_i^*.

[6] Such non-cooperative solution concepts are defined and discussed in Hammond (2004), as well as some in the game theory textbooks cited there — for example, Fudenberg and Tirole (1991) or Osborne and Rubinstein (1994).

6.4. SOME SPECIAL CARDINAL GAMES

6.4.1. *Generalized Zero-Sum Games*

The two-person game $G = \langle N, S^N, v^N \rangle$ with $N = \{1, 2\}$ is said to be a *two-person generalized zero-sum game* if there exist strictly increasing strategy contingent affine transformations of the form described in Section 6.3 — namely,

$$\begin{aligned} \tilde{v}_1(s_1, s_2) &\equiv \alpha_1(s_2) + \rho_1 v_1(s_1, s_2) \\ \text{and } \tilde{v}_2(s_1, s_2) &\equiv \alpha_2(s_1) + \rho_2 v_2(s_1, s_2) \end{aligned}$$

— such that $\tilde{v}_1 + \tilde{v}_2 \equiv 0$. This will be true if and only if

$$v_2(s_1, s_2) \equiv -\rho v_1(s_1, s_2) + \alpha_2^*(s_1) + \alpha_1^*(s_2)$$

for suitable functions $\alpha_2^*(s_1)$, $\alpha_1^*(s_2)$, and a suitable positive constant ρ. These transformations are more general than those allowed in the constant weighted sum games of Section 6.1.2 because the additive constants can depend on the other player's strategy.

For ordinary two-person zero-sum games there are well known special results such as the maximin theorem, and special techniques such as linear programming. Obviously, one can adapt these to two-person generalized zero-sum games.

6.4.2. *Generalized Cardinal Team Games*

The game $G = \langle N, S^N, v^N \rangle$ is said to be a *generalized cardinal team game* if each player's utility function can be expressed as an increasing strategy contingent affine transformation $v_i(s^N) \equiv \alpha_i(s_{-i}) + \rho_i v^*(s^N)$ of a common cardinal utility function v^*. Then the best reply correspondences and Nash equilibrium set will be identical to those in the cardinal team game with this common utility function.

In such a game, note that i's gain to deviating from the strategy profile s^N by choosing s_i' instead is given by

$$v_i(s_i', s_{-i}) - v_i(s_i, s_{-i}) = \rho_i[v^*(s_i', s_{-i}) - v^*(s_i, s_{-i})].$$

In the special case when $\rho_i = 1$ for all $i \in N$, this implies that G is a *potential game*, with v^* as the *potential function*. Because of this restriction on the constants ρ_i, however, this definition due to Monderer and Shapley (1996) involves implicit interpersonal comparisons. See Ui (2000) in particular for further discussion of potential games. Morris and Ui (2005) describe games with more general constants ρ_i as *weighted potential games*. They also consider *generalized potential games* which are best response equivalent to cardinal team games.

7. Quantal Response Equilibria

7.1. STOCHASTIC UTILITY

Given any feasible set $F \in \mathcal{F}$, ordinary decision theory considers a choice set $C(F) \subset F$. On the other hand, *stochastic decision theory* considers a simple *choice lottery*

$q(\cdot, F) \in \Delta(F)$ defined for each $F \in \mathcal{F}$. Specifically, let $q(x, F)$ denote the probability of choosing $x \in F$ when the agent is presented with the feasible set F.

Following the important choice model due to Luce (1958, 1959), the mapping $u : X \to \mathbb{R}_+$ is said to be a *stochastic utility function* in the case when $q(x, F) = u(x)/\sum_{y \in F} u(y)$ for all $x \in F$. In this case $q(x, F)$ is obviously invariant to transformations of u that take the form $\tilde{u}(x) \equiv \rho u(x)$ for a suitable mutiplicative constant $\rho > 0$. Thus, u is a positive-valued function defined up to a ratio scale. And whenever $x, y \in F \in \mathcal{F}$, the utility ratio $u(x)/u(y)$ becomes equal to the choice probability ratio $q(x, F)/q(y, F)$.

Much econometric work on discrete choice uses the special *multinomial logit* version of Luce's model, in which $\ln u(x) \equiv \beta U(x)$ for a suitable *logit utility* function U on $\Delta(Y)$ and a suitable constant $\beta > 0$. Then the formula for $q(x, F)$ takes the convenient loglinear form

$$\ln q(x, F) = \ln u(x) - \ln\left(\sum_{y \in F} u(y)\right) = \alpha + \beta U(x)$$

where the normalizing constant α is chosen to ensure that $\sum_{x \in F} q(x, F) = 1$. Obviously, this expression for $\ln q(x, F)$ is invariant under transformations taking the form $\tilde{U}(x) \equiv \gamma + U(x)$ for an arbitrary constant γ. A harmless normalization should be to choose utility units so that $\beta = 1$. In which case, whenever $x, y \in F \in \mathcal{F}$, the utility difference $U(x) - U(y)$ becomes equal to the logarithmic choice probability ratio $\ln[q(x, F)/q(y, F)]$.

7.2. LOGIT EQUILIBRIUM

Consider the normal form game $G = \langle N, S^N, v^N \rangle$, as in Section 6.1. For each player $i \in N$, assume that the multinomial logit version of Luce's model applies directly to the choice of strategy $s_i \in S_i$. Specifically, assume that there is a stochastic utility function of the form $f_i(s_i, \pi_i) = \exp[\beta_i V_i(s_i, \pi_i)]$, for some positive constant β_i. Then each player $i \in N$ has a *logit response function* $\pi_i \mapsto p_i(\pi_i)(\cdot)$ mapping $\Delta(S_{-i})$ to $\Delta(S_i)$ which satisfies

$$\ln[p_i(\pi_i)(s_i)] = \beta_i V_i(s_i, \pi_i) - \rho_i(\pi_i)$$

for all $\pi_i \in \Delta(S_{-i})$ and all $s_i \in S_i$, where the normalizing constant $\rho_i(\pi_i)$ is defined as the weighted exponential mean $\ln\left\{\sum_{s_i \in S_i} \exp[\beta_i V_i(s_i, \pi_i)]\right\}$.

Following McKelvey and Palfrey (1995), a *logit equilibrium* is defined as a profile $\bar{\mu}^N \in \prod_{i \in N} \Delta(S_i)$ of independent mixed strategies satisfying $\bar{\mu}_i(s_i) = p_i(\bar{\pi}_i)(s_i)$ for each player $i \in N$ and each strategy $s_i \in S_i$, where $\bar{\pi}_i = \bar{\mu}^{N\setminus\{i\}} = \prod_{h \in N\setminus\{i\}} \bar{\mu}_h$. In fact, such an equilibrium must be a fixed point of the mapping $p : D \to D$ defined on the domain $D := \prod_{i \in N} \Delta(S_i)$ by $p(\mu^N)(s^N) = \langle p_i(\mu^{N\setminus\{i\}})(s_i) \rangle_{s_i \in S_i}$. Note that this mapping, and the associated set of logit equilibria, are invariant under all increasing affine transformations of the form $\tilde{v}_i(s^N) \equiv \alpha_i(s_{-i}) + \delta_i v_i(s^N)$ provided that we replace each β_i with $\tilde{\beta}_i := \beta_i/\rho_i$. Indeed, one allowable transformation makes each $\tilde{\beta}_i = 1$, in which case each transformed utility difference satisfies

$$v_i(s_i, \bar{s}_{-i}) - v_i(s'_i, \bar{s}_{-i}) = \ln[p_i(1_{\bar{s}_{-i}})(s_i)/p_i(1_{\bar{s}_{-i}})(s'_i)]$$

where $1_{\bar{s}_{-i}}$ denotes the degenerate lottery that attaches probability 1 to the strategy profile $\bar{s}_{-i}$. Once again, utility differences become equal to logarithmic probability ratios.

8. Evolutionary Stability

8.1. REPLICATOR DYNAMICS IN CONTINUOUS TIME

Let $G = \langle N, S^N, v^N \rangle$ be a game with cardinal utility, as defined in Section 6.1. Suppose that each $i \in N$ represents an entire population of players, rather than a single player. Suppose too that there are large and equal numbers of players in each population. All players are matched randomly in groups of size $\#N$, with one player from each population. The matching occurs repeatedly over time, and independently between time periods. At each moment of time every matched group of $\#N$ players plays the game G. Among each population i, each strategy $s_i \in S_i$ corresponds to a player type. The proportion $\sigma_i(s_i)$ of players of each such type within the population i evolves over time. Assuming suitable random draws, each player in population i encounters a probability distribution $\pi_i \in \Delta(S_{-i})$ over other players' type profiles $s_{-i} \in S_{-i}$ that is given by

$$\pi_i(s_{-i}) = \bar{\pi}_i(\langle s_j \rangle_{j \in N \setminus \{i\}}) = \prod_{j \in N \setminus \{i\}} \sigma_j(s_j)$$

The expected payoff $V_i(s_i, \pi_i)$ experienced by any player of type s_i in population i is interpreted as a measure of (relative) "biological fitness". It is assumed that the rate of replication of that type of player depends on the difference between that measure of fitness and the average fitness $\mathbb{E}_{\sigma_i} V_i(\cdot, \pi_i)$ over the whole population i. It is usual to work in continuous time and to treat the dynamic process as deterministic because it is assumed that the populations are sufficiently large to eliminate any randomness.[7] Thus, one is led to study a *replicator dynamic process* in the form of simultaneous differential equations which determine the proportional net rate of growth $\hat{\sigma}_i(s_i) := \frac{d}{dt} \ln \sigma_i(s_i)$ of each type of player in each population.

8.2. STANDARD REPLICATOR DYNAMICS

Following the ideas of Taylor and Jonker (1978) and Taylor (1979), the *standard replicator dynamics* (Weibull, 1995) occur when the differential equations imply that the proportional rate of growth $\hat{\sigma}_i(s_i)$ equals the measure of *excess fitness* defined by

$$E_i(s_i; \sigma_i, \pi_i) := V_i(s_i, \pi_i) - \mathbb{E}_{\sigma_i} V_i(\cdot, \pi_i)$$

[7] See Boylan (1992) and Duffie and Sun (2004) for a discussion of this.

for each $i \in N$ and each $s_i \in S_i$. In this case, consider affine transformations which take each player's payoff function from v_i to $\tilde{v}_i(s^N) \equiv \alpha_i(s_{-i}) + \delta_i v_i(s^N)$, where the multiplicative constants δ_i are all positive. This multiplies by δ_i each excess fitness function $E_i(s_i; \sigma_i, \pi_i)$, and so the transformed rates of population growth. Thus, these utility transformations in general speed up or slow down the replicator dynamics within each population. When $\delta_i = \delta$, independent of i, all rates adjust proportionately, and it is really just like measuring time in a different unit. Generally, however, invariance of the replicator dynamics requires all the affine transformations to be translations of the form $\tilde{v}_i(s^N) \equiv \alpha_i(s_{-i}) + v_i(s^N)$, with each $\delta_i = 1$, in effect. This is entirely appropriate because each utility difference $v_i(s_i, \bar{s}_{-i}) - v_i(s'_i, \bar{s}_{-i})$ equals the difference $E_i(s_i; \sigma_i, 1_{\bar{s}_{-i}}) - E_i(s'_i; \sigma_i, 1_{\bar{s}_{-i}})$ in excess fitness, which is independent of σ_i, and so equals the difference $\hat{\sigma}_i(s_i) - \hat{\sigma}_i(s'_i)$ in proportional rates of growth.

8.3. ADJUSTED REPLICATOR DYNAMICS

Weibull (1995) also presents a second form of *adjusted replicator dynamics*, based on Maynard Smith (1982). The proportional rates of growth become

$$\hat{\sigma}_i(s_i) = \frac{E_i(s_i; \sigma_i, \pi_i)}{\mathbb{E}_{\sigma_i} V_i(\cdot, \pi_i)} = \frac{V_i(s_i, \pi_i)}{\mathbb{E}_{\sigma_i} V_i(\cdot, \pi_i)} - 1$$

for each $i \in N$ and each $s_i \in S_i$. Then the above affine transformations have no effect on rates of population growth in the case when $\tilde{v}_i(s^N) \equiv \delta_i v_i(s^N)$, for arbitrary positive constants δ_i that can differ between populations. Thus, different utility functions are determined up to non-comparable ratio scales. Indeed, each utility ratio $v_i(s_i, \bar{s}_{-i})/v_i(s'_i, \bar{s}_{-i})$ equals the excess fitness ratio $E_i(s_i; \sigma_i, 1_{\bar{s}_{-i}})/E_i(s'_i; \sigma_i, 1_{\bar{s}_{-i}})$, which is independent of σ_i, and so equals the ratio $\hat{\sigma}_i(s_i)/\hat{\sigma}_i(s'_i)$ of the proportional rates of growth.

9. Consequentialist Foundations

9.1. CONSEQUENTIALIST GAME FORMS

Let X denote a fixed domain of possible consequences. A *consequentialist game form* is a triple $\Gamma = \langle N, S^N, \gamma \rangle$ where:

(i) N is a finite set of *players*;
(ii) each player $i \in N$ has a *strategy set* S_i, and $S^N = \prod_{i \in N} S_i$ is the set of *strategy profiles*;
(iii) there is an *outcome function* $\gamma : S^N \to X$ which specifies what consequence results from each strategy profile in the domain S^N.

Consider any fixed profile w^N of individual utility functions $w_i : X \to \mathbb{R}$ defined on the consequence domain X. Given any consequentialist game form Γ, there is a unique corresponding game $G^\Gamma(w^N) = \langle N, S^N, u^N \rangle$ with $u_i(s^N) \equiv w_i(\gamma(s^N))$ for all

$s^N \in S^N$ and all $i \in N$. There is also a best reply correspondence

$$\bar{s}_{-i} \mapsto\!\!\!\to B_i^\Gamma(\bar{s}_{-i}; w_i) := \arg\max_{s_i \in S_i} w_i(\gamma(s_i, \bar{s}_{-i}))$$

and a (possibly empty) pure strategy Nash equilibrium set $E^\Gamma(w^N)$.

9.2. ORDINAL INVARIANCE

An obvious invariance property is that $B_i^\Gamma(\bar{s}_{-i}; w_i) \equiv B_i^\Gamma(\bar{s}_{-i}; \tilde{w}_i)$ for all possible Γ, which is true if and only if w_i and $\tilde{w}_i$ are ordinally equivalent functions on the domain X, for each $i \in N$. Similarly, all the other pure strategy solution concepts mentioned in Section 5.2.4, especially the pure strategy Nash equilibrium set $E^\Gamma(w^N)$, are preserved for all possible Γ if and only if the two profiles w^N and $\tilde{w}^N$ are ordinally equivalent. In this sense, we have reverted to the usual form of ONC invariance, rather than the SCONC invariance property that applies when just one game is being considered. This is one reason why the theory set out in Hammond (2004), for instance, does consider the whole class of consequentialist game forms.

9.3. CARDINAL INVARIANCE

A similar invariance concept applies when each player i's strategy set S_i is replaced by $\Delta(S_i)$, the set of mixed strategies, and the outcome function $\gamma : S^N \to X$ is replaced by a lottery outcome function $\gamma : \Delta(S^N) \to \Delta(X)$. Then all the players' best reply correspondences are preserved in all consequentialist game forms Γ if and only if the two profiles w^N and $\tilde{w}^N$ are cardinally equivalent. Similarly for any other solution concepts that depend only on the players' belief contingent preference orderings $R_i(\pi_i)$.

10. Concluding Remarks

Traditionally, game theorists have contented themselves with specifying a single numerical payoff function for each player. They do so without any consideration of the units in which utility is measured, or what alternative profiles of payoff functions can be regarded as equivalent. This paper will have succeeded if it leaves the reader with the impression that considering such measurement issues can considerably enrich our understanding of the decision-theoretic foundations of game theory. A useful by-product is identifying which games can be treated as equivalent to especially simple games, such as two-person zero-sum games, or team games.

Finally, it is pointed out that the usual utility concepts in single-person decision theory can be derived by considering different players' objectives in the whole class of consequentialist game forms, rather than just in one particular game.

Acknowledgements

A very preliminary version of some of the ideas discussed in this paper was presented to a seminar in May 2002 at the Università Cattolica del Sacro Cuore in Milan. My thanks to Luigi Campiglio for inviting me, and to the audience for their questions and comments. The present version (February 2005) is offered as a tribute to my friend and colleague Christian Seidl, with whom (and also Salvador Barberà) it has been my privilege to co-edit the *Handbook of Utility Theory.*

References

Aumann, R.J. 1985. "An Axiomatization of the Non-Transferable Utility Value", *Econometrica* 53, 599–612.

Bossert, W., and J.A. Weymark. 2004. "Utility in Social Choice", in: S. Barberà, P.J. Hammond, and C. Seidl (eds.): *Handbook of Utility Theory, Vol. 2: Extensions*, Boston: Kluwer Academic Publishers, ch. 20, 1099–1177.

Boylan, R. 1992. "Laws of Large Numbers for Dynamical Systems with Randomly Matched Individuals", *Journal of Economic Theory* 57, 473–504.

Dagan, N., and R. Serrano. 1998. "Invariance and Randomness in the Nash Program for Coalitional Games", *Economics Letters* 58, 43–49.

D'Aspremont, C., and L. Gevers. 1977. "Equity and the Informational Basis of Collective Choice", *Review of Economic Studies* 44, 199–209.

D'Aspremont, C., and L. Gevers. 2002. "Social Welfare Functionals and Interpersonal Comparability", in: K.J. Arrow, A.K. Sen, and K. Suzumura (eds.): *Handbook of Social Choice and Welfare, Vol. I*, Amsterdam: North-Holland, ch. 10, 459–541.

Duffie, D., and Y.N. Sun. 2004. "The Exact Law of Large Numbers for Independent Random Matching". Preprint available at `http://www.stanford.edu/~duffie/lln-I.pdf`.

Fisher, I. (1892) "Mathematical Investigations in the Theory of Value and Prices" *Transactions of the Connecticut Academy of Arts and Sciences* 9: 1–124.

Fudenberg, D., and J. Tirole. 1991. *Game Theory*, Cambridge, Mass.: MIT Press.

Hammerstein, P., and R. Selten. 1994. "Game Theory and Evolutionary Biology", in: R.J. Aumann and S. Hart (eds.): *Handbook of Game Theory with Economic Applications*, Vol. 2, Amsterdam: North-Holland, ch. 28, 929–993.

Hammond, P.J. 2004. "Expected Utility in Non-Cooperative Game Theory", in: S. Barberà, P.J. Hammond, and C. Seidl (eds.): *Handbook of Utility Theory, Vol. 2: Extensions*, Boston: Kluwer Academic Publishers, ch. 18, 979–1063.

Kaneko, M., and M.H. Wooders. 2004. "Utility Theories in Cooperative Games", in: S. Barberà, P.J. Hammond, and C. Seidl (eds.): *Handbook of Utility Theory, Vol. 2: Extensions*, Boston: Kluwer Academic Publishers, ch. 19, 1065–1098.

Kıbrıs, Ö. 2004a. "Ordinal Invariance in Multicoalitional Bargaining", *Games and Economic Behavior* 46, 76–87.

Kıbrıs, Ö. 2004b. "Egalitarianism in Ordinal Bargaining: The Shapley–Shubik Rule", *Games and Economic Behavior* 49, 157–170.

Luce, R.D. 1958. "An Axiom for Probabilistic Choice Behavior and an Application to Choices among Gambles (Abstract)", *Econometrica* 26, 318–319.

Luce, R.D. 1959. *Individual Choice Behavior*, New York: John Wiley.

Marschak, J., and R. Radner. 1972. *Economic Theory of Teams*, New Haven: Yale University Press.

Maynard Smith, J. 1982. *Evolution and the Theory of Games*, Cambridge: Cambridge University Press.

McKelvey, R.D., and T.R. Palfrey. 1995. "Quantal Response Equilibria for Normal Form Games", *Games and Economic Behavior* 10, 6–38.

McLean, R.P. 2002. "Values of Non-Transferable Utility Games", in R.J. Aumann and S. Hart (eds.): *Handbook of Game Theory with Economic Applications*, Vol. 3, Amsterdam: North-Holland, ch. 55, 2077–2120.

Monderer, D., and L.S. Shapley. 1996. "Potential Games", *Games and Economic Behavior* 14, 124–143.

Mongin, P., and C. d'Aspremont. 1998. "Utility Theory and Ethics", in: S. Barberà, P.J. Hammond, and C. Seidl (eds.): *Handbook of Utility Theory, Vol. 1: Principles*, Boston: Kluwer Academic Publishers, ch. 10, 371–481.

Morris, S., and T. Ui. 2004. "Best Response Equivalence", *Games and Economic Behavior* 49, 260–287.

Morris, S., and T. Ui. 2005. "Generalized Potentials and Robust Sets of Equilibria", *Journal of Economic Theory* (in press).

Nash, J.F. 1950. "The Bargaining Problem", *Econometrica* 28, 155–162.

Osborne, M.J., and A. Rubinstein. 1994. *A Course in Game Theory*, Cambridge, Mass.: MIT Press.

Pareto, V. 1896. *Cours d'économie politique*, Lausanne: Rouge.

Roberts, K.W.S. 1980. "Interpersonal Comparability and Social Choice Theory", *Review of Economic Studies* 47, 421–439.

Roth, A.L. 1979. *Models of Bargaining*, Berlin: Springer Verlag.

Samet, D., and Z. Safra. 2005. "A Family of Ordinal Solutions to Bargaining Problems with Many Players", *Games and Economic Behavior* 50, 89–108.

Sen, A.K. 1970. "Interpersonal Aggregation and Partial Comparability", *Econometrica* 38, 393–409. Reprinted with correction in: A.K. Sen, *Choice, Welfare and Measurement*, Oxford: Basil Blackwell, 1982.

Sen, A.K. 1973. *On Economic Inequality*, Oxford: Clarendon Press.

Sen, A.K. 1974. "Informational Bases of Alternative Welfare Approaches: Aggregation and Income Distribution", *Journal of Public Economics* 3, 387–403.

Sen, A.K. 1977. "On Weights and Measures: Informational Constraints in Social Welfare Analysis", *Econometrica* 45, 1539–1572.

Sen, A.K. 1979. "Interpersonal Comparisons of Welfare", in: M. Boskin (ed.): *Economics and Human Welfare: Essays in Honor of Tibor Scitovsky*, New York, Academic Press. Reprinted in: A.K. Sen, *Choice, Welfare and Measurement*, Oxford: Basil Blackwell, 1982.

Shapley, L. 1969. "Utility Comparisons and the Theory of Games", in: G.T. Guilbaud (ed.): *La Décision: Agrégation et dynamique des ordres de préférence*, Paris: Editions du Centre National de la Recherche Scientifique, 251–263.

Taylor, P.D. 1979, "Evolutionarily Stable Strategies with Two Types of Player", *Journal of Applied Probability* 16, 76–83.

Taylor, P.D., and L.B. Jonker. 1978. "Evolutionarily Stable Strategies and Game Dynamics", *Mathematical Biosciences* 40, 145–156.

Thomson, W. 1994. "Cooperative Models of Bargaining", in: R.J. Aumann and S. Hart (eds.): *Handbook of Game Theory with Economic Applications*, Vol. 2, Amsterdam: North-Holland, ch. 35, 1237–1284.

Ui, T. 2000. "A Shapley Value Representation of Potential Games", *Games and Economic Behavior* 31, 121–135.

Von Neumann, J. 1928. "Zur Theorie der Gesellschaftsspiele", *Mathematische Annalen* 100, 295–320. Reprinted in: A.H. Taub (ed.): *Collected Works of John von Neumann*, Vol. VI, Oxford: Pergamon Press, 1963, 1–26. Translated as "On the Theory of Games of Strategy" in: A.W. Tucker and R.D. Luce (eds.): *Contributions to the Theory of Games*, Vol. IV, Princeton: Princeton University Press, 1959, 13–42.

Von Neumann, J., and O. Morgenstern. 1944 (3rd edn. 1953). *Theory of Games and Economic Behavior*, Princeton: Princeton University Press.

Weibull, J.W. 1995. *Evolutionary Game Theory*, Cambridge, Mass.: MIT Press.

Peter J. Hammond
Department of Economics
Stanford University
Stanford, CA 94305–6072
U.S.A.
peter.hammond@stanford.edu

COMPENSATED DEMAND AND INVERSE DEMAND FUNCTIONS: A DUALITY APPROACH

SUSANNE FUCHS–SELIGER
Universität Karlsruhe

1. Introduction

In this paper a model of consumer behavior will be developed based on the individual's preferences on the price space. We consider inverse demand functions which assign, to every commodity bundle x, that market price the individual is willing to pay for x when income M prevails. If the direct demand function $x = h(p, M) = (\frac{M}{2p_1}, \frac{M}{2p_2})$ is given, then the inverse demand function corresponding to it, is $p = P(x, M) = (\frac{M}{2x_1}, \frac{M}{2x_2})$. Demand function $h(p, M)$ and inverse demand function $P(x, M)$ are dual concepts describing consumer behavior. Inverse demand functions are useful when prices do not exist or are artificially distorted. They often are a convenient tool for modelling market behavior of a monopolistic firm (see Varian, 1978, p. 53). We will also study compensated inverse demand functions; for any quantity vector x and any comparison price vector p^0 a compensated inverse demand function gives the price vector p the individual is prepared to pay for x given that he or she is maintained on the same indifference level.

The analysis in this article will be based on preference relations which are not generally assumed to be transitive and complete. Therefore, a quite general framework for inverse demand will be used.

Finally, relationships between distance functions, representing the individual's preferences on the price space, and compensated demand functions will be established.

2. The Model

Modelling consumer's behavior we will assume the following hypotheses:

(P1) $\succeq$ is a relation on the strictly positive n-dimensional vector space $\mathbb{R}^n_{++}$. Every $p \in \mathbb{R}^n_{++}$ represents an income-normalized price vector, i.e. $p = \frac{P}{M}$, where $P \in \mathbb{R}^n_{++}$ are the market prices, and M is the income of the individual, where $M > 0$.

(P2) $\succeq$ is transitive and complete.

U. Schmidt and S. Traub (eds.), Advances in Public Economics: Utility, Choice and Welfare 51-60.

(P3) $\succeq$ is continuous, i.e.

(P3.1) $\{p \in \mathbb{R}^n_{++} \mid p^0 \succeq p\}$ is closed in $\mathbb{R}^n_{++}$ for every $p^0 \in \mathbb{R}^n_{++}$ (lower semicontinuity).

(P3.2) $\{p \in \mathbb{R}^n_{++} \mid p \succeq p^0\}$ is closed in $\mathbb{R}^n_{++}$ for every $p^0 \in \mathbb{R}^n_{++}$ (upper semicontinuity).

(P4) $p^1 < p^2 \Longrightarrow p^1 \succ p^2$, where $\succ$ is the asymmetric part of $\succeq$ [1]

(P5) For every sequence $< p^k >, p^k \in \mathbb{R}^n_{++}$, such that $\lim_{k\to\infty} p^k = p^0 \not> 0$ it follows: For every $p \in \mathbb{R}^n_{++}$ there exists a positive number N such that $p^k \succ p$ for all $k > N$.

The statement $p \succeq p'$ means: the consumer either finds p preferable to p' or he is indifferent between the two price systems p and p'. (P4) should be interpreted in the following way: if the price vector p^1 for a certain commodity bundle x is lower than p^2, then the individual prefers p^1 to p^2. (P5) should be interpreted analogously. It should be stressed that the above hypotheses are not all needed for the following results. Even transitivity or completeness of $\succeq$ can be deleted for some proceeding statements. However, if we assume (P1) to (P3) then by Debreu's theorem we immediately obtain

LEMMA 1. *Assume (P1), (P2) and (P3), then $\succeq$ can be represented by a continuous real-valued function $v : \mathbb{R}^n_{++} \longrightarrow \mathbb{R}_+$, $v(p) = s$, which represents the relation $\succeq$, i.e. $p^1 \succeq p^2 \Longleftrightarrow v(p^1) \geqq v(p^2)$, $\forall p^1, p^2 \in \mathbb{R}^n_{++}$ (see Debreu, 1959). The function v can be considered as an "indirect utility function."*

3. Inverse Demand Functions

An inverse demand function characterizes those prices the individual is willing to pay for a certain amount of goods. Formally this means:
Let $X \subseteq \mathbb{R}^n_+$ be a commodity space, then

$$b : X \longrightarrow \mathbb{R}^n_+,\ b(x) = p,$$

is called an inverse demand function, or more generally,

$$b : X \longrightarrow 2^{\mathbb{R}^n_{++}},\ b(x) \neq \emptyset,$$

is called an inverse demand correspondence.

By $B(x)$ we will denote all those income-normalized price vectors at which x is available, i.e. $B(x) = \{p \in \mathbb{R}^n_{++} \mid px \leqq 1\}$. It has been shown (see Fuchs-Seliger, 1999, Theorem 1, pp. 241–242).

LEMMA 2. *The correspondence $B : \mathbb{R}^n_+ \longrightarrow 2^{\mathbb{R}^n_{++}}$, $B(x) = \{p \in \mathbb{R}^n_{++} \mid px \leqq 1\}$, is lower hemicontinuous on $\mathbb{R}^n_+$. Lower hemicontinuity is defined by:*
The correspondence $f : S \to 2^T$, $(S, T \subseteq \mathbb{R}^n)$ is called lower hemicontinuous on S, if for every $x^0 \in S$ and every sequence $< x^k >, x^k \in S$, converging to x^0, and for every $y^0 \in f(x^0)$ there exists a sequence $< y^k >$ converging to y^0 with $y^k \in f(x^k)$.

[1] $p^1 < p^2$ means, $p^1_i < p^2_i\ \forall i \leqq n$.

The inverse demand function corresponds to the indirect utility function which is the dual counterpart to the (direct) utility function to which the (direct) demand function corresponds. Given the indirect utility function v or, more generally, a preference relation $\succeq$ on $\mathbb{R}^n_{++}$, a given inverse demand function is called "consistent with $\succeq$", if for all $x \in \mathbb{R}^n_{++}$,

$$b(x) = \{p \in \mathbb{R}^n_{++} \mid p \in B(x) \wedge \forall p' \in B(x) : \ p' \succeq p\}.$$

By interpretation, $b(x)$ coincides with the set of those income-normalized price vectors which, according to his preferences, the consumer is prepared to pay at most for x. Otherwise the firms would produce an amount less than x. In the light of (P4), any price system lower than p would not be accepted for x by the firm.

The above definition of consistency is built in analogy to rationality of demand correspondences with respect to a given relation R on $X \subseteq \mathbb{R}^n_+$, i.e.

$$h(p) = \{x \in X \mid x \in B'(p) \wedge \forall y \in B'(p) : \ xRy\},$$

where $B'(p) = \{z \in X \mid pz \leqq 1\}$. Hence $h(p)$ consists of those commodity bundles which, according to the individual's opinion, are the best ones at the income-normalized price vector p, and which the consumer, according to rationality, also chooses.

The question arises which conditions have to be imposed on $\succeq$ such that $b(x) \neq \emptyset$. The crucial difficulty is that $B(x)$ is not closed. If $X = \mathbb{R}^n_+$, then $B'(p)$ for every $p \in \mathbb{R}^n_{++}$ is a compact set and thus, the application of the finite intersection property yields that $h(p) \neq \emptyset$, if R is complete, transitive and continuous on $\mathbb{R}^n_+$ (see Hildenbrand and Kirman, 1988). Even transitivity and completeness of R can be replaced by weaker properties (see Fuchs-Seliger and Mayer, 2003, for instance). Since $B(x)$ is not closed, the assumption that $\succeq$ be a continuous ordering on $\mathbb{R}^n_{++}$ does not imply that $b(x) \neq \emptyset$. Since according to Lemma 1 the relation $\succeq$ can be represented by a continuous indirect utility function $v : \mathbb{R}^n_{++} \longrightarrow \mathbb{R}$ one can apply a former result in (Fuchs-Seliger, 1999, Theorem 7, p. 245) and obtain

THEOREM 1. *Let the commodity space be* $X = \mathbb{R}^n_{++}$ *and assume (P1) to (P5). Then* $b(x) \neq \emptyset$, $\forall x \in \mathbb{R}^n_{++}$, *if* b *is consistent with* $\succeq$.

The proof of this assertion in Fuchs-Seliger (1999), Theorem 7, uses the following property:

(γ) For every sequence $< p^k >$, $p^k \in \mathbb{R}^n_{++}$, $[p^k \rightarrow p^0 \not> 0] \Longrightarrow [v(p^k) \rightarrow \infty]$.

If we examine that proof, then we realize that condition (γ) is used for one conclusion only (see Fuchs-Seliger, 1999, p. 243). However, this conclusion, namely $p^0 > 0$, also follows if we apply (P5) taking into consideration that in that proof we have $v(p^k) > v(p)$ instead of $p^k \succ p$ for all $k > N$.

REMARK 1. *It can be immediately seen that condition (γ) is more restrictive than (P5). Since, if we assume that the sequence* $< v(p^k) >$ *is divergent if* $p^k \rightarrow p^0 \not> 0$, *then for every $p' \in \mathbb{R}^n_{++}$ and $s' = v(p')$ there exists k_0 such that for all $k \geqq k_0$, $v(p^k) > v(p')$. By representability we thus have, $p^k \succ p'$, $\forall k \geqq k_0$. From this (P5) immediately follows.*

In the preceding theorem it will be shown that strict concavity of $\succeq$ implies single-valuedness of the inverse demand correspondence. Remember that strict concavity is defined in the following way:

Let Y be a convex set, $p, p' \in Y$ with $p \neq p'$, then:
$p \succeq p' \Longrightarrow p \succ \lambda p + (1-\lambda)p'$, $\forall \lambda \in (0,1)$.

THEOREM 2. *Let $\succeq$ satisfy (P1) to (P5) and be strictly concave, then $b(x)$ is single-valued if b is consistent with $\succeq$. Moreover if $\succeq$ is homothetic*[2]*, then b is homogeneous of degree -1.*

PROOF. Proof of single-valuedness: Suppose there exists $x^0 \in \mathbb{R}^n_{++}$ and $p', p'' \in \mathbb{R}^n_{++}$, $p' \neq p''$, such that $p', p'' \in b(x^0)$. Hence, by the definition of b, $p' \succeq p''$. Strict concavity implies $p' \succ p(t) = tp' + (1-t)p''$ for $t \in (0,1)$. Since $p'x^0 \leqq 1$ and $p''x^0 \leqq 1$, we also obtain $p(t)x^0 \leqq 1$. Hence $p(t) \in B(x^0)$. This result together with $p' \succ p(t)$ is contradicting to the definition of $b(x^0)$.
In order to show homogeneity of degree -1 consider $x^0 \in \mathbb{R}^n_{++}$ and $\lambda > 0$. Then

$$\begin{aligned} b(\lambda x^0) &= \{p \in \mathbb{R}^n_{++} \mid p\lambda x^0 \leqq 1 \quad \wedge\ \forall p' : (p'\lambda x^0 \leqq 1 \Rightarrow p' \succeq p)\} \\ &= \tfrac{1}{\lambda}\{\lambda p \in \mathbb{R}^n_{++} \mid \lambda p x^0 \leqq 1 \ \wedge\ \forall \lambda p' : (p'\lambda x^0 \leqq 1 \Rightarrow \lambda p' \succeq \lambda p)\} \\ &= \tfrac{1}{\lambda}\{q \in \mathbb{R}^n_{++} \mid q x^0 \leqq 1 \quad \wedge\ \forall q' : (q' x^0 \leqq 1 \Rightarrow q' \succeq q)\} \\ &= \lambda^{-1} b(x^0). \end{aligned}$$

■

4. Inverse Compensated Demand Correspondences

We will now define the inverse counterpart to compensated demand functions. Therefore, we preliminarily introduce the inverse (or indirect) expenditure function

$$\begin{aligned} C(x,p) &= \min_{p' \in \mathbb{R}^n_{++}} \{p'x \mid p \succeq p'\} \text{ for } (x,p) \in \mathbb{R}^{2n}_{++}, \text{ or more generally} \\ C^0(x,p) &= \inf_{p' \in \mathbb{R}^n_{++}} \{p'x \mid p \succeq p'\} \text{ for } (x,p) \in \mathbb{R}^{2n}_{++}. \end{aligned}$$

$C(x,p)$ indicates the amount of money which enables a consumer, who faces a certain output x, to maintain a particular standard of living when prices have changed.

REMARK 2. *In order that $C^0(x,p)$ is well defined we only need reflexivity of $\succeq$. If additionally $\succeq$ is decreasing, then $C^0(x,p) > 0$.*

[2] $\succeq$ is called "homothetic", if $x \succeq y \Longrightarrow \lambda x \succeq \lambda y$, $\forall \lambda > 0$.

We will now present conditions implying that $C(x,p)$ is well defined.

LEMMA 3. *Assume (P1), (P3.1), (P4) and (P5) and let* $\succeq$ *be reflexive. Then* $C(x,p)$ *is well defined for all* $(x,p) \in \mathbb{R}^{2n}_{++}$.

PROOF. Consider $(p^0, x^0) \in \mathbb{R}^{2n}_{++}$, then by the former remark, $\inf\{p'x^0 \mid p^0 \succeq p', p' \in \mathbb{R}^n_{++}\} = C^0(x^0, p^0)$ is well defined. Therefore, in every ϵ^i-neighborhood of $C^0(x^0, p^0)$, $\epsilon^i > 0$, there is a value $p^i x^0$ with $p^i \in \mathbb{R}^n_{++}$ such that $p^0 R p^i$ and $C^0(x^0, p^0) + \epsilon^i > p^i x^0 \geqq C^0(x^0, p^0)$.

Let $\epsilon^i = \frac{1}{i}$, $\forall i \geqq 1$. The sequence $< p^i >$ is bounded and hence there exists a convergent subsequence of $< p^i >$. Without loss of generality let this be $< p^i >$ itself. By $(P5)$, $< p^i >$ converges to a vector $\tilde{p} > 0$. Otherwise, if $\tilde{p} \not> 0$, then by $(P5)$ there exists $K \in \mathbb{R}_{++}$ such that $p^j P p^0$, $\forall j > K$, in contradiction to the construction of $< p^i >$. Since we have $p^0 R p^i$, $\forall i \geqq 1$, the lower semicontinuity yields, $p^0 R \tilde{p}$ and thus $C^0(x^0, p^0) \in \{p'x^0 \mid p^0 R p', p' \in \mathbb{R}^n_{++}\}$. ■

Examining the above proof, one can see that (P4) is not needed. However, with regard of the interpretation of this system of axioms, (P4) will be also kept. We will now consider those price vectors which solve the optimization problem

$$\min_{p' \in \mathbb{R}^n_{++}} \{p'x \mid p \succeq p'\}.$$

and write

$$\delta(x,p) = \arg \min_{p' \in \mathbb{R}^n_{++}} \{p'x \mid p \succeq p'\},\ \forall (x,p) \in \mathbb{R}^{2n}_{++}.$$

$\delta : \mathbb{R}^{2n}_{++} \longrightarrow 2^{\mathbb{R}^n_{++}}$ will be called "inverse compensated demand correspondence". One can also show

LEMMA 4. *If (P1), (P3), (P4) and (P5) is assumed, and if* $\succeq$ *is complete, then*

$$\delta(x,p) = \arg \min_{p' \in \mathbb{R}^n_{++}} \{p'x \mid p \sim p'\},\ \forall (x,p) \in \mathbb{R}^{2n}_{++},$$

where $\sim$ *is the symmetric part of* $\succeq$.

PROOF. In order to obtain a contradiction, suppose $p' \succ p^0$ for some $p^0 \in \delta(x', p')$. Since $\succeq$ is complete, and upper semicontinuous there would exist an ϵ-neighborhood $U_\epsilon(p^0)$ of p^0 such that $p' \succ p$ for all $p \in U_\epsilon(p^0)$. Especially, there exists $\tilde{p} \in U_\epsilon(p^0)$ such that $\tilde{p} < p^0$ and $p' \succ \tilde{p}$. Since $\tilde{p}x' < p^0 x'$ we obtain a contradiction to $p^0 \in \delta(x', p')$. ■

Using the notion of upper hemicontinuity, one can show that the correspondence $\delta(\cdot, p^0)$ for every $p^0 \in \mathbb{R}^n_{++}$is upper hemicontinuous on $\mathbb{R}^n_{++}$. If a correspondence is compact-valued, then upper hemicontinuity can be defined by (see Hildenbrand and Kirman, 1988).

Let $F : S \to 2^T$, where $S, T \subseteq \mathbb{R}^n$, be such that for every $x \in S$, $F(x)$ is compact. Then F is called "upper hemicontinuous" at $x^0 \in S$, if for every sequence $< x^k >$ with $\lim_{k\to\infty} x^k = x^0$ and for every sequence $< y^k >$ with $y^k \in F(x^k)$, there exists a convergent subsequence of $< y^k >, < y^{kj} >$, such that $\lim_{j\to\infty} y^{kj} = y \in F(x^0)$. F is called upper hemicontinuous if it is upper hemicontinuous at every $x \in S$.

In order to apply the above definition, we firstly demonstrate the compact-valuedness of $\delta(x^0, p^0)$ for $x^0 \in \mathbb{R}^n_{++}$.

THEOREM 3. *Assume (P1), (P3.1), (P4) and (P5) and let $\succeq$ be reflexive, then the following statements hold for every $p^0 \in \mathbb{R}^n_{++}$:*

a) the correspondence $\delta(\cdot, p^0)$ is compact-valued on $\mathbb{R}^n_{++}$,
b) $\delta(\cdot, p^0)$ is upper hemicontinuous on $\mathbb{R}^n_{++}$.

PROOF.

a) Firstly, let us show that $\delta(x^0, p^0)$ is closed for every $x^0 \in \mathbb{R}^n_{++}$. Therefore, let us consider a sequence $< p^k >, p^k \in \delta(x^0, p^0)$, such that $\lim_{k\to\infty} p^k = \tilde{p}$. By definition of $C(x^0, p^0), p^k x^0 \leqq p' x^0$, for all p' such that $p^0 \succeq p'$. Thus, $\tilde{p} x^0 \leqq p' x^0$. Since $p^0 \succeq p^k$, $\forall k$, lower semicontinuity of $\succeq$ implies, $p^0 \succeq \tilde{p}$. Hence, $\tilde{p} \in \delta(x^0, p^0)$.
In order to obtain a contradiction suppose that $\delta(x^0, p^0)$ is not bounded. Then there will exist a sequence $< p^k >$, $p^k \in \delta(x^0, p^0)$, such that the ith component of p^k, p^k_i converges to ∞, i.e. $p^k_i \to \infty$, and $p^k x^0 > p^0 x^0$ for all $k > N$. Since, by reflexivity we have $p^0 \succeq p^0$ and since $p^k \in \delta(x^0, p^0)$, we obtain $p^k x^0 \leqq p^0 x^0$, contradicting the previous result. Thus, $\delta(x^0, p^0)$ is bounded and closed, hence compact.

b) Let $< x^k >$, $x^k \in \mathbb{R}^n_{++}$, be a sequence, such that $\lim_{k\to\infty} x^k = \tilde{x} \in \mathbb{R}^n_{++}$, and let $p^k \in \delta(x^k, p^0)$. Since $\succeq$ is reflexive, the definition of $\delta(x^k, p^0)$ yields, $p^k x^k \leqq p^0 x^k$. Since $< x^k >$ is convergent, it is also bounded. Hence, in view of $p^k x^k \leqq p^0 x^k$, $< p^k >$ is also bounded. Thus, there exists a convergent subsequence $< p^{kj} >$ of $< p^k >$, such that $\lim_{j\to\infty} p^{kj} = \tilde{p}$. Suppose $\tilde{p} \not> 0$, then in view of (P5) there exists $N > 0$, such that for every $j > N$, $p^{kj} \succ p^0$. A contradiction to $p^0 \succeq p^{kj}$. Hence, $\tilde{p} > 0$, and in view of lower semicontinuity of $\succeq$, $p^0 \succeq \tilde{p}$.
Let us now consider an arbitrary price vector $\hat{p}$, such that $p^0 \succeq \hat{p}$. This together with $p^{kj} \in \delta(x^{kj}, p^0)$ implies, $p^{kj} x^{kj} \leqq \hat{p} x^{kj}$, $\forall j$. From this we obtain $\lim_{j\to\infty} (p^{kj} x^{kj}) \leqq \hat{p} \cdot \lim_{j\to\infty} x^{kj}$, and thus $\tilde{p}\tilde{x} \leqq \hat{p}\tilde{x}$. Since $\hat{p}$ was an arbitrary price vector with $p^0 \succeq \hat{p}$, we obtain: $\forall p' : [p^0 \succeq p' \Longrightarrow \tilde{p}\tilde{x} \leqq p'\tilde{x}]$.
This together with $p^0 \succeq \tilde{p}$ implies $\tilde{p} \in \delta(\tilde{x}, p^0)$.

■

Since every upper hemicontinuous and single-valued correspondence F is a continuous function (see Hildenbrand and Kirman, 1988) we immediately obtain the following conclusion:

COROLLARY 1. *Assume the conditions of Theorem 3. Then $\delta(\cdot, p^0)$ is continuous on $\mathbb{R}^n_{++}$ if $\delta(\cdot, p^0)$ is single-valued.*

The application of Theorem 3 also yields:

COROLLARY 2. *Assume the conditions of Theorem 3, and additionally let $\succeq$ be strictly concave. Then $\delta(\cdot, p^0)$ is continuous on $\mathbb{R}^n_{++}$.*

Moreover one can also show that Shephard's Lemma follows (see Shephard, 1974, and Fuchs-Seliger, 1995). Preliminarily it should be noted that $C(\cdot, p^0)$ is a concave function, following immediately from the definition of $C(\cdot, p^0)$.

THEOREM 4. *Let $\succeq$ be reflexive and strictly concave. Furthermore, assume (P1), (P3.1), (P4) and (P5). Then for every $p \in \mathbb{R}^n_{++}$,*

$$\frac{\partial C(x,p)}{\partial x_i} = \delta_i(x,p), \ \forall x \in \mathbb{R}^n_{++}.$$

PROOF. Consider $p^0 \in \mathbb{R}^n_{++}$ and the commodity bundles $x \in \mathbb{R}^n_{++}$ and $x + \Delta x$. Write $\Delta C(x, p^0) = C(x + \Delta x, p^0) - C(x, p^0)$. Then by definition:

$$\begin{aligned} \Delta C(x,p^0) &= (x+\Delta x)\cdot\delta(x+\Delta x,p^0) - x\cdot\delta(x,p^0) \qquad (1)\\ &= x\cdot\delta(x+\Delta x,p^0) - x\cdot\delta(x,p^0) + \Delta x\cdot\delta(x+\Delta x,p^0). \end{aligned}$$

The definition of δ yields $p^0 \succeq \delta(x + \Delta x, p^0)$ and $p^0 \succeq \delta(x, p^0)$, and thus, $x \cdot \delta(x + \Delta x, p^0) - x \cdot \delta(x, p^0) \geqq 0$.

This, together with (1) implies $\Delta C(x, p^0) \geqq \Delta x \cdot \delta(x + \Delta x, p^0)$. For any $j \leqq n$, suppose $\Delta x = (0, \ldots, 0, \Delta x_j, 0, \ldots, 0)$. Then we obtain, $\Delta C(x, p^0) \geqq \Delta x_j \cdot \delta_j(x + \Delta x, p^0)$.

If $\Delta x_j > 0$, then $\frac{\Delta C(x,p^0)}{\Delta x_j} \geqq \delta_j(x + \Delta x, p^0)$. If $\Delta x_j < 0$, then the converse holds.

Since the concavity of $C(\cdot, p^0)$ implies that $C(\cdot, p^0)$ is right- and left-hand differentiable and since $\delta(\cdot, p^0)$ is continuous on $\mathbb{R}^n_{++}$.

$$\lim_{\substack{\Delta x_j > 0\\ \Delta x_j \to 0}} \frac{\Delta C(x,p^0)}{\Delta x_j} \geqq \lim_{\Delta x_j \to 0} \delta_j(x+\Delta x,p^0) = \delta_j(x,p^0) \geqq \lim_{\substack{\Delta x_j < 0\\ \Delta x_j \to 0}} \frac{\Delta C(x,p^0)}{\Delta x_j}. \qquad (2)$$

Otherwise, the concavity of $C(\cdot, p^0)$ implies

$$\lim_{\substack{\Delta x_j < 0\\ \Delta x_j \to 0}} \frac{\Delta C(x,p^0)}{\Delta x_j} \geqq \lim_{\substack{\Delta x_j > 0\\ \Delta x_j \to 0}} \frac{\Delta C(x,p^0)}{\Delta x_j}.$$

From this result together with (2) the assertion follows. ■

5. Distance Functions and Inverse Compensated Demand

If we interpret prices as the individual's readiness to pay for a certain amount of goods, then prices indirectly reflect her or his estimation of these goods. We will now consider a method of evaluating prices by distance functions, which can be considered as a special kind of indirect utility functions evaluating prices in comparison to a fixed reference price system. It will be seen that transitivity of the preference relation is not needed in order to obtain first insights.

We will consider a special type of distance functions which are Minkowski-gauge functions, defined by

$$\gamma(x, C) = inf\{\lambda > 0 \mid x \in \lambda C\}, \text{where } C \subset \mathbb{R}^n, \ C \neq \emptyset, \ C \text{ convex.}$$

The above definition will be used for defining a distance function in consumer theory. Therefore, let $R(p') = \{p \in \mathbb{R}^n_{++} \mid p \succeq p'\}$ and define the distance function d^0 by

$$d^0(p, R(p')) = \inf\{t \in \mathbb{R}_{++} \mid p \in tR(p')\},$$

where p' is a reference price vector, or in another version,

$$d^0(p, p') = \inf\{t \in \mathbb{R}_{++} \mid \frac{p}{t} \succeq p'\},$$

under the supposition that infimum exists. We can immediately see that $d^0(p, p')$ is well defined if $\succeq$ is decreasing and thus satisfies $(P4)$. If we additionally assume that $\succeq$ is upper semicontinuous then it immediately follows that

$$d(p, p') = \min\{t \in \mathbb{R}_{++} \mid \frac{p}{t} \succeq p'\}, \quad \forall p, p' \in \mathbb{R}^n_{++}$$

is well defined.

Thus we have

LEMMA 5. *Let $\succeq$ satisfy $(P1)$, $(P3.2)$ and $(P4)$. Then for every $p' \in \mathbb{R}^n_{++}$*

a) $d(p, p')$ is well defined,
b) $d(\cdot, p')$ is homogeneous of degree 1.

PROOF. [for b)]

$$\begin{aligned} d(\lambda p, p') &= min\{t \in \mathbb{R}_{++} \mid \tfrac{\lambda p}{t} \succeq p'\} = \lambda min\{\tfrac{t}{\lambda} \in \mathbb{R}_{++} \mid \tfrac{\lambda p}{t} \succeq p'\} \\ &= \lambda min\{t' \in \mathbb{R}_{++} \mid \tfrac{p}{t'} \succeq p'\} = \lambda d(p, p'), \quad \forall \lambda > 0. \end{aligned}$$

■

Instead of $d(\cdot, p')$ we can define another version of a distance function which Newman (1987) calls *S-gauge* function (an abbreviation of Shephard-gauge function). It is defined by

$$D(p, p') = max\{t \in \mathbb{R}_{++} \mid p' \succeq \frac{p}{t}\}.$$

In economics this kind of distance functions are mostly used. It can be easily shown that the assertions of the following lemma hold.

LEMMA 6. *Let $\succeq$ satisfy $(P1)$, $(P3.1)$ and $(P4)$. Then for every $p' \in \mathbb{R}^n_{++}$:*

a) $D(p, p')$ is well defined,
b) $D(\cdot, p')$ is homogeneous of degree 1.

Since $\succeq$ is increasing, thick indifference spaces are excluded and we obtain

THEOREM 5. *Assume $(P1)$, $(P3)$ and $(P4)$ and additionally let $\succeq$ be complete. Then for all $p, p' \in \mathbb{R}^n_{++}$*

$$d(p, p') = D(p, p').$$

PROOF. Firstly, in order to obtain a contradiction, suppose $D(p, p') > d(p, p')$ for some $p, p' \in \mathbb{R}^n_{++}$. By definition $\frac{p}{d(p,p')} \succeq p'$ and $p' \succeq \frac{p}{D(p,p')}$.

Consider $\lambda = \frac{D(p,p')+d(p,p')}{2}$, then $p^1 = \frac{p}{d(p,p')} > \frac{p}{\lambda} > \frac{p}{D(p,p')} = p^2$, and thus by $(P4)$ $p^1 \prec \frac{p}{\lambda} \prec p^2$. Hence, by definition $\neg(p' \succeq \frac{p}{\lambda})$ and $\neg(\frac{p}{\lambda} \succeq p')$. This is a contradiction to the completeness of $\succeq$. If, in contrary, we suppose that $d(p, p') > D(p, p')$ we obtain a contradiction by an analogous way of argumentation. ■

We will now demonstrate that $D(p, p')$ represents the relation $\succeq$, given the reference price vector p'.

THEOREM 6. *Assume $(P1)$ to $(P4)$ and let $p^0 \in \mathbb{R}^n_{++}$. Then $D(p^0, \cdot)$ represents the relation $\succeq$, i.e.*

$$p^1 \succeq p^2 \iff D(p^0, p^1) \geqq D(p^0, p^2).$$

PROOF. Assume $p^1 \succeq p^2$. In view of the definition of $D(\cdot)$ and $d(\cdot)$,

$$\frac{p^0}{d(p^0, p^1)} \succeq p^1 \text{ and } \frac{p^0}{d(p^0, p^2)} \succeq p^2, \quad \text{and } p^1 \succeq \frac{p^0}{D(p^0, p^1)} \text{ and } p^2 \succeq \frac{p^0}{D(p^0, p^2)}.$$

Since in view of the previous theorem $d(p, \tilde{p}) = D(p, \tilde{p})$ for all $p, \tilde{p} \in \mathbb{R}^n_{++}$ we obtain

$$p^1 \sim \frac{p^0}{D(p^0, p^1)} \text{ and } p^2 \sim \frac{p^0}{D(p^0, p^2)} \tag{3}$$

Suppose $D(p^0, p^1) < D(p^0, p^2)$. Then in view of $(P4)$, $\frac{p^0}{D(p^0,p^1)} \prec \frac{p^0}{D(p^0,p^2)}$. This together with (3) and $(P2)$ implies $p^1 \prec p^2$, a contradiction.

Hence, $D(p^0, p^1) \geqq D(p^0, p^2)$.

In order to show the converse, assume $D(p^0, p^1) \geqq D(p^0, p^2)$. Thus, $\frac{p^0}{D(p^0,p^1)} \leqq \frac{p^0}{D(p^0,p^2)}$. In case of equality, $p^1 \sim \frac{p^0}{D(p^0,p^1)} \sim \frac{p^0}{D(p^0,p^2)} \sim p^2$, and thus by $(P2)$, $p^1 \sim p^2$.

If $\frac{p^0}{D(p^0,p^1)} < \frac{p^0}{D(p^0,p^2)}$ then in view of $(P4)$ and the previous equivalence it follows $p^1 \succ p^2$. ■

The above result is important because it proves that the distance function $D(p, p^0)$ represents the relation $\succsim$ on the price space for any reference price vector p^0.

The above result together with Theorem 4 and the definition of $D(\cdot)$ and $\delta(\cdot)$ immediately yields

THEOREM 7. *Let* $\succsim$ *satisfy* (*P*1) *to* (*P*5). *Then*

a) $C(x,p) = \min_{p' \in \mathbb{R}^n_{++}} \{p'x \mid D(p,p') = 1\}$.

b) $\delta(x,p) = \arg\min_{p' \in \mathbb{R}^n_{++}} \{p'x \mid D(p,p') = 1\}$.

c) If $\delta(x,p)$ *is single-valued, then* $\frac{\partial C(x,p)}{\partial x_i} = \arg\min_{p' \in \mathbb{R}^n_{++}} \{p'x \mid D(p,p') = 1\}$.

From the above results we can conclude that the partial derivatives of $C(x,p)$ with respect to x_i gives that price system p' which minimizes the expenditure for x and for which $D(p,p') = 1$ holds.

The previous analysis has shown that we can build a model of consumer behavior, when prices are not given but depend on the supply of goods and the consumer's willingness to pay for a certain amount of goods.

References

Debreu, G. 1959. *Theory of Value*, New York: J. Wiley.

Fuchs-Seliger, S. 1995. "On Shephard's Lemma and the Continuity of Compensated Demand Functions", *Economics Letters* 48, 25–28.

Fuchs-Seliger, S. 1999. "A Note on Duality in Consumer Theory", *Economic Theory* 13, 239–246.

Fuchs-Seliger, S. 2002. "An Analysis of Distance Functions in Consumer Theory", in: G. Bosi, S. Holzer, and R. Isler (eds.): *Proceedings of the Conference "Utility Theory and Applications"*, Trieste, 69–89.

Fuchs-Seliger, S., and O. Mayer. 2003. "Rationality without Transitivity", *Journal of Economics* 80(1), 77–87.

Hildenbrand, W., and A.P. Kirman. 1988. *Introduction to Equilibrium Analysis*, Amsterdam: North Holland.

Newman, P. 1987. "Gauge Functions", in: *The New Palgrave–A Dictionary of Economics*, Vol. II, 484–488.

Shephard, R. W. 1974. *Indirect Production Functions*, Meisenheim am Glan: Anton Hain.

Varian, H. 1978. *Microeconomic Analysis*, New York: W. Norton and Company.

Susanne Fuchs-Seliger
Institut für Wirtschaftstheorie und Operations Research
Universität Karlsruhe
Kollegium am Schloss
D-76128 Karlsruhe
Germany
seliger@wior.uni-karlsruhe.de

SHADOW PRICES FOR A NONCONVEX PUBLIC TECHNOLOGY IN THE PRESENCE OF PRIVATE CONSTANT RETURNS

JOHN A. WEYMARK
Vanderbilt University

1. Introduction

One of the best-known results in optimal taxation theory is the production efficiency theorem of Diamond and Mirrlees (1971). This theorem shows that if commodity taxes are chosen optimally, the profits of the private sector are taxed at a 100% rate, and a mild demand regularity condition is satisfied, then the vector of optimal aggregate net outputs of the public and private production sectors is efficient. An implication of this theorem is that the appropriate shadow prices for public sector managers are the private producer prices. Hence, if the production technology of the public sector is convex, then the optimal public production maximizes profits on this production set at these prices.

However, in practice, taxes are not set optimally, which limits the applicability of the production efficiency theorem. Nevertheless, when the public technology is convex and some of the private sector firms have constant-returns-to-scale technologies, Diamond and Mirrlees (1976) have shown that public sector shadow prices should be set equal to the private producer prices in some circumstances, even if taxes are not optimal.

To state this result more precisely, it is necessary to describe the main features of the model considered by Diamond and Mirrlees. There are n goods. The economy has two types of private firms: (i) profit-maximizing competitive firms with constant-returns-to-scale technologies (the C-sector) and (ii) firms whose optimal net outputs only depend on producer prices and, possibly, on aggregate quantities. In choosing the values of its instruments, the government is assumed to choose its production plan optimally from a convex production set and it must ensure that all markets clear, but it is not constrained to set optimal taxes. Furthermore, the government is assumed to complete its transactions using the private producer prices and not to have preferences for the distribution of its revenue between taxes and receipts from its productive operations, nor for the distribution of production between sectors of the economy.

U. Schmidt and S. Traub (eds.), Advances in Public Economics: Utility, Choice and Welfare, 61-71.

Diamond and Mirrlees' theorem, informally stated above, shows that the private producer prices are the appropriate shadow prices for the public sector if it is optimal for public production to be efficient and if the optimal net outputs of $n-1$ firms in the C-sector are linearly independent. Diamond and Mirrlees (1976) have also shown that in the absence of the linearly independent C-sector outputs, the profits of the C-sector firms evaluated using the public sector shadow prices are all zero, but these shadow prices need not equal the private producer prices. These two shadow pricing theorems have been shown to be special cases of more general results by Drèze and Stern (1987, Section 2.3.5), Guesnerie (1979, Section 3.2), and Guesnerie (1995, Section 4.1), to whom the reader is referred for further discussion.

One of the traditional justifications for producing goods in the public sector is the presence of significant nonconvexities in the production technologies of these goods.[1] It is therefore of interest to determine if private producer prices are the correct shadow prices for the managers of the public sector in an economy in which all of Diamond and Mirrlees' assumptions (including the existence of the linearly independent C-sector outputs) are satisfied except for the convexity of the public production possibility set. In this article, I show that they are, but the scope for using these prices to decentralize the optimal public production may be limited. Specifically, the optimal public net outputs need only maximize profits using the private producer prices on a subset of the public production set. The size of this subset, which could be quite large, depends on the magnitudes of the optimal C-sector outputs. I also present sufficient conditions for profit maximization using these prices to identify the optimal public production plan on the whole public production set.[2]

In Section 2, I present Diamond and Mirrlees' shadow pricing theorems for a convex public technology. My shadow pricing theorems for a nonconvex public technology are developed in Section 3. Some concluding remarks follow in Section 4.

2. A Convex Production Technology

In this section, I introduce the model and present the two shadow pricing theorems for a convex public technology due to Diamond and Mirrlees (1976). In order to focus on essentials, I shall sacrifice some of the generality of their results in my presentation.

There are n commodities. There are J private firms, indexed by $j = 1, \ldots, J$. The production possibility set of firm j is $Y^j \subset \Re^n$ and its vector of net outputs is $y^j \in Y^j$.[3] It is assumed that some private firms have constant-return-to-scale technologies. The set of such firms is C. Thus, Y^j is a cone for all $j \in C$. The other private firms (if any) constitute the set R.

[1] See Bös (1985) for a discussion of the various reasons for organizing production in the public sector or for publicly regulating the prices at which private firms operate.

[2] The techniques employed by Drèze and Stern (1987) and Guesnerie (1979, 1995) do not require the public production set to be convex. However, if it is nonconvex, their theorems only show that infinitesimal changes in the public production from the optimum do not increase profits evaluated using the private producer prices.

[3] $\Re^n$ is the n-dimensional Euclidean space. The origin in $\Re^n$ is denoted by 0_n.

Producer prices are $p \gg 0_n$.[4] Each private firm is a competitive profit maximizer. At the prices p, the set of optimal net supplies for firm j is $y^j(p)$. Thus, $y^j(\cdot)$ is the supply correspondence of the jth firm. For firms in the R-sector, but not for firms in the C-sector, $y^j(\cdot)$ could be a function.

The government's production possibility set is $Z \subset \Re^n$. The vector of net outputs of the public sector is $z \in Z$. The government transacts with the private sector using the producer prices p. Thus, the profit (loss if negative) of the public sector from its production activities is pz.

It is only necessary to consider the aggregate demand behavior of the consumer sector of the economy. Consumer prices are $q \gg 0_n$. The aggregate net demand vector is $x \in \Re^n$. This aggregate net demand vector depends on q and the net (of tax) profits of the individuals in this economy. After-tax profits are functions of the producer prices p and the variables τ related to profit taxation. Different interpretations of τ are possible. For example, if all firms are taxed at at common rate ρ, then $\tau = \rho$. Alternatively, if all profits are distributed to individuals who are then taxed on their profit income at possibly person-specific tax rates, then τ is the vector of these tax rates. It is assumed that given q, p, and τ, the vector of aggregate net demands $x(q, p, \tau)$ is uniquely determined. Hence, $x(\cdot)$ is a function.

Market clearing requires that

$$x(q, p, \tau) = \sum_{j=1}^{J} y^j + z, \tag{1}$$

where $y^j \in y^j(p)$ for all $j = 1, \ldots, J$ and $z \in Z$. By Walras' Law, satisfaction of (1) is equivalent to requiring the government to balance its budget. Letting $T(p, \tau)$ denote the government's revenue from profit taxation, the government's budget is balanced if

$$(q - p)x(q, p, \tau) + T(p, \tau) + pz = 0. \tag{2}$$

The vector $t = q - p$ is the vector of (specific) commodity tax rates. As is standard in the optimal commodity tax literature, it is assumed that the government chooses t indirectly through the choice of p and q, rather than directly.

It is assumed that for all $z \in Z$, there is sufficient flexibility in the choice of p, q, and τ so that the market-clearing conditions (1) or, equivalently, the government budget constraint (2) is satisfied. It is not assumed that the government can necessarily choose the commodity and profit taxes optimally, although this is not ruled out either. For example, because of political constraints, some or all of the commodity taxes may be fixed during the period being considered.

From (2), it follows that for given p, the choice of z only affects the set of q and τ compatible with government budget balance through its effect on the public sector profits pz. Following Diamond and Mirrlees (1976), it is assumed that the q and τ

[4] The following conventions are used for vector inequalities: for all $x, y \in \Re^n$, $x \gg y$ if $x_i > y_i$ for all $i = 1, \ldots, n$ and $x > y$ if $x_i \geq y_i$ for all $i = 1, \ldots, n$ and $x \neq y$.

required for the government budget constraint to be satisfied are uniquely determined by the values of p and pz. Hence,

$$q = \phi(p, pz) \tag{3}$$

and

$$\tau = \psi(p, pz) \tag{4}$$

for some functions ϕ and ψ.

Let P denote the set of admissible producer prices. These are the producer prices that are feasible. This set may be quite restricted. For example, if the aggregate production technology in the C-sector is linear and $\bar{p}$ is orthogonal to every net output vector on the efficient frontier of this production set, then, up to a positive factor of proportionality, $\bar{p}$ is the only feasible producer price vector if this sector of the economy is to operate.

Substituting (3) and (4) into $x(q, p, \tau)$, we obtain a 'reduced-form' of the aggregate net demands, $\tilde{x}(p, pz)$. The market clearing condition can then be rewritten as

$$\tilde{x}(p, pz) = \sum_{j=1}^{J} y^j + z, \tag{5}$$

where $y^j \in y^j(p)$ for all $j = 1, \ldots, J$ and $z \in Z$.

Social welfare is assumed to only depend on the consumption of individuals. The social welfare function need not be individualistic in the sense of only depending on an individual's consumption indirectly through its effects on this person's utility. Taking note of (3) and (4), we can express the social welfare function in indirect form as $V(p, pz)$.

The government chooses $z \in Z$, $p \in P$, and $y^j \in y^j(p)$, $j = 1, \ldots, J$, to maximize $V(p, pz)$ subject to (5). It is assumed that a solution $(z^*, p^*, y^{1*}, \ldots, y^{J*})$ to this problem exists.

It is also assumed that any optimal public production vector z^* is (weakly) efficient; i.e., there is no other $z \in Z$ for which $z \gg z^*$. It is not assumed that public production necessarily involves all commodities. As a consequence, Z could have an empty interior. Efficiency implies that z^* is on the relative frontier of Z.[5] Because z^* is efficient, if, as Diamond and Mirrlees assume, Z is convex, then z^* can be supported by a set of shadow prices $s > 0_n$. Hence, it is possible to decentralize production in the public sector by providing the managers of the public sector with the shadow prices s and instructing them to choose z to maximize profits at these prices.

Because it has not been assumed that commodity taxes are chosen optimally and that profits are taxed at a 100% rate, it is not possible to use the Diamond and Mirrlees

[5] The vector z is in the *relative interior* of Z if there exists a relative neighborhood of z contained in Z. A *relative neighborhood* of z is the set formed by the intersection of a neighborhood of z in $\Re^n$ with the minimal hyperplane containing Z. If every relative neighborhood of z contains elements of both Z and its complement, then z is on the *relative frontier* of Z. For a more formal treatment of relative interiors and relative frontiers, see Arrow and Hahn (1971, p. 376).

(1971) production efficiency theorem to conclude that the public sector shadow prices should equal (up to a factor of proportionality) the optimal private sector producer prices p^*. Nevertheless, if Z is convex, then at the shadow prices s that support z^*, it must be the case that the value of the optimal net supply y^{j*} of any private sector firm with a constant-returns-to-scale technology must be zero. In other words, if it is feasible to transfer the proportion θ of a C-sector firm's production y^{j*} to the public sector, then there is no change in social welfare.[6]

THEOREM 1 (Diamond and Mirrlees, 1976). *If (i) aggregate net demand depends in reduced form on producer prices and public sector profits, (ii) the public sector makes its transactions using the private sector producer prices, (iii) social welfare only depends on consumers' demands, (iv) any optimal public production is efficient, and (v) Z is convex, then for any solution $(z^*, p^*, y^{1*}, \ldots, y^{J*})$ to the government's optimization problem, there exists a vector of shadow prices $s > 0$ such that z^* maximizes sz on Z and such that*

$$sy^{j*} = 0 \tag{6}$$

for all $j \in C$.

My statement of Theorem 1 differs from that of Diamond and Mirrlees in three respects. First, they do not require the firms in the R-sector to be competitive profit maximizers. Instead, they assume that the net supplies of these firms depend in reduced form on producer prices and public sector profits, as has been assumed for the consumer sector. Their assumption permits some R-sector firms to exhibit monopoly power. Second, Diamond and Mirrlees also permit social welfare to depend on the net supplies of the firms in the R-sector. Modifying the model in this way does not affect the conclusion that the indirect social welfare function can be written as a function of producer prices and public sector profits, which is the only feature of the social welfare function that is used in the proof of Theorem 1. All of the other results presented here remain valid with these assumptions concerning the form of the social welfare function and the behavior of the R-sector firms.

Third, instead of assuming that z^* is efficient, Diamond and Mirrlees merely assume that z^* is on the relative frontier of Z. If, for example, Z is bounded from below, z^* can be on the relative frontier of Z without being efficient. When this is the case, at least one of the shadow prices must be negative. The practical appeal of Diamond and Mirrlees' version of Theorem 1 depends on z^* being efficient and, in their informal remarks, they assume that it is.[7]

The model employed in this shadow pricing theorem can also be extended in a number of other ways without affecting the conclusions of the theorem. For example, the model can be reformulated so as to allow for some kinds of consumption externalities, to allow for some forms of non-market clearing, and to allow for price vectors that differ

---

[6] If $\theta < 0$, then production is being transferred from the public sector to the C-sector firm.

[7] See, for example, Diamond and Mirrlees (1976, p. 41).

between consumers (e.g., by region) or between firms (e.g., because of intermediate goods taxation). In addition, by reinterpreting the model in intertemporal terms, Theorem 1 becomes a theorem about optimal social discount rates. See Diamond and Mirrlees (1976, Section 5) for details.

While, in general, the optimal shadow prices need not equal the private sector producer prices p^*, Diamond and Mirrlees (1976, p. 45) have identified a special case in which s must be proportional to p^* and, hence, can be set equal to p^*. This special case occurs when there are $n-1$ C-sector firms whose optimal net supply vectors y^{j*} are linearly independent. Diamond and Mirrlees do not state this theorem formally, nor do they provide a complete proof of this result. However, because the argument used to establish this theorem is needed in the next section to help prove Theorem 3, I include a complete proof here.

THEOREM 2 (Diamond and Mirrlees, 1976). *If, in addition to the assumptions of Theorem 1, there are $n-1$ C-sector firms whose optimal net supply vectors are linearly independent in the solution $(z^*, p^*, y^{1*}, \ldots, y^{J*})$ to the government's optimization problem, then the public sector shadow prices s are proportional to the optimal private sector producer prices p^*.*

PROOF. Let $C' \subseteq C$ be a set of $n-1$ firms whose optimal net supply vectors y^{j*} are linearly independent. Let A be the matrix whose rows are the net supply vectors of the firms in C'. By assumption, the rank of A is $n-1$. By a standard theorem in linear algebra, the dimension of the kernel of the linear mapping f defined by A is equal to one.[8] It follows from (6) that s is in the kernel of f. Because each C-sector firm has a constant-returns-to-scale technology, $p^* y^{j*} = 0$ for all $j \in C'$. Thus, p^* is also in the kernel of f. Because the kernel is one-dimensional (and both s and p^* are nonzero), s and p^* must be proportional to each other. ■

3. A Nonconvex Public Technology

If Z is nonconvex and the optimal public production z^* is efficient, it may not be possible to decentralize the production of z^* by specifying a set of public sector shadow prices and instructing the public managers to maximize profits using these prices. Nevertheless, there may exist shadow prices that serve as the correct guides for public decision-making in a neighborhood of z^*. That is, there exists a $\delta > 0$ such that z^* maximizes shadow profits on

$$Z_\delta = \{z \in Z \mid \|z - z^*\| < \delta\}. \tag{7}$$

Theorem 3 shows that if the assumptions of Theorem 2 are satisfied except for the convexity of Z, then the private producer prices p^* are the correct shadow prices to use in order for z^* to maximize shadow profits in some neighborhood of z^*.

[8] See, for example, Zelinsky (1968, Theorem 5.3.2).

THEOREM 3. *If (i) aggregate net demand depends in reduced form on producer prices and public sector profits, (ii) the public sector makes its transactions using the private sector producer prices, (iii) social welfare only depends on consumers' demands, (iv) any optimal public production is efficient, and (v) there are* $n-1$ *C-sector firms whose optimal net supply vectors are linearly independent in the solution* $(z^*, p^*, y^{1*}, \ldots, y^{J*})$ *to the government's optimization problem, then there exists a* $\delta > 0$ *such that* z^* *maximizes* p^*z *on* Z_δ*.*

PROOF. Let C' be a set of $n-1$ C-sector firms whose optimal net supply vectors y^{j*} are linearly independent. Note that in order for these net supplies to be linearly independent, $y^{j*} \neq 0_n$ for all $j \in C'$. The independence of these supply vectors also implies that there is a unique hyperplane H containing all vectors of the form $z = z^* + \sum_{j \in C'} \lambda_j y^{j*}$. (Negative λ_j are permissible.) Choose $\delta > 0$ so that for all $z \in H$ for which $\|z - z^*\| < \delta$, there exist $\lambda_j < 1$ for all $j \in C'$ such that $z = z^* + \sum_{j \in C'} \lambda_j y^{j*}$.

Let $\hat{z}$ be any such vector. Because the technologies of the C-sector firms are cones and $\lambda_j < 1$ for all $j \in C'$, $\hat{y}^j = (1 - \lambda_j) y^{j*} \in Y^j$. If $\hat{z} \in Z$, this transfer of production between the public and private sectors is feasible for the economy. Because profits of the C-sector firms are zero both before and after the transfer using the prices p^*, the revenue from profit taxation is unchanged. Aggregate net outputs are also unchanged, so the market clearing condition (5) is also satisfied. Hence, $(\hat{z}, p^*, \hat{y}^1, \ldots, \hat{y}^J)$ is also a solution to the government's optimization problem, where $\hat{y}^j = y^{j*}$ for all $j \notin C'$. By assumption, $\hat{z}$ must be efficient. Thus, the hyperplane H containing $\hat{z}$ does not intersect the relative interior of Z in Z_δ.

Because z^* is efficient, there exists a normal s to H with $s > 0_n$ for which z^* maximizes s^*z on Z_δ. Because $sz = sz^*$ for all $z \in H$, it follows from the definition of H that $sy^{j*} = 0$ for all $j \in C'$. Because the optimal net supply of any firm in $C \backslash C'$ is a linear combination of the optimal net supplies of the firms in C', it then follows that $sy^{j*} = 0$ for all $j \in C$. The argument used in the proof of Theorem 2 shows that s must be proportional to p^*. ■

The existence of the $n-1$ linearly independent optimal C-sector production vectors implies that it is possible to move locally in any direction from z^* on the hyperplane H defined in the proof of Theorem 3 by making a combination of feasible changes in the scale of operations of these producers and transferring the resulting production to the public sector. Whenever the resulting public production vector is feasible, it must be optimal, and so must be efficient. Thus, the nonnegative normal p^* to H serves as a vector of shadow prices for optimal public decision-making in a neighborhood of z^*.

If there are fewer than $n-1$ linearly independent optimal C-sector production vectors, then there is no longer a unique hyperplane containing all vectors of the form $z = z^* + \sum_{j \in C'} \lambda_j y^{j*}$. Any such hyperplane may contain a feasible public production arbitrarily close to z^* that is not obtainable from a combination of feasible changes in the scale of operations of the C-sector producers. The argument used to establish Theorem 3 can then no longer be employed to argue that this public production vector is efficient. Hence, shadow prices defined using this hyperplane may not decentralize the optimal public production locally. For example, if there are three goods, one C-sector firm who produces good two using good one as an input, and the public sector produces goods two and three using good one as an input, then it is only possible to conclude that feasible changes in z^* that are proportional to the C-sector firm's net supply vector are on the frontier of Z. In Theorem 1, convexity of Z guarantees that at least one of the hyperplanes described above does not intersect the relative interior of Z, and so can be used to define shadow prices (which need not be proportional to p^*) that decentralize public production globally.

As is clear from the proof of Theorem 3, the choice of δ is bounded from above because it is only possible to scale down the production of any C-sector firm a finite amount before it ceases to operate. It is for this reason that it may not be possible to use the private producer prices p^* to decentralize the optimal public production globally. Nevertheless, the neighborhood of z^* for which profit maximization using the prices p^* identifies z^* as an optimal production may be quite large. For example, suppose that there are two goods, one C-sector firm, and that the C-sector firm and the public sector firm both produce good two using good one as an input. By scaling down the production of the private firm, it is possible to transfer up to $|y^{1*}|$ units of the input to the public firm. As it is also possible to transfer production from the public to the private sector, the reasoning used in the proof of Theorem 3 applies for any $z \in Z$ for which $0 \leq |z_1| \leq |z_1^* + y_1^{1*}|$. The larger $|y_1^{1*}|$ is, the larger the neighborhood of z^* for which the producer prices p^* decentralize the optimal public production. More generally, if the size of the C-sector is large as measured by the distance of these firms' optimal net supply vectors from the origin, then the neighborhood Z_δ on which z^* necessarily maximizes profits at the prices p^* is also large. This limited form of decentralization may be perfectly adequate in practice.

If the nonconvex regions of Z are located close to z^*, it may well be the case that z^* not only maximizes p^*z on Z_δ, it may also maximize p^*z on all of Z. For example, consider replacing the public sector technology by its convex hull $ch(Z)$. Suppose that any optimal public production in this new economy must also be efficient. If the solution to the government's optimization problem is unchanged when the public technology is enlarged in this way, it follows from Theorem 2 that z^* maximizes p^*z on $ch(Z)$ and, hence, on Z, not just on Z_δ. Thus, if the assumptions of Theorem 3 hold and the solution to the government's optimization problem is invariant to the convexification of the public sector technology, then the optimal public production z^* can be decentralized globally using the prices p^*.

THEOREM 4. *If (i) aggregate net demand depends in reduced form on producer prices and public sector profits, (ii) the public sector makes its transactions using the private sector producer prices, (iii) social welfare only depends on consumers' demands, (iv) any optimal public production is efficient, (v)* $(z^*, p^*, y^{1*}, \ldots, y^{J*})$ *is a solution to the government's optimization problem when the public sector technology is either* Z *or* $ch(Z)$*, and (vi) there are* $n-1$ C*-sector firms whose optimal net supply vectors are linearly independent, then* z^* *maximizes* p^*z *on* Z.

Replacing the public technology with its convex hull relaxes the constraints facing the government. In general, one would expect this expansion of the public sector technology set to increase the optimal value of the social welfare function. However, Theorem 5 shows that if the assumptions of Theorem 2 hold when the technology is $ch(Z)$ and the public production vector z° that maximizes profits on Z using the producer prices p^* in the solution to the government's optimization problem for the convexified technology is unique, then the optimal public production z^* in $ch(Z)$ is in fact in Z. Thus, the assumptions of Theorem 4 are satisfied and the public sector's optimal production vector for the actual technology Z can be decentralized globally using the optimal private producer prices. Note that it has not been assumed that z^* and z° are the same, nor has it been assumed that they yield the same profits with the prices p^*. Rather, these conclusions are implications of the theorem.

THEOREM 5. *If (i) aggregate net demand depends in reduced form on producer prices and public sector profits, (ii) the public sector makes its transactions using the private sector producer prices, (iii) social welfare only depends on consumers' demands, (iv) any optimal public production is efficient, (v) there are $n-1$ C-sector firms whose optimal net supply vectors are linearly independent in the solution $(z^*, p^*, y^{1*}, \ldots, y^{J*})$ to the government's optimization problem when the public sector technology is $ch(Z)$, and (vi) z° uniquely maximizes p^*z on Z, then $z^* = z^\circ$.*

PROOF. When the public technology is $ch(Z)$, the assumptions of Theorem 2 are satisfied. Hence, z^* maximizes p^*z on $ch(Z)$. Because z^* is in $ch(Z)$, there exists a positive integer K such that for all $k = 1, \ldots, K$, there exists a vector $z^k \in Z$ and a scalar $\mu_k > 0$ with $\sum_{k=1}^{K} \mu_k = 1$ such that $z^* = \sum_{k=1}^{K} \mu_k z^k$. Because z^* maximizes p^*z on $ch(Z)$, it then follows that $p^*z^k = p^*z^*$ for all $k = 1, \ldots, K$. Thus, each of the z^k maximizes p^*z on Z. By assumption, z° uniquely maximizes p^*z on Z. Hence, $K = 1$ and $z^* = z^1 = z^\circ$. ■

The assumption in Theorem 5 that z° uniquely maximizes p^*z on Z is essential. If, for example, $z^* \in ch(Z) \setminus Z$ and z^* is a strict convex combination of z^1 and z^2, both of which maximize p^*z on Z, then it is possible that social welfare is lower with either z^1 and z^2 than with z^* because neither z^1 nor z^2 is part of a feasible allocation with the prices p^*. In such a situation, convexifying the technology Z increases social welfare, and the assumptions of Theorem 4 do not apply.

4. Concluding Remarks

Diamond and Mirrlees (1976, p. 45) note that a limitation of their shadow pricing theorems is that they assume that optimal public production is efficient, rather than deducing efficiency from more fundamental properties of the model. To illustrate the limitations of this assumption, they cite examples from Diamond and Mirrlees (1971) in which aggregate production efficiency is not optimal. However, even if the sum of the private and public net outputs is not on the frontier of the aggregate production possibilities set, it does not follow that public production must be inefficient. In fact, Weymark (1981) has shown that with relatively weak assumptions about the production technologies, any net output vector in the aggregate production possibilities set can be obtained as the sum of net outputs that are efficient for each firm.[9] Hence, it is not restrictive to assume that public production is efficient provided that it is possible to obtain any net output vector that is efficient for the private sector in the aggregate using the available policy instruments. This will be the case if all private firms are competitive profit maximizers with convex technologies and any nonnegative producer price vector is feasible.

The theorems presented in this article for a nonconvex public technology Z show that if there is enough independence in the optimal supplies of the C-sector firms, then the optimal public production z^* maximizes profits using the private producer prices over some region of Z containing z^*. This region may be quite large. If the solution to the government's optimization problem is invariant to the replacement of Z by its convex hull, then z^* maximizes profits at these prices on all of Z. Whether convexifying the public technology changes the optimal public production depends on where on the frontier of Z that z^* is located. This dependence is reminiscent of the finding by Moore et al. (1972) that simply changing the resource endowment can affect whether Pareto optimal allocations in a first-best economy with a nonconvex aggregate production technology can be decentralized as competitive equilibria. As is the case here, the circumstances that they have identified in which it is possible to decentralize Pareto optima depend on properties of a convexified version of the economy. It would be of interest to see if the techniques that Moore, Whinston, and Wu introduced to analyze their problem can be adapted to provide further insight into the situations in which private producer prices can be used to globally decentralize optimal public production in the kind of second-best environments considered in this article.

References

Arrow, K. J., and F. Hahn. 1971. *General Competitive Analysis*, San Francisco: Holden-Day.

Bös, D. 1985. "Public Sector Pricing", in: A. J. Auerbach and M. Feldstein (eds.): *Handbook of Public Economics*, Vol. 1, Amsterdam: North-Holland, 129–211.

Diamond, P. A., and J. A. Mirrlees. 1971. "Optimal Taxation and Public Production I: Production Efficiency", *American Economic Review* 61, 8–27.

Diamond, P. A., and J. A. Mirrlees. 1976. "Private Constant Returns and Public Shadow Prices", *Review of Economic Studies* 43, 41–47.

Drèze, J., and N. Stern. 1987. "The Theory of Cost–Benefit Analysis", in: A. J. Auerbach and M. Feldstein (eds.): *Handbook of Public Economics*, Vol. 2. Amsterdam: North-Holland, 909–989.

Guesnerie, R. 1979. "General Statements on Second Best Pareto Optimality", *Journal of Mathematical Economics* 6, 169–194.

[9] His formal theorem assumes that the technologies are convex, but, as he notes, the convexity assumption is not needed for his result if the aggregate private production set and the public production set are bounded above by hyperplanes that are not parallel to each other.

Guesnerie, R. 1995. *A Contribution to the Pure Theory of Taxation*, Cambridge: Cambridge University Press.

Moore, J. C., A. B. Whinston, and J. S. Wu. 1972. "Resource Allocation in a Non-convex Economy", *Review of Economic Studies* 39, 303–323.

Weymark, J. A. 1981. "On Sums of Production Set Frontiers", *Review of Economic Studies* 48, 179–183.

Zelinsky, D. 1968. *A First Course in Linear Algebra*, New York: Academic Press.

John A. Weymark
Department of Economics
Vanderbilt University
VU Station B #351819
2301 Vanderbilt Place
Nashville, TN 37235–1819
U.S.A.
john.weymark@vanderbilt.edu

A GLANCE AT SOME FUNDAMENTAL PUBLIC ECONOMICS ISSUES THROUGH A PARAMETRIC LENS

CHRISTOS KOULOVATIANOS
Universität Wien

1. Introduction

In this paper I am suggesting a few shortcuts that simplify complex matters in public economics in order to gain additional insights from these one grasps by reading textbooks. I am using parametric models that take the general textbook-style analysis a step further: not only they provide analytical solutions, but they also reveal the role of primitives for reaching specific qualitative conclusions on more advanced questions.

I believe that the identification and use of parametric models in the public economics analysis is a fruitful complement to the study of questions through general theoretical treatments. It can help substantially in boosting the scholar's economic intuition. Models can help as guides for forming good questions and for reaching answers beyond the immediate scope of the general analysis. The reason behind this special potential role of carefully selected parametric models is that they can preserve important information about economic primitives that is contained within specific parameters. Moreover, some models are able to both carry and exhibit this information of key primitives in analytical solutions and also to reveal the relative importance of these primitives for answers to each examined general question and mechanism.

In what follows, I am pointing out my objective and conclusions in each section separately.

2. A Pure Exchange Economy

Textbooks teach us that in pure exchange economies with secured property rights of individuals over endowments of consumable private goods and with the only proviso on primitives that preferences of individuals are convex, the two welfare theorems hold. This analysis is a very powerful benchmark for introducing both the allocative power of private markets, because the competitive-equilibrium allocations have many strong properties, and also for looking at ways of reallocating welfare through lump-sum transfers. The 'advanced' question I want to examine is: "*how does preference*

U. Schmidt and S. Traub (eds.), Advances in Public Economics: Utility, Choice and Welfare, 73-104.

heterogeneity influence the competitive allocation of resources and lump-sum transfer policies?"

Let's use a familiar parametric example. Consider a 2–person–2–good exchange economy with primitives summarized by Table I. Both individuals have secured property rights over their endowment.

TABLE I.

	Individual A	Individual B
Utility function	$\alpha \ln(x) + (1-\alpha)\ln(y)$	$\beta \ln(x) + (1-\beta)\ln(y)$
Endowment	$(\hat{x}_A, \hat{y}_A)$	$(\hat{x}_B, \hat{y}_B)$

2.1. COMPETITIVE (DECENTRALIZED) EQUILIBRIUM

During the bargaining process of exchange the two individuals examine any proposed vector of prices (p_x, p_y). We will find the demands of each individual for each of the two goods as functions of prices (p_x, p_y) and the rest of the fundamentals given in Table I.

2.1.1. *Partial-equilibrium Demands*

Fix an arbitrary price vector, (p_x, p_y). The maximization problem of individual A is:

$$\max_{(x,y)} \left[\alpha \ln(x) + (1-\alpha)\ln(y)\right]$$
$$\text{subject to : } p_x x + p_y y \leq p_x \hat{x}_A + p_y \hat{y}_A \ .$$

The resulting demands for A in decentralized equilibrium, denoted as "DE", are

$$x_A^{DE} = \alpha \left(\hat{x}_A + \frac{p_y}{p_x}\hat{y}_A\right) , \tag{1}$$

where the symbol x_A^{DE} stands for "demand of individual A for good x in the decentralized equilibrium (DE)", and,

$$y_A^{DE} = (1-\alpha)\left(\frac{p_x}{p_y}\hat{x}_A + \hat{y}_A\right) . \tag{2}$$

Due to the fact that the functional structure of individual B's problem is symmetric to the functional structure of A's problem, it is straightforward to see that B's demand functions will be the same as these of A, given by (1) and (2), except from some different parameters. Namely,

$$x_B^{DE} = \beta \left(\hat{x}_B + \frac{p_y}{p_x}\hat{y}_B\right) \tag{3}$$

and

$$y_B^{DE} = (1-\beta)\left(\frac{p_x}{p_y}\hat{x}_B + \hat{y}_B\right). \tag{4}$$

2.1.2. *Market-clearing Prices*

Market-clearing conditions simply require that aggregate demand meets aggregate supply for each good. These conditions are,

$$x_A^{DE} + x_B^{DE} = \hat{x}_A + \hat{x}_B \tag{5}$$

$$y_A^{DE} + y_B^{DE} = \hat{y}_A + \hat{y}_B \tag{6}$$

and using these conditions together with the demand functions, the decentralized-equilibrium price vector (normalized using good x as the numeraire) is,

$$\left(1, \frac{p_y^{DE}}{p_x^{DE}}\right) = \left(1, \frac{(1-\alpha)\,\hat{x}_A + (1-\beta)\,\hat{x}_B}{\alpha\hat{y}_A + \beta\hat{y}_B}\right). \tag{7}$$

2.1.3. *Interpretations*

So, what can make good y relatively more expensive? Equation (7) reveals a lot, since, after all, when markets are efficient, as it is the case here, prices reveal all the information about primitives and endowment allocations.

(i) Keeping the distribution of endowments constant, it is transparent that if both individuals have a strong relative preference for y, i.e. the case where both α and β are low $\frac{p_y^{DE}}{p_x^{DE}}$ increases.

(ii) Keeping preference parameters, α and β constant, a low level of total endowment of y, i.e. the case where both $\hat{y}_A$ and $\hat{y}_B$ are low, scarcity of y makes y more expensive.

(iii) Consider that individual A has a lot of x, i.e. $\hat{x}_A$ is high, and also A prefers more y, i.e. α is low, so, $(1-\alpha)\,\hat{x}_A$ is high. The price of y will be higher: individual B will exploit this weakness of A, it will extract most of the endowment of A in terms of units of x, by setting a higher price for y.

2.1.4. *General Equilibrium*

Using the equilibrium price vector and the demand functions, the decentralized-equilibrium demanded quantities are given by Table II.

2.1.5. *Pareto Allocations*

The first welfare theorem states that if all goods are private in an exchange economy and each individual has convex preferences over these private goods, then a decentralized, completely free trade of endowments will always end up in a Pareto efficient

TABLE II.

Good	Individual A	Individual B
x_i^{DE}	$\alpha\left[\hat{x}_A + \frac{(1-\alpha)\hat{x}_A+(1-\beta)\hat{x}_B}{\alpha\hat{y}_A+\beta\hat{y}_B}\hat{y}_A\right]$	$\beta\left[\hat{x}_B + \frac{(1-\alpha)\hat{x}_A+(1-\beta)\hat{x}_B}{\alpha\hat{y}_A+\beta\hat{y}_B}\hat{y}_B\right]$
y_i^{DE}	$(1-\alpha)\left[\frac{\alpha\hat{y}_A+\beta\hat{y}_B}{(1-\alpha)\hat{x}_A+(1-\beta)\hat{x}_B}\hat{x}_A + \hat{y}_A\right]$	$(1-\beta)\left[\frac{\alpha\hat{y}_A+\beta\hat{y}_B}{(1-\alpha)\hat{x}_A+(1-\beta)\hat{x}_B}\hat{x}_B + \hat{y}_B\right]$

outcome. Pareto efficiency of a chosen trade means that no other trade can make a person better off without making at least one of the other individuals worse off. Therefore, once all individuals agree upon a Pareto efficient outcome, no other trade can be commonly agreed-upon, since at least one person will be worse off if any other alternative is chosen.

Since our example above meets the sufficient conditions of the first welfare theorem, we know that the demanded quantities and the equilibrium price vector constitute a Pareto efficient equilibrium. We know this since the marginal rate of substitution between the two goods is equal to the commonly agreed equilibrium price for both individuals. This means that the indifference curves of the two individuals are tangent at the equilibrium point. But moving from the point of tangency will make at least one individual worse off, i.e. the decentralized equilibrium is, indeed, Pareto efficient.

In this section we may forget about initial endowments for the moment, and focus on finding all possible points with the Pareto efficiency property. Technically, this means that we should look for all the possible demands where: (i) the marginal rate of substitution between the two goods for both individuals is equal; and also (ii) markets clear. In other words, we are looking for points in the Edgeworth box where the indifference curves of the two individuals are tangent.[1]The market-clearing conditions are:

$$x_A + x_B = X , \tag{8}$$
$$y_A + y_B = Y , \tag{9}$$

where X and Y are the total resources of each good in the overall economy.[2]

In general, since we don't care about the initial allocation of endowments, we will be varying the demands of individual A only, and we will be expressing the demands of B as the remaining quantity from total resources. So, (x_A, y_A) will be the demands of A, and $(X - x_A, Y - y_A)$ will be the demands of B. Therefore, the Pareto efficient set is all possible vectors (x_A, y_A) and $(X - x_A, Y - y_A)$, such that:

$$\frac{\frac{\partial u^A(x_A,y_A)}{\partial x_A}}{\frac{\partial u^A(x_A,y_A)}{\partial y_A}} = \frac{\frac{\partial u^B(X-x_A,Y-y_A)}{\partial(X-x_A)}}{\frac{\partial u^B(X-x_A,Y-y_A)}{\partial(Y-y_A)}} \tag{10}$$

[1] Being in the Edgeworth box guarantees market clearing, that total supply equals total demand.

[2] Remember that, graphically, the aggregate quantities X and Y are the dimensions of the Edgeworth box.

Using the specific functions of our example, (10) gives:

$$\frac{\alpha}{1-\alpha}\frac{y_A}{x_A}=\frac{\beta}{1-\beta}\frac{Y-y_A}{X-x_A}\ . \tag{11}$$

So, the points satisfying (11) are Pareto efficient. Solving this last expression for y_A we get:

$$y_A=\frac{Y}{\frac{\alpha(1-\beta)}{(1-\alpha)\beta}\left(\frac{X}{x_A}-1\right)+1} \tag{12}$$

Equation (12) can draw the Pareto efficient set in the Edgeworth box. It is easy to verify that this will be an increasing function, since:

$$\frac{\partial y_A}{\partial x_A}=\frac{\frac{\alpha(1-\beta)}{(1-\alpha)\beta}\frac{X}{x_A^2}Y}{\left[\frac{\alpha(1-\beta)}{(1-\alpha)\beta}\left(\frac{X}{x_A}-1\right)+1\right]^2}>0\ .$$

Also: $x_A=0\Rightarrow y_A=0$ and $x_A=X\Rightarrow y_A=Y$, i.e. the Pareto-efficient line passes through the southwest and northeast corners of the Edgeworth box.

2.2. THE SOCIAL PLANNER'S CHOICE

The (utilitarian) Social Planner's problem can be expressed as:

$$\max_{(x_A,y_A,x_B,y_B)}\ \varphi\left[\alpha\ln\left(x_A\right)+(1-\alpha)\ln\left(y_A\right)\right]+(1-\varphi)\left[\beta\ln\left(x_B\right)+(1-\beta)\ln\left(y_B\right)\right]$$

$$\text{subject to}:\quad \begin{array}{l} x_A+x_B=X\ , \\ y_A+y_B=Y\ , \end{array}$$

where φ is the weight the Social Planner puts on the utility of individual A. Two key necessary conditions are

$$\frac{x_B}{x_A}=\frac{\beta\left(1-\varphi\right)}{\alpha\varphi}\quad\text{and}\quad\frac{y_B}{y_A}=\frac{\left(1-\beta\right)\left(1-\varphi\right)}{\left(1-\alpha\right)\varphi}\ .$$

So, using the two constraints it is

$$x_A^{SP}=\frac{\alpha\varphi X}{\alpha\varphi+\beta\left(1-\varphi\right)}\ ,$$

$$x_B^{SP}=\frac{\beta\left(1-\varphi\right)X}{\alpha\varphi+\beta\left(1-\varphi\right)}\ ,$$

$$y_A^{SP}=\frac{\left(1-\alpha\right)\varphi Y}{\left(1-\alpha\right)\varphi+\left(1-\beta\right)\left(1-\varphi\right)}\ ,$$

and

$$y_B^{SP}=\frac{\left(1-\beta\right)\left(1-\varphi\right)Y}{\left(1-\alpha\right)\varphi+\left(1-\beta\right)\left(1-\varphi\right)}\ .$$

2.2.1. *Implementation of Pareto Optimal Allocations*

There are infinite transfer policies that the Social Planner can adopt in order to enforce her best-preferred demands. Let's characterize these transfers.

If the after-transfer endowments are $\left(\left(\hat{x}_A^{SP}, \hat{y}_A^{SP}\right), \left(\hat{x}_B^{SP}, \hat{y}_B^{SP}\right)\right)$, we know from the analysis of competitive equilibrium that the decentralized-equilibrium price of y in terms of units of good x will be:

$$\frac{(1-\alpha)\,\hat{x}_A^{SP} + (1-\beta)\,\hat{x}_B^{SP}}{\alpha\hat{y}_A^{SP} + \beta\hat{y}_B^{SP}} ,$$

but we want this price ratio to be equal to the Social Planner's preferred one, i.e.

$$\frac{(1-\alpha)\,\hat{x}_A^{SP} + (1-\beta)\,\hat{x}_B^{SP}}{\alpha\hat{y}_A^{SP} + \beta\hat{y}_B^{SP}} = \frac{(1-\alpha)\,\varphi + (1-\beta)\,(1-\varphi)}{\alpha\varphi + \beta\,(1-\varphi)}\frac{X}{Y} .$$

If, for example, we want to replicate x_A^{SP} in decentralized equilibrium with after-transfer endowments $\left(\left(\hat{x}_A^{SP}, \hat{y}_A^{SP}\right), \left(\hat{x}_B^{SP}, \hat{y}_B^{SP}\right)\right)$, then it must be that:

$$x_A^{SP} = \alpha\left[\hat{x}_A^{SP} + \frac{(1-\alpha)\,\varphi + (1-\beta)\,(1-\varphi)}{\alpha\varphi + \beta\,(1-\varphi)}\frac{X}{Y}\hat{y}_A^{SP}\right] .$$

Solving this expression for $\hat{y}_A^{SP}$, we can see that, as long as all after-transfer endowments are positive, if the Social Planner chooses an arbitrary $\hat{x}_A^{SP}$, then she can give the following after-transfer endowments:

$$\left(\hat{x}_A^{SP}, \frac{\varphi Y}{(1-\alpha)\,\varphi + (1-\beta)\,(1-\varphi)} - \frac{\alpha\varphi + \beta\,(1-\varphi)}{(1-\alpha)\,\varphi + (1-\beta)\,(1-\varphi)}\frac{Y}{X}\hat{x}_A^{SP}\right) \qquad (13)$$

and

$$\left(X - \hat{x}_A^{SP}, Y - \frac{\varphi Y}{(1-\alpha)\,\varphi + (1-\beta)\,(1-\varphi)} + \frac{\alpha\varphi + \beta\,(1-\varphi)}{(1-\alpha)\,\varphi + (1-\beta)\,(1-\varphi)}\frac{Y}{X}\hat{x}_A^{SP}\right) \qquad (14)$$

It is transparent that the role of individual preferences and also of the social Planner's preferences over individual utilities, captured by parameter φ, determine the optimal allocations of the social planner. The logic of the mapping of preferences to decentralized-equilibrium allocations that was expressed in points (i) through (iii) above is also vivid in the Social Planner's choice. This is because the constant preference intensities captured by α and β retain the same logic for all available initial endowments, X and Y, giving a great facility to welfare analysis.

3. Economy with Production

Bator (1957) provided an elegant diagrammatic analysis for explaining the mechanics of general equilibrium in private economies with production. Yet, unlike the case of pure exchange economies, the optimal redistributive policies of productive factors by a Social Planner who wishes to implement her own policies cannot be depicted graphically. This section undertakes the task of shedding some light on the determinants of the redistributive policies of the Social Planner through a parametric model.

Consider the same individuals as above, but now the two individuals are, instead, endowed with capital, k, and labor, l, namely:

TABLE III.

	Individual A	Individual B
utility function	$\alpha \ln(x) + (1-\alpha)\ln(y)$	$\beta \ln(x) + (1-\beta)\ln(y)$
endowment	$(\hat{k}_A, \hat{l}_A)$	$(\hat{k}_B, \hat{l}_B)$

Both individuals have secured property rights over their endowment. Capital and labor can be used to produce the final goods, x and y, through the productive operation of competitive companies that use the technologies,

$$x = k_x^{\chi} l_x^{1-\chi} \quad \text{and} \quad y = k_y^{\psi} l_y^{1-\psi} ,$$

where k_x, k_y, l_x, l_y are the quantities of the intermediate factors employed in each productive operation.

3.1. EFFICIENT PRODUCTION

Since the exchange of intermediate goods is free, two sectors are formed, each specializing in the production of a final good. At this point it is irrelevant who provides the intermediate factors. This is because intermediate goods move freely from company to company, up to the point that the rental prices for each intermediate good (r for capital and w for labor), become equal across companies for the same good, through arbitrage. Therefore, individuals A and B are indifferent between disposing their resources of total factors to one firm and not the other.

Given an arbitrary price vector $((r,w),(p_x,p_y))$, the two firms maximize their profits. The firm for producing good x has a profit function $\pi_x(k_x,l_x) = p_x k_x^{\chi} l_x^{1-\chi} - rk_x - wl_x$.

$$\max_{(k_x,l_x)} p_x k_x^{\chi} l_x^{1-\chi} - rk_x - wl_x$$

The first-order (necessary conditions) give:

$$\frac{1-\chi}{\chi}\frac{k_x}{l_x} = \frac{w}{r} \tag{15}$$

and symmetrically for the sector of good y,

$$\frac{1-\psi}{\psi}\frac{k_y}{l_y} = \frac{w}{r} . \tag{16}$$

Equations (15) and (16) correspond to the marginal rate of technical substitution for each final good. The fact that in equilibrium they must be equal, shows that production has to be Pareto efficient. If we denote the total inelastic supply of the two intermediate goods as:

$$\hat{k}_A + \hat{k}_B = K \;, \tag{17}$$

and

$$\hat{l}_A + \hat{l}_B = L \;, \tag{18}$$

then market clearing in the intermediate-goods markets (total demand equals total supply) gives:

$$k_x + k_y = K = \hat{k}_A + \hat{k}_B \;, \tag{19}$$

and

$$l_x + l_y = L = \hat{l}_A + \hat{l}_B \;. \tag{20}$$

What is the Pareto efficient set for production? It must satisfy: (i) market clearing (which can be represented geometrically by just being in the Edgeworth box); and (ii) that the marginal rate of technical substitution is the same across the two sectors of production. The condition satisfying (ii) is given by combining equations (15) and (16):

$$\frac{1-\chi}{\chi}\frac{k_x}{l_x} = \frac{1-\psi}{\psi}\frac{k_y}{l_y} \;.$$

Using the market clearing equations (19) and (20), we can see that $k_y = K - k_x$ and $l_y = L - l_x$. Therefore, the Pareto efficient set for production is given by demand bundles of (k_x, l_x) that satisfy:

$$\frac{1-\chi}{\chi}\frac{k_x}{l_x} = \frac{1-\psi}{\psi}\frac{K-k_x}{L-l_x} \;. \tag{21}$$

Now the goal is to express intermediate-good demands as functions of $\frac{w}{r}$ only. Equations (15), (16), (19), and (20) help us transform the non-linear set of initial conditions into a simple system of linear equations. Solving this linear system, we obtain:

$$k_x = \frac{\frac{w}{r}L - \frac{1-\psi}{\psi}K}{\frac{1}{\chi} - \frac{1}{\psi}} \;, \tag{22}$$

$$k_y = \frac{\frac{1-\chi}{\chi}K - \frac{w}{r}L}{\frac{1}{\chi} - \frac{1}{\psi}} \;, \tag{23}$$

$$l_x = \frac{\frac{1-\chi}{\chi}}{\frac{1}{\chi} - \frac{1}{\psi}}\left(L - \frac{1-\psi}{\psi}\frac{r}{w}K\right) \;, \tag{24}$$

and

$$l_y = \frac{\frac{1-\psi}{\psi}}{\frac{1}{\chi} - \frac{1}{\psi}}\left(\frac{1-\chi}{\chi}\frac{r}{w}K - L\right) \;. \tag{25}$$

Equations (22) through (25) provide important insights about efficient allocation in production. Specifically, more of a productive factor is allocated in a sector if

(i) the relative factor intensity in the particular sector is high,
(ii) the total available quantity of the production factor is high relative to the total quantity of the other production factor,
(iii) the relative price of the production factor is low.

The fact that factor intensities in this parametric model are constant helps the mechanics of points (i) through (iii) be carried through the rest of the analysis. So, a useful set of intuitive ideas is retained, independently from the factor price vector, (r, w), and also from the aggregate-resource availability, K and L.

3.2. PRODUCTION POSSIBILITIES

The Production Possibilities Frontier (PPF) is the maximum total output of Y that can be produced for any pre-assigned total quantity of good X. So, the total productive resources, (K, L), must be utilized efficiently in production. In this section we will restrain the concept to a joint relationship between total produced quantities and final-good prices, something like two joint supply curves. This will facilitate us in finding the total quantities directly after we specify the final-goods price vector at a later stage, when we also analyze the exchange of consumers. A key relationship between the PPF and final goods prices: the slope of any point of the PPF is the "Rate of Product Transformation"$= -\frac{dY}{dX}$.

We are confronted with constant returns to scale in production and, as we know, profits in this case are zero. The zero-profit condition paves our way to characterizing efficient production:

$$\pi_x = 0 \Rightarrow p_x X = rk_x + wl_x \overset{(15)}{\Longrightarrow} p_x X = rk_x + \frac{1-\chi}{\chi} rk_x \Rightarrow p_x X = \frac{rk_x}{\chi} \overset{(22)}{\Longrightarrow}$$

$$p_x X = \frac{\psi wL - (1-\psi) rK}{\psi - \chi} . \tag{26}$$

Similarly, from the zero-profit condition for the production of good Y, we get:

$$p_y Y = \frac{(1-\chi) rK - \chi wL}{\psi - \chi} . \tag{27}$$

Dividing (27) by (26), we have:

$$\frac{p_y Y}{p_x X} = \frac{(1-\chi) rK - \chi wL}{\psi wL - (1-\psi) rK} \Rightarrow \frac{Y}{X} = \frac{p_x}{p_y} \frac{(1-\chi) K - \chi \frac{w}{r} L}{\psi \frac{w}{r} L - (1-\psi) K} . \tag{28}$$

Now we want to eliminate the intermediate-good price ratio $\frac{w}{r}$ from equation (28) and keep only Y^{DE}, X^{DE} and $\frac{p_x}{p_y}$ in the expression. Profit maximization in the sector for good x implies that

$$\chi p_x \left(\frac{k_x}{l_x}\right)^{\chi-1} = r \overset{(15)}{\Longrightarrow} \frac{r}{p_x} = \chi^{\chi} (1-\chi)^{1-\chi} \left(\frac{w}{r}\right)^{\chi-1} . \tag{29}$$

Similarly,

$$\psi p_y \left(\frac{k_y}{l_y}\right)^{\psi-1} = r \overset{(16)}{\Longrightarrow} \frac{r}{p_y} = \psi^{\psi} (1-\psi)^{1-\psi} \left(\frac{w}{r}\right)^{\psi-1} . \tag{30}$$

Dividing (30) by (29), we reach the desired relationship:

$$\frac{w}{r} = \left[\frac{\chi^{\chi} (1-\chi)^{1-\chi}}{\psi^{\psi} (1-\psi)^{1-\psi}}\right]^{\frac{1}{\chi-\psi}} \left(\frac{p_x}{p_y}\right)^{\frac{1}{\chi-\psi}} . \tag{31}$$

Substituting (31) into (28) we obtain:

$$\frac{Y}{X} = \frac{p_x}{p_y} \frac{(1-\chi) K - \chi \left[\frac{\chi^{\chi}(1-\chi)^{1-\chi}}{\psi^{\psi}(1-\psi)^{1-\psi}}\right]^{\frac{1}{\chi-\psi}} \left(\frac{p_x}{p_y}\right)^{\frac{1}{\chi-\psi}} L}{\psi \left[\frac{\chi^{\chi}(1-\chi)^{1-\chi}}{\psi^{\psi}(1-\psi)^{1-\psi}}\right]^{\frac{1}{\chi-\psi}} \left(\frac{p_x}{p_y}\right)^{\frac{1}{\chi-\psi}} L - (1-\psi) K} , \tag{32}$$

which is a PPF equation that shows the unique relationship between total final-good produced quantities and final-good prices.

3.3. CONSUMER CHOICE

Consumers receive income from renting their endowments of intermediate goods. So, given an arbitrary price vector $((r, w), (p_x, p_y))$, the maximization problem of individual A is:

$$\max_{(x,y)} [\alpha \ln(x) + (1-\alpha) \ln(y)]$$
$$\text{subject to} \; : \; p_x x + p_y y \leq r\hat{k}_A + w\hat{l}_A .$$

Solving this problem leads to

$$x_A = \alpha \frac{r}{p_x} \left(\hat{k}_A + \frac{w}{r}\hat{l}_A\right)$$

and, after using (29), it is

$$x_A^{DE} = \alpha \chi^{\chi} (1-\chi)^{1-\chi} \left(\frac{w}{r}\right)^{\chi-1} \left(\hat{k}_A + \frac{w}{r}\hat{l}_A\right) . \tag{33}$$

Similarly,

$$y_A^{DE} = (1-\alpha) \psi^{\psi} (1-\psi)^{1-\psi} \left(\frac{w}{r}\right)^{\psi-1} \left(\hat{k}_A + \frac{w}{r}\hat{l}_A\right) , \tag{34}$$

$$x_B^{DE} = \beta \chi^{\chi} (1-\chi)^{1-\chi} \left(\frac{w}{r}\right)^{\chi-1} \left(\hat{k}_B + \frac{w}{r}\hat{l}_B\right) , \tag{35}$$

and

$$y_B^{DE} = (1-\beta)\,\psi^{\psi}\,(1-\psi)^{1-\psi}\left(\frac{w}{r}\right)^{\psi-1}\left(\hat{k}_B + \frac{w}{r}\hat{l}_B\right). \tag{36}$$

The symbol x_A^{DE} stands for "demand of individual A for good x in the decentralized equilibrium (DE)." The goal now is to find the factor price ratio, $\frac{w}{r}$. This can be done by looking at the market-clearing conditions of one of the two markets, say, the market of final good x. Consumer demands are such that individual A spends α of her total income on good x, whereas B, spends β of her total income on good x. Namely:

$$\left.\begin{array}{l} p_x x_A = \alpha\left(r\hat{k}_A + w\hat{l}_A\right) \\ p_x x_B = \beta\left(r\hat{k}_B + w\hat{l}_B\right) \end{array}\right\} \Rightarrow p_x X = r\left(\alpha\hat{k}_A + \beta\hat{k}_B\right) + w\left(\alpha\hat{l}_A + \beta\hat{l}_B\right). \tag{37}$$

On the other hand, the zero-profit feature of perfect competition in production yields equation (26). Equating (26) and (37) results in:

$$\frac{w^{DE}}{r^{DE}} = \frac{\alpha\hat{k}_A + \beta\hat{k}_B + \frac{(1-\psi)K}{\psi-\chi}}{\frac{\psi L}{\psi-\chi} - \alpha\hat{l}_A - \beta\hat{l}_B}. \tag{38}$$

So, (31) combined with (38) give:

$$\frac{p_y^{DE}}{p_x^{DE}} = \frac{\chi^{\chi}(1-\chi)^{1-\chi}}{\psi^{\psi}(1-\psi)^{1-\psi}}\left(\frac{\alpha\hat{k}_A + \beta\hat{k}_B + \frac{(1-\psi)K}{\psi-\chi}}{\frac{\psi L}{\psi-\chi} - \alpha\hat{l}_A - \beta\hat{l}_B}\right)^{\chi-\psi}. \tag{39}$$

Therefore, the normalized final-goods price vector is:

$$\left(1, \frac{\chi^{\chi}(1-\chi)^{1-\chi}}{\psi^{\psi}(1-\psi)^{1-\psi}}\left(\frac{\alpha\hat{k}_A + \beta\hat{k}_B + \frac{(1-\psi)K}{\psi-\chi}}{\frac{\psi L}{\psi-\chi} - \alpha\hat{l}_A - \beta\hat{l}_B}\right)^{\chi-\psi}\right).$$

Equations (38) and (39) give the decentralized-equilibrium prices. You can see that these prices contain information about the structure of technology, preferences and the initial intermediate-good allocation of endowments. Substituting the equilibrium prices into the consumer- and factor demand functions that we found above, we obtain the equilibrium demanded quantitities. In particular, plugging the particular factor price ratio $\frac{w^{DE}}{r^{DE}}$ into the demand functions, the decentralized-equilibrium consumer demanded quantitites are given by Table IV.

Moreover, plugging the particular factor price ratio $\frac{w^{DE}}{r^{DE}}$ into the factor demand functions, the decentralized-equilibrium factor demanded quantities are given by Table V.

TABLE IV. Consumer demands in decentralized equilibrium

Good	Individual A
x_A^{DE}	$\alpha\chi^{\chi}(1-\chi)^{1-\chi}\left(\frac{\alpha\hat{k}_A+\beta\hat{k}_B+\frac{(1-\psi)K}{\psi-\chi}}{\frac{\psi L}{\psi-\chi}-\alpha\hat{l}_A-\beta\hat{l}_B}\right)^{\chi-1}\left(\hat{k}_A+\frac{\alpha\hat{k}_A+\beta\hat{k}_B+\frac{(1-\psi)K}{\psi-\chi}}{\frac{\psi L}{\psi-\chi}-\alpha\hat{l}_A-\beta\hat{l}_B}\hat{l}_A\right)$
y_A^{DE}	$(1-\alpha)\psi^{\psi}(1-\psi)^{1-\psi}\left(\frac{\alpha\hat{k}_A+\beta\hat{k}_B+\frac{(1-\psi)K}{\psi-\chi}}{\frac{\psi L}{\psi-\chi}-\alpha\hat{l}_A-\beta\hat{l}_B}\right)^{\psi-1}\left(\hat{k}_A+\frac{\alpha\hat{k}_A+\beta\hat{k}_B+\frac{(1-\psi)K}{\psi-\chi}}{\frac{\psi L}{\psi-\chi}-\alpha\hat{l}_A-\beta\hat{l}_B}\hat{l}_A\right)$
Good	Individual B
x_B^{DE}	$\beta\chi^{\chi}(1-\chi)^{1-\chi}\left(\frac{\alpha\hat{k}_A+\beta\hat{k}_B+\frac{(1-\psi)K}{\psi-\chi}}{\frac{\psi L}{\psi-\chi}-\alpha\hat{l}_A-\beta\hat{l}_B}\right)^{\chi-1}\left(\hat{k}_B+\frac{\alpha\hat{k}_A+\beta\hat{k}_B+\frac{(1-\psi)K}{\psi-\chi}}{\frac{\psi L}{\psi-\chi}-\alpha\hat{l}_A-\beta\hat{l}_B}\hat{l}_B\right)$
y_B^{DE}	$(1-\beta)\psi^{\psi}(1-\psi)^{1-\psi}\left(\frac{\alpha\hat{k}_A+\beta\hat{k}_B+\frac{(1-\psi)K}{\psi-\chi}}{\frac{\psi L}{\psi-\chi}-\alpha\hat{l}_A-\beta\hat{l}_B}\right)^{\psi-1}\left(\hat{k}_B+\frac{\alpha\hat{k}_A+\beta\hat{k}_B+\frac{(1-\psi)K}{\psi-\chi}}{\frac{\psi L}{\psi-\chi}-\alpha\hat{l}_A-\beta\hat{l}_B}\hat{l}_B\right)$

TABLE V. Production-factor demands in decentralized equilibrium

Sector	Capital	Labor
x	$k_x^{DE}=\frac{\frac{\alpha\hat{k}_A+\beta\hat{k}_B+\frac{(1-\psi)K}{\psi-\chi}}{\frac{\psi L}{\psi-\chi}-\alpha\hat{l}_A-\beta\hat{l}_B}L-\frac{1-\psi}{\psi}K}{\frac{1}{\chi}-\frac{1}{\psi}}$	$l_x^{DE}=\frac{\frac{1-\chi}{\chi}}{\frac{1}{\chi}-\frac{1}{\psi}}\left(L-\frac{1-\psi}{\psi}\frac{\frac{\psi L}{\psi-\chi}-\alpha\hat{l}_A-\beta\hat{l}_B}{\alpha\hat{k}_A+\beta\hat{k}_B+\frac{(1-\psi)K}{\psi-\chi}}K\right)$
y	$k_y^{DE}=\frac{\frac{1-\chi}{\chi}K-\frac{\alpha\hat{k}_A+\beta\hat{k}_B+\frac{(1-\psi)K}{\psi-\chi}}{\frac{\psi L}{\psi-\chi}-\alpha\hat{l}_A-\beta\hat{l}_B}L}{\frac{1}{\chi}-\frac{1}{\psi}}$	$l_x^{DE}=\frac{\frac{1-\psi}{\psi}}{\frac{1}{\chi}-\frac{1}{\psi}}\left(\frac{1-\chi}{\chi}\frac{\frac{\psi L}{\psi-\chi}-\alpha\hat{l}_A-\beta\hat{l}_B}{\alpha\hat{k}_A+\beta\hat{k}_B+\frac{(1-\psi)K}{\psi-\chi}}K-L\right)$

3.4. THE SOCIAL PLANNER'S ALLOCATION

The Social Planner's problem is:

$$\max_{\substack{((x_A,y_A),(x_B,y_B))\\((k_x,l_x),(k_y,l_y))\\(X,Y)}} \varphi\left[\alpha\ln(x_A)+(1-\alpha)\ln(y_A)\right]+(1-\varphi)\left[\beta\ln(x_B)+(1-\beta)\ln(y_B)\right]$$

$$\begin{aligned} \text{s.t.}\quad x_A+x_B &\leq X\,,\\ y_A+y_B &\leq Y\,,\\ X &\leq k_x^{\chi}l_x^{1-\chi}\,,\\ Y &\leq k_y^{\psi}l_y^{1-\psi}\,,\\ k_x+k_y &\leq K\,,\\ l_x+l_y &\leq L\,. \end{aligned}$$

If E^{SP} is the desired allocation by the Social Planner, then by redistributing

TABLE VI. Social planner's optimal demands in decentralized Equilibrium

Good	Individual A
x_A^{SP}	$\alpha\chi^{\chi}(1-\chi)^{1-\chi}\left(\frac{\alpha\hat{k}_A^{SP}+\beta\hat{k}_B^{SP}+\frac{(1-\psi)K}{\psi-\chi}}{\frac{\psi L}{\psi-\chi}-\alpha\hat{l}_A^{SP}-\beta\hat{l}_B^{SP}}\right)^{\chi-1}\left(\hat{k}_A^{SP}+\frac{\alpha\hat{k}_A^{SP}+\beta\hat{k}_B^{SP}+\frac{(1-\psi)K}{\psi-\chi}}{\frac{\psi L}{\psi-\chi}-\alpha\hat{l}_A^{SP}-\beta\hat{l}_B^{SP}}\hat{l}_A^{SP}\right)$
y_A^{SP}	$(1-\alpha)\psi^{\psi}(1-\psi)^{1-\psi}\left(\frac{\alpha\hat{k}_A^{SP}+\beta\hat{k}_B^{SP}+\frac{(1-\psi)K}{\psi-\chi}}{\frac{\psi L}{\psi-\chi}-\alpha\hat{l}_A^{SP}-\beta\hat{l}_B^{SP}}\right)^{\psi-1}\left(\hat{k}_A^{SP}+\frac{\alpha\hat{k}_A^{SP}+\beta\hat{k}_B^{SP}+\frac{(1-\psi)K}{\psi-\chi}}{\frac{\psi L}{\psi-\chi}-\alpha\hat{l}_A^{SP}-\beta\hat{l}_B^{SP}}\hat{l}_A^{SP}\right)$
Good	Individual B
x_B^{SP}	$\beta\chi^{\chi}(1-\chi)^{1-\chi}\left(\frac{\alpha\hat{k}_A^{SP}+\beta\hat{k}_B^{SP}+\frac{(1-\psi)K}{\psi-\chi}}{\frac{\psi L}{\psi-\chi}-\alpha\hat{l}_A^{SP}-\beta\hat{l}_B^{SP}}\right)^{\chi-1}\left(\hat{k}_B^{SP}+\frac{\alpha\hat{k}_A^{SP}+\beta\hat{k}_B^{SP}+\frac{(1-\psi)K}{\psi-\chi}}{\frac{\psi L}{\psi-\chi}-\alpha\hat{l}_A^{SP}-\beta\hat{l}_B^{SP}}\hat{l}_B^{SP}\right)$
y_B^{SP}	$(1-\beta)\psi^{\psi}(1-\psi)^{1-\psi}\left(\frac{\alpha\hat{k}_A^{SP}+\beta\hat{k}_B^{SP}+\frac{(1-\psi)K}{\psi-\chi}}{\frac{\psi L}{\psi-\chi}-\alpha\hat{l}_A^{SP}-\beta\hat{l}_B^{SP}}\right)^{\psi-1}\left(\hat{k}_B^{SP}+\frac{\alpha\hat{k}_A^{SP}+\beta\hat{k}_B^{SP}+\frac{(1-\psi)K}{\psi-\chi}}{\frac{\psi L}{\psi-\chi}-\alpha\hat{l}_A^{SP}-\beta\hat{l}_B^{SP}}\hat{l}_B^{SP}\right)$

any initial factor endowment allocation so that so that E^{SP} is implemented after the redistribution, even if markets are set free thereafter. It suffices to redistribute productive factors, since our analysis has shown that any initial factor allocation gives rise to a unique competitive general equilibrium. Once the Social Planner has chosen her best-preferred allocation, she can focus on the her optimal allocation of production factors and focus on redistributing just production factors. The Social Planner can implement her desired equilibrium by re-allocating endowments of production factors through lump-sum transfers according to the demand quantities given by Table 4, but viewed this time as functions of the endowment vectors $\left(\left(\hat{k}_A^{SP},\hat{l}_A^{SP}\right),\left(\hat{k}_B^{SP},\hat{l}_B^{SP}\right)\right)$.

If, for example, the social planner's allocation of demands for the final good (the result from solving the Social Planner's problem), is

$$\left(\left(x_A^{SP},y_A^{SP}\right),\left(x_B^{SP},y_B^{SP}\right)\right),$$

the optimal transfer of endowments leading to the vector

$$\left(\left(\hat{k}_A^{SP},\hat{l}_A^{SP}\right),\left(\hat{k}_B^{SP},\hat{l}_B^{SP}\right)\right),$$

is given by the solution to the system of equations given by Table VI. Table VI comes from plugging the formula (38) into the formulas of Table IV, and by setting the vector of individual factor endowments as the vector of unknowns.

The four equations of Table IV comprise a system of four equations with four unknowns, after the levels of the Social Planner's preferred allocation of final goods is computed. Yet, equations (19) and (20) reveal that it is four equations with two unknowns, thus, the policies are indefinite and infinite. The important insight of Table VI is that it gives the logic through which the Social Planner will allocate the factor inputs among individuals. The mechanics of the decentralized equilibrium are key for determining the lump-sum transfers. Preferences and factor intensities in production determine the direction of transfers.

4. Market Failures

The goal of this section is to provide a parametric example of how private markets would fail to provide the optimal level of public infrastructure, if there are externalities in production.

Consider an economy with M identical firms, needing only private labor as an input, but also needing infrastructure, denoted by Q, in order to operate, e.g. roads. The employed technology of firm $j \in \{1, ..., M\}$ is

$$y_{j,f} = l_{j,f}^{\alpha} Q^{1-\alpha} , \tag{40}$$

where $l_{j,f}$ is the units of hired labor by firm j to be used for producing the firm's private good, $y_{j,f}$. To provide one unit of infrastructure, one needs to spend one unit of time, so, if each firm $i \in \{1, ..., M\}$ provides $l_{i,q}$ units of its own hired labor in order to contribute to infrastructure, the production function of firm $j \in \{1, ..., M\}$ is

$$y_{j,f} = l_{j,f}^{\alpha} \left(\sum_{i=1}^{M} l_{i,q} \right)^{1-\alpha} . \tag{41}$$

There are also N identical households with utility derived by consumption, c_h, and leisure, $1 - l_h$, where 1 is the total time of the household and l_h its labor supply, with utility function of the form

$$\theta \ln (c_h) + (1 - \theta) \ln (1 - l_h) , \tag{42}$$

where $\theta \in (0, 1)$.

4.1. COMPETITIVE (DECENTRALIZED) EQUILIBRIUM

We start with the firm's problem. A single firm j hires her private resource $l_{j,f}$ the use of which is excludable by others. The firm also contributes to the building of infrastructure, by hiring $l_{j,q}$ units of labor in order to build infrastructure Q, a good that can be freely used by all other firms. Since the cost of use of Q is zero, all firms enjoy a positive externality by it. Yet, in the competitive setup where free markets provide Q, all firms undertake a part of the cost for its provision: in particular, a firm j has to pay $wl_{j,q}$, where w is the wage per unit of labor, that is formed in the free market in general equilibrium. So, a firm j maximizes the following objective:

$$\max_{(l_{j,f}, l_{j,q})} l_{j,f}^{\alpha} \left(\sum_{i=1}^{M} l_{i,q} \right)^{1-\alpha} - w \left(l_{j,f} + l_{j,q} \right)$$

that leads to,

$$l_q = \frac{1}{M}\frac{1-\alpha}{\alpha} l_f \; . \tag{43}$$

Since each firm has decreasing returns to scale, all firms have positive profits. In order to derive the optimal profits of a firm, it is:

$$\left.\begin{aligned} \pi_f &= y_f - w\left(l_f + l_q\right) \\ w l_f &= \alpha y_f \\ w l_q &= \tfrac{(1-\alpha)}{M} y_f \end{aligned}\right\} \Rightarrow \pi_f = \frac{M-1}{M}\left(1-\alpha\right) y_f \; . \tag{44}$$

So, we are done with characterizing the behavior of firms up to this point. Let's see the household behavior now. The problem faced by one of the identical households is:

$$\max_{(c_h, l_h)} \theta \ln\left(c_h\right) + \left(1-\theta\right)\ln\left(1-l_h\right)$$

subject to:

$$c_h = w l_h + d_h \; ,$$

where d_h is the dividend given to each household out of the profits made by the firms. The necessary conditions are $\frac{1-\theta}{\theta}\frac{c_h}{1-l_h} = w$ and $c_h = w l_h + d_h$.

The market-clearing conditions are:

$$\begin{aligned} \text{labor:} &\quad M\left(l_f + l_q\right) = N l_h \; , \\ \text{profits:} &\quad M \pi_f = N d_h \; , \\ \text{final good:} &\quad M y_f = N c_h \; , \\ \text{infrastructure:} &\quad M l_q = Q \; . \end{aligned}$$

Combining all the results so far yields the equilibrium solution summed up in Table VII.

An important remark is that firms understand that, due to the externality in production there is a discrepancy between their private cost and private benefit when infrastructure is provided via the free market. The reason is that the cost of providing a unit of Q is w for a single firm, yet the same firm benefits from the units of Q that it has provided plus the units of Q that all other firms have provided as well. Compared to the decentralized equilibrium of economies without externalities, when a production externality is present each firm tends to transfer part of their cost for providing Q to all other firms. On first grounds, this is easy to see from equation (43), which gives the allocation of factor demands by a single firm between labor for the final good and labor for infrastructure, Q. In particular, (43) says that the higher the number of the firms, the smaller the fraction out of total labor demand that the firm allocates to providing Q. This is the point where we can argue mathematically that as the number of firms, M, increases, all firms tend to re-allocate the burden of providing infrastructure to other firms. As every firm does this, a smaller fraction of total, economy-wide private resources goes to infrastructure.

TABLE VII. Decentralized equilibrium

Prices	
Final good (normalized)	Labor
$p = 1$	$w^{DE} = a^{\alpha}(1-\alpha)^{1-\alpha}$
Household choices	
Consumption Demand	Labor Supply
$c_h^{DE} = \frac{\theta a^{\alpha}(1-\alpha)^{1-\alpha}}{\theta\left(\alpha+\frac{1-\alpha}{M}\right)+1-\theta}$	$l_h^{DE} = \frac{\theta\left(\alpha+\frac{1-\alpha}{M}\right)}{\theta\left(\alpha+\frac{1-\alpha}{M}\right)+1-\theta}$
Factor Demands	
Labor for the final good	Labor for infrastructure
$l_f^{DE} = \frac{N}{M}\frac{\alpha\theta}{\theta\left(\alpha+\frac{1-\alpha}{M}\right)+1-\theta}$	$l_q^{DE} = \frac{N}{M^2}\frac{(1-\alpha)\theta}{\theta\left(\alpha+\frac{1-\alpha}{M}\right)+1-\theta}$
Firm profits	Dividends to households
$\pi_f^{DE} = \frac{M-1}{M^2}\frac{N\theta a^{\alpha}(1-\alpha)^{2-\alpha}}{\theta\left(\alpha+\frac{1-\alpha}{M}\right)+1-\theta}$	$d_h^{DE} = \frac{M-1}{M}\frac{\theta a^{\alpha}(1-\alpha)^{2-\alpha}}{\theta\left(\alpha+\frac{1-\alpha}{M}\right)+1-\theta}$
Total Output	Infrastructure
$Y^{DE} = N\frac{\theta a^{\alpha}(1-\alpha)^{1-\alpha}}{\theta\left(\alpha+\frac{1-\alpha}{M}\right)+1-\theta}$	$Q^{DE} = \frac{N}{M}\frac{(1-\alpha)\theta}{\theta\left(\alpha+\frac{1-\alpha}{M}\right)+1-\theta}$

This observation is also transferred to the general-equilibrium mechanics of infrastructure provision. It is easy to see that:

$$\frac{\partial Q^{DE}}{\partial M} < 0 \, .$$

Another important remark is the response of labor in general equilibrium. It is:

$$\frac{\partial l_h^{DE}}{\partial M} < 0 \, .$$

Obviously, as the number of firms increases and private markets fail more and more to internalize the externality, the general-equilibrium labor demand and supply fall.

4.2. THE SOCIAL PLANNER

The Social Planner's problem is:

$$\max_{\substack{(c_h, l_h) \\ (l_f, l_q)}} \; N\left[\theta \ln(c_h) + (1-\theta)\ln(1-l_h)\right]$$

$$\text{subject to:} \quad \begin{aligned} Nc_h &\leq Ml_f^{\alpha}(Mlq)^{1-\alpha} \\ M(l_f + l_q) &\leq Nl_h \end{aligned}$$

The Social Planner internalizes the externality fully, since she considers the aggregate economy constraint, $Nc_h \leq Ml_f^{\alpha}(Mlq)^{1-\alpha}$. Since the Social Planner's control variables are all the control variables by all households and all firms in the economy, she also keeps track of the direct interactions among all agents. In this economy there is an externality in production. Therefore, *non-market-mechanism related interactions among firms in the free market are included fully in the aggregate economy constraint,* $Nc_h \leq Ml_f^{\alpha}(Mlq)^{1-\alpha}$*. This observation in the structure of the problem of the Social Planner suffices to prove that she will fully internalize the externality.*

On the contrary, free markets will internalize the externality partially, as we saw from the decentralized-equilibrium solution. The extent to which free markets internalize the externality has to do with the number of the firms in the economy, M, since the higher the M, the more firms tend to re-allocate private resources used for the provision of Q^{DE} to all the other firms. In other words, *the higher the* M*, the less free markets internalize the externality.*

The Social Planner can do no otherwise than internalizing the externality fully, due to considering her constraint $Nc_h \leq Ml_f^{\alpha}(Mlq)^{1-\alpha}$ *in her problem, irrespective of the value of* M. Moreover, *the Social Planner can exploit constant returns to scale,* since the sum of the exponents in the aggregated Cobb-Douglas production function, $Ml_f^{\alpha}(Mlq)^{1-\alpha}$, is equal to one.

In a similar fashion, the results are summarized in Table VIII.

TABLE VIII. Social-planner equilibrium

Shadow prices	
Final good (normalized)	Labor
$p_{shadow} = 1$	$w_{shadow}^{SP} = M^{1-\alpha}\alpha^{\alpha}(1-\alpha)^{1-\alpha}$
Household choices	
Consumption Demand	Labor Supply
$c_h^{SP} = M^{1-\alpha}\alpha^{\alpha}(1-\alpha)^{1-\alpha}\theta$	$l_h^{SP} = \theta$
Factor demands	
Labor for the final good	Labor for infrastructure
$l_f^{SP} = \alpha\theta\frac{N}{M}$	$l_q^{SP} = (1-\alpha)\theta\frac{N}{M}$
Total Output	Infrastructure
$Y^{SP} = M^{1-\alpha}\alpha^{\alpha}(1-\alpha)^{1-\alpha}\theta N$	$Q^{SP} = (1-\alpha)\theta N$

4.3. COMPARISONS

Tables VII and VIII enable us to make direct algebraic comparisons in order to cross-validate the theoretical conclusions stated in the question. In particular, through formula substitutions we can see that:

$$\begin{aligned}
l_h^{SP} &= \theta \geq \frac{\theta\left(\alpha + \frac{1-\alpha}{M}\right)}{\theta\left(\alpha + \frac{1-\alpha}{M}\right) + 1 - \theta} = l_h^{DE} , \\
c_h^{SP} &= M^{1-\alpha}\alpha^{\alpha}\left(1-\alpha\right)^{1-\alpha}\theta \geq \frac{\theta\alpha^{\alpha}\left(1-\alpha\right)^{1-\alpha}}{\theta\left(\alpha + \frac{1-\alpha}{M}\right) + 1 - \theta} = c_h^{DE} , \\
l_f^{SP} &= \alpha\theta\frac{N}{M} \geq \frac{N}{M}\frac{\alpha\theta}{\theta\left(\alpha + \frac{1-\alpha}{M}\right) + 1 - \theta} = l_f^{DE} , \\
l_q^{SP} &= \left(1-\alpha\right)\theta\frac{N}{M} \geq \frac{1}{M}\frac{\left(1-\alpha\right)\theta\frac{N}{M}}{\theta\left(\alpha + \frac{1-\alpha}{M}\right) + 1 - \theta} = l_q^{DE} , \\
Q^{SP} &= \left(1-\alpha\right)\theta N \geq \frac{1}{M}\frac{\left(1-\alpha\right)\theta N}{\theta\left(\alpha + \frac{1-\alpha}{M}\right) + 1 - \theta} = Q^{DE} , \\
Y^{SP} &= M^{1-\alpha}\alpha^{\alpha}\left(1-\alpha\right)^{1-\alpha}\theta N \geq \frac{a^{\alpha}\left(1-\alpha\right)^{1-\alpha}\theta N}{\theta\left(\alpha + \frac{1-\alpha}{M}\right) + 1 - \theta} = Y^{DE} , \\
u_h^{SP} &= \ln\left\{\left[M^{1-\alpha}\alpha^{\alpha}\left(1-\alpha\right)^{1-\alpha}\theta\right]^{\theta}\left(1-\theta\right)^{1-\theta}\right\} \\
&\geq \ln\left\{\frac{\left[\alpha^{\alpha}\left(1-\alpha\right)^{1-\alpha}\theta\right]^{\theta}\left(1-\theta\right)^{1-\theta}}{\theta\left(\alpha + \frac{1-\alpha}{M}\right) + 1 - \theta}\right\} = u_h^{DE}
\end{aligned}$$

with equality if and only if $M = 1$. We can defend the above inequalities in various ways. Whenever there is ambiguity due to the presence of M in the expressions, one can take derivatives with respect to M and check whether the statement is true in the domain of $M \geq 1$.

5. Voting

The logic behind the Meltzer-Richard (1981) model of redistributive voting can be illustrated through a parametric example.

Consider an economy of N households with different labor productivity. Households consume a single final good. The production function of the consumable good is a linear function, given by:

$$F\left(l_1, l_2, ..., l_h, ..., l_N\right) = \sum_{h=1}^{N} \varepsilon_h l_h ,$$

where ε_h is the structural productivity of the $h - th$ household and l_h stands for the supplied labor hours of the $h - th$ household. We can see that the production function distinguishes the types of labor according to the skill of each household. We take the vector of structural productivities $(\varepsilon_1, \varepsilon_2, ..., \varepsilon_N)$ of each household as N exogenously given parameters. Since production technology exhibits constant returns to scale (zero profits), it is the same to assume that, instead of having a large number, M, of identical firms, there is only one firm (i.e. $M = 1$).

5.1. THE PROBLEM OF THE FIRM

The firm needs to determine how many units of each type of labor to hire. Its problem is:

$$\max_{(l_1, l_2, ..., l_h, ..., l_N)} \sum_{h=1}^{N} \varepsilon_h l_h - \sum_{h=1}^{N} w_h l_h \ ,$$

where w_h is the wage per unit of working time of the $h-th$ household with productivity ε_h. Apparently, the demand function for each household type is given by the following relationship,

$$w_h = \varepsilon_h \ , \tag{45}$$

i.e. a perfectly elastic demand function for each type. Given that equation (45) gives that wages are necessarily tied to the exogenous productivity parameters ε_h, we will use ε_h instead of w_h, for all $h \in \{1, ..., N\}$ from now on.

5.2. GOVERNMENT

The elected government taxes labor income by imposing a flat marginal income tax rate, τ, and by redistributing the average tax revenues to each household as a lump-sum amount, i.e.

$$T = \frac{1}{N} \tau \sum_{h=1}^{N} \varepsilon_h l_h \ . \tag{46}$$

The fiscal budget is balanced.

5.3. HOUSEHOLDS

All households derive utility from the consumption of the final good and from leisure. All households have the same utility function, given by:

$$U(c_h, 1 - l_h) = \theta \ln(c_h) + (1 - \theta) \ln(1 - l_h) \ ,$$

with $\theta \in (0, 1)$. Given the fiscal intervention of the elected government, the household problem is:

$$\max_{(c_h, l_h)} \theta \ln(c_h) + (1 - \theta) \ln(1 - l_h)$$

subject to:

$$c_h \leq (1 - \tau) \varepsilon_h l_h + T \ .$$

The first-order conditions are,

$$\frac{1-\theta}{\theta}\frac{c_h}{1-l_h} = (1-\tau)\,\varepsilon_h \,, \tag{47}$$

$$c_h = (1-\tau)\,\varepsilon_h l_h + T \,. \tag{48}$$

Now, combining (47) with (48), it is

$$c_h = \theta\left[(1-\tau)\,\varepsilon_h + T\right] \,, \tag{49}$$

$$l_h = \theta - (1-\theta)\,\frac{T}{(1-\tau)\,\varepsilon_h} \,. \tag{50}$$

We define the average productivity as $\varepsilon_\mu = 1/N \sum_{h=1}^{N} \varepsilon_h$. In order to pin down the level of the lump-sum transfer, T, we must see that (46) together with (50) imply

$$T = \frac{(1-\tau)\,\tau\theta\varepsilon_\mu}{1-\theta\tau} \,. \tag{51}$$

Equation (51) shows how the lump-sum trasfer, T, is expressed as a function of the policy parameter τ only, and also as a function of the economic fundamentals of the model, after the stage of competitive equilibrium and fiscal-budget balancing are incorporated in to the problem. Equation (51) can now be substituted to the supply and demand functions (49) and (50) as:

$$(49) \overset{(51)}{\Longrightarrow} c_h = \theta\,(1-\tau)\,\frac{\varepsilon_h + \theta\,(\varepsilon_\mu - \varepsilon_h)\,\tau}{1-\theta\tau} \,, \tag{52}$$

$$(50) \overset{(51)}{\Longrightarrow} l_h = \theta - (1-\theta)\,\frac{\theta\tau}{1-\theta\tau}\frac{\varepsilon_\mu}{\varepsilon_h} \,, \tag{53}$$

and the optimal leisure time is given by

$$(53) \Rightarrow 1 - l_h = (1-\theta)\,\frac{\varepsilon_h + \theta\,(\varepsilon_\mu - \varepsilon_h)\,\tau}{(1-\theta\tau)\,\varepsilon_h} \,. \tag{54}$$

Substituting (52) and (54) into the utility function of household $h \in \{1, ..., N\}$, it is

$$V_h(\tau) = \ln\left[\theta^\theta \left(\frac{1-\theta}{\varepsilon_h}\right)^{1-\theta}\right] + \theta\ln(1-\tau) + \ln\left[\varepsilon_h + \theta\,(\varepsilon_\mu - \varepsilon_h)\,\tau\right] - \ln(1-\theta\tau) \,. \tag{55}$$

It is a matter of algebra to check that the preferences over τ, represented by equation (55), are single-peaked. Single peakedness leads to the median voter winning the majority elections and imposing her best-preferred policy, τ_m (best τ of the median).

$$V_h'(\tau) = 0 \Rightarrow \theta\left[-\frac{1}{1-\tau} + \frac{\varepsilon_\mu - \varepsilon_h}{\varepsilon_h + \theta\,(\varepsilon_\mu - \varepsilon_h)\,\tau} + \frac{1}{1-\theta\tau}\right] = 0 \tag{56}$$

Two remarks can be made from equation (56).

Remark 1: the best-preferred tax rate of the voter with the average productivity is zero. To see this, set $\varepsilon_h = \varepsilon_\mu$ in equation (56), to obtain

$$\frac{1}{1-\theta\tau} = \frac{1}{1-\tau} \Rightarrow (1-\theta)\,\tau = 0 \Rightarrow \tau = 0\,.$$

Remark 2: if there are no tax disincentives for labor supply (in this model, set $\theta = 1$, i.e. leisure is not valued at all and the labor supply is inelastic) the best-preferred tax rate of any voter $h \in \{1, ..., N\}$ with $\varepsilon_h < \varepsilon_\mu$ is 100%. To see this, set $\theta = 1$ and observe that, from equation (55), the value function $V_h(\tau)$ becomes,

$$V_h(\tau) = \ln\left[\varepsilon_h + (\varepsilon_\mu - \varepsilon_h)\,\tau\right]\ ,$$

so, apparently, $\tau = 100\%$, the maximum possible, maximizes $V_h(\tau)$ if $\varepsilon_h < \varepsilon_\mu$. What went wrong with the post-socialist countries is that the planners of the leading party did not realize that in human behavior it is not $\theta = 1$ (i.e. people have no labor disutility as long as they work for the society), but it is $\theta \in (0, 1)$, i.e. people value their own personal leisure and work incentives are very important. With taxes 100% and $\theta \in (0, 1)$, there is no labor supply in this model, and labor supply had been very low in the post-socialist countries.

The winning tax of the median voter, τ_m, in this model will be given by:

$$\tau_m = \frac{(1+\theta)\,\varepsilon_\mu - 2\varepsilon_m + \sqrt{(1-\theta)\,(\varepsilon_\mu - 2\varepsilon_m)\left[(1+3\theta)\,\varepsilon_\mu - 2\,(1+\theta)\,\varepsilon_m\right]}}{2\theta^2\,(\varepsilon_\mu - \varepsilon_m)}\,.$$

The higher the difference between the median and the mean, the higher the party polarization and the higher the elected tax rate.

For dealing with political polarization all we need is a better understanding of how the economy works. Left-wing or right-wing ideologies are very old and obsolete. Yet, non-thinking social masses still try to understand even the simplest economic matters under the narrow rationale of such outdated ideologies and political parties still utilize the lack of thinking by voters. Democracies give excellent chances to implement packages of consumption, property and income taxes that can minimize polarization and overall distortions. Addressing the behavior of microeconomic units correctly, leads to positive answers to deep economic and political issues.

6. Externalities and Growth

Paul Romer's (1986) study was the first attempt to link technical change with economic behavior and the market mechanism. This model can be considered as a modification of the Ramsey-Cass-Koopmans model with production that exhibits an externality: knowledge spillovers originated by the aggregate stock of capital in the economy. The presence of an externality implies that the first welfare theorem does not hold. In other words, the pursuit of personal interest by each economic unit in the economy under perfect competition does not lead to a Pareto-optimal equilibrium. This means that there are ways to increase the welfare of some individuals without having to decrease the welfare of others. So, the competitive, decentralized equilibrium leads to lower welfare compared to the equilibrium dictated by a benevolent utilitarian social planner. The reason behind this discrepancy is the fact that individual economic agents find suboptimal for them to internalize the externality. On the contrary, the social planner can do so.

Problems may arise with estimating the impact of the externality in production, especially while eliciting it from aggregate data. Nevertheless, this model is very useful as a basis for many other models in the literature. Therefore, instead of suggesting a parametric model that leads to a closed-form solution in the infinite-horizon case, I present a two-period that reveals, in my opinion, both the mechanics of endogenous growth and the sources of inefficiency of the competitive-equilibrium dynamic allocation.

6.1. THE TWO-PERIOD MODEL OF PAUL ROMER: A DIAGRAMMATIC ANALYSIS

6.1.1. *Households*

Imagine an economy inhabited by M identical households, where M is a large finite number. Households live for only two periods, $t = 0, 1$. Each household does not value leisure and it supplies inelastically one unit of labor each period. So, all households together supply aggregately M units of labor to production. Households draw utility from the consumption of a composite good each period. Since households live for two periods, this single good is treated as two different goods, consumption "today," c_0, and consumption "tomorrow," c_1. The preferences of an arbitrary household $j \in \{1, ..., M\}$ are represented in the positive orthant of consumption, $(c_{j,0}, c_{j,1})$ by the following twice continuously differentiable function:

$$U(c_{j,0}, c_{j,1}) = u(c_{j,0}) + \beta u(c_{j,1}) \ ,$$

with $\beta \in (0,1)$ and for all $t \in \{0,1\}$, $u_1(c_{j,t}) > 0$, $u_{11}(c_{j,t}) < 0$, $\lim_{c_{j,t} \to 0} u_1(c_{j,t}) = \infty$ and $\lim_{c_{j,t} \to \infty} u_1(c_{j,t}) = 0$. The function $U(c_{j,0}, c_{j,1})$ has the extra property of representing homothetic preferences. In other words, $u(c_{j,t})$ is such that for all $\xi > 0$ and all $(c_{j,0}, c_{j,1})$ the marginal rate of substitution is equal to the marginal rate of substitution at point $(\xi c_{j,0}, \xi c_{j,1})$, meaning that:

$$\frac{u_1(c_{j,0})}{\beta u_1(c_{j,1})} = \frac{u_1(\xi c_{j,0})}{\beta u_1(\xi c_{j,1})} \ .$$

Consumable goods can be transformed into capital goods without any extra cost, "one to one" (they have the same price each period). In period 0 all households hold assets that claim capital. The level of capital goods held in period 0 by each household is determined exogenously. We assume that all households start with the same wealth, i.e. $k_{j,0} = k_0 > 0$ for all $j \in \{1, ..., M\}$. Therefore, aggregate capital is given by: $K_0 = Mk_0 > 0$. Households can choose which level of capital they wish to hold in period 1, so for all $j \in \{1, ..., M\}$, $k_{j,1}$ is a choice variable. They are constrained, however, by a terminal condition about their capital holdings at the end of period 1: they cannot leave debt after the end of period 1, so, we denote this condition as: $k_{j,2} \geq 0$. We can say immediately that, since consumable and capital goods are one-to-one transformable to each other, rational households could always consume any positive amount of capital that could be left unexploitable in period 1, increasing in this way their utility. Therefore, we can say in advance that the terminal condition will be: $k_{j,2} = 0$.

6.1.2. *Firms*

Production of consumables/capital goods takes place through the entrepreneural activity of N firms, where N is an exogenously given large finite number. Each firm $i \in \{1, ..., N\}$ has access to the exact same technology as all the other firms. Technology in each period $t \in \{0, 1\}$ is represented by the following three-input production function:

$$y_{i,t} = F\left(k_{i,t}, K_t, l_{i,t}\right) ,$$

where variables $k_{i,t}$ and $l_{i,t}$ are physical capital and labor employed by firm i in period t. The presence of variable $K_t \equiv \sum_{i=1}^{N} k_{i,t}$ in the production function of any firm $i \in \{1, ..., N\}$ captures the central hypothesis of Paul Romer that aggregate knowledge of the economy is embodied into aggregate capital stock that is used in production. The level of K_t in each time period affects positively the knowledge ("to know how") of each firm, without the firm undertaking any additional cost, like research activities. This means that aggregate capital is a positive *externality* for a single individual firm, each firm enjoys a *knowledge spillover*. The economic intuition behind this externality is that as more machines are used in the aggregate economy, more is known about using them, so the productivity of both capital and labor used by a single firm will increase with more aggregate capital in the overall economy.

The exogenously given number of firms N is "large enough," meaning that each firm in the overall final-product market is like "a drop in the ocean" compared to all the remaining $N - 1$ firms. Even if the firm shuts down its operation it cannot generate any scarcity with respect to the total supply of the final good or with respect to total demand for capital. So, each firm $i \in \{1, ..., N\}$ has negligible market power and it is a price taker with respect to the final good, and with respect to the prices of the two intermediate goods, capital and labor.

In order to refine his results, Paul Romer (1986) assumed the following on the representative firm's production function.

For all $i \in \{1, ..., N\}$, for all $t \in \{0, 1\}$ and for all $(k_{i,t}, K_t, l_{i,t})$:

(i) $F_n\left(k_{i,t}, K_t, l_{i,t}\right) > 0$, $n \in \{1, 2, 3\}$, i.e. positive marginal product with respect to each productive input,
(ii) $F_{nn}\left(k_{i,t}, K_t, l_{i,t}\right) < 0$, $n \in \{1, 2, 3\}$, i.e. decreasing marginal product with respect to each productive input,
(iii) $F_{12}\left(k_{i,t}, K_t, l_{i,t}\right) > 0$, and $F_{32}\left(k_{i,t}, K_t, l_{i,t}\right) > 0$, i.e. the marginal product of $k_{i,t}$, and $l_{i,t}$ with respect to K_t is increasing,

(iv) for all $\xi > 1$:

(iv.a) $F(\xi k_{i,t}, \xi K_t, \xi l_{i,t}) > \xi F(k_{i,t}, K_t, l_{i,t})$, i.e. increasing returns to scale with respect to all productive inputs,

(iv.b) $F(\xi k_{i,t}, \xi K_t, l_{i,t}) = \xi F(k_{i,t}, K_t, l_{i,t})$, i.e. constant returns to scale with respect to inputs $(k_{i,t}, K_t)$,

(iv.c) $F(\xi k_{i,t}, K_t, \xi l_{i,t}) = \xi F(k_{i,t}, K_t, l_{i,t})$, i.e. constant returns to scale with respect to inputs $(k_{i,t}, l_{i,t})$.

Moreover, the depreciation rate is $\delta \in [0, 1]$.

We should first observe that it is necessary to assume a vector for capital $(K_0, K_1) >> 0$, with strictly positive elements. The initial aggregate capital of the economy, K_0, is given as an initial condition, so we know it is positive. But it is important to restrict our attention to a strictly positive potential K_1 as well. The complete determination of K_1 is something that does not concern us now, and as each firm is like a "drop in the ocean," it cannot control aggregate capital. Therefore, the profit-maximization problem of a firm $i \in \{1, ...N\}$ is:

$$\max_{(k_{i,t}, l_{i,t})} F(k_{i,t}, K_t, l_{i,t}) - R_t k_{i,t} - w_t l_{i,t} \qquad t \in \{0, 1\} \ .$$

The first-order necessary optimality conditions are:

$$R_t = F_1(k_{i,t}, K_t, l_{i,t}) \qquad t \in \{0, 1\} \ , \tag{57}$$

$$w_t = F_3(k_{i,t}, K_t, l_{i,t}) \qquad t \in \{0, 1\} \ . \tag{58}$$

These first order conditions can be sufficient for a global maximum, if

$$F_{11}F_{33} - F_{13}^2 \geq 0 \ ,$$

for all $(k_{i,t}, K_t, l_{i,t}) >> 0$, $t \in \{0, 1\}$. Since $F_{11}(\cdot), F_{33}(\cdot) < 0$ for $(K_0, K_1) >> 0$, the last inequality implies that the objective function is strictly quasi-concave with respect to variables $(k_{i,t}, l_{i,t})$ for any given vector $(K_0, K_1) >> 0$. With $F_{11}, F_{33} < 0$ and $F_{11}F_{33} - F_{13}^2 \geq 0$, the Hessian of function F with respect to variables $(k_{i,t}, l_{i,t})$ for any given vector $(K_0, K_1) >> 0$, is negative semidefinite.

Substitution of (57) and (58) into the objective function gives:

$$\pi(k_{i,t}, K_t, l_{i,t}) = F(k_{i,t}, K_t, l_{i,t}) - [F_1(k_{i,t}, K_t, l_{i,t}) k_{i,t} + F_3(k_{i,t}, K_t, l_{i,t}) l_{i,t}] \ ,$$

$t \in \{0, 1\}$. Given our assumption (iv.c) of constant returns to scale with respect to the vector $(k_{i,t}, l_{i,t})$, Euler's theorem concerning homogeneous functions implies that

$$F_1(k_{i,t}, K_t, l_{i,t}) k_{i,t} + F_3(k_{i,t}, K_t, l_{i,t}) l_{i,t} = F(k_{i,t}, K_t, l_{i,t}) \ ,$$

making the optimal profits of the firm equal to 0 ($\pi(k_{i,t}, K_t, l_{i,t}) = 0$).

Since the profit function is globally concave and its global maximum is the value 0, a simple refinement on the potential organization of the firms is enforced endogenously.

There is a large set of scenarios that we must consider about the market share that each firm could take, in order to draw conclusions about the equilibrium firm organization. Groups of firms could cooperate in order to form coalitions that could affect prices and gain monopolistic power. Potential coalitions could (partially) control K_1, and behave according to additionally evaluating and rewarding the marginal effects of K_1 in their productive activity. Given Paul Romer's interpretation of knowledge embodiment into physical capital, a more intuitive way of saying "firms could invest more after considering the marginal effects of K_1", is: "firms could invest into research on ideas that transform physical capital into more productive one and this knowledge would spill over all producers costlessly." For implementing such a collusive agreement two types of problems can arise:

(i) A potential coalition needs to enforce regulations and undertake monitoring costs that would prevent firms from shirking, i.e. from avoiding to invest "enough" in research.
(ii) Even if a coalition could overcome problem (i) and costlessly enforce rules in a universal coalition of all the N firms, there could always be new entrants who could "free ride." Profits for such entrants would be higher, driving the rest of the firms out of the market.[3]

Problems (i) and (ii) are typical in industrial organization whenever there are externalities. In decentralized equilibrium, any collusive equilibrium can be undermined either from inside or outside a coalition. Therefore, each firm operates non-cooperatively in decentralized equilibrium and uses conditions (57) and (58) in order to give shape to its dominant factor-demand/product supply strategy. From the symmetry of technology for each firm, comes a symmetry of strategies for all firms, giving the following equilibrium conditions:

$$k_{i,t} = \frac{K_t}{N} \qquad \text{for all } i \in \{1, ..., N\} \ , t \in \{0,1\} \ , \tag{59}$$

and

$$l_{i,t} = \frac{M}{N} \qquad \text{for all } i \in \{1, ..., N\} \ , t \in \{0,1\} \ . \tag{60}$$

Labor supply is determined from the fact that households supply M working hours altogether. Firm equilibrium demand for capital in period 0 is also known to us already, since K_0 is exogenously given and all households are identical even in this respect, they are all initially endowed with assets claiming $\frac{K_0}{M}$ units of physical capital. As we will see below, the homogeneity of households and their symmetry of economic

[3] Entrants could sell the final good down to zero-profit prices for them. The assumption of increasing returns to scale (assumption (iv.a)), in conjunction with Euler's theorem about homogeneous functions would simply mean that the coalition of incumbent firms would end up paying capital "too much:" incumbents would make negative profits at the equilibrium supply prices of the entrants, because they would have to reward (spend on) the research they undertake. The entrants would avoid this cost, benefited by the externality, and they would make zero profits. Hence all incumbent firms would shut down operation.

actions will imply that in period 1, they will also hold $\frac{K_1}{M}$ units of physical capital. But this amount is to be determined by their consumer optimizing behavior.

Now we focus on characterizing the full decentralized equilibrium algebraically. We must first figure out the borrowing constraints. In period 0 the constraint of a household $j \in \{1, ..., M\}$ is given by:

$$c_{j,0} + k_{j,1} = (1 + R_0 - \delta)\, k_{j,0} + w_0 \; . \tag{61}$$

Since in equilibrium rational households that meet the constraint $k_{j,2} \geq 0$ will not leave any capital leftovers (they can always consume them and increase their utility, so they cannot attain a maximum if $k_{j,2} > 0$), the constraint becomes $k_{j,2} = 0$. Shifting (61) one period ahead and imposing $k_{j,2} = 0$, we get:

$$c_{j,1} = (1 + R_1 - \delta)\, k_{j,1} + w_1 \; . \tag{62}$$

So, the problem of the household reads as follows:

$$\begin{array}{llcl} \max\limits_{\{c_{j,0}, c_{j,1}, k_{j,1}\}} & u(c_{j,0}) + \beta u(c_{j,1}) & & \\ \text{subject to:} & c_{j,0} + k_{j,1} & = & (1 + R_0 - \delta)\, k_{j,0} + w_0 \; , \\ c_{j,1} & & = & (1 + R_1 - \delta)\, k_{j,1} + w_1 \; , \end{array}$$

given $(K_0, K_1) >> 0$ and $k_{j,0} = \frac{K_0}{M}$. Solving this problem we obtain,

$$\frac{u_1(c_{j,0})}{\beta u_1(c_{j,1})} = (1 + R_1 - \delta) \; . \tag{63}$$

So, in equilibrium the representative household links the marginal rate of substitution between today's and tomorrow's consumption with the gross effective interest rate, exactly as we link income values over time in finance.

6.1.3. *Decentralized Equilibrium*

DEFINITION. (Decentralized Equilibrium, DE) *Given the economic fundamentals U (preferences of households) and F (productive technology of firms), a decentralized equilibrium is: (i) a set of capital and labor demands by all firms,* $\left\{\left(k_{i,t}^{DEfirm}, l_{i,t}^{DEfirm}\right)\right\}_{i=1}^{N}$, $t \in \{0, 1\}$, *such that all firms maximize their profits; (ii) a set of consumption demands and capital supplies by all households* $\left\{\left(c_{j,t,}^{DEhousehold}, k_{j,t}^{DEhousehold}\right)\right\}_{j=1}^{M}$, $t \in \{0, 1\}$, *such that all households maximize their utility; (iii) a set of prices* $\left(1, R_t^{DE}, w_t^{DE}\right)$, $t \in \{0, 1\}$, *such that markets clear, i.e.* $\sum_{i=1}^{N} k_{i,t}^{DEfirm} = \sum_{j=1}^{M} k_{j,t}^{DEhousehold} = K_t^{DE}$, $\sum_{j=1}^{M} c_{j,t}^{DE} = C_t^{DE}$, $t \in \{0, 1\}$.

As it was stressed above, all households $j \in \{1, ..., M\}$ will demand the same quantities of consumption, i.e. $c_{j,t}^{DE} = c_t^{DE} = \frac{C_t^{DE}}{M}$, and they will also supply the same quantities of capital, i.e. $k_{j,t}^{DEhousehold} = k_t^{DEhousehold} = \frac{K_t^{DE}}{M}$, $t \in \{0,1\}$. Also, all firms $i \in \{1,...,N\}$ will demand the same quantities of capital, i.e. $k_{i,t}^{DEfirm} = k_t^{DEfirm} = \frac{K_t^{DE}}{N}$, and they will also demand the same quantities of labor, $l_{i,t}^{DEfirm} = l_t^{DEfirm} = \frac{M}{N}$, $t \in \{0,1\}$. Therefore, using (57) and (58), decentralized-equilibrium prices for $t \in \{0,1\}$ will be given by:

$$R_t^{DE} = F_1\left(\frac{K_t^{DE}}{N}, K_t^{DE}, \frac{M}{N}\right) , \tag{64}$$

and

$$w_t^{DE} = F_3\left(\frac{K_t^{DE}}{N}, K_t^{DE}, \frac{M}{N}\right) . \tag{65}$$

Using (63) and (64), household demands for consumption will be driven by:

$$\frac{u_1\left(c_0^{DE}\right)}{\beta u_1\left(c_1^{DE}\right)} = 1 + F_1\left(\frac{K_t^{DE}}{N}, K_t^{DE}, \frac{M}{N}\right) - \delta , \tag{66}$$

and conditions (61) and (62). Combining (66) with (61) and (62), we can also get the equilibrium level of K_1^{DE}.

The strategy of our diagrammatic exposition is to isolate preferences from all the rest of the economic determinants and behavior: technology (production and capital-storage technology from one period to another), profit maximization of firms and all market-clearing conditions. We will therefore depict everything in the commodity space of consumptions in each period. Without loss of generality, we will work on the commodity space of *aggregate* consumptions. We are allowed to do this, since we have assumed that preferences are homothetic.[4]The reason we also use the space of aggregate consumptions is that comparison with the Social Planner's solution is easier.

If we aggregate (61) and (62) and use (64) and (65) and use assumption (iv.c) (constant returns to scale with respect to the vector $(k_{i,t}, l_{i,t})$) and Euler's theorem about homogeneous functions, we get:

$$C_0 + K_1 = F(K_0, K_0, M) + (1-\delta) K_0 , \tag{67}$$

and

$$C_1 = F(K_1, K_1, M) + (1-\delta) K_1 . \tag{68}$$

We now want to "insert" (67) into (68) in order to get the production-possibility frontier for the decentralized equilibrium (PPF^{DE}). We must be careful here: since neither the households, nor the firms assume that they affect aggregate prices, we should substitute (67) only in the first variable entry of function F in (68). Namely:

$$C_1 = F(F(K_0, K_0, M) + (1-\delta) K_0 - C_0, K_1, M) + (1-\delta) K_1 . \tag{69}$$

---

[4] Later on, while explaining the social planner's problem I will explain more about the convenience of assuming homothetic preferences.

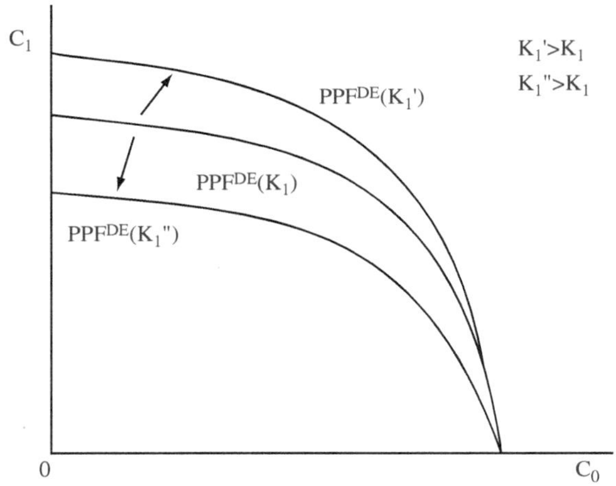

Figure 1.

Note that:

$$\frac{\partial C_1}{\partial C_0} = -F_1 \left(F \left(K_0, K_0, M\right) + \left(1-\delta\right) K_0 - C_0, K_1, M\right) - \left(1-\delta\right) < 0 \; , \tag{70}$$

and

$$\frac{\partial^2 C_1}{\partial C_0^2} = F_{11} \left(F \left(K_0, K_0, M\right) + \left(1-\delta\right) K_0 - C_0, K_1, M\right) < 0 \; , \tag{71}$$

with the last two equations justifying the shape of the curve PPF^{DE}, as this is depicted in Figure 1. In the same figure, we can also see how the PPF^{DE} depends on the externality K_1. When K_1 increases, the whole curve shifts upwards, but it is always connected to the point $(F(K_0, K_0, M) + (1-\delta) K_0, 0)$, i.e. the case where we consume everything in the first period. There is one diagram left. The one that determines the general equilibrium demands and prices. This is depicted in Figure 2. What is important to note there is that the position of the PPF^{DE} is determined by K_1^{DE}, where K_1^{DE} equals the length of the segment of the C_0 axis pointed out by the bracket. The latter is the outcome of the coincidence of the slope between the $\text{PPF}^{DE}\left(K_1^{DE}\right)$ and the marginal rate of substitution, both of which determine the gross effective interest rate.

6.1.4. *The Social Planner*

Let's first make clear that, due to the homotheticity of preferences, when the social planner maximizes $MU(c_0, c_1)$ *under any constraints*, it is equivalent to maximizing $U(Mc_0, Mc_1) = U(C_0, C_1)$ *under the same constraints.* Remember that from the fact that utility functions are *ordinal* representations of preference systems and *not*

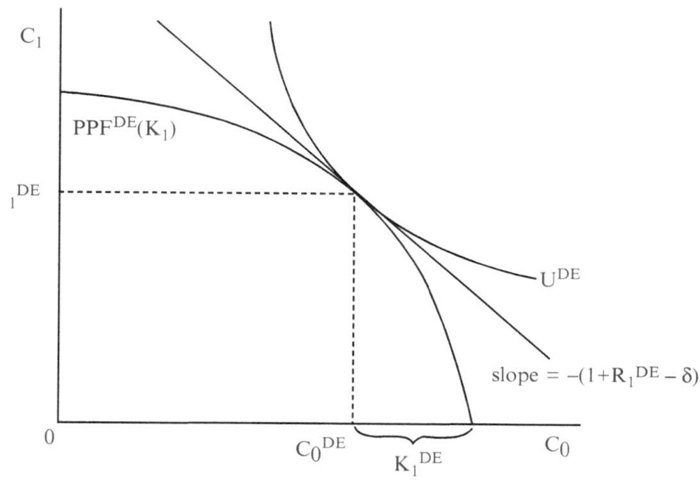

Figure 2.

cardinal, any monotonic transformation of $U(c_0, c_1)$ would lead to the same optimal demand system for a given arbitrary set of constraints. The definition of a homothetic utility function is that $U(c_0, c_1)$ is a monotonic transformation of a generic linearly homogeneous function $h(c_0, c_1)$ with respect to the vector (c_0, c_1), i.e. $U(c_0, c_1) = g(h(c_0, c_1))$, where $g(\cdot)$ is strictly increasing. Since $h(c_0, c_1) = \frac{1}{M} h(Mc_0, Mc_1)$ from the definition of linear homogeneity, $U(C_0, C_1) = U(Mc_0, M_1) = g(h(Mc_0, Mc_1))$. It is easy to see that $MU(c_0, c_1) = Mg\left(\frac{1}{M} h(Mc_0, Mc_1)\right)$ is a monotonic transformation of $U(C_0, C_1)$, hence maximizing $U(C_0, C_1)$ is equivalent to maximizing $MU(c_0, c_1)$ under the same constraints.

The social planner's problem is:

$$\max_{\{C_0, C_1, K_1\}} u(C_0) + \beta u(C_1)$$

subject to:

$$C_0 + K_1 = F(K_0, K_0, M) + (1 - \delta) K_0 , \tag{72}$$

$$C_1 = F(K_1, K_1, M) + (1 - \delta) K_1 . \tag{73}$$

The social planner is able to observe and control the externality, therefore we can write equations (72) and (73) as follows:

$$C_0 + K_1 = [F(1, 1, M) + 1 - \delta] K_0 , \tag{74}$$

$$C_1 = [F(1, 1, M) + 1 - \delta] K_1 , \tag{75}$$

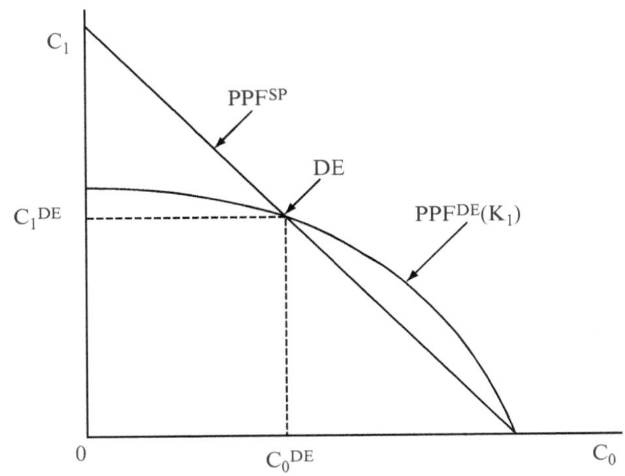

Figure 3.

since she can control both the direct contribution of K_1 in production and its indirect effect through the knowledge spillover. Solving, we now find:

$$\frac{u_1\left(C_0^{SP}\right)}{\beta u_1\left(C_1^{SP}\right)} = 1 + F\left(1, 1, M\right) - \delta \ . \tag{76}$$

Equations (76), (74) and (75), together with the fact that the planner will distribute incomes, demands and supplies equally across individual households and firms, fully determine the social-planner equilibrium. In order to draw the production possibility frontier of the social planner (PPF^{SP}), we substitute (74) into (75) and we get:

$$C_1 = \left[F\left(1, 1, M\right) + 1 - \delta\right]\left\{\left[F\left(1, 1, M\right) + 1 - \delta\right] K_0 - C_0\right\} \ . \tag{77}$$

Obviously:

$$\frac{\partial C_1}{\partial C_0} = 1 + F\left(1, 1, M\right) - \delta \ , \tag{78}$$

and

$$\frac{\partial^2 C_1}{\partial C_0^2} = 0 \ . \tag{79}$$

i.e. the PPF^{SP} is a straight line.

We must see that the gross effective interest rate of the social planner (in equation (76)), is always greater than any decentralized-equilibrium interest rate. This is due to the fact that the social planner rewards the externality, because she can control it and utilize it in her calculations. Note that capital-market clearing conditions imply

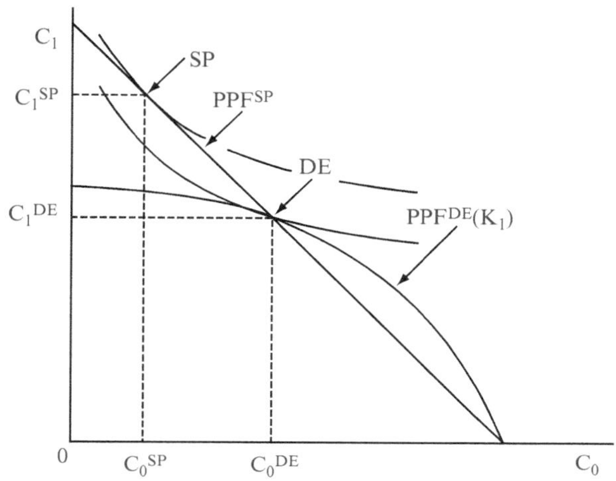

Figure 4.

that, independently of how much K_1^{DE} is, the gross-effective interest rate must be: $1+F_1\left(\frac{K_1^{DE}}{N},K_1^{DE},\frac{M}{N}\right)-\delta$.

$$\begin{aligned}
F(1,1,M) &= \frac{N}{K_1^{DE}}F\left(\frac{K_1^{DE}}{N},K_1^{DE},\frac{M}{N}\right) \quad \text{using (iv.b) and (iv.c) and Euler's theorem}\\
&= \frac{N}{K_1^{DE}}\left[F_1\left(\frac{K_1^{DE}}{N},K_1^{DE},\frac{M}{N}\right)\frac{K_1^{DE}}{N}+F_3\left(\frac{K_1^{DE}}{N},K_1^{DE},\frac{M}{N}\right)\frac{M}{N}\right]\\
&\quad \text{using (iv.c)}\\
&= F_1\left(\frac{K_1^{DE}}{N},K_1^{DE},\frac{M}{N}\right)+F_3\left(\frac{K_1^{DE}}{N},K_1^{DE},\frac{M}{N}\right)\frac{M}{K_1^{DE}}\\
&> F_1\left(\frac{K_1^{DE}}{N},K_1^{DE},\frac{M}{N}\right).
\end{aligned}$$

Figure 3 shows that the equilibrium $\left(C_0^{DE},C_1^{DE}\right)$ is on the PPF^{SP}. This follows from the fact that capital-market clearing implies:

$$C_1^{DE}=F\left(K_1^{DE},K_1^{DE},M\right)+(1-\delta)K_1^{DE}, \tag{80}$$

and

$$C_1^{SP}=F\left(K_1^{SP},K_1^{SP},M\right)+(1-\delta)K_1^{SP}. \tag{81}$$

Subsituting $K_1^{DE}=F(K_0,K_0,M)+(1-\delta)K_0-C_0^{DE}$ into (80) gives:

$$C_1^{DE}=[F(1,1,M)+1-\delta]\left[F(K_0,K_0,M)+(1-\delta)K_0-C_0^{DE}\right], \tag{82}$$

which proves it.

The fact that the social planner's allocation implies a higher welfare level comes from a simple revealed-preference argument, as shown diagrammatically by Figure 4.

References

Bator, F.M. 1957. "The Simple Analytics of Welfare Maximization", *American Economic Review* 47, 22–59.

Meltzer, A.H., and S.F. Richard. 1981. "A Rational Theory of the Size of Government", *Journal of Political Economy* 89(5), 914–927.

Romer, P.A. 1986. "Increasing Returns and Long-Run Growth", *Journal of Political Economy* 94, 1002–1037.

Christos Koulovatianos
Institut für Volkswirtschaftslehre
Universität Wien
Hohenstaufengasse 9
A-1010 Wien
Österreich
christos.koulovatianos@univie.ac.at

RENT SEEKING IN PUBLIC PROCUREMENT

DIETER BÖS
Universität Bonn

MARTIN KOLMAR
Universität Mainz

1. Introduction

Consider two private firms that compete for an indivisible public project which one of the firms will eventually carry out. In contrast to many other theoretical papers on procurement,[1] we do not assume that the government procurement agency chooses one of the firms by means of an auction process. The agency rather selects the private contractor by means of negotiations. This approach corresponds to economic practice, where in most cases public purchasing is based on negotiations and not on auctions. In the US, for example, it is not the sealed-bid auction, but competitive negotiation that *"is by far the most common method by which the government purchases products and services with a value in excess of the simplified acquisition threshold of $ 100,000"* (Tiefer and Shook, 1999, p. 77).

Procurement by negotiations is in general inefficient, in contrast to an optimal auction. Given this inefficiency, it makes sense to look for contractual arrangements which might improve the efficiency of imperfect procurement procedures. A temporal separation of award and actual contracting is such an arrangement. Such a separation has been made obligatory for EU procurement by a ruling of the European Court of Justice in 1999.[2] Therefore, countries like Germany or Austria, which have not yet separated award and contract, will have to change their procurement law accordingly,[3] whereas in other countries, like France, Belgium and Italy, award and contract have been separated for a long time.[4]

---

[1] See, for instance, Laffont and Tirole (1987).

[2] The judgment of the European Court of Justice, October 2, 1999, is an interpretation of the Council Directive 89/665/EEC.

[3] Although Austria already changed its procurement law, this obviously was not satisfactory for the EU. Hence, further litigations are pending before the EU Court of Justice.

[4] In the US federal procurement award and contract are unified. However, a post-award (=post-contract) protest may lead to an extraordinary termination of the initial contract, thus effectively separating award and contract. See Tiefer and Shook (1999, p. 496).

U. Schmidt and S. Traub (eds.), Advances in Public Economics: Utility, Choice and Welfare, 105-118.

The government procurement agency should make a contract with the highest-quality firm, as corresponds to a setting of negotiated procurement (whereas procurement by sealed-bid auction always is based on price). When the award is given, each firm knows the quality of the project it is offering but not the quality of the other firm's project, whereas the procurement agency does not observe either quality. However, the agency and the other firm observe a signal which refers to the reputation of the firm and which is positively correlated with the quality that is achieved if the project is carried out by this very firm.

The basic logic of this paper is as follows. Assume that award and contract are separated in time. Then, during the time span between award and contract, any firm has an incentive to engage in rent-seeking activities in order to influence the probability that it gets the contract. The procurement agency can use the rent-seeking outlays as information about the true quality of the project because high-quality firms will engage more heavily in rent-seeking activities than low-quality firms. Thus, it becomes more probable that the procurement agency writes the contract with the high-quality firm. Whether the improvement in the agency's informational status implies an efficiency gain or not, depends on the specification of rent-seeking activities. If the activities are zero-sum in nature (corruption), efficiency increases, whereas in the case of negative-sum rent seeking (lobbying), the positive information effect has to be compared with the negative effect of wasted lobbying outlays.

If award and contract are unified, the agency will choose the competitor with the higher expected qualification for the project. As we shall see, this is the competitor with the higher observable reputation signal. The potential sellers will anticipate this decision rule of the agency. With a temporal separation of award and contract, however, the agency can give the award to the inferior-looking firm, that is, the firm with the lower reputation signal. This changes the position of the private competitors, because they know that the contract will eventually be signed with this inferior-looking competitor unless the agency is induced to revoke its award decision. A superior-looking firm, that did not get the award, may use the time span between award and actual contracting to induce the agency to revoke its award decision. Rent seeking is one way to try to achieve such a revocation. Direct negotiations between the potential sellers would be another way. It turns out that it can be rational for the agency to give the award to the inferior-looking firm: this strategy may be a vehicle by which the procurement agency extracts further information about the unobservable qualities of the projects offered by the two potential sellers.

The present paper is a sequel to Bös and Kolmar (2003), where we assumed that the private firms *negotiate* in the time span between award and contract: the firm that did not get the award tries to bribe the successful awardee in order to get the contract. This possibility of firms' negotiations is not treated in the present paper. In contrast, in this paper the private firms engage in rent seeking.

The paper is organized as follows: In Section 2 we present the model and sketch the benchmark case of non-separated award and contract. In Section 3 we extend the game by separating award and contracting and deal with the rent-seeking activities of the private firms. Section 4 concludes.

2. The Model

A government procurement agency wants to purchase an indivisible project. The agency is risk neutral and maximizes the benefit-cost difference of the project. Two private firms, indexed $k = i, j$, are interested in carrying out the project. Both firms are risk-neutral profit maximizers. The firm that gets the award will in the following be called the winner, whereas its counterpart will be called the loser. It is not necessarily the winner with whom the agency makes the contract. The award may be revoked and, in such a case, the agency will make the contract with the loser.

2.1. THE VARIABLES AND THEIR VERIFIABILITY

The benefit-cost difference of the project is the surplus that results from the game. It is denoted by $q_k \in [\underline{q}, \overline{q}]$ if the project is carried out by seller k. Abbreviating we shall denote q_k as 'quality' of the project and of seller k, respectively. Both at the awarding stage and at the contracting stage, the procurement agency cannot observe the qualities offered by the private firms. However, it observes signals $e_k > 0$ which can be thought of as exogenously given reputations of the firms. Any signal is positively correlated with quality. Let $f_k(q) := f(q \mid e_k)$ be the probability that a project of quality q is realized if the signal is e_k and $F_k(q) := F(q \mid e_k) = \int_{\underline{q}}^{q} f_k(r)dr$ be the associated distribution function. Then for $\widetilde{e}_k \geq \hat{e}_k$ we assume

$$F(q \mid \widetilde{e}_k) \leq F(q \mid \hat{e}_k). \tag{1}$$

This assumption implies first-order stochastic dominance: higher quality is more probable the higher a seller's reputation signal.

The reputation signals are not verifiable before a court (although they are common knowledge): reputation could only be described by many characteristics, some of which cannot actually be measured but are subjective in nature. The quality is non-verifiable private information both at the awarding and at the contracting stage. However, ex post, when the project has actually been carried out, quality becomes known to everyone and becomes verifiable.

Since the procurement agency is a risk-neutral quality maximizer, at the early stages of the game it aims at maximizing expected quality. Let us define $\mu_k = E[q \mid e_k]$, as the expected quality q given signal e_k. It can be shown that the ranking of expected qualities and of reputation signals is identical:

$$\mu_i \geq \mu_j \Leftrightarrow e_i \geq e_j. \tag{2}$$

This can easily be proved. We have $\mu_k = \int_{\underline{q}}^{\overline{q}} q f_k(q)dq = \left(\overline{q} - \int_{\underline{q}}^{\overline{q}} F_k(q)dq\right)$. Hence, $\mu_i \geq \mu_j \Leftrightarrow \int_{\underline{q}}^{\overline{q}} (F_i(q) - F_j(q))\, dq \leq 0 \Leftrightarrow e_i \geq e_j$. The last equivalence follows from our assumption of first-order stochastic dominance.

A procurement contract that can be signed ex-ante can specify the firm that will carry out the project and a price that is paid to this firm. However, empirically most prices specified in ex-ante procurement contracts turn out to be subject to renegotiation during the realization of the project. In this paper we make the simplifying assumption that an ex-ante specified price has no influence on the ex-post renegotiated price between the procurement agency and the successful contractor. Since an ex-ante specified price has no influence on the negotiations ex-post, we omit it as an explicit strategy variable. We are not interested in the exact process of this negotiation and therefore follow the literature[5] by assuming that the ex-post price π for the seller is some fraction $\alpha \in [0, 1]$ of the surplus of the project, that is, of the quality q. The remaining fraction $\beta(= 1 - \alpha)$ goes to the procurement agency.[6] Anticipating this division of surplus, at the moment of contracting each firm knows exactly what it will get if it becomes contractor (since it knows its own quality). The agency only knows the expected payment it will face if signing the contract with a particular firm.

2.2. THE STAGES OF THE GAME

We consider the following sequential setting:

- at date 0, the qualities and the reputation signals are given;
- at date 1, the award is given to one of the firms (the winner);
- at date 2, the loser may use political channels to influence the procurement agency by rent-seeking activities (which will, of course, give rise to counteractions of the winner);
- at date 3, if the firms' rent seeking gives a signal that the loser's quality is higher than the winner's, then the procurement agency will revoke the award. In this case, the loser becomes the agency's contractor. Otherwise, the award is confirmed, and the procurement agency enters into a contract with the winner;
- at date 4, the project is carried out by the private contractor, and the surplus is divided between the procurement agency and the firm. By way of example, if the project has been carried out by firm i, at date 4 the quality of the completed project is observed by the procurement agency and the price $\pi = \alpha q_i$ is paid to i.

2.3. A BENCHMARK

As a benchmark we consider the situation where award and contract are not separated. In this case, the timing of events is as follows:

- at date 0, the qualities and the reputation signals are given;
- at date 1, one firm is selected by the procurement agency; this firm simultaneously is the awardee and the contractor;
- at date 2, the project is carried out and the surplus is divided between the agency and the firm.

[5] See Aghion and Tirole (1994), Che and Hausch (1999), Edlin and Reichelstein (1996) and Grossman and Hart (1986).

[6] α and β are exogenously given in our model.

We solve this three-stage game by backward induction. The agency's payoff at date 2 is βq_k if seller k had been chosen as contractor. At date 1, therefore, the agency compares the expected qualities and gives the award to the firm with higher expected quality given the respective reputation signal. We have already shown that the expected quality is higher, the higher the reputation signal. Therefore, the agency will give the award to the firm with higher reputation signal.

The resulting allocation is inefficient because the procurement agency makes no use of the information held by the private firms. By separating award and contract, the agency can extract at least part of this information and, thus, increase its expected payoff.

3. Rent Seeking

Following the literature on rent seeking, we distinguish between corruption and lobbying:[7]

- Assume first that the rent-seeking payments are bribes that are encashed by the procurement agency, that is, rent seeking is zero-sum in nature. This case of rent seeking corresponds closely to what might be called *corruption* of the agency.
- Assume second that the rent-seeking payments are wasted, that is, rent seeking is negative-sum in nature. This case of rent seeking is more closely related to the common-sense interpretation of *lobbying*.

Comparing both types of rent seeking shows immediately that corruption ceteris paribus leads to a higher level of welfare because nothing is wasted. On the other hand, corruption is seen as morally condemnable and, therefore, is explicitly forbidden in almost every country.

The equilibrium strategies of the agency and of the firms are the same for both types of rent seeking (Subsection 3.1). However, corruption and lobbying are differently to be treated when it comes to the normative evaluation of the consequences of rent seeking (Subsections 3.2 and 3.3).

3.1. EQUILIBRIUM STRATEGIES

The gap between the awarding and the contracting stage can be used for rent-seeking activities in order to change the ex-ante decision of the procurement agency.[8] Each firm spends R_k dollars for rent seeking, thereby influencing the probability $x(R_i, R_j)$ that the contract is signed with the winner. Without limitation of generality we assume that firm i is the winner and firm j is the loser.

At date 3 the procurement agency announces the final contractor and signs a contract with this firm. We assume that the agency uses the following decision rule

[7] See Hillman and Riley (1989), Hillman and Samet (1987), Körber and Kolmar (1996), Nitzan (1994).

[8] For the modelling of rent-seeking contests see Dixit (1987), Baik and Shogren (1992) and Nitzan (1994).

in order to determine the final contractor:[9]

$$x(R_i, R_j) = \begin{cases} 1 & \text{if } R_i \geq R_j\,, \\ 0 & \text{if } R_i < R_j\,, \end{cases} \qquad (DR). \tag{3}$$

This decision rule is based on the fact that R_k is higher, the higher a firm's quality: since the gross profit at stake, αq_k, is higher for the high-quality firm, in equilibrium this firm always spends more on rent seeking than the inferior-quality firm as we will prove shortly. Therefore, $R_j > R_i$ reveals the information to the agency that $q_j > q_i$, so that the award should be revoked and the contract signed with the high-quality loser j.[10] Note that the winner i has the advantage that he will become the contractor if $R_i = R_j$. Hence, we have an asymmetric contest of the sellers.

It is plausible to assume a sequential bargaining structure at date 2: the loser, who wants a revocation of the award, has to make the first move (date $2a$). The winner follows after observing the loser's rent-seeking activity (date $2b$). Both firms anticipate the agency's decision rule DR. Applying backward induction, we calculate the firms' optimal rent-seeking expenditures.

Date 2b: The winner's profit $\Pi_i(R_i, R_j)$ can be written as

$$\Pi_i(R_i, R_j) = \begin{cases} \alpha q_i - R_i & \text{if } R_i \geq R_j \\ -R_i & \text{if } R_i < R_j \end{cases}. \tag{4}$$

The optimal strategy of the winner can be easily derived from this profit equation:

$$R_i^* = \begin{cases} R_j & \text{if } \alpha q_i \geq R_j \\ 0 & \text{if } \alpha q_i < R_j \end{cases}. \tag{5}$$

Date 2a: The loser anticipates that the agency's decision rule would give him a profit $\Pi_j(R_i, R_j)$:

$$\Pi_j(R_i, R_j) = \begin{cases} \alpha q_j - R_j & \text{if } R_j > R_i \\ -R_j & \text{if } R_j \leq R_i \end{cases}. \tag{6}$$

However, since he cannot observe the winner's expenditures R_i, he can only find his own optimal expenditures by maximizing his expected profit $E\Pi_j$:

$$E\Pi_j = prob[R_j > R_i]\,\alpha q_j - R_j. \tag{7}$$

This expectation still contains the unobservable variable R_i. However, the loser's probability of winning the contest can be rewritten as follows. We know from the winner's reaction function that $prob[R_j > R_i] = prob[R_j > \alpha q_i] = F_i(R_j/\alpha)$. Therefore, the loser solves the following optimization problem:

$$\max_{R_j} E\Pi_j = F_i(R_j/\alpha)\,\alpha q_j - R_j \tag{8}$$

[9] As will be shown shortly, this decision rule is part of a Nash equilibrium of the game.

[10] The award-winning low-quality firm, in such a case, cannot sue the agency for compensation because its quality is not verifiable and the firm never enters stage 4 of the game where quality becomes verifiable.

under the restrictions that $R_j \geq 0$ and $F_i(R_j/\alpha)\,\alpha q_j - R_j \geq 0$. Accordingly, the loser's optimal strategy can be characterized as follows:[11]

LEMMA 1. *The loser's optimal strategy is either $R_j^* = 0$ or the optimum is characterized by $R_j^* > 0 \,\wedge\, f_i(R_j^*/\alpha)\, q_j = 1$.*

PROOF. See Appendix A.1. ■

The lemma is intuitive: whenever the loser engages in rent seeking, he will invest until the marginal return on investment is equal to the marginal costs. Marginal costs are equal to 1 whereas the marginal return on investment is equal to the increase in the probability of winning the contest $(1/\alpha)\, f_i(R_j^*/\alpha)$ times the gross profit αq_j.

In the following we have to distinguish between two cases: in the first, $R_j^* = 0$ is the equilibrium strategy of the loser. In this case, the winner always spends $R_i^* = 0$ and wins the contest. No information is revealed and, therefore, the agency will always make the contract with the winner, as indicated by the DR strategy. Hence, a separation of award and contract is neutral with respect to the efficiency of the resulting allocation.

In the second case, $R_j^* > 0$ is the optimal strategy for the loser. It follows immediately that the loser has no incentive to overinvest, that is, $R_j^* \leq \alpha q_j$ Assume to the contrary that $R_j^* > \alpha q_j$. In this case we have $E\Pi_j = F_i(R_j^*/\alpha)\,\alpha q_j - R_j^* \leq \alpha q_j - R_j^* < 0$. However, this contradicts the assumption that R_j^* is a maximum, since the loser can always guarantee himself a zero expected profit by choosing $R_j = 0$.

3.2. THE CASE OF A CORRUPT PROCUREMENT AGENCY

We are now in the position to prove the following result:

DEFINITION. *A state is efficiency-improving if it entails a higher sum of payoffs for all players, that is, for the procurement agency, the loser and the winner.*

PROPOSITION 1. *A separation of award and contract is efficiency-improving if rent-seeking activities have the character of corruption.*

PROOF. If $R_j^* = 0$, nothing changes compared to the situation where award and contract are not separated. If $R_j^* > 0$, we get

$$R_j^* \;\leq\; \alpha q_j \qquad\qquad \text{(loser's strategy)},$$

$$R_i^* \;=\; \begin{cases} R_j^* & \text{if } \alpha q_i \geq R_j^* \\ 0 & \text{if } \alpha q_i < R_j^* \end{cases} \qquad\qquad \text{(winner's strategy)}.$$

We have to prove the following statements: a) the award is revoked if and only if this is a change for the better; in other words, whenever the contract is signed with the

[11] For the problems of existence and uniqueness of an interior solution see Appendix $A.2$.

loser, the loser has the higher quality, b) the procurement agency sticks to its strategy DR and c) there is a strictly positive probability that the award is revoked.

In order to prove a) we have to distinguish two cases:

1. $R_j^* > 0, R_i^* = 0$. In this case we have $\alpha q_j \geq R_j^* > \alpha q_i$ and, therefore, revoking the award is always a change for the better.
2. $R_j^* > 0, R_i^* = R_j^*$. In this case the award is never revoked.

We can therefore conclude that revoking the award always leads to an efficiency improvement. This implies immediately that DR is optimal for the procurement agency (which proves statement b). Finally, let us turn to the proof of statement c): what is the probability for the case $R_j^* > 0$ and $R_i^* = 0$? The first-order condition in Lemma 1 allows the following explicit calculation of R_j^*:[12]

$$R_j^* = \alpha f_i^{-1}(1/q_j) =: \alpha\phi(q_j), \tag{9}$$

where $\phi(q_j)$ is a shorthand for $f_i^{-1}(1/q_j)$. Therefore, for given q_j the probability for $R_j^* > \alpha q_i$ is $prob\,[\alpha q_i < \alpha\phi(q_j)] = prob\,[q_i < \phi(q_j)] = F_i(\phi(q_j))$. Thus, the probability of an efficiency-improving revocation of the award is equal to

$$\int_{\underline{q}}^{\overline{q}} F_i(\phi(q_j))\, f_j(q_j) dq_j > 0. \tag{10}$$

Summarizing, the agency gets a (weakly) higher payoff, the sum total of the loser's and the winners' payoffs are (weakly) increased by the separation of award and contract that allows for corruption. The rent-seeking expenditures R_k are pure transfers that are not welfare-relevant. Therefore, compared with a situation of unified award and contract, efficiency is improved. ∎

Proposition 1 has shown that the separation of award and contract is efficiency improving compared with the benchmark where award and contract are unified. Note, however, that the result is still imperfect.[13] Figure 1 gives a graphical illustration of the result. Assume that the loser's quality is q_j as indicated in the figure. A first-best solution requires that firm i signs the contract whenever $q_i \geq q_j$, that is, if quality i lies in the interval b of the figure. Vice versa, the first best requires that firm j signs the contract whenever $q_i < q_j$, that is, if quality i lies in the interval a. Now assume that the award has been given to firm i. As we have proved, the firms' rent seeking activities reverse the award if $\alpha q_i \leq R_j^* \leq \alpha q_j \Leftrightarrow q_i \leq \phi(q_j) \leq q_j$. Therefore, a separation of award and contract improves upon the nonseparation if q_i lies in the interval c, that is, if the loser is considerably better than the winner. If the difference between the sellers is small (interval m, for 'middle'), it is still the award-winning

[12] The inversion of the density function is well-defined because Π_j is strictly convex in an environment around R_j^*.

[13] This is a consequence of the impossibility theorem by Myerson and Satterthwaite (1983).

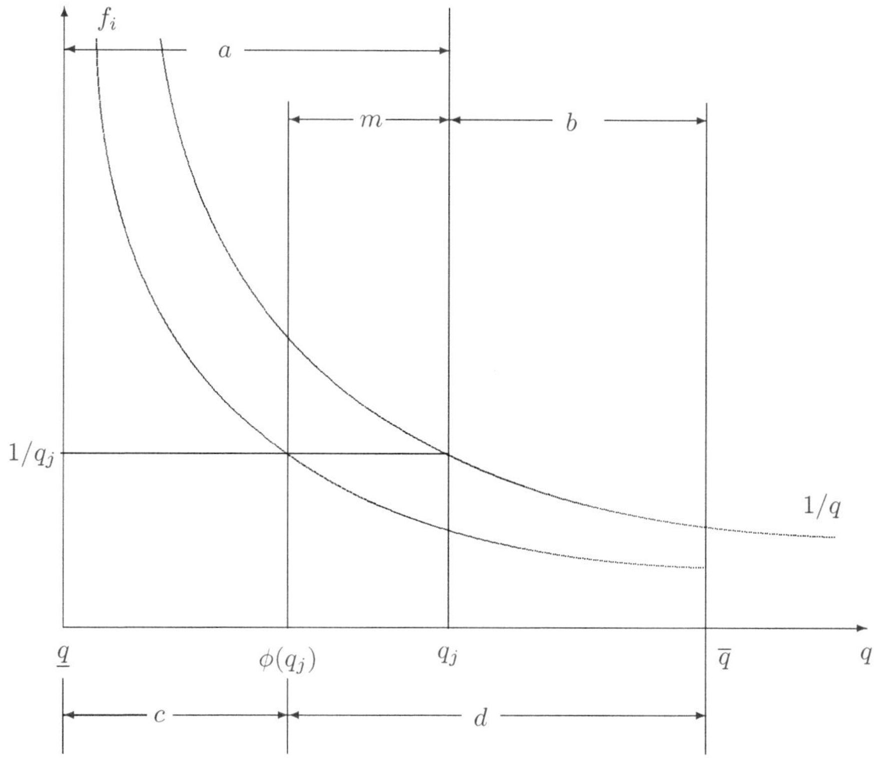

Figure 1. Efficiency-improving rent-seeking activities.

seller i who ends up signing the contract, despite his inferior quality. The creation of flexibility due to the separation of award and contract allows for the self-correction of imperfect decision rules, but only if the initial decision yielded 'large' losses.

It remains to be shown that the agency's revocation strategy is part of a Nash equilibrium of the game. Assume that $R_j^* > 0, R_i^* = 0$.[14] In that case, the rent-seeking activities reveal the information to the procurement agency that $q_j \geq q_i$ and, therefore, at date 3 revocation is the optimal strategy of the procurement agency.

Let us, finally, step back to date 1. The procurement agency anticipates the firms' rent-seeking activities, and its own decision rule (DR). It will be the optimal strategy of the agency to give the award to that firm for which date 2 rent seeking promises the highest ex-post payoff.

Assume first that the procurement agency always gives the award to the firm with the better signal, $e_i \geq e_j$. Then, the expected payoff of the agency is as follows: the

[14] And therefore $q_i \leq \phi(q_j) \leq q_j$.

agency always gets $\beta\mu_i$. Furthermore, in all cases where the award is revoked it gets $\beta(q_j - q_i) > 0$ in addition to $\beta\mu_i$. This additional payoff results from the separation of award and contract. Its expected value can be calculated as follows.

For a given q_j, the expected value of q_i given that $q_i \leq \phi(q_j)$ is

$$E[q \mid q_i \leq \phi(q_j)] = \int_{\underline{q}}^{\phi(q_j)} q \frac{f_i(q)}{F_i(\phi(q_j))} dq. \tag{11}$$

Therefore, the agency's expected additional payoff for a given q_j is equal to

$$\beta F_i(\phi(q_j)) \left(q_j - \int_{\underline{q}}^{\phi(q_j)} q \frac{f_i(q)}{F_i(\phi(q_j))} dq \right). \tag{12}$$

Taking expectations over q_j gives the expected additional payoff of the agency:

$$g(i) := \beta \int_{\underline{q}}^{\overline{q}} F_i(\phi(q_j)) q_j f_j(q_j) dq_j - \beta \int_{\underline{q}}^{\overline{q}} \int_{\underline{q}}^{\phi(q_j)} q f_i(q) dq f_j(q_j) dq_j. \tag{13}$$

Summarizing, an agency that always gives the award to the firm with the higher reputation signal faces an expected payoff of

$$G(i) := \beta\mu_i + g(i). \tag{14}$$

By the same procedure we can calculate the expected payoff of an agency that always gives the award to the firm with the lower reputation signal:[15]

$$G(j) := \beta\mu_j + g(j). \tag{15}$$

Summarizing, at date 1, the procurement agency should give the award to firm i if and only if

$$G(i) - G(j) \geq 0. \tag{16}$$

This condition implies the following result:

PROPOSITION 2. *It may be optimal for the procurement agency to give the award to the seller with the inferior signal.*

PROOF. The proof follows the same lines as the proof in Appendix A in Bös and Kolmar (2003). ■

What is the intuition for this surprising result? Without any rent-seeking activities, the procurement agency loses $\beta(\mu_j - \mu_i)$ by giving the award to i, the firm with the lower reputation signal. However, this loss can be overcompensated by a revocation of the award following the firms' rent seeking.

---

[15] $g(j)$ is equal to $g(i)$ after interchanging the indices i and j.

By giving the award to the lower-quality firm i, the agency has made an error. Rent seeking may correct this error. If rent seeking corrected mistakes from the award stage perfectly, the optimal award strategy of the agency would be indeterminate from an efficiency point of view. However, this cannot be guaranteed. There is always[16] the intermediate interval m where mistakes are not corrected. If q_i and q_j are relatively close, the separation has no positive influence on the efficiency of the allocation. On the other hand, the separation of award and contract successfully reduces the probability of decision errors if these errors would have implied relatively large losses. The procurement agency's decision of whom to give the award, therefore, depends on the contingent expected value of the projects in the 'intermediate' ranges where the projects of both sellers have relatively similar qualities. Therefore, there are cases for which it is reasonable for the procurement agency to give the award to the low-quality firm because its performance contingent on a restricted interval of q exceeds the performance of the other firm *despite the fact that its overall performance is worse.*

3.3. THE CASE OF LOBBYING

Let us finally turn to the analysis of rent-seeking contests where the investments are pure lobbying. The equilibrium strategies of the players are not affected by this change of interpretation, but the normative implications are. This is due to the fact that lobbying outlays are pure waste. Relating the case of lobbying to the benchmark, we obtain:

PROPOSITION 3. *In contrast to the case of corruption, a separation of award and contract is not necessarily efficiency-improving if rent-seeking activities have the character of lobbying.*

PROOF. The expected gain of a separation of award and contract is equal to the expected difference of the value of the game where award and contract are separated and the value of the game where award and contract are not separated, that is,

$$E[\Delta] = \int_{\underline{q}}^{\overline{q}} \left[F_i(\phi(q_j))\, q_j + \int_{\phi(q_j)}^{\overline{q}} q_i f_i(q_i) dq_i \right] f_j(q_j) dq_j - \int_{\underline{q}}^{\overline{q}} q_i f_i(q_i) dq_i. \tag{17}$$

The expected lobbying outlays for a given q_j, ΣR, are $\alpha\phi(q_j) + prob[\alpha q_i \geq \alpha\phi(q_j)]\, \alpha\phi(q_j)$. Recall that $prob[\alpha q_i \geq \alpha\phi(q_j)] = 1 - F_i(\phi(q_j))$. Therefore, the expected lobbying outlays are

$$E[\Sigma R] = \int_{\underline{q}}^{\overline{q}} \left[2 - F_i(\phi(q_j)) \right] \alpha\phi(q_j)\, f_j(q_j) dq_j. \tag{18}$$

If a separation of award and contract leads to lobbying activities of both sellers, the resulting equilibrium is efficiency-improving if

$$E[\Delta] - E[\Sigma R] > 0. \tag{19}$$

[16] By way of exception, there is no interval m if $\phi(q_j) = q_j$. However, this case is not interesting at all. $\phi(q_j) \to q_j$ if $q_j \to 0$. Therefore, in this case a reward given to winner i should never be revoked.

Substituting (17) and (18) reveals that this inequality is fulfilled if

$$\int_{\underline{q}}^{\overline{q}} \left[\underbrace{F_i(\phi(q_j))\, q_j}_{\geq 0} + \underbrace{\Big[F_i(\phi(q_j)) - 2\Big]\alpha\phi(q_j)}_{<0} - \underbrace{\int_{\underline{q}}^{\phi(q_j)} q_i f_i(q_i) dq_i}_{>0} \right] f_j(q_j) dq_j > 0.$$

Because of $0 \leq F_i(\cdot) \leq 1$, the first term is positive, and the second term negative. Thus, the effect on net profits is ambiguous. ■

It may be noted that, as in the case of corruption, it may be optimal for the procurement agency to give the award to the seller with the inferior signal.

4. Conclusion

The separation of award and contract in public procurement may improve upon erroneous decisions of a procurement agency. The firms' rent-seeking activities reveal information to the agency that otherwise would have been unavailable. It has been shown that a separation of award and contract is efficiency-improving if the procurement agency is corrupt or if the wasted lobbying expenditures are only a small fraction of the surplus of the project.

Surprisingly, the expected surplus of the project may be maximized if the award is given to a seller with an inferior quality signal. The intuition for this result is as follows: rent seeking will correct a wrong ex-ante decision if the quality of the award-winning firm is very low whereas the quality of the loser is very high. Thus, the expected payoffs of different awarding strategies differ only with respect to intermediate values of project quality. It can be the inferior-quality firm that has a better contingent performance for these intermediate qualities despite the fact that the unconditional expected quality is below that of the other firm.

Appendix

A.1. PROOF OF LEMMA 1

The Lagrangean of the loser, seller j, is

$$\mathcal{L} = F_i(R_j/\alpha)\,\alpha q_j - R_j + \lambda R_j + \mu\left(F_i(R_j/\alpha)\,\alpha q_j - R_j\right), \tag{A.1}$$

which yields the following Kuhn-Tucker first-order conditions:

$$R_j : (1+\mu)\left(f_i(R_j/\alpha)\, q_j - 1\right) + \lambda \leq 0 \wedge R_j \geq 0$$
$$\wedge\ R_j\left((1+\mu)\left(f_i(R_j/\alpha)\, q_j - 1\right) + \lambda\right) = 0, \tag{A.2}$$
$$\lambda : R_j \geq 0 \wedge \lambda \geq 0 \wedge \lambda R_j = 0, \tag{A.3}$$
$$\mu : F_i(R_j/\alpha)\,\alpha q_j - R_j \geq 0 \wedge \mu \geq 0 \wedge \mu\left(F_i(R_j/\alpha)\,\alpha q_j - R_j\right) = 0. \tag{A.4}$$

These conditions give rise to 3^3 possible cases which in turn have to be analyzed. There are two qualitatively different types of solutions that have to be distinguished: First, $R_j = 0$ may turn out to be optimal. This leads directly to part 1 of lemma 1 irrespective of the specification of parameter values. Second, $R_j > 0$ may turn out to be optimal. Then $f_i(R_j/\alpha)\,q_j - 1 = 0$ has to be fulfilled. Note that this result holds both for interior and for corner solutions. For $R_j > 0$, conditions (A.2) require $(1+\mu)\,(f_i(R_j/\alpha)q_j - 1) = 0$,[17] and since $\mu \geq 0$, this always implies $f_i(R_j/\alpha)\,q_j - 1 = 0$, regardless of whether we have an interior solution where $F_i(R_j/\alpha)\,\alpha q_j - R_j \geq 0$ is not binding ($\mu = 0$), or we have a corner solution where $F_i(R_j/\alpha)\,\alpha q_j - R_j = 0$, and $\mu > 0$. ■

A.2. REMARKS ON EXISTENCE AND UNIQUENESS OF INTERIOR SOLUTIONS

Since the winner's density function enters the f.o.c. $f_i(R_j^*/\alpha)\,q_j = 1$, it is not guaranteed that the Kuhn-Tucker conditions characterize a unique maximum. Due to its lack of structure the condition might characterize a local minimum and even if it characterizes a maximum, it need not be unique. In order to characterize a local maximum we need $(1/\alpha)\,f_i'(R_j^*/\alpha)\,q_j \leq 0$ at R_j^*. Fortunately, we do not require existence or uniqueness of an interior solution in this context. All we need is $R_j^* > 0 \wedge f_i(R_j^*/\alpha)\,q_j = 1$ for every local maximum. If there are several ones, we will use the convention that the loser chooses that with the highest expected profit Π_j.

Acknowledgements

We gratefully acknowledge helpful comments by G. Gyárfás, M. Hagedorn, S. Marjit, C. Lülfesmann and J. Pietzcker and the participants of seminars in Bonn, Konstanz, London (LSE), Saarbrücken and York.

References

Aghion, P., and J. Tirole. 1994. "The Management of Innovation", *Quarterly Journal of Economics* 109(4), 1185–1209.

Baik, K. H., and J. F. Shogren. 1992. "Strategic Behavior in Contests: Comment", *American Economic Review* 82(1), 359–362.

Bös, D., and M. Kolmar. 2003. "On the Separation of Award and Contract in Public Procurement", *Finanzarchiv* 59(4), 425–442.

Che, Y.-K., and D. B. Hausch. 1999. "Cooperative Investments and the Value of Contracting", *American Economic Review* 89(1), 125–147.

Dixit, A. 1987. "Strategic Behavior in Contests", *American Economic Review* 77(5), 891–898.

Edlin, A. S., and S. Reichelstein. 1996. "Holdups, Standard Breach Remedies, and Optimal Investment", *American Economic Review* 86(3), 478–501.

Grossman, S. J., and O. Hart. 1986. "The Costs and Benefits of Ownership: A Theory of Vertical and Lateral Integration", *Journal of Political Economy* 94(4), 691–719.

Hillman, A. L., and J. Riley. 1989. "Politically Contestable Rents and Transfers", *Economics and Politics* 1, 17–39.

[17] $\lambda = 0$ in this case, as can be seen from conditions (A.3).

Hillman, A. L., and D. Samet. 1987. "Dissipation of Contestable Rents by a Small Number of Contenders", *Public Choice* 54(1), 63–82.
Körber, A. and M. Kolmar. 1996. "To Fight or not to Fight? An Analysis of Submission, Struggle, and the Design of Contests", *Public Choice* 88(3–4), 381–392.
Laffont, J. J., and J. Tirole. 1987. "Auctioning Incentive Contracts", *Journal of Political Economy* 95, 921–937.
Myerson, R. B., and M. A. Satterthwaite. 1983. "Efficient Mechanisms for Bilateral Trading", *Journal of Economic Theory* 29(2), 265–281.
Nitzan, S. 1994. "Modelling Rent-Seeking Contests", *European Journal of Political Economy* 10(1), 41–60.
Tiefer, C., and W. A. Shook. 1999. *Government Contract Law*, Durham, NC: Carolina Academic Press.

Dieter Bös (†)

Martin Kolmar
Lehrstuhl für Theoretische Volkswirtschaft
Universität Mainz
Jakob-Welder-Weg 4
D-55128 Mainz
Germany
kolmar@uni-mainz.de

A NEW SUBJECTIVE APPROACH TO EQUIVALENCE SCALES: AN EMPIRICAL INVESTIGATION

CARSTEN SCHRÖDER
Universität Kiel

ULRICH SCHMIDT
Universität Hannover

1. Introduction

The measurement of inequality and poverty requires comparisons of households with differing quantitative and qualitative compositions. The most prominent instrument for such comparisons are equivalence scales. In general an equivalence scale is given by the income ratio of two households with differing compositions but an identical living standard. Three different approaches for deriving equivalence scales are discussed in the literature: expert based methods, methods based on consumption data, and subjective methods.

Expert equivalence scales are derived from needs and market baskets defined by specialists. These definitions are, however, arbitrary even if they are based on scientific data, because needs for food and even more for superior consumption goods cannot be defined in an objective way.[1] Moreover, the outcomes of this method may be distorted due to divergent prices between the subgroups of the population.

Consumption oriented approaches pursue the aim of deriving preferences from demand data Single equation models refer to absolute expenditure or relative expenditure shares of a single good as welfare criteria. In contrast to this, extended models simultaneously consider several categories of goods. The main problem of these approaches is the assumption of identical consumption structures which are assumed to be independent of the chosen income level. This assumption is, however, rejected by our empirical data. Furthermore, there may be discrepancies between consumption and expenditure, especially in the short run: Expenditure may take place in a single period while the good is consumed during several periods. Analogously to the expert based scales, most of the consumption oriented approaches assume prices to be identical for all individuals. Another problem arises if preferences and lifestyles

[1] Cf. Townsend (1962), Friedman (1965), Rein (1974), and Atkinson (1983).

U. Schmidt and S. Traub (eds.), Advances in Public Economics: Utility, Choice and Welfare, 119-134.

of individuals depend on the demographic characteristics of the household. Since expenditures for different categories of goods, used as welfare indicators, are then affected by the lifestyle, equivalence scales will be distorted.[2]

In our opinion the subjective method has several advantages for the empirical evaluation of equivalence scales. Therefore, we employ a subjective approach in which equivalence scales are derived from evaluations of respondents. The most popular study with a subjective approach was conducted by Kapteyn and van Praag (1976). Here, an individual has to state the income amounts which correspond, in her own familiar circumstances, to specified utility levels, for instance "very bad", "bad", "insufficient", "sufficient", "good", and "very good".[3] This approach, characterized by the specification of utility levels, is also used in most of the subjective analyzes of the poverty line.[4] A controversial underlying assumption is the existence of a cardinal welfare function with a specific functional form. Moreover, utilizing the dimension "utility" is problematic since this leads to a significant correlation between stated income levels and the real income of the respondents.[5] Kapteyn and van Praag (1976) refer to this phenomenon as preference drift. According to Coulter et al. (1992) these are the fundamental problems of the subjective approach. Both problems are avoided in our approach, first presented in Koulovatianos et al. (2005). Instead of utility levels, different net incomes of a reference one adult household are presented to the subjects. Then, the demography of the household is changed (number of adults and/or children) and subjects have to specify the net income which the modified household would need in order to reach an identical living standard. Our approach possesses the typical advantages of the original subjective method: Several assumptions which are necessary for the two other approaches are avoided, especially the assumption of identical lifestyles.[6] In addition to this, the subjective approach takes account of different prices between the subgroups of the population.[7] However, we want to emphasize that we do not regard our approach as superior to the one of Kapteyn and van Praag (1976). Instead, we think that both approaches are complements.

The empirical study relying on our approach is mainly devoted to two questions. First, a characteristic property of equivalence scales discussed in the literature is the fact that they do not depend on income. For instance, an 80 percent higher income is assigned to a couple rather than to a single, irrespective of the single's initial income. However, our empirical study demonstrates that the weights for household members vary with income, that is, the share of the living costs of children and the second adult in the family budget decreases with increasing reference income of the reference household. This point was already discussed in Koulovatianos et al. (2005), the present paper provides an additional analysis. The main focus of our paper is the

---

[2] Cf. e.g. Coulter et al. (1992).

[3] Rainwater (1974) extended this approach to hypothetical families. Dubnoff (1985), on the other hand, specified income levels and asked for the corresponding utilities.

[4] For a detailed critique of this approach cf. Hartog (1988) and Seidl (1994).

[5] Cf. especially Goedhart et al. (1977) and Kapteyn et al. (1984).

[6] Cf. Klein (1986), p. 288.

[7] Compare van der Gaag and Smolensky (1982).

second point, namely the question whether the scale values for children depend on the number of parents living in the household. The only two investigations of this question we are aware of are based on income and consumption data. Both evaluate higher weights for children in two parent families. We will argue that this result is not plausible and it is also rejected by our analysis: According to our respondents, the weights for children in one parent families are evidently higher than those in two parent families.

This paper is organized as follows. In the next section we describe the data collection and the structure of the employed questionnaire. Section 3 is devoted to the question whether the evaluated equivalence scales do depend on the reference income. The weights for children living in one parent or two parent families are compared in Section 4. An approximation of an equivalence scale function which reflects both dependencies is presented in Section 5. Section 6 concludes.

Single adult household without a child	Reference income	Two adult household without a child	?
One parent household with 1 child	?	Two parent household with 1 child	?
One parent household with 2 children	?	Two parent household with 2 children	?
One parent household with 3 children	?	Two parent household with 3 children	?

Figure 1. Questionnaire structure.

2. The Survey

For our analysis we use the German data reported in Koulovatianos et al. (2005). This data was collected in 1999 by the Institut für Finanzwissenschaft und Sozialpolitik of the Christian–Albrechts-Universität zu Kiel. The questionnaire is subdivided into two sections. In the first section, the subjects have to evaluate five situations which differ in the reference net income of a household with a single adult. Adults are assumed to be at an age between 35 and 55, children between 7 and 11. The five reference net incomes for a single adult per month are 1000, 2500, 4000, 5500 and 7000 Deutschmarks. Then, the demography of the household is changed (number of adults and/or children) and the subjects have to answer the following question: "How much income does the household with the new demography need in order to enjoy the same living standard as the childless one parent household (with given reference income)?" The participants were asked to complete the resulting table (Figure 1) for five reference income levels.

The second section of the questionnaire asked for several personal characteristics of the respondents: family status, occupation, net income of the household per month, etc. A breakdown of our sample can be taken from Table A.I in the Appendix.

We received data from 180 subjects, of which 13 had to be excluded: Seven questionnaires were incomplete and six respondents offended the plausibility axiom. Such an offence was identified either (a) if the stated income strictly decreased with increasing number of household members, or (b) if the specified income for a childless two adult household was more than twice the reference income for a single, or (c) if the stated income for a given demography in the lower income class exceeded the income for the same demography in a higher income class.

3. Income Dependence of Equivalence Scales

3.1. RESULTS OF PREVIOUS STUDIES

In general, the literature only considers equivalence scales which are independent of income. Consumption oriented approaches refer to this assumption as "Independence of Base" (Lewbel, 1989) or "Equivalence Scale Exactness" (Blackorby and Donaldson, 1988). This constancy assumption can be justified with at least two arguments. First, constant scales are easier to evaluate and mathematically more convenient.[8] Second, income dependencies may be considered as empirically irrelevant or insignificant.[9] However, these assumptions have serious implications which can be illustrated by the following example of Conniffe (1992). Consider two identical households, each consisting of two adults and two children, which differ only in their monthly income. Suppose the weights equal 1.0 for an adult and 0.5 for a child such that the sum of weights for each household is 3.0. If the first household has an income of \$ 3000, the "costs" of each adult are \$ 1000 and the "costs" of each child are \$ 500. While this seems to be plausible, things change if the income of the second household, is, say 50 times, higher such that an adult now receives an amount of \$ 50000 and each child \$ 25000 per month. According to Conniffe (1992), this is no longer plausible, particularly for the children costs.

In the following we will give a brief overview of studies which have already taken into account a possible income dependence of equivalence scales. The first empirical study dealing with income dependencies was conducted by Seneca and Taussig (1971). They consider families with identical gross incomes but different numbers of children. Using two different market baskets in their expenditure based method, they evaluate a tax schedule which guarantees an identical living standard for all families, given identical gross income. From this tax schedule they finally calculate the resulting equivalence scales for the single family compositions. Their results show that the gains

[8] Compare for example Conniffe (1992).

[9] Compare for example Merz and Faik (1995).

in taxation and, thus, the corresponding weights for children decrease with increasing gross income. However, their study applies only to families with at least two children and consequently yields no results for the first child. In contrast, our study provides a clear negative income dependency also for the first child. Furthermore, our study allows to analyze the relation of the weight for the second adult to the reference income of a single adult, as well as the relation between children weights and number of parents living in the household.

An expenditure based approach is also used by van Hoa (1986) to evaluate the weights for each additional child as a function of the household income. Three income classes (low, middle, high) are considered. The results of van Hoa show that the weights for children first decline from 0.41 for the low income class to 0.14 for the middle, but then increase to 0.21 for the high income class. An economic argument for this increase is missing. In our opinion this result is not plausible and it is also rejected by our data. Furthermore, the weights for additional children are specified without considering the total number of children already living in the household.

In order to obtain expenditure based equivalence scales which are independent of the chosen level of utility or income, most studies employ an expenditure system relying on the above mentioned independence of base (IB) assumption or equivalence scale exactness (ESE). However, a direct empirical test by Dickens et al. (1993) rejects this assumption and shows that it may cause seriously distorted scale values. Consequently, they conclude that, in general, non linear models have to be employed which in turn lead to income dependent equivalence scales. This result is also supported by the empirical analysis of Missong and Stryck (1998) which shows that, in contrast to the linear model, marginal consumption quota for different goods typically vary significantly with the given income level. However, even if the independence of base assumption could be accepted, the resulting model does not necessarily lead to constant equivalence scales. Conniffe (1992) can show in his theoretical analysis that also in the linear model the scale values for households may converge with increasing income towards a constant value which equals unity regardless of the number of "dependants" in the household. A dependant is defined as a person "with an income too low to purchase subsistence quantities of commodities even when forming part of a two adult household."[10]

A first approach for relaxing the IB/ESE assumption in the consumption oriented approach was suggested by *Donaldson and Pendakur* (2004) introducing two different classes of equivalent-income functions that are generalizations of those functions corresponding to IB/ESE equivalence scales. Using Canadian expenditure data, they derive equivalence scales that slightly decrease with increasing household income.

Finally, Aaberge and Melby (1998) determine income dependent equivalence scales by using the minimal social security pensions and child allowances of Norway. The equivalence scale of household type z in relation to a one adult reference household

[10] Conniffe (1992, p. 433).

type r is calculated as

$$E(z, y(r)) = 1 + \frac{m(z) - m(r)}{y(r)} \tag{1}$$

where $m(r)$ and $y(r)$ represent the minimum and the disposable income of the reference household r and $m(z)$ is the minimum income of household type z. Although this method encounters the argument that income dependent equivalence scales are mathematically inconvenient it has nevertheless several undesirable properties. The formula implies first that the income elasticity of the weights for children and the second adult are identical. Second, a bisection of the weights for the second adult and the children occurs if disposable income is doubled. The results of our study strongly reject both properties. Furthermore, since the analysis of Aaberge and Melby (1998) relies on expert based institutional scales, all the criticism discussed in Section 2 can be applied.

3.2. THE RESULTS OF OUR STUDY

Table I gives an overview of our results. Abbreviations represent demography and reference income of the household: A indicates an adult, C a child, and the adjacent number is the reference income.

The value of EAACC4000 for example is the equivalence scale (E) for a two parent household with two children at a reference income of 4000 Deutschmarks. Thus, it corresponds to the income divided by 4000 Deutschmarks which is necessary for this household in order to obtain the same standard of living as a reference single adult household with an income of 4000 Deutschmarks. The values of all equivalence scales in the table clearly decrease with increasing reference income. The only exception is the change from EAA5500 to EAA7000 but this increase is given by only 0.1 percent and it is, moreover, insignificant. All other scale values are negatively correlated with the reference income on a significance level of 1 percent (other significance levels are marked). For the calculation of these significance levels, we arranged the single scale values for a given demography in increasing order of the reference income level. Then, for each scale value we tested whether it is lower than the scale value of the next income class in the row below.

Altogether, our study provides strong evidence for the decrease of equivalence scales with increasing reference income. This can be emphasised by the fact that 91 percent of the subjects responded with incomes leading to decreasing scale values over all income levels and all household types. Only two subjects stated income values corresponding to constant scale values. 13 subjects declared income values causing increases of single scale values, especially for households with two adults and no child. Restricting attention to the scale values for children, only seven out of the 13 respondents remained stating single incomes corresponding to increasing scale values.

The decrease can also be illustrated as follows: The scale values at a reference income of 1000 Deutschmarks are on average 1.64 times higher than the corresponding values at a reference income of 7000 Deutschmarks. The highest value 1.9 of this relation occurs between two parent households with three children (EAACCC1000

TABLE I. Household equivalence scales

	Min.	*Max.*	*Mean*	*Std.d.*	*T*
EAC1000	1.10	2.50	1.570	.230	—
EAC2500	1.00	1.68	1.241	.114	21.586
EAC4000	1.00	1.60	1.173	.110	11.435
EAC5500	1.00	1.45	1.128	.089	10.405
EAC7000	1.00	1.50	1.113	.088	5.027
EACC1000	1.20	3.00	2.020	.398	—
EACC2500	1.00	2.00	1.436	.195	24.240
EACC4000	1.00	2.00	1.314	.181	13.678
EACC5500	1.00	1.82	1.233	.150	13.017
EACC7000	1.00	1.71	1.205	.146	6.673
EACCC1000	1.30	5.00	2.473	.612	—
EACCC2500	1.08	2.50	1.629	.283	23.259
EACCC4000	1.00	2.50	1.449	.254	15.418
EACCC5500	1.00	2.09	1.339	.210	14.897
EACCC7000	1.00	1.90	1.294	.201	7.603
EAA1000	1.20	2.00	1.753	.205	—
EAA2500	1.00	2.00	1.495	.266	13.417
EAA4000	1.00	2.00	1.458	.279	*3.222
EAA5500	1.00	2.00	1.388	.264	8.135
EAA7000	1.00	2.00	1.389	.272	$^{\diamond}$-0.184
EAAC1000	1.30	3.50	2.269	.325	—
EAAC2500	1.00	2.56	1.718	.319	22.742
EAAC4000	1.00	2.56	1.610	.329	8.424
EAAC5500	1.00	2.24	1.508	.311	10.438
EAAC7000	1.00	2.29	1.493	.317	**1.544
EAACC1000	1.50	4.50	2.725	.498	—
EAACC2500	1.00	3.40	1.919	.395	24.550
EAACC4000	1.00	2.89	1.753	.373	10.861
EAACC5500	1.00	2.56	1.615	.360	12.536
EAACC7000	1.00	2.57	1.587	.365	*2.731
EAACCC1000	1.60	6.00	3.174	.749	—
EAACCC2500	1.08	4.20	2.115	.474	24.025
EAACCC4000	1.00	3.22	1.885	.435	12.156
EAACCC5500	1.00	2.91	1.726	.416	12.261
EAACCC7000	1.00	2.88	1.677	.413	3.886

Note. *Min.* denotes the lowest value stated. *Max.* denotes the highest value stated. *Std.d.* denotes the standard deviation and T is the t statistic. * denotes significance at the 0.5 percent level. ** denotes significance at the 10 percent level. $^{\diamond}$ denotes insignificance. All other values are significant at the 1 percent level.

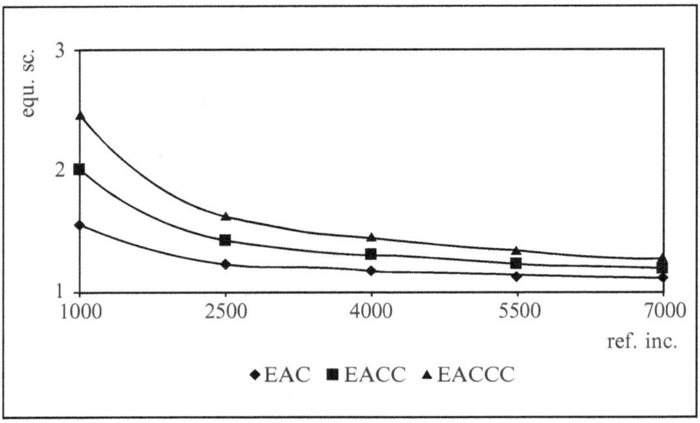

Figure 2. Single adult equivalence scales.

and EAACCC7000) and the lowest between the two adult households without children (EAA1000 and EAA7000). Therefore, we can conclude that the income dependency of the children weights is stronger than of the weight of the second adult in the household.

For the lowest reference income, our scale values do not differ significantly from most of the values reported in the literature. But since our equivalence scales decrease with increasing reference income, the values in the higher reference income classes are lower than those in most other studies. Note that the strongest decrease of the scale values between two consecutive income classes occurs when raising the reference income from 1000 to 2500 Deutschmarks. Since a monthly income of 1000 Deutschmarks equals roughly the German social assistance for single adults, this result indicates that also poverty measurement should not employ constant equivalence scales. For instance, countries with a lower level of social assistance should consequently use higher scale values. Also poverty comparisons between different countries may be distorted if they rely on constant equivalence scales.

A summary of our results is provided by Figures 2 and 3. Figure 2 represents the households consisting of a single adult with one, two, or three children, while Figure 3 is concerned with two adult households without a child and with one, two, or three children.

3.3. EXPLANATIONS

Economies of scale due to decreasing expenditure shares for basic goods like food are perhaps the most important explanation for the negative correlation between the equivalence scales and the reference income level. While budget shares for basic goods decrease with increasing income, budget shares increase for those goods which can be regarded as public goods for the household members. Especially in the low income

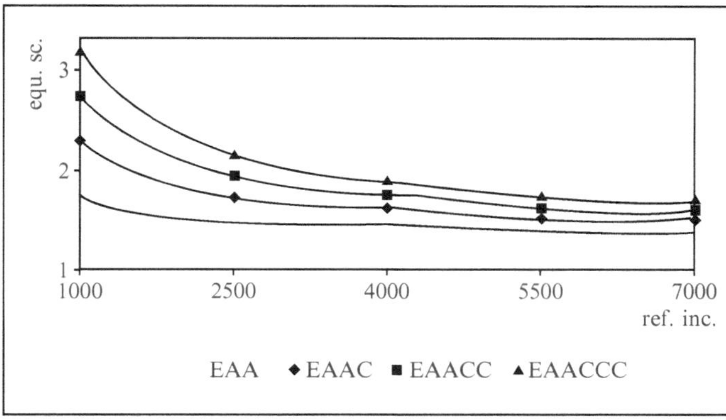

Figure 3. Two adults equivalence scales.

classes the public good component of basic goods like food is quite small but their budget share is quite high. Therefore, it is plausible that scale values are a convex function of reference income as in Figures 2 and 3.

Another explanation for decreasing equivalence scales may be derived from the studies of Caplovitz (1967) and Piachaud (1974) which show that prices for goods differ between the subgroups of the population. Especially the members of the low income classes are not able to take advantage of favorable purchases due to missing liquidity, technically insufficient possibilities (no freezer for example), and close quartered living space. There exists also discrimination against members of the low income classes, for example in the housing market.

Nelson (1993) explains the drop of weights for children as income rises by the hypothesis that parents limit expenditure for children since they are worried about spoiling them. This is underlined in our study by the fact that despite of multiplying the reference income by a factor of seven from the lowest to the highest income class, mean absolute incomes for children only rise by a factor of 1.4. In contrast to this, the income elasticity of the weight for the second adult is evidently lower, possibly due to the aim of representing the household by status symbols in an adequate way. In this context also the argument of Stolz (1983) should be noticed, who explains the income elasticity of the equivalence scales by a correlation between consumption patterns and the social position of an individual.

4. A Comparison of Weights for Children in One Parent and Two Parent Households

4.1. RESULTS OF PREVIOUS STUDIES

The dependency of children weights on the number of parents living in the household has hardly been taken into account in the literature until now. Even corresponding to scales from the OECD or the social legislation in Germany, a child who lives in a one parent family should get the same absolute income as a child living in a two parent family. Employing an expenditure based approach, Merz and Faik (1995) as well as Lancaster and Ray (1998) empirically estimate separate scale values for children living in one parent and two parent households without interpreting them in this context. The results of both studies imply higher income amounts for children in two parent than for children in one parent families.

4.2. THE RESULTS OF OUR STUDY

Table II presents an overview of our results. The values presented in the columns 2-4 represent the minimal, maximal and mean absolute incomes for children cumulated over all children in the household. Again, the abbreviations represent the demography and the reference income of the household: A indicates an adult, C a child, and the adjacent number is the reference income. Thus, for instance the value ICCAA4000 represents the additional income amount (I) a household consisting of two adults and two children given a reference income of 4000 Deutschmarks needs in order to reach the same living standard as the childless two adult household.

In the column *Diff.* the mean income for children in a two parent household is subtracted from the mean income for children in a one parent household. Except for one insignificant exception, all differences are positive. The significance of these differences was examined by a T-test which confirms that the additional income needed in order to keep the same living standard for children in a one parent family is significantly higher than for those in a two parent family with the same reference income. This result is true for all five reference income classes. The mean difference, which can be interpreted as a bonus for one parent households, is 48.33 Deutschmarks. Except for the marked ones, all cases are significant at the 0.05 level.

In Table III, the additional income amounts for children (not cumulated) are expressed in terms of children weights (W). There are two possibilities for standardization: On the one hand the additional income amounts for children can be divided by the reference income of a single adult. This method does not take into account whether it is a one parent or a two parent family. On the other hand, the income amounts for children in a two parent family can also be divided by the income of the two parent family in the relevant reference income class. To simplify comparisons, the last standardization is used since analyzes in the literature in general refer to the income of a two parent household. The abbreviations are the same as above. Consequently, the value WCCAA4000 is the additional amount of income for the second child, divided by the income for a two adult household at a reference income of 4000 Deutschmarks, the household needs in order to keep its standard of living if demography changes from one child to two children. All weights for children living in a one parent family are evidently and significantly higher than those for children living in two parent families.

TABLE II. Cumulated incomes for children

	Min.	*Max.*	*Mean*	*Std.d.*	*Diff.*	*T*
ICA1000	100	1500	569.521	230.138		—
ICAA1000	100	1500	516.228	224.885	53.294	3.566
ICCA1000	200	2000	1020.359	397.968		—
ICCAA1000	200	2500	972.036	422.167	48.323	2.916
ICCCA1000	300	4000	1473.353	611.777		—
ICCCAA1000	300	4000	1420.958	684.209	52.395	2.526
ICA2500	0	1700	603.293	284.708		—
ICAA2500	0	2400	557.485	296.396	45.808	2.984
ICCA2500	0	2500	1090.419	488.326		—
ICCAA2500	0	3500	1061.258	533.042	29.162	⋆1.511
ICCCA2500	200	3750	1572.036	708.256		—
ICCCAA2500	200	5500	1550.898	780.320	21.138	◇.820
ICA4000	0	2400	689.820	439.556		—
ICAA4000	0	3840	608.323	429.475	81.497	3.848
ICCA4000	0	4000	1255.389	723.654		—
ICCAA4000	0	5160	1179.401	702.151	75.988	2.921
ICCCA4000	0	6000	1797.006	1015.567		—
ICCCAA4000	0	6480	1708.006	1008.129	89.000	2.651
ICA5500	0	2500	704.790	491.685		—
ICAA5500	0	3520	662.275	480.644	42.515	2.181
ICCA5500	0	4500	1283.533	825.195		—
ICCAA5500	0	5280	1248.862	865.006	34.671	◇1.240
ICCCA5500	0	6000	1861.617	1153.869		—
ICCCAA5500	0	7040	1863.713	1255.997	-2.096	◇-.048
ICA7000	0	3500	788.922	612.972		—
ICAA7000	0	4480	728.988	579.414	59.934	2.133
ICCA7000	0	5000	1435.928	1018.458		—
ICCAA7000	0	6720	1383.587	1034.636	52.341	⋆1.442
ICCCA7000	0	6300	2058.563	1404.133		—
ICCCAA7000	0	8960	2017.599	1466.647	40.964	◇.910

Note. *Min.* denotes the lowest value stated. *Max.* denotes the highest value stated. *Std.d.* denotes the standard deviation. *Diff.* means difference and *T* is the t statistic. ⋆ denotes significance at the 0.5 percent level. ⋆⋆ denotes significance at the 10 percent level. ◇ denotes insignificance. All other values are significant at the 1 percent level.

4.3. EXPLANATIONS

The higher values of the weights for children in one parent families compared with those in two parent families can be explained by two reasons. Since a couple needs a higher income than a single, in order to reach the same standard of living, the costs

TABLE III. Weights for children

	Min.	*Max.*	*Mean*	*Std.d.*	*T*
WCA1000	.10	1.50	.570	.230	—
WCAA1000	.05	.75	.297	.129	18.215
WCCA1000	.00	1.00	.451	.223	—
WCCAA1000	.00	.92	.262	.148	14.641
WCCCA1000	.00	2.20	.453	.270	—
WCCCAA1000	.00	1.25	.256	.171	12.137
WCA2500	.00	.68	.241	.114	—
WCAA2500	.00	.60	.149	.077	10.637
WCCA2500	.00	.50	.195	.097	—
WCCAA2500	.00	.60	.134	.073	9.196
WCCCA2500	.00	.60	.193	.106	—
WCCCAA2500	.02	.42	.132	.072	15.599
WCA4000	.00	.60	.173	.110	—
WCAA4000	.00	.60	.103	.068	12.853
WCCA4000	.00	.50	.141	.082	—
WCCAA4000	.00	.31	.098	.057	9.808
WCCCA4000	.00	.50	.135	.084	—
WCCCAA4000	.00	.31	.090	.057	10.264
WCA5500	.00	.45	.128	.089	—
WCAA5500	.00	.40	.084	.055	10.476
WCCA5500	.00	.36	.105	.068	—
WCCAA5500	.00	.24	.075	.051	16.214
WCCCA5500	.00	.36	.105	.068	—
WCCCAA5500	.00	.46	.079	.061	10.683
WCA7000	.00	.50	.113	.088	—
WCAA7000	.00	.40	.072	.052	11.798
WCCA7000	.00	.30	.092	.065	—
WCCAA7000	.00	.20	.065	.044	6.092
WCCCA7000	.00	.30	.089	.063	—
WCCCAA7000	.00	.20	.063	.043	8.940

Note. *Min.* denotes the lowest value stated. *Max.* denotes the highest value stated. *Std.d.* denotes the standard deviation. *Diff.* means difference and T is the t statistic. All values are significant at the 0.5 percent level.

for children of the two parent household are divided by a higher income value. This technical effect is a result of the construction of the weights and causes higher children weights in one parent families. On the other hand, even the absolute income amounts stated for children in one parent families are higher than those in two parent families. Since the absolute costs for children in one parent families are probably higher due to higher expenditure for external child care this result is plausible.

5. Functional Representation and Estimation of Equivalence Scales

This section proposes a particular function for the representation of our results. According to our function the equivalence scale $E(a, c, y)$ for a household consisting of a adults and c children is at the reference income level y given by:

$$E(a, c, y) = 1 + \frac{D(a-1)}{y^G} + \frac{dc^f}{y^g + a}. \tag{2}$$

For the parameters D, d, f, and G, g our fitting yields the following values: $D = 19.22$, $d = 75.25$, $f = 0.91$, $G = 0.43$, and $g = 0.73$. These values imply that all scale values are a decreasing and convex function of reference income.

The structure of our function is intuitively plausible: A single adult reference household always receives a value of unity, since in this case both the second and third term on the right side equal zero. In two adult households the third term again equals zero while the second one is always positive but decreasing with the reference income level. If there are children in the household the second term is positive. The value of this quotient increases sub-proportionally with the number of children and decreases with increasing reference income and increasing number of adults (one or two) in the household (corresponding to the bonus for one parent households). Note that we have as result of our estimation $g > G$ which implies that the children weights are more sensitive to changes of the reference income than the weight for the second adult.

Table A.II in the Appendix compares the observed mean values of the equivalence scales with the estimates on basis of our function. Obviously, the chosen functional form fits the data rather good.

6. Conclusion

We have presented equivalence scales derived from a survey where subjects have been asked to assess the income needs of different hypothetical households given five levels of reference income of a reference household. We find that equivalence scales obtained negatively depend on the level of reference income. This finding strongly questions the results of previous studies where equivalence scales have been assumed to be constant. Obviously, this constancy assumption either means an overestimation of the needs of "rich" or the underestimation of the needs of "poor" multi-person households or the mis-specification of the needs of both. Second, the number of adults in the household turns out to be an important criterion for the evaluation of children needs. According to our respondents, the income needs of children are an increasing function of the number of adult household members. It is, therefore, necessary to broaden economic models with respect to this interaction.

Appendix

TABLE A.I. Breakdown of the sample

	N	*Share*		N	*Share*
Gender			Partner in the household		
Female	71	.43	*Yes*	97	.58
Male	96	.57	*No*	70	.42
Number of children in the household			Occupational group		
None	123	.73	*Welfare Recipient*	2	.01
One	18	.11	*Unemployed*	5	.03
Two	15	.10	*Blue-collar worker*	10	.06
More than two	11	.06	*White-collar worker*	96	.58
Number of Brothers and Sisters			*Pupil, student, trainee*	34	.20
None	31	.19	*Self-employed*	7	.04
One	55	.33	*Pensioner*	10	.06
Two	47	.28	*Housewife, houseman*	3	.02
More than two	34	.20	Education		
Net income of the household[a]			*No finished education*	1	.01
<1750	32	.20	*Finished ext. element. school*	21	.13
1750–3249	44	.26	*Finished secondary school*	39	.23
3250–4749	37	.22	*Finished German*		
4750–6249	37	.22	*secondary school*	65	.39
>6249	17	.10	*University degree*	41	.24

Note. [a] values in Deutschmarks.

TABLE A.II. Empirical means and estimated values

	Mean	*Estim.*		*Mean*	*Estim.*
	—		*EAA1000*	1.75	1.99
	—		*EAA2500*	1.49	1.66
	—		*EAA4000*	1.46	1.54
	—		*EAA5500*	1.39	1.47
	—		*EAA7000*	1.39	1.43
EAC1000	1.57	1.49	*EAAC1000*	2.27	2.47
EAC2500	1.24	1.25	*EAAC2500*	1.72	1.91
EAC4000	1.17	1.18	*EAAC4000*	1.61	1.72
EAC5500	1.13	1.14	*EAAC5500*	1.51	1.61

Table continues.

TABLE A.II.

Continuation of Table A.II.

	Mean	*Estim.*		*Mean*	*Estim.*
EAC7000	1.11	1.12	*EAAC7000*	1.49	1.54
EACC1000	2.02	1.91	*EAACC1000*	2.73	2.90
EACC2500	1.44	1.47	*EAACC2500*	1.92	2.13
EACC4000	1.31	1.33	*EAACC4000*	1.75	1.87
EACC5500	1.23	1.26	*EAACC5500*	1.61	1.74
EACC7000	1.21	1.22	*EAACC7000*	1.59	1.65
EACCC1000	2.47	2.32	*EAACCC1000*	3.17	3.31
EACCC2500	1.63	1.68	*EAACCC2500*	2.12	2.34
EACCC4000	1.45	1.48	*EAACCC4000*	1.89	2.02
EACCC5500	1.34	1.38	*EAACCC5500*	1.73	1.85
EACCC7000	1.29	1.32	*EAACCC7000*	1.68	1.75

Note. *Mean* gives the average equivalence scale of the sample. *Estim.* gives the estimate using the parameters of the functional form chosen.

References

Aaberge, R., and I. Melby 1998. "The Sensitivity of Income Inequality to Choice of Equivalence Scales," *Review of Income and Wealth* 44, 565–569.

Atkinson, A. B. 1983. *The Economics of Inequality*, Oxford.

Blackorby, C., and D. Donaldson 1988. "Adult-Equivalence Scales and the Economic Implementation of Interpersonal Comparisons of Well-Being," University of British Columbia, Discussion Paper No. 88–27.

Caplovitz, D. 1967. it The Poor Pay More, New York: The Free Press.

Conniffe, D. 1992. "The Non-Constancy of Equivalence Scales," *Review of Income and Wealth* 38, 429–443.

Coulter, F. A. E., F. A. Cowell, and S. P. Jenkins 1992. "Differences in Needs and Assessment of Income Distributions," *Bulletin of Economic Research* 44, 77–124.

Dickens, R., V. Fry, and P. Pashardes 1993. "Non-Linearities and Equivalence Scales," *The Economic Journal* 103, 359–368.

Donaldson, D., and K. Pendakur 2004. "Equivalent-expenditure Functions and Expenditure-dependent Equivalence Scales," *Journal of Public Economics* 88, 175–208.

Dubnoff, S. 1985. "How much Income is Enough? Measuring Public Judgements," *Public Opinion Quarterly* 49, 285–299.

Faik, J. 1995. *Äquivalenzskalen, Theoretische Erörterungen, empirische Ermittlung und verteilungsbezogene Anwendung für die Bundesrepublik Deutschland*, Berlin: Duncker and Humblot.

Friedman, R. D. 1965. *Poverty, Definition and Perspective*, Washington D. C: American Enterprise Institute.

Goedhart, T., V. Halberstadt, A. Kapteyn, and B. M. S. van Praag 1977. "The Poverty Line. Concept and Measurement," *Journal of Human Resources* 12, 503–520.

Hartog, J. 1988. "Poverty and the Measurement of Individual Welfare. A Review of A. J. M. Hagenaars' The Persception of Poverty," *Journal of Human Resources* 23, 243–266.

Kapteyn, A., S. van de Geer, and H. van de Stadt 1984. *The Impact of Changes in Income and Family Composition on Subjective Measures of Well-Being*, Netherlands Central Bureau of Statistics, Department for Statistics of Income and Consumption, Voorburg.

Kapteyn, A., and B. M. S. van Praag 1976. "A New Approach to the Construction of Family Equivalence Scales," *European Economic Review* 7, 313–335.

Klein, T. 1994. "Einkommen und Bedarf im Haushaltszusammenhang - Äquivalenzskalen als Instrument der Wohlfahrtsmessung," in: Hauser, R., N. Ott, and G. Wagner (eds.), *Mikroanalytische Grundlagen der Gesellschaftspolitik*, vol. 2, Berlin: Akademie-Verlag, 278–294.

Klein, T. 1986. *Aquivalenzskalen - Ein Literatursurvey*, SfB 3-working paper 195, Frankfurt am Main and Mannheim.

Koulovatianos, C., C. Schröder, and U. Schmidt 2005. "On the Income Dependence of Equivalence Scales," *Journal of Publics Economics* forthcoming.

Lancaster, G., and R. Ray 1998. "Comparison of Alternative Models of Household Equivalence Scales: The Australian Evidence on Unit Record Data," *The Economic Record* 74, 1–14.

Lewbel, A. 1989. "Household Equivalence Scales and Welfare Comparisons," *Journal of Public Economics* 39, 377–391.

Merz, J., and J. Faik 1995. "Equivalence Scales Based on Revealed Preference Consumption Expenditures, The Case of Germany," *Jahrbücher für Nationalökonomie und Statistik* 214, 425–447.

Missong, M., and I. Stryck 1998. "Lineare Ausgabensysteme, Existenzminima und Sozialhilfe," *Jahrbücher für Nationalökonomie und Statistik* 217, 574–587.

Nelson, J. A. 1993. "Independent of Base Equivalence Scales Estimation Using United States Micro-Level Data," *Annales DEconomie et de Statistique* 29, 43–63.

Piachaud, D. 1974. *Do the Poor Pay More?*, London: Child Poverty Action Group.

Rainwater, L. (1974), *What Money Buys: Inequality and the Social Meanings of Income*, New York.

Rein, M. 1974. "Problems in the Definition and Measurement of Poverty," in: Townsend, P. (ed.), *The Concept of Poverty*, London: Heinemann, 46–63.

Seidl, C. 1994. "How Sensible is the Leyden Individual Welfare Function of Income," *European Economic Review* 38, 1633–1659.

Seneca, J. J., and M. K. Taussig 1971. "Family Equivalence Scales and Personal Income Tax Exemptions for Children," *The Review of Economics and Statistics* 53, 253–262.

Stolz, I. 1983. *Einkommensumverteilung in der Bundesrepublik Deutschland, Eine theoretische und empirische Untersuchung*, Frankfurt am Main and New York: Campus Verlag.

Townsend, P. 1962. "The Meaning of Poverty," *British Journal of Sociology* 13, 210–227.

Van der Gaag, J., and E. Smolensky 1982. "True Household Equivalence Scales and Characteristics of the Poor in the United States," *The Review of Income and Wealth* 28, 17–28.

Van Hoa, T. 1986. "Measuring Equivalence Scales: A New System-Wide Method," *Economics Letters* 20, 95–99.

Carsten Schröder
Institut für Volkswirtschaftslehre
Universität Kiel
D-24098 Kiel
Germany
u2261@bwl.uni-kiel.de

Ulrich Schmidt
Lehrstuhl für Finanzmarkttheorie
Universität Hannover
Königsworther Platz 1
D-30167 Hannover
Germany
U.Schmidt@mbox.vwl.uni-hannover.de

UTILITY INDEPENDENCE IN HEALTH PROFILES: AN EMPIRICAL STUDY

ANA M. GUERRERO
Universidad de Alicante

CARMEN HERRERO
Universidad de Alicante & IVIE

1. Introduction

Quality-adjusted life years (QALYs) are the most frequently used outcome measure in cost utility analysis. In cost utility analysis the benefits of health care programs are not expressed in monetary terms but rather in utility terms. They provide a straightforward procedure to combine quantity of life and quality of life into one single index measure. Each possible outcome of a medical treatment can be described by means of a health profile that indicates the states of health an individual will experience over his lifespan, after treatment. These possible health profiles can be assigned a particular number of QALYs. Thus, QALYS, interpreted as a utility model, assign a utility index to every individual health profile. QALYs have the advantage of being easy to calculate, and of having an intuitively appealing interpretation. Their disadvantage is that they require the individual preference relation to satisfy some restrictive conditions. Given the importance of the QALY measure and the many discussions about its appropriateness, further insights into such restrictive conditions are important.

In a risk environment, the utility functions for evaluating health profiles come from the analysis of individual preferences over lotteries on health profiles. The methodology used to analyze those preferences is based on the multi-attribute evaluation theories (see Krantz et al., 1971, Keeney and Raiffa, 1976, Miyamoto, 1983, 1988) where the attributes in a health profile are the health status levels in the various periods. Under expected utility, two different utility functions representing individual preferences over lotteries on health profiles are obtained whenever individual preferences satisfy certain properties (see Bleichrodt, 1995, Bleichrodt and Gafni, 1995). If individual preferences satisfy *additive independence* the utility function over health profiles is additive, whereas when individual preferences satisfy the weaker property of *mutual utility independence* (see Keeney and Raiffa, 1976, Miyamoto, 1988), a multi-

U. Schmidt and S. Traub (eds.), Advances in Public Economics: Utility, Choice and Welfare, 135-150.

plicative utility function is obtained. This property states that conditional preferences for lotteries on every subset of the attributes in a health profile are independent of its complement. As an example of the meaning of this property, in a riskless environment, it says that preferences between profiles that contain the same health state in period t do no depend upon the severity of the health state in period t, whatever t is.

Mutual utility independence is equivalent to the simultaneous fulfilment of two weaker assumptions: *initial utility independence, and final utility independence.* These two assumptions state that conditional preferences for lotteries over the final (initial) health states are independent of its complement, the initial (final) health states. Obviously, if mutual utility independence is fulfilled, then both initial and final utility independence hold. For the reverse implication, substitute preferential by utility independence in Theorem 1, Section 4 in Gorman (1968).

The adequacy of the QALY model to represent individual preferences on health profiles has been criticized. Some authors defend that the utility of a health profile cannot be determined by adding or multiplying the single period utilities of health states (see Krabbe and Bonsel, 1998, Richardson et al., 1996, Kuppermann et al., 1997). On the contrary, this utility should be elicited with respect to the entire profile. If the utility of a health state in a single period depends on either preceding or subsequent periods in the profile, then this criticism may have merit. In this respect, Loomes and McKenzie (1989) say:

> ...an individual who experiences several months of moderate discomfort as part of a treatment which he expects to result in improvements may place a rather different value on the experience compared with an individual for whom the same period in the same state of discomfort is seen as a phase in a degenerative illness, with a much lower expectation of recovery.

The general message of this statement is that, in choosing between alternative treatments, the long run, that is, the possibility of recovery, matters. Sequence effects and the preference for *happy endings* have been also reported extensively (see Krabbe and Bonsel, 1998, Ross and Simonson, 1991). That is, changes in the final health states that could involve changes in the life horizon can affect the individual's evaluation of her initial health states and, thus, final utility independence could be violated in certain cases.

In a recent paper (Guerrero and Herrero, 2005), we relax the mutual utility independence assumption by only assuming initial utility independence. The resulting utility function is just a generalization of the additive or multiplicative utility functions traditionally used to evaluate health profiles. The main reason to explore such a generalization was made on the grounds of previous criticisms that may indicate that, in the individual evaluation of health profiles, *mutual utility independence* could be too strong a requirement. Since, as mentioned before, *mutual utility independence* is equivalent to the simultaneous fulfilment of two weaker independence assumptions, it seemed natural to ask whether either of them, and in particular, *initial utility independence* is more adequate to explain individual preferences.

In this paper we empirically address the problem of testing the adequacy of the assumption of *mutual utility independence* by comparing the fulfillment of the two weaker assumptions of *initial utility independence* and *final utility independence.* To do so, we carried out a survey using three different sets of questionnaires, administered to three different groups of people. The subjects of the first group were students from the University of Alicante, between 18 and 20 years old, the second group of agents were people between 21 and 64 and, finally, the third group of people were older than 65. In the survey all agents answer a total of 22 questions, where they were confronted with choices between pairs of medical treatments, some of them risky, and some others riskless. Those questions give rise to 8 tests of independence for each individual: 4 tests of *initial independence*, two of them in a risky context and the rest in a riskless one, and 4 tests of *final independence*, all of them in a riskless context. At an aggregate level, we determine whether most of the subjects satisfy or violate *initial (final) independence* for each test. At an individual level, we determine whether most of the tests satisfy or violate *initial (final) independence* for each subject.

The importance of the study is clear. If *mutual utility independence* is satisfied, we can be persuaded of the adequacy of the QALY model to represent preferences on health profiles. If, on the contrary, it is violated, we may think that alternative models of the holistic type could be more appropriate to represent such preferences. In particular, the more supported *initial independence* is, the better the semiseparable model in Guerrero and Herrero (2005) is for representing preferences on health profiles.

The paper is structured as follows. In Section 2, different independence assumptions are presented as well as some previous studies commented. Section 3 describes the design used in the survey to test initial and final independence. The results are commented in Section 4. Discussion in Section 5 close the paper. A complete description of the health states, as well as of the tests for all groups of people are presented in Appendices A.1 and A.2.

2. Independence Assumptions and Background

Different independence assumptions have been used in the literature, in dealing with preferences over risky profiles when health varies over time. We briefly summarize them.

Additive independence Additive independence holds when preferences between risky alternative treatments only depend upon the marginal probability distributions of the health states, rather than on their joint probability distributions (see Bleichrodt & Quiggin, 1997). Under additive independence, an individual have identical preferences between treatments A and B, where the results of A and B are, respectively, $L_A = [(x_t, x_{-t}), 1/2; (x_t^a, x_{-t}^a)]$, and $L_B = [(x_t, x'_{-t}), 1/2; (x_t^b, x_{-t}^b)]$, for all t, all x_t, and for all $x_{-t}, x'_{-t}, x_t^a, x_{-t}^a, x_t^b$, and x_{-t}^b., where x_t, x_t^a, x_t^b represent health states at period t, and $x_{-t}, x'_{-t}, x_{-t}^a$, and x_{-t}^b stand for different health profiles at any period different from t.

Under additive independence (and expected utility), the utility function for health profiles has an additive form (see Bleichrodt and Quiggin, 1997).

Mutual utility independence Mutual utility independence holds when preferences between risky treatments involving only changes at an specific period do not depend on the severity at which health state at that period is held fixed. Under mutual utility independence, an individual has identical preferences between treatments A and B, where the results of A and B are, respectively $L_A = [(x_t, x_{-t}), p; (x_t, y_{-t})]$, and $L_B = [(y_t, x_{-t}), p; (y_t, y_{-t})]$, for all t, all x_t, y_t, all p, and all x_{-t}, y_{-t}.

Under mutual utility independence (and expected utility), the utility function over health profiles has a multiplicative form (see Bleichrodt and Gafni, 1995). In a non-risky scenario this property is called *mutual preferential independence.*

Initial utility independence Initial utility independence holds when preferences between risky treatments involving changes only at the final periods do not depend on the severity at which health states at the initial periods are held fixed. Under initial utility independence, an individual has identical preferences between treatments A and B, where the results of A and B are, respectively, $L_A = [(\overleftarrow{x}_{t-1}, \overrightarrow{x}_t), p; (\overleftarrow{x}_{t-1}, \overrightarrow{y}_t)]$, and $L_B = [(\overleftarrow{y}_{t-1}, \overrightarrow{x}_t), p; (\overleftarrow{y}_{t-1}, \overrightarrow{y}_t)]$, for all t, all $\overleftarrow{x}_{t-1}, \overleftarrow{y}_{t-1}$, all p, and all $\overrightarrow{x}_t, \overrightarrow{y}_t$, where $\overleftarrow{x}_{t-1}, \overleftarrow{y}_{t-1}$ represent the health states enjoyed in certain health profiles up to period $t-1$, and $\overrightarrow{x}_t, \overrightarrow{y}_t$ stand for the health states enjoyed from period t onwards.

Under initial utility independence (and expected utility), the utility function over health profiles has a semi-separable form (see Guerrero and Herrero, 2005). In a non-risky scenario this property is called *initial preferential independence.* Whenever there is no possibility of misunderstanding, we will simply refer to *initial independence*, both for the risky and riskless scenarios.

Final utility independence Final utility independence holds when preferences between risky treatments involving changes only at the initial periods do not depend on the severity at which health states at the final periods are held fixed. Under final utility independence, an individual has identical preferences between treatments A and B, where the results of A and B are, respectively, $L_A = [(\overleftarrow{x}_{t-1}, \overrightarrow{x}_t), p; (\overleftarrow{y}_{t-1}, \overrightarrow{x}_t)]$,and $L_B = [(\overleftarrow{x}_{t-1}, \overrightarrow{y}_t), p; (\overleftarrow{y}_{t-1}, \overrightarrow{y}_t)]$, for all t, all $\overleftarrow{x}_{t-1}, \overleftarrow{y}_{t-1}$, all p, and all $\overrightarrow{x}_t, \overrightarrow{y}_t$. In a non-risky scenario, this property is called *final preferential independence.* As before, if there is no possibility of misunderstanding, we will refer to *final independence.*

Clearly, under expected utility, independence for risky choices imply also independence for riskless choices, while the reverse is not true. When expected utility is challenged, then tests for both the risky and the riskless cases should be studied independently.

Treadwell (1998) tested mutual preferential independence (the riskless version of mutual utility independence). He found that mutual preferential independence hold in 36 out of the 42 tests he performed. Spencer (2003) tested additive independence but her results are poorly consistent with additive independence.

Additional studies for the case in which health does not vary over time have addressed the utility independence of survival duration and quality of life. Miyamoto and Eraker (1988) obtained a positive answer to that question, while Bleichrodt and Johannesson (1997) found evidence against. Abellan et al. (2004) tested the predictive validity of different multiplicative models, obtaining that power models outperform linear and exponential models.

3. Method

3.1. SUBJECTS

The subjects of the study were 135 people, divided into three age groups. *Young,* 49 students from the University of Alicante, between 18 and 20 years old, enrolled in different undergraduate studies. *Middle,* 47 people between 20 and 65 years old, with different professional activities, and *Elderly,* 39 retired people of over 65. These two last groups involve people who were patients in a health center, their relatives or friends and some nurses. Our sample then, seems to be more representative of the general population than when students alone are considered. In all cases, a personal interview, conducted by the authors, was performed.

3.2. HEALTH STATES

Four health states were used in the questionnaires. The health states were indicated by capital letters: from A, "excellent health" to D, "severe", with two intermediate health states, B and C. In order to describe the health states, we considered just two of the five dimensions used in the EuroQol EQ–5D:[1] (1) usual activities (e.g. work, study, housework, family or leisure activities), and (2) pain or discomfort. These two dimensions have been chosen because they are related to two effects on health conditions observed in many diseases. Both dimensions have 3 levels. The dimensions, their levels and the health states are shown in Appendix A.1. These health states are naturally ordered so that A is perceived as better than B, B better than C, and C better than D.

3.3. HEALTH PROFILES

Different health care programs or medical treatments may give rise to different individual benefits that can come described by different health profiles. An individual health profile describes the quality of life over the individual lifespan, that is, her health states in the various periods of life. The attributes in a health profile are the health status levels in the various periods. Here these attributes are described by using "chronic intervals" in which a certain (chronic) health state is experienced during some consecutive periods of life. A typical health profile is described by two or three different chronic intervals. For example, the health profile $A_{10}B_{10}C_2$ has three

[1] The five dimensions used in the EuroQol EQ–5D are: (1) Mobility; (2) Self-care; (3) Usual activities (e.g. work, study, housework, family or leisure activities); (4) Pain/Discomfort; (5) Anxiety/Depression.

chronic intervals: the first one made out of 10 years in health state A, the second one made out of another 10 years in health state B, and finally, a chronic interval of 2 years in health state C. In all cases, and whenever those profiles were presented to the subjects, they were understood as possible profiles they would enjoy from now onwards. These profiles were also considered as *final*, in the sense that they identified the individual's future case history as complete, i.e., the total number of years of each chronic interval, the health state during each chronic interval, the sequence, and the time of death. For the Young group, we presented profiles of a maximum horizon of 55 years. This duration was reduced to 30 years for the Middle group of agents, and to 15 for the Elderly group. The health profiles proposed to the agents were quite diverse. They did not have a fixed life-span, namely, duration of life was a relevant variable. Moreover, health profiles were made up from chronic intervals that could be of different duration. They corresponded to non-constant health profiles, so that the states of health were different during different periods.

3.4. DESIGN AND MATERIALS

The agents in each age group were given a questionnaire with 22 different questions. In all the questions, we asked participants to imagine a hypothetical condition, and to choose between two medical treatments that result on two different health profiles. The hypothetical conditions used were related to renal failure, headache, back pain, rheumatism and accident injuries. An example of the sort of questions posed to the agents in which two alternatives treatments, one certain (T1) and the other contingent (T2), were proposed, is the following.

"You have been diagnosed as having renal failure. During the next 4 years, however, you will not suffer from any symptoms. There are two different treatments, to be applied in 4 years time.

T1: If you choose this treatment, you will live for 15 years more in health state B. After that 15 year-period, you will die.

$$A_4B_{15}$$

T2: With the alternative treatment (a transplant), and provided it is successful (likelihood 95%), you will live for 26 more years in excellent health (A) following which, you will die. If the treatment fails (likelihood 5%), you will live in a severe state (D) for 10 years, and then you will die.

95% chance of A_{30}
5% chance of A_4D_{10}

What treatment would you prefer? Tick either T1 (if you prefer the first treatment), T2, (if you prefer the second treatment)."

The comparisons between choices made in these questions were used to create the tests of initial and final independence. These tests are described for the three age-groups in Appendix A.2: the former are tests 1–4 and the later are tests 5–8.

In order to test *initial utility independence* there were 8 questions in which the individuals have to choose between two health profiles that have in common the initial health states. The question of the example is one of those. Initial utility independence tests were performed by confronting the choices in two questions involving two pairs of health profiles in which we have changed the health state appearing in the common initial periods. By way of example in test 1 (for the young group) we confront the choice made in the previous question with the choice made in a question involving these two health profiles T1': D_4B_{15} and T2': 95% chance of D_4A_{26}; 5% chance of D_{14}. In this test the preferences of an individual satisfy initial utility independence if, simultaneously, she prefers T1 to T2 and T1' is preferred to T2', or if, simultaneously, she prefers T2 to T1 and T2' is preferred to T1'. From the choices made in the 8 questions we have made 4 tests of initial independence. Two out of them were tests in which decisions were made in a risky scenario: a contingent situation is presented to the agent. Thus, two alternative profiles are possible, each one with some probability. Uncertainty is associated with the application of a certain medical treatment in such a way that there is a high probability (95% for young people, and 90% otherwise) of success, and a low probability (5% and 10% respectively) of failure. Probabilities were chosen in line with the usual likelihood of success physicians consider suitable to propose a given medical treatment to a patient.

In testing the property of final independence, we have to deal with profiles tied at the final periods. Thus, in this case, unlike the initial independence tests, when choosing between two treatments, the profiles coming from them should have identical duration and, moreover, health states should coincide at the last periods of life. Fulfilling these conditions in a risky scenario is rather counterintuitive. That is why we only tested the property of final independence in a riskless context. It is satisfied if the preference order of health profiles involving only changes on the initial health states does not depend on the final health states held fixed. Note that changes in the final health states could also involve changes in the life horizon. In order to test final preferential independence there were also 8 questions in which the individuals had to choose between two health profiles that have in common the final health states. Final independence tests were performed by confronting the choices in two questions involving two pairs of health profiles in which we have changed the health state appearing in the common final periods. By way of example, in test 5 (for the young group) we confront the choice made in a question involving these two health profiles, T1: D_3A_{52} and T2: $B_{15}A_{40}$, with the choice made in a question involving these two health profiles, T1': $D_3A_{12}C_{40}$ and T2': $B_{15}C_{40}$. In this test the preferences of an individual satisfy final independence if, simultaneously, she prefers T1 to T2 and T1' is preferred to T2', or if, simultaneously, she prefers T2 to T1 and T2' is preferred to T1'. From the choices made in the 8 questions we have made 4 tests of final preferential independence.

There were 6 consistency tests that completed the choices made by the individuals, and were only added to verify that individuals choices were consistent. Note that, among the tests performed in the context of certainty, there were 6 of the type known as replacement tests (see Treadwell, 1998): the alternative health situations presented in any given test are not dominant, in the sense that neither of them is clearly preferred to the other.

In Appendix A.2 we describe the tests of initial utility independence and the tests of final preferential independence.

3.5. PROCEDURE

The subjects were individually interviewed by the authors. First, they read a brief description of each of the different health states presented in Appendix A.1. It was emphasized in the instructions that only one of the four health states would be experienced during any given interval of time. It was also explained that their choices should be based exclusively on their own opinions about the proposed situations without taking the effects of these situations on their family and/or friends into account. All individuals faced 22 choices each. The pairs of questions corresponding to each of the independence tests were placed far from each other in the questionnaire (to avoid memory effects). Moreover, each choice appeared on a separate sheet of paper, to discourage references to choices other than the current one. In this way, we avoided identical answers, made by inertia, in pairs of questions belonging to the same test. In facing every choice, the subjects were asked to imagine that they are experiencing a particular illness or accidental injury, that could be treated with two alternative treatments causing two different health profiles. They were then asked about the treatment they would prefer in the case of suffering such illness or accidental injury. At every choice, the interviewers explained at least two alternative real situations underlying each health profile. Thus, it was quite likely that individuals could imagine and assess such situations. The real situations included some of the following health conditions: cardiovascular conditions, renal failure, headache, back pain, AIDS, rheumatism and accidental injuries. The participants generally required about 40 minutes to make all of their choices, after which, they were debriefed.

4. Results

All the participants agreed on state D being worse than state C, C being worse than state B, and B being worse than state A. As for the independence tests, we present the results at both the aggregate and the individual level.

4.1. AGGREGATE ANALYSIS

We analyzed the choices made by each individual between both pairs of health situations in every independence test. From these choices, we obtained, at an aggregate level, the proportion of individuals who satisfy the independence property in each test. To do so, we performed a simple application of the "sign-matching tests" introduced in Miyamoto et al. (1997). We computed an "independence score" for each test and for each subject. Since the questionnaire was only filled-in once, each test was coded as 1, if independence was satisfied by that subject, and 0 if independence was violated. The mean value of the independence score for each of the tests represents the proportion of individuals satisfying initial utility (final preferential) independence in each test and it is an estimate of the true mean probability that responses to the given test will be consistent with these independence properties. If the mean value of the independence score for test n exceeds (is less than) .5, then we can say that the results for test n are *qualitatively consistent (inconsistent)* with initial utility (final preferential) independence. It is known that if a statistical test shows that the mean value of independence score is significantly greater than .5 at the α (we will consider $\alpha = .05$) level of significance then evidence is strong that the population mean of independence scores is greater than .5. In this study we use a binomial test that is an appropriate statistical test. If it shows that this mean value is significantly greater than (less than) .5, we can say that this mean value is *significantly in favor (in violation)* of initial utility (final preferential) independence.

The mean independence scores for the 4 initial utility independence tests for young, middle and elderly groups are qualitatively in favor of initial independence, and all the 95% confidence intervals does not overlap .5. Therefore the results are also significantly in favor of initial utility independence in the statistical sense mentioned above.

The mean independence scores for the 4 final preferential independence tests are: greater than .5 for the young group; greater than .5 in tests 6 and 8 and equal to .5 in tests 5 and 7, for the middle group; less than .5 for the elderly group. The 95% confidence intervals for the 4 final preferential independence tests: does not overlap .5 in tests 5 and 6, but overlap .5 in tests 7 and 8, for the young group; overlap .5 for both the middle and the elderly group. Therefore, the results in the four tests of the young group and in tests 6 and 8 for the middle group are qualitatively in favor of final independence, whereas only the results in tests 5 and 6 for the young group are significantly in favor of final preferential independence. Consequently, the results of all the tests for the middle and elderly are significantly inconsistent with final preferential independence. If we concentrate on the results across ages initial independence is equally fulfilled, independently of age, while final independence is less fulfilled as age increases.

4.2. INDIVIDUAL ANALYSIS

Here we consider individual choices, rather than group choices. We analyze whether our individuals' preferences fulfill initial independence and/or final independence. We determine whether independence is significantly satisfied or violated, for each of the 135 individuals separately. To do so, we also perform a simple application of the "sign-matching tests". We computed an "independence score" for each subject for each test. Since the questionnaire was only filled-in once, each test was coded as 1, if independence was satisfied by that subject and 0, if independence was violated. The mean independence scores for each subject represent the proportions of independence tests satisfied by each subject. If the mean values for *initial (final) independence* tests in a subject were equal or higher than .5, it would indicate a qualitatively satisfaction of *initial utility (final preferential) independence* for this subject. Considering the total sample of 135 individuals, the percentage of individuals satisfying initial independence is 94.807%, while the percentage of individuals satisfying final independence, is 66.106%. Both independence assumptions are simultaneously satisfied by 60.737% of the individuals. This individual analysis indicates that the property of *initial independence* is better fulfilled than the property of *final independence.*

TABLE I. Proportion of individuals satisfying Initial Independence (*II*) or Final Independence (*FI*)

% total sample	*II*	*FI*
Young	97.95	77.55
Middle	93.61	74.46
Elderly	92.3	41.66

If we disaggregate the individual analysis for each group, we obtain that: (1) For the Young group the percentage of individuals satisfying *initial utility independence* (*II*) is 97.95 %, whereas the percentage of those satisfying *final preferential independence* (*FI*) is 77.55%; (2) For the Middle group the percentage of individuals satisfying *initial utility independence* (*II*) is 93.61 %, whereas the percentage of individuals satisfying *final preferential independence* (*FI*) is 74.46%; (3) For the Elderly group the percentage of individuals satisfying *initial utility independence* (*II*) is 92.3%, whereas the percentage of those satisfying *final preferential independence* (*FI*) is 41.66%. These results are summarized in Table 1.

The percentage of individuals fulfilling final preferential independence is much lower for the *Elderly* group than for any of the other groups. Nonetheless, the percentages of people fulfilling *initial utility independence* are quite similar across ages.

5. General discussion

In our study we obtained a differentiated behavior in dealing with independence across ages. While it was more commonly satisfied than violated for young and middle aged people, this was not the case for elderly people. Indeed if we focus on the individual level, *initial independence* is reliably satisfied, whereas *final independence* is less better fulfilled as age increases. Some of the tests were performed in a context of risk, which is the most natural context in which to deal with health evaluations. It is noteworthy, however, that there are no significant differences in the results obtained in this experiment whether we consider the tests under either certainty or risk. Our findings do not challenge the satisfaction of the property of mutual utility (preferential) independence, but clearly show that one part of the independence property (i.e., *initial independence*) is much better fulfilled than the other part (i.e, *final independence*), and in particular, as age increases.

There are other empirical studies in the literature, related to ours. In the following sequel, we try to compare their results to our own findings.

In Hall et al. (1992) it was observed that, in some cases, the cause-of-death can explain different evaluations of identical health profiles that ended in death from different causes. A similar effect was observed in some of our tests on fertility conditions. Such findings contradict the additive structure of the QALY model which makes no allowance for a cause-of-death or type-of-condition effect.

In Krabbe and Bonsel (1998) evidence of a sequence effect in health is reported. Decreasing health profiles were less attractive to subjects than similar increasing health profiles. These sequential effects also contradict the additive structure in the QALY model.

In an experiment without sequence effects Richardson et al. (1996) also found no evidence of the fulfilment of additive utility independence. Their study highlights the differences between two different approaches to the measurement of multi-phase health states: 1) The holistic evaluation approach, in which subjects were asked to adopt the long-term perspective of a prospective patient and judge the entire course of subsequent events and 2) the conventional QALY approach, obtained by adding-up the present value of independently assessed QALYs in each state. The main reason given for the discrepancy observed between these two different approaches is not the framing of the empirical analysis, but rather the negative discount rates applied by individuals in the evaluation of health profiles. These discount rates increase the relative importance of the last years of life in the health profiles.

Our results hold, regardless of the size and valence of the subject's discount rates. Our tests of independence are satisfied or violated, regardless of time discounting. Nonetheless, negative discount rates are more compatible with *initial independence* than with *final independence*. If the final periods are more important than the initial periods in the evaluation of a health profile, then it seems natural to assume that changes in health states in the final periods should influence the valuation of such a health profile more than changes in the initial periods. Consequently, sequence effects contradict the additive structure with positive or zero discount rates in the QALY model, although they may well be consistent with models that only require initial independence.

Something similar can be said of the results in Kuppermann et al. (1997). They suggest that, at least from the perspective of an individual, preferences for the various sequences of events that may follow a specific pre-natal diagnostic decision are not necessarily separable and additive. Our selection of health profiles are close to the health profiles selected by Kupperman in the sense that ours also represent health outcome paths derived from real situations. Unlike Kuppermann et al., our health profiles do not present salient cross-interval influences that would be expected to produce independence violations.

Finally, Treadwell (1998) presents a study supporting preferential independence and thus, the application of the QALY model. Our findings are very similar to his *for the young group.* As such, when restricted to students as respondents, we quite agree with his results. There are, nonetheless, significant differences as age increases, an aspect that is not explored there. In some sense, we can think of our study as complementary to Treadwell's, since we include not only additional age groups, but risky profiles as well. Furthermore, at the individual level, the better adequacy of the *initial independence* assumption over the *preferential independence* becomes apparent. Unlike Treadwell, in our independence tests we consider health profiles of different life-spans. His health profiles are all 30 years long; likewise, "chronic" periods in our health profiles are of variable duration. His are all of 10 years. Finally, we consider more health states (4 instead of 3) explained by two attributes, and ours are also associated with a greater amount of illnesses, some of which are associated with severe conditions.

In summarizing, we faced the following question: can individual preferences on discrete health states be used to deduce individual preferences on health profiles? If so, is the additive QALY model the right one to represent such preferences? To answer these questions, we designed a survey to test the fundamental assumptions behind the QALY model, namely, preferential independence. Our results indicate not only that the independence assumption is fulfilled in many cases, *but* also that the assumption of *initial independence* is better fulfilled than the assumption of *preferential independence*, and in particular, as age increases. Our results, as well as those obtained by other authors, are better explained by a *semi-separable* structure than by an additive structure in the QALY model. Even though the semiseparable model seems to represent individual preferences better, it is far more complicated to estimate. We, therefore, face a trade-off between simplicity and accuracy in the representation of individual preferences.

Appendix

A.1. HEALTH STATE DESCRIPTIONS

USUAL ACTIVITIES

- Able to perform all usual activities (e.g. work, study, housework, family or leisure activities) **without problems.**
- **Not** able to perform **many** usual activities.
- **Not** able to perform **any** usual activity.

PAIN/ DISCOMFORT

- **No** pain or discomfort.
- **Often** light to moderate pain or discomfort.
- **Often** moderate to severe pain or discomfort.

We presented four health states to the subjects in our study. They are described by combining different levels of the two previous attributes. The health states are called A, B, C, D, and they are chosen so that

$$A \succ B \succ C \succ D$$

We define each health state as follows:

- A Able to perform all usual activities **without problems.** **No** pain or discomfort.
- B Able to perform all usual activities **without problems.** **Often** light to moderate pain or discomfort.
- C **Not** able to perform **many** usual activities. **Often** light to moderate pain or discomfort.
- D **Not** able to perform **any** usual activity. **Often** moderate to severe pain or discomfort.

A.2. DESCRIPTION OF INDEPENDENCE TESTS

Young Group

Initial Independence tests (1–4)

Test 1
T1: 5% chance of A_4D_{10}
95% chance of A_{30}
T2: A_4B_{15}
T1': 5% chance of D_{14}
95% chance of D_4A_{26}
T2': D_4B_{15}

Test 2
T1: 5% chance of C_4D_{10}
95% chance of C_4A_{26}
T2: C_4B_{15}
T1': 5% chance of D_{14}
95% chance of D_4A_{26}
T2': D_4B_{15}

Test 3
T1: A_4B_{30}
T2: $A_{31}D_3$
T1': D_4B_{30}
T2': $D_4A_{27}D_3$

Test 4
T1: A_4B_{30}
T2: $A_{31}D_3$
T1': C_4B_{30}
T2': $C_4A_{27}D_3$

Final Independence tests (5–8)

Test 5
T1: D_3A_{52}
T2: $B_{15}A_{40}$
T1': $D_3A_{12}C_{40}$
T2': $B_{15}C_{40}$

Test 6
T1: D_3A_{17}
T2: $B_{15}A_5$
T1': $D_3A_{12}B_5$
T2': B_{20}

Test 7
T1: $B_8D_4C_{30}$
T2: C_{42}
T1': $B_8D_4A_{30}$
T2': $C_{12}A_{30}$

Test 8
T1: B_8D_9
T2: $C_{12}D_5$
T1': $B_8D_4B_5$
T2': $C_{12}B_5$

Middle Group

Initial Independence tests (1–4)

Test 1
T1: 10% chance of B_5D_{20}
90% chance of $B_5A_{20}D_5$
T2: $B_5A_{10}B_{10}$
T1': 10% chance of D_{25}
90% chance of $D_5A_{20}D_5$
T2': $D_5A_{10}B_{10}$

Test 2
T1: 10% chance of D_{10}
90% chance of D_4B_{21}
T2: $D_4A_{14}C_2$
T1': 10% chance of A_4D_6
90% chance of A_4B_{21}
T2': $A_{18}C_2$

Test 3
T1: $A_{24}D_6$
T2: A_5B_{25}
T1': $D_5A_{19}D_6$
T2': D_5B_{25}

Test 4
T1: $D_6B_{16}D_8$
T2: D_6C_{24}
T1': $A_6B_{16}D_8$
T2': A_6C_{24}

Final Independence tests (5–8)

Test 5
T1: D_2A_{28}
T2: $B_{10}A_{20}$
T1': $D_2A_8D_{20}$
T2': $B_{10}D_{20}$

Test 6
T1: D_2A_9
T2: $B_{10}A_1$
T1': $D_2A_8D_1$
T2': $B_{10}D_1$

Test 7
T1: $B_4D_2A_{24}$
T2: C_6A_{24}
T1': B_4D_{26}
T2': C_6D_{24}

Test 8
T1: $B_4D_2A_1$
T2: C_6A_1
T1': B_4D_3
T2': C_6D_1

Elderly group

Initial Independence tests (1–4)

Test 1
T1: 10% chance of B_2D_{11}
90% chance of $B_2A_{10}D_3$
T2: $B_2A_5B_6$
T1': 10% chance of D_{13}
90% chance of $D_2A_{10}D_3$
T2': $D_2A_5B_6$

Test 2
T1: 10% chance of D_5
90% chance of D_2B_{11}
T2: $D_2A_7C_1$
T1': 10% chance of A_2D_3
90% chance of A_2B_{11}
T2': A_9C_1

Test 3
T1: $A_{12}D_3$
T2: A_5B_{10}
T1': $D_5A_7D_3$
T2': D_5B_{10}

Final Independence tests (5–8)

Test 5
T1: D_1A_{14}
T2: B_5A_{10}
T1': D_1A_5
T2': B_5A_1

Test 6
T1: D_1A_5
T2: B_5A_1
T1': $D_1A_4D_1$
T2': B_5D_1

Test 7
T1: $B_2D_1A_{12}$
T2: C_3A_{12}
T1': B_2D_{13}
T2': C_3D_{12}

Test 4
T1: $D_3B_8D_4$
T2: D_3C_{12}
T1': $A_3B_8D_4$
T2': A_3C_{12}

Test 8
T1: $B_2D_1A_3$
T2: C_3A_3
T1': B_2D_4
T2': C_3D_3

Acknowledgements

Thanks are due to John Miyamoto and Han Bleichrodt for helpful comments. Financial support from the Spanish Ministry of Education (SEJ2004-08011), Generalitat Valenciana (GROUPOS03-086), Fundacion BBVA (BBVA1-04X), and from the Instituto Valenciano de Investigaciones Económicas are gratefully acknowledged.

References

Abellan, J. M., J. L. Pinto, I. Mendez, and X. Badia. 2004. *A Test of the Predictive Validity of Non-linear QALY Models Using TTO Utilities*, WP 741, Universitat Pompeu Fabra.

Bleichrodt, H. 1995. QALYs and HYEs: "Under What Conditions Are They Equivalent?", *Journal of Health Economics* 14, 17–37.

Bleichrodt, H., and A. Gafni. 1995. "Time Preference, the Discounted Utility Model and Health", *Journal of Health Economics* 15, 49–66.

Bleichrodt, H., and J. Quiggin. 1997. "Characterizing QALYs Under a General Rank Dependent Utility Model", *Journal of Risk and Uncertainty* 15, 151–1.

Bleichrodt, H., and M. Johannesson. 1997. "The Validity of QALYs: An Empirical Test of Constant Proportional Tradeoff and Utility Independence", *Medical Decision Making* 17, 21–32.

Gorman, W. M. 1968. "The Structure of Utility Functions", *Review of Economic Studies*, 367–390.

Guerrero, A., and C. Herrero. 2005. "A Semi-separable Utility Function for Health Profiles", *Journal of Health Economics* 24, 33–54.

Hall J., K. Gerard, G. Salkeld, and J.A. Richardson. 1992. "A Cost Utility Analysis of Mammography Screening in Australia", *Social Sciences and Medicine* 34, 993–1004.

Keeney, R. L., and H. Raiffa. 1976. *Decisions with Multiple Objectives: Preferences and Value Trade-offs*, New York: Wiley.

Krabbe, P. F. M., and G. J. Bonsel. 1998. "Sequence Effects, Health Profiles, and the QALY model", *Medical Decision Making* 18, 178–186.

Krantz, D.H., R.D. Luce, P. Suppes, and A. Tversky. 1971. *Foundations of Measurement. Volume I: Additive and Polynomial Representations*, New York: Academic Press.

Kuppermann M., S. Shiboski, D. Feeny, E. P. Elkin., and A. E. Washington. 1997. "Can Preference Scores for Discrete States Be Used to Derive Preference Scores for an Entire Path of Events? An Application to Prenatal Diagnosis", *Medical Decision Making* 17, 152–159.

Loomes, G., and L. McKenzie. 1989. "The Use of QALYs in Health Care Decision Making", *Social Science and Medicine* 28, 299–308.

Miyamoto, J. M. 1983. "Measurement Foundations for Multi-attribute Psychophysical Theories Based on First Order Polynomials" *Journal of Mathematical Psychology* 27, 152–182.

Miyamoto, J. M. 1988. "Generic Utility Theory: Measurement Foundations and Applications in Multi-attribute Utility Theory", *Journal of Mathematical Psychology* 32, 357–404.

Miyamoto J. M., J. W. Lundell, and S. Tu . 1997. *Sign Matching Tests for Ordinal Independence in Paired Comparison and Rating Data*, Working paper, Seattle, Washington: Department of Psychology, University of Washington.

Miyamoto J. M., and S. A. Eraker. 1988. "A Multiplicative Model of Utility of Survival Duration and Health Quality", *Journal of Experimental Psychology: General* 117, 3–20.

Richardson J., J. Hall, and G. Salkeld. 1996. "The Measurement of Utility in Multiphase Health States", *International Journal of Technology Assessment in Health Care* 12, 151–162.
Ross, W.T., and I. Simonson. 1991. "Evaluations of Pairs of Experiences: A Preference for Happy Endings", *Journal of Behavioral Decision Making* 4, 273–282.
Spencer A. 2003. "A Test of the QALY Model when Health Varies over Time", *Social Sciences and Medicine* 57, 1697–1706.
Treadwell J. R. 1998. "Tests of Preferential Independence in the QALY Model", *Medical Decision Making* 18, 418–428.

Carmen Herrero
Departamento de Fundamentos de Análisis Económico
Universidad de Alicante
Campus San Vicente
E-03071 Alicante
Spain
Carmen.Herrero@ua.es

Ana M. Guerrero
Departamento de Fundamentos de Análisis Económico
Universidad de Alicante
Campus San Vicente
E-03071 Alicante
Spain
anague_4@hotmail.com

CONSTRUCTING A PREFERENCE-ORIENTED INDEX OF ENVIRONMENTAL QUALITY

A Welfare-Theoretic Generalization of the Concept of Environmental Indices

MICHAEL AHLHEIM
Universität Hohenheim
OLIVER FRÖR
Universität Hohenheim

1. Introduction

In the literature on environmental indices these measures are typically seen as informational tools for the communication between environmental experts, politicians and the public at large. To this end environmental indices are presumed to make complex and detailed information on the state of the environment simpler and more lucid. They may serve as a means of resource allocation, of judging and comparing the quality of different locations, of measuring the success of environmental policy or of informing the public on the development of environmental quality in a country or in certain geographic regions. This multipurpose character of environmental indices implies the well-known dilemma inherent in this concept: on the one hand environmental indices should be easy to understand and to interpret also for laymen and on the other hand the information they convey should not be trivial or too superficial. Their construction implies a reduction of complex multidimensional environmental specifics to a single number which obviously goes along with a considerable loss of information as compared to the original data set underlying the respective indices. The reason why one is willing to accept this loss of information is the hope that more people will be interested in such a condensed informational tool than in the complex data set on which it is based. Clearly, the dilemma between comprehensibility and scientific profoundness is not easy to resolve. Looking at the main environmental indices used today one might get the impression that the intention to find the middle ground between these two claims has led to constructions that are neither much noticed in the public nor very instructive from a scientific point of view. So, today there is not much left of the euphoria of the early days. In spite of the fact that most countries and also supranational institutions like the OECD (cf. OECD 2001) have implemented

U. Schmidt and S. Traub (eds.), Advances in Public Economics: Utility, Choice and Welfare, 151-172.

systems of environmental indicators to monitor and illustrate the success of their environmental policy these indicators are largely unknown to most people as well as to most politicians (see also Wiggering and Müller, 2004).

Since environmental indices are supposed to inform scientists, politicians and the public of changes in the state of the environment they are regarded as a yardstick for the success of environmental policy as a whole and en detail. As long as environmental indices reflect the knowledge and opinion of experts only as it is typical of most indices today, they cannot be expected to attract much attention: on the one hand the scientific information they contain is too highly aggregated and, therefore, too superficial to be of interest to the scientific community and on the other hand common people do not find in these indices what they are interested in since the informational content is not oriented by people's preferences. This latter point might also be responsible for the indifference of most politicians to environmental indices since they are mainly interested in the perception of their environmental policy efforts by their voters and not in the objective results of this policy, as is well-known from public choice theory.

Against this political background we suggest to construct a class of indices which are grounded on household preferences instead of expert opinion. In particular, we propose to use household preferences as an aggregator for the valuation of environmental changes (air quality, water quality, climate, traffic, radiation etc.) when constructing an overall environmental index. Since such an index reflects people's attitudes towards environmental changes as well as the perception and valuation of these changes by the people it may represent a significant element of communication between politicians and their voters regarding the success of environmental policy. It should be noted that, of course, such a "People's Index of Environmental Quality" cannot substitute completely for traditional expert indices but it can complement them.

The fundamental dilemma of environmental indices, i. e. how to convey exact expert information and attract public attention at the same time, can be solved by separating these tasks. If pure expert indices are freed from the burden of being popular they may contain more detailed and more exact information and, therefore, they might turn out to be more satisfactory for the scientific community[1] while preference-oriented indices on the other hand might develop to be attractive instruments of information among politicians, the media and the people. It is well-known that environmental policy can be successful only if it is accepted and supported by the people and if it becomes part of the social norms guiding people when they have to make non-economic decisions. Therefore, a preference-based index of environmental policy as proposed here might provide an attractive link between policy makers on the one hand and "the people" on the other. A regular (e.g. annual) publication of such an index would keep politicians as well as the public at large informed about

[1] Within the scientific community the so-called pressure-state-response framework (PSR) for environmental indicators has become very popular and has also been adopted as official framework by EUROSTAT. For a detailed presentation of this concept and practical issues see Markandya and Dale (2001).

developments in the main sectors of our natural environment filtered through the preferences of the citizens concerned by these developments.

The paper is organized as follows: Section 2 contains a short overview of the most important existing environmental indices and of their main characteristics. In Section 3 we discuss the construction and the main features of descriptive environmental indices and indicators. In Section 4 we propose the construction of a preference-based environmental index and discuss the possibilities for its empirical assessment and practical implementation. The last section contains some concluding remarks.

2. Environmental Indices in Practice

Before we propose a preference-oriented environmental index we want to give a short overview over the most important environmental indices which are used now in the practice of environmental monitoring. While we will focus on descriptive indices of environmental states, we will include two normative indices, as well. There exists a variety of different indices in the literature, therefore, this selection doesn't claim to be comprehensive. However, the examples were chosen so as to reflect the main developments up to date.

2.1. DESCRIPTIVE ENVIRONMENTAL INDICES

The most popular descriptive indices are the Environmental Quality Index (EQI) for Canada (cf. Inhaber, 1974), the Hope and Parker Index (HPI) for the UK, France and Italy (Hope and Parker, 1990, 1995), the Mirror of Cleanliness (MoC) for the Netherlands (den Butter, 1992) and the Korean Composite Environmental Index (CEI) described in Kang (2002). A conceptually slightly different variety has been developed by Ten Brink et al. (1991) known as the Ecological Dow Jones (EDJ) which found its applications also mainly in the Netherlands. The construction of all mentioned descriptive indices follows a two-step procedure. In a first step, suitable indicators representative for an environmental issue are selected or created from underlying data. Subsequently, the set of these indicators is aggregated to an overall index number using an appropriate aggregator function.

Within the first group of indices it can be observed that the importance of the respective index as an information tool for the public increases over time. The Canadian EQI was designed as a pure index of the state of the environment that was to serve as an information tool for the administration and national statistics. This is reflected by the fact that the first step of the index construction procedure, the creation of the set of indicators from environmental data, strictly follows the criteria of environmental experts, while the second step follows a purely arbitrary aggregation procedure in which an equal importance of the single indicators is assumed. As a consequence, the set of indicators reflects very specific and well weighted information and could serve as an informational basis for policy making in the respective environmental issues. The final index number of the EQI, however, seems to contain little information as the assumption of equal importance of environmental issues is highly doubtful.

A conceptually similar approach has been taken for the MoC whereas the level of environmental data is not as detailed as in the EQI. On the contrary, the computation of a pollution index was meant to be particularly simplified by the use of selected environmental quantities that were found to be representative, i.e. indicative, of some pollution theme. Still no solution could be proposed as to the determination of the relative importance of the pollution themes in an objective way.

In contrast to the Canadian EQI and the MoC, the Hope and Parker Index shifts the focus of the environmental index away from the pure expert index to an index that on the one hand takes people's perceptions of the different environmental issues into account and on the other hand aims at creating an information tool specifically for the broader public (cf. Hope and Parker, 1990, 1995). While the selection and creation of the set of indicators is based on expert knowledge the (additive) aggregation to the final index number of the HPI considers people's preferences for the determination of the aggregation weights. To this end the weights for the indicators are determined by public opinion surveys concerning people's state of worry with respect to the various environmental issues. The index is meant to be published on a monthly basis.

A refinement of the HPI can be found in the Korean CEI (cf. Kang, 2002). This index makes use of the respective core indicators for "environmental themes" recommended by the OECD (cf. OECD, 2001). Furthermore, the determination of the final aggregation weights follows a strict hierarchical process in which the respondent to a public survey will produce a priority list of the various environmental themes and will also state the degree of seriousness concerning each theme. Consequently, the CEI reflects the public's trade-offs between the various environmental themes in a more consistent way.

Finally, an index that does not make use of any measured environmental data but is simply based on changes of abundances of indicator species in representative ecosystems is the so-called "Ecological Dow Jones" described in Ten Brink et al. (1991). As such, this index is a pure expert index and completely ignores public preferences toward the various species or ecosystems.

2.2. NORMATIVE INDICES

A different type of environmental indices are normative indices which combine the measurement of certain indicator values with a normative statement. One form of normative indices are achievement indices that are designed to measure and visualize the extent to which a specific environmental goal, i. e. the normative statement, has already been attained. Another form can be seen in the comparison of a state index with a normative statement of sustainability. Examples of these two forms are given in the following.

The first example is the German Environmental Index (DUX) which was developed in the year 1999 for the specific purpose of conveying information about the effectiveness of national environmental policy to the general public. The degree of target achievement of six theme-related sub-indices is computed separately and subsequently added up to form an overall score of achievement of German environmental policy. While no weighting according to public preferences is included in the index, its computational simplicity and close connection to policy making are characteristics that could in principle lead to considerable perception in the broader public. The second example for an achievement index recently found in the literature, the Health-related Environmental Index (HEI) proposed by Wheeler (2004), refrains from the calculation of an overall index number and stops at the level of a set of four health-related indicators which he, however, calls "indices". The aim of this set of indicators is to inform policy makers and the public about spatial inequity with respect to environmental (living) conditions in order to identify those regions within a country that should be given a high priority for environmental improvements. The construction of these indicators is based on the relation of measured environmental data, e.g. ambient pollutant concentration in a certain region, to a threshold value (i.e. the target) considered acceptable from a health-related point of view. As such, this set of indicators is purely based on expert knowledge.

The so-called Ecological Footprint (EF) as an example of a sustainability index represents a normative index in the sense that it allows the direct comparison to a normative measure of sustainability (cf. Rees, 1992, 2000, Chambers et al., 2000). However, in contrast to the simplicity of the DUX its conceptual approaches of "carrying capacity" and "bioproductive areas" of a country is highly problematic from a scientific as well as from a computational point of view. While aggregate index numbers are without doubt very appealing for policy making and for the information of the public the EF has certainly reached a limit of validity.

Of all the described indices the DUX had the best chances of becoming an influential index for German environmental policy due to its clear and simple message of target achievement and to its embedding into the German environmental administration. However, the DUX has failed to prove operational mainly because of delays in data collection and inconsistent data categories among the various administrative bodies.

3. The General Structure of Environmental Indices

In the literature the terms "environmental index" and "environmental indicator" are not always used in a consistent way. In our presentation we follow Ott (1978, p. 8) in defining an environmental indicator as a function of environmental data and an environmental index as a function of environmental indicators.

While an environmental index describes the condition of "the environment" as a whole environmental indicators are more specific. It is common practice that each indicator characterizes a particular aspect of the environment like the classical environmental media water, soil or air quality. In the more recent literature these media have been extended by the so-called environmental themes climate, landscape, radiation, noise etc. For simplicity's sake in what follows we shall treat the traditional environmental media (water, air, soil etc.) as a subset of the more comprehensive category of "environmental themes" since all arguments relevant for this paper hold for "media" as well as for "themes".

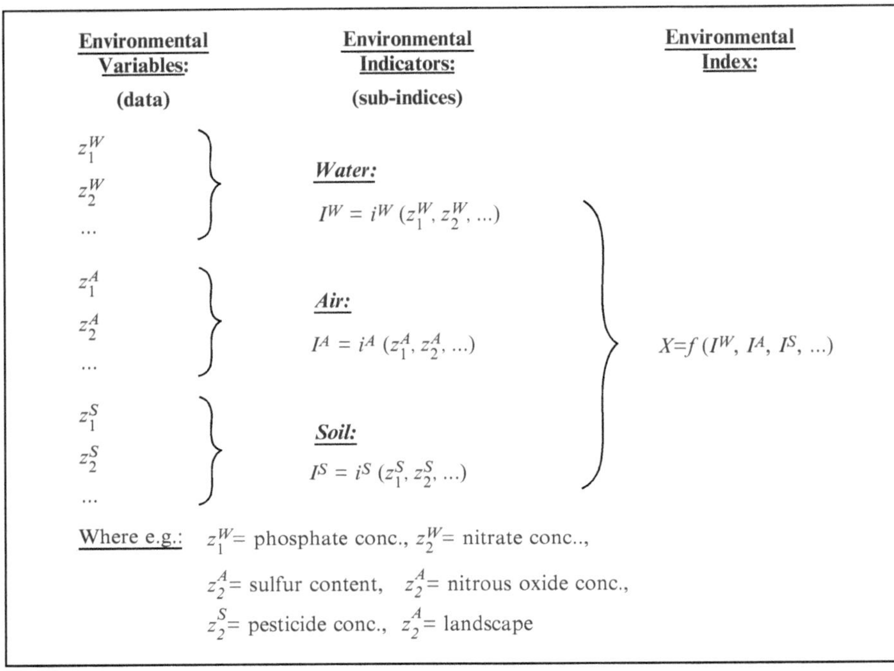

Figure 1. The relation between environmental data, indicators and indices.

3.1. ENVIRONMENTAL INDICATORS

The first step of constructing an environmental index consists in the collection of data pertaining to the various environmental themes mentioned above. Then these data are aggregated to theme related indicators (water, air, soil, climate ...) where each indicator is a mathematical function defined on the variables characterizing the respective medium or theme. These indicators serve as arguments of a mathematical function that describes the overall state of the environment by a single number, the environmental index. Therefore, indicators are often also referred to as sub-indices. The relation between environmental data, indicators and indices is illustrated in Figure 1. Figure 1 illustrates that at each stage of this aggregation process information is lost on the one hand while simplicity and intelligibility of the environmental "message" is gained on the other. Obviously, there is no single "correct" way of aggregating e.g. air pollution data (nitrogen oxides, sulphur dioxide, carbon dioxide etc.) to form an air quality indicator. There is always a certain degree of arbitrariness inherent in the choice of an aggregation function

$$I^j = i^j\left(z_1^j, z_2^j, \ldots\right) \quad (j = A, W, S, \ldots). \tag{1}$$

If more than one variable is to be included in an indicator I^j, it is common practice to normalize these values (i. e. by dividing them by some reference or base value $\bar{z}_k^j$) so that I^j as well as z_k^j become dimensionless numbers where $k = 1, 2, \ldots, K$ denotes the various data or variables characterizing the environmental medium or theme $j = A, W, S, \ldots$ (air, water, soil ...)[2]. If $(\partial I^j / \partial z_k^j) > 0$ and variables z_k^j represent pollutants, the indicator I^j is a pollution indicator, while it is an environmental quality indicator if z_k^j stands for something positive for the environment (like e.g. the number of species per acre of land).

An aggregator function for environmental indicators that is very popular in practice is the weighted sum of the measured data (see e.g. the German DUX, the Ecological Dow Jones Index or the indices proposed by Hope and Parker, 1990, or Ten Brink et al., 1991):

$$I^j = \sum_{k=1}^{K} a_k \cdot z_k^j \,. \tag{2}$$

Such a linear aggregation implies that the influence of the different variables on the value of the indicator is constant no matter how high the concentration of the respective pollutant is. Things are different if instead of such a mechanical aggregation form a so-called functional aggregator like a CES function[3] with the general form

$$I^j = \left(\sum_{k=1}^{K} a_k \cdot \left(z_k^j \right)^{\varrho} \right)^{1/\varrho} \tag{3}$$

is used. Here the absolute weight of a pollutant within an indicator changes as its quantity changes. For $\varrho > 1$ the relative weight of a pollutant $\frac{\partial I^j / \partial z_k^j}{\partial I^j / \partial z_n^j}$ increases c. p. with its quantity while for $\varrho < 1$ it is just the other way round. Of course, there are many other possibilities of aggregating environmental variables which have different implications with respect to the relative weights of the various pollutants (for a thorough treatment of these problems cf., e.g. Ott, 1978) but for practical environmental indicators mostly either a weighted sum or a CES function is used as an aggregator.

The question which kind of aggregator should be used cannot be answered in general. It depends on the environmental theme or medium to be described by the indicator and on the kind of variables z_k^j. At least in cases where the variables z_k^j describe more or less technical data whose consequences for the environment as a whole cannot be comprehended by laymen, aggregation should be based on the advice of natural scientists or environmental experts.

---

[2] Normalization is, of course, only possible and meaningful for ratio-scale measurable variables, like e.g. masses or pollutant loads (cf. Ebert and Welsch, 2004). For interval-scale measurable variables, like e.g. most commonly used temperature units, normalization yields meaningless numbers unless transformed to their origin unit (e.g. Kelvin in this case).

[3] CES stands for "Constant Elasticity of Substitution".

3.2. ENVIRONMENTAL INDICES

Another aggregation process is needed to obtain an overall environmental index X based on the various theme- or media-related environmental indicators, i. e.

$$X = X(\pi) \quad \text{where} \quad \pi = [I^A, I^W, I^S, \ldots] \,. \tag{4}$$

Here the vector π represents the environmental profile to be valued by the index X. This profile consists of the theme-related indicators or sub-indices for air, water, soil etc. Again, we have the choice between a multitude of different aggregation functions. Also at this stage the most popular and most wide-spread aggregation form is the weighted sum of the indicators so that

$$X = \sum_{j=A,W,S,\ldots} b_j \cdot I^j \,. \tag{5}$$

This implies that the absolute weights of the different environmental media or themes in the overall index are constant no matter what their actual state is:

$$\frac{\partial X}{\partial I^j} = b_j = const \,. \tag{6}$$

Accordingly, the weight relation between two different indicators, i. e. their marginal rate of substitution

$$MRS_{r,j} = -\frac{dI^j}{dI^r}\bigg|_{\mathrm{dX=0}} = \frac{\partial X/\partial I^r}{\partial X/\partial I^j} = \frac{b_r}{b_j} \quad (r,j = A, W, S, \ldots) \tag{7}$$

is also constant along the index level curves (i. e. for $X = const.$). The marginal rate of substitution between e.g. water and air $MRS_{W,A}$ indicates by how much the indicator for water quality I^W must increase if the indicator for air I^A decreases by an infinitesimally small unit and the value of the overall index X is to be constant. It denotes how large an increase in water quality is necessary in order to compensate for a marginal deterioration of air quality so that the overall index is constant. This can be illustrated graphically in a $(I^W \times I^A)$-diagram like Figure 2 where the MRS between water and air quality equals the slope of the level curves for different values X_1, X_2 and X_3 of the index X. Such a level curve is the locus of all $(I^W - I^A)$-combinations that generate the same value of the index function $X(I^A, I^W, I^S, \ldots)$. For the linear aggregator (5), which is quite popular in practice, these level curves are straight lines with a negative slope equal to $(-b_r/b_j)$ as shown in Figure 2. It follows that this aggregation form implies a constant compensation scheme even in extreme cases where one of the media under consideration is nearly destroyed (like "air" in point B in Figure 2). Even then a further loss of quality of this medium can be compensated by the same improvement of another medium like water in Figure 2 as in a situation where the quality of all media is well-balanced like in point A in Figure 2.

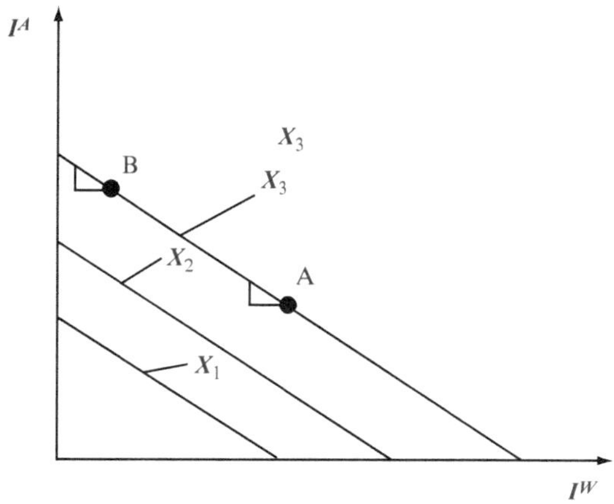

Figure 2. Trade-off between water and air quality with a linear aggregator.

The question arises if the marginal trade-off between e.g. water and air quality is really independent of the actual condition of the two media. Would it not be more plausible to assume that the relative importance of an environmental medium like air quality or an environmental theme like traffic or noise increases as its general condition deteriorates? This would definitely be more in accordance with what most people feel. Nevertheless, the linear aggregation form (5) is rather common in practice. It is used e.g. for one of the most important German environmental indices, the so-called DUX ("Deutscher Umwelt Index"), which is published monthly by the Umweltbundesamt. Choosing the weighted sum of media and theme related indicators as an overall environmental index is also proposed e.g. by Hope and Parker (1990, 1995) for the U.K. They recommend to consider people's preferences when fixing the weights of the different themes in the overall sum [the b_j in (5) above]. Though this is an improvement compared to the determination of these weights by expert opinion only we are still left with the problem of constant compensation rates between sub-indices.

As an alternative aggregator the already mentioned CES function is also quite popular in practice (see e.g. Inhaber, 1974, den Butter, 1992, or den Butter and van der Eyden, 1998). Applied to our aggregation problem here it assumes the general form

$$X = \left(\sum_{j=W,A,S,\ldots} b_j \cdot \left(I^j\right)^{\varrho} \right)^{1/\varrho} . \tag{8}$$

Here, the influence of the different media on the index value varies with the value of the respective indicator

$$\frac{\partial X}{\partial I^j} = b_j \cdot (I^j)^{\varrho)-1} \left(\sum_r b_r \cdot (I^r)^{\varrho} \right)^{\frac{1-\varrho}{\varrho}} \tag{9}$$

and the marginal rate of substitution between the values of two different indicators

$$MRS_{j,r} = -\frac{dI^j}{dI^r}\bigg|_{\mathrm{dX=0}} = \frac{b_r}{b_j} \cdot \left(\frac{I^r}{I^j} \right)^{\varrho-1} \tag{10}$$

varies with the environmental quality mix expressed by the ratio (I^r/I^j):

$$\frac{\partial MRS_{j,r}}{\partial I^r} = \frac{(\varrho - 1) \cdot b_r \, (I^r)^{\varrho-2}}{b_j \, (I^j)^{\varrho-1}} \tag{11}$$

as can be seen from Figure 3. In Figure 3 the standard case of a CES-based environmental quality index is shown where the value of X increases as the values of the media related environmental quality indicators I^j increase, i. e. $X_1 < X_2 < X_3$. For an environmental quality index the parameter ϱ is typically chosen smaller than one in the aggregator function (8) which leads to convex level curves as shown in Figure 3. The trade-off between different media depicted there seems to be quite plausible from an empirical point of view. The relative weights of the different media change along a level curve of the index X, i. e. for a changing mix of air and water quality with X being constant (e.g. at a level $X = X_3$). In an extreme situation like in point B where air quality is low compared to water quality it takes a much higher increase in water quality to compensate for a further loss in air quality than in a more balanced environmental situation like point A. Such a flexible compensation scheme where the relative importance of an environmental medium increases as its quality decreases seems to be more in accordance with our everyday experience than the rigid compensation type of the linear aggregator (5).

Nevertheless, in the literature on environmental indices it is often suggested to use the additive aggregation form (5) for the computation of environmental indices from media- or theme-related sub-indices. In most contributions it is recommended to choose the coefficients of the different media in this aggregation process according to the suggestions of environmental experts. Other authors propose to choose these aggregation weights in accordance with people's preferences which are to be assessed in opinion surveys. This proposal was made e.g. by Hope and Parker (1990, 1995) for an environmental index for the U.K. Using a CES aggregator as proposed e.g. by Inhaber (1974), den Butter (1992), or den Butter and van der Eyden (1998) is even closer to human preferences towards environmental themes as we think. As will be explained below we propose to go even one step further and base the whole construction of an environmental index on people's preferences and not only on the choice of single coefficients. Such a preference-oriented environmental index might represent a most useful complement to traditional natural science-oriented environmental indices.

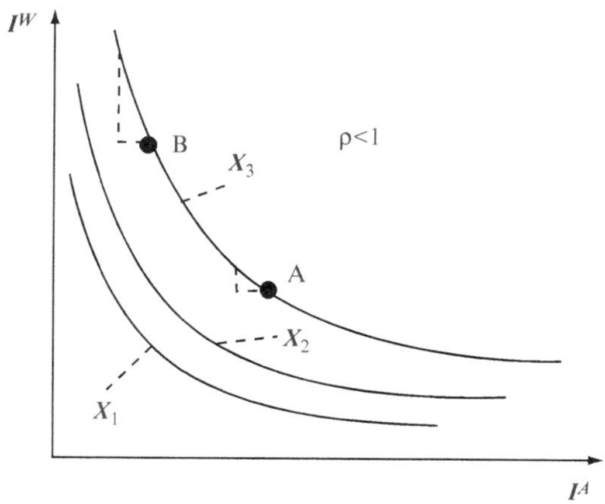

Figure 3. Trade-off between water and air quality with a CES aggregator.

3.3. THE ROLE OF TIME

Until now we have ignored the significance of time in our discussion of environmental indices. But environmental indices have, of course, to be located precisely in time because environmental quality is not constant but changes in time. In this context we have to make a difference between environmental state indices and environmental change indices.

3.3.1. *Environmental State Indices*

A descriptive environmental index like (4) describes the state of environmental quality at a certain point in time. To make this clear we rewrite (4) as

$$X^t = X(\pi^t) \tag{12}$$

where the vector π^t is the environmental profile at time t

$$\pi^t = [I_t^A, I_t^W, I_t^S, \ldots] \tag{13}$$

that describes the various facets of environmental quality at that point. Depicting the state of the environment alone is useful only if some reference state of the environment exists to which the actual state can be compared at least implicitly. If we know e.g. that a value of "2" or less of the index means that environmental quality is hazardous to human health we implicitly compare the actual value of the index to this reference value, i. e. if the index takes on a value of "8" we know that everything is fine. Without knowing that a value of "2" means danger to man we would not know how to interpret the actual value of "8". Therefore, even if an environmental index is defined as a state index, i. e. in terms of an absolute value, it is implicitly interpreted in relation to some reference level of the index which signifies danger or bliss or a "typical" or average state of the environment. If we want to make this comparison explicit we define an environmental change index rather than an environmental state index.

3.3.2. *Environmental Change Indices*

An environmental change index typically compares two different states of the environment. Therefore, change indices are often based directly on state indices like X^t discussed above. If r and t denote two different states of the environment we can, therefore, define:

$$CX^{r,t} = CX\left(\pi^r, \pi^t\right) = \frac{X\left(\pi^t\right)}{X\left(\pi^r\right)} = \frac{X^t}{X^r} \tag{14}$$

The index X^r for the reference state r of the environment to which the actual state t is compared might stand for some hypothetical threshold or critical value of environmental quality. It could also represent a historical value of the index like the value it assumed in the preceding time period ("last year") or at the starting point of a time series. In this case the change index describes the development of environmental quality over time. This is, of course, the most interesting use of change indices.

From a formal point of view descriptive environmental change indices like CX in (14) are "classical" index measures like e.g. price or quantity indices and can, therefore, be characterized by the so-called Identity Axiom and the Monotonicity Axiom going back to Irving Fisher (1927):

<u>Identity Axiom for Descriptive Indices</u>

$$CX^{t,t} = CX\left(\pi^t, \pi^t\right) \equiv 1 \tag{15}$$

<u>Monotonicity Axiom for Descriptive Indices</u>

$$\begin{aligned} \pi^r > \pi^s \quad &\Rightarrow \quad CX\left(\pi^t, \pi^r\right) > CX\left(\pi^t, \pi^s\right) \\ \pi^r > \pi^s \quad &\Rightarrow \quad CX\left(\pi^r, \pi^t\right) < CX\left(\pi^r, \pi^s\right) \end{aligned} \tag{16}$$

where $\pi^r > \pi^s$ means that at least one element of the environmental profile π^r is greater than the respective element of π^s and no element of π^r is smaller than the respective element of π^s.

If we want to illustrate the change of environmental quality over several successive time periods using a descriptive environmental index, it is desirable that the mathematical structure of this index allows to link the different indices characterizing single time periods together. The resulting "chain index" describes the overall change of environmental quality from the starting period to the actual period correctly. This refers to be the so-called Circularity Condition going back to Irving Fisher (1927):

<u>Circularity Condition</u>

$$CX\left(\pi^{t-1}, \pi^t\right) \cdot CX\left(\pi^t, \pi^{t+1}\right) = CX\left(\pi^{t-1}, \pi^{t+1}\right) \tag{17}$$

The Circularity Condition makes it possible to link an arbitrary number of successive environmental change indices starting from some base year $t = 0$ in order to judge the change of environmental quality over the whole time horizon covered by these period indices. This leads to an environmental "chain index" according to

$$CX^{0,t} = CX^{0,1} \cdot CX^{1,2} \cdot \ldots \cdot CX^{t-1,t} = \prod_{\tau=1}^{t} CX\left(\pi^{\tau-1}, \pi^{\tau}\right) . \tag{18}$$

Such an index can be interpreted in direct analogy to the common price and quantity indices known from statistics. One can observe how it changes from one year to the next and one can compare this index for several years to see how environmental quality changes over the whole time span of observation. Circularity according to (17) guarantees intertemporal consistency of the index.

The axioms and time-related consistency conditions discussed in this section were defined for descriptive environmental index measures. Such indices aggregate theme-related environmental indicators or sub-indices in a purely mechanical way, mostly as a weighted sum.

In the next section we propose a different kind of environmental index that values an environmental profile in accordance with people's preferences. Such a preference-oriented index reflects how people feel about the changes of environmental quality to be valued. Therefore, the aggregation of the environmental sub-indices has to be based on the principles of welfare theory in this case. That means that for preference-based indices there exists a theoretical foundation for the aggregation of the theme-related sub-indices. In the next section we shall propose such a preference-oriented index and we shall scrutinize its theoretical properties in the light of the axioms and consistency conditions considered here. Further, we shall discuss the possibilities for its empirical assessment.

4. A Preference-based Environmental Index

4.1. THEORETICAL CONCEPT

The most important complication of constructing a preference-oriented environmental index is that such an index cannot be based on measurable facts alone like $X(\pi)$ but has to rely on people's perceptions of environmental quality and on their stated preferences with respect to this quality. The objective is to build an index describing the state of the environment filtered through people's preferences. At this point we have to refer to microeconomic household theory where preferences are typically described by a consumer's direct utility function

$$U_h = u_h\left(y_h, \pi\right) . \tag{19}$$

Here U_h is the utility level an individual h realizes with a vector y_h of market consumption goods and an environmental profile π (which is the same for all households).

If we want to construct an index valuing environmental quality according to people's preferences we have to rely on interviews in order to obtain a comprehensive valuation of the environment.[4] The problem is that it is quite difficult for people to state the absolute value or utility they obtain from a specific environmental situation.[5] Instead one usually needs a reference situation against which one can value the actual situation. If we want to assess e.g. the value of a bottle of wine we implicitly compare the situation where we drink this bottle to a situation without it. But what would be a situation without environment? Apparently, such a reference situation does not make much sense.

The obvious choice of a suitable reference situation for the (relative) valuation of the actual state of the environment would be some previous state of the environment which people have experienced personally and which is close enough in time so that they can still remember it. For example, one could assess an environmental index on an annual basis so that people compare the actual environmental situation as characterized by the actual environmental profile π^t to last year's environmental profile π^{t-1}.

It is clear that a preference-based environmental index has to be defined on an individual basis, i. e. it has to consider individual preferences. In a second step one has to think about aggregating the individual environmental indices to a representative social or overall environmental index which is compatible with the descriptive natural science-based environmental indices.

For a preference-based index it obviously does not make sense to postulate the monotonicity axiom (15) directly. Since we now regard the environment through the filter of people's preferences we rather have to make sure first of all that these preferences are truly mirrored by the index. We expect a preference-based individual environmental change index $PCX_h\left(\pi^{t-1}, \pi^t\right)$ to indicate reliably if the individual prefers the actual situation to the previous one or not. We call this the

<u>Indicator Condition</u>

$$u_h\left(y_h, \pi^t\right) \gtreqless u_h\left(y_h, \pi^{t-1}\right) \quad \Leftrightarrow \quad PCX_h\left(\pi^{t-1}, \pi^t\right) \gtreqless 1 . \tag{20}$$

In the case of strict monotonicity of the preference ordering the Indicator Condition implies the fulfilment of the Monotonicity Axiom but it is important to note that for preference-based indices monotonicity is only a derived property and not a postulate. Preference-based indices are linked directly to a consumer's preferences but only indirectly to the environmental profile. So, what we want is a measure for the utility change induced by changes in environmental quality.

---

[4] It is well-known that valuation methods which do without interviewing people (the so-called indirect valuation methods) can assess only the use value of environmental goods which represents only a small part of their total value (see e.g. Ahlheim, 2003, p. 29 ff.)

[5] Of course, one could make them value their satisfaction with the environment on a Likert scale but this is much too imprecise to be useful for the construction of an environmental index.

4.2. EMPIRICAL ASPECTS

Since a consumer's utility function is not empirically observable we propose to construct an index which is based on the household's money-metric utility function

$$M_h = m_h\left(p, \pi, U_h\right) \tag{21}$$

which measures utility in monetary terms. This function expresses the utility level U_h realized by a household h as the minimum amount of money the household would have to spend in order to attain this utility level when market prices are given by the price vector p and environmental quality is given by the environmental profile π. The money-metric utility function m_h provides a description of an individual's well-being which is equivalent to the corresponding direct utility function.

The money-metric utility function m_h is strictly monotonically increasing in the utility level U_h, i. e.

$$\frac{\partial m_h}{\partial U_h}\left(p, \pi, U_h\right) > 0\,. \tag{22}$$

It can also be shown (see e.g. Ahlheim, 1993, p. 41 ff.) that the money-metric utility function is strictly monotonically decreasing in environmental quality π:

$$\frac{\partial m_h}{\partial \pi_j}\left(p, \pi, U_h\right) < 0 \quad (j = A, W, S, \ldots)\,. \tag{23}$$

This is plausible if we consider that higher environmental quality with all other things being equal means a higher level of utility so that it needs less market consumption (and, therefore, less expenditures) to maintain the same utility level as before. For other properties of the money-metric utility function see e.g. Ahlheim (1993, p. 39 ff.) or Ahlheim (1998, p.492 ff.).

Since the money-metric utility function is strictly monotonic in utility we can now specify our preference-based index of environmental change from a time period $t-1$ (e.g. "last year") to period t ("this year") as

$$PCX_h^{t-1,t} = \frac{m_h\left(p^{t-1}, \pi^{t-1}, U_h^t\right)}{m_h\left(p^{t-1}, \pi^{t-1}, U_h^{t-1}\right)} \tag{24}$$

where p^{t-1} is the market price vector of last year and π^{t-1} is last year's environmental quality. Analogously, U_h^{t-1} is the utility level that the consumer realized last year while U_h^t is his actual utility level. In principle, this index is based on the quantity indices and welfare indices put forward e.g. by Allen (1975), Pollak (1978) or Deaton and Muellbauer (1980). It reflects the change in people's well-being or utility from a time period $t-1$ to the following period t in index form. With additional assumptions we must now focus this index on environmental changes only.

From the strict monotonicity of the money-metric utility function in utility it follows that this index is a true welfare indicator in the sense of the indicator condition (20), i. e.

$$PCX_h^{t,t-1} \gtreqless 1 \quad \Leftrightarrow \quad U_h^t \gtreqless U_h^{t-1} \tag{25}$$

The index PCX according to (24) compares two expenditure amounts: former real expenditures $m_h\left(p^{t-1}, \pi^{t-1}, U_h^{t-1}\right)$ on the one hand and the hypothetical expenditures $m_h\left(p^{t-1}, \pi^{t-1}, U_h^t\right)$ on the other where the latter describes the minimum amount of money the household would have to spend in order to realize the actual utility level U_h^t with former market good prices p^{t-1} and the former environmental profile π^{t-1}. If we denote former expenditures by E_h^{t-1} and actual expenditures by E_h^t we can write

$$m_h\left(p^{t-1}, \pi^{t-1}, U_h^{t-1}\right) = E_h^{t-1} \text{ and } m_h\left(p^t, \pi^t, U_h^t\right) = E_h^t \,. \tag{26}$$

Both terms can easily be assessed empirically since they represent expenditures that have actually been made.

Things are different with hypothetical expenditures $m_h\left(p^{t-1}, \pi^{t-1}, U_h^t\right)$ which cannot be observed directly so that we have to assess them indirectly. We can reformulate this term according to

$$\begin{aligned} m_h\left(p^{t-1}, \pi^{t-1}, U_h^t\right) &= m_h\left(p^{t-1}, \pi^{t-1}, U_h^t\right) - m_h\left(p^t, \pi^{t-1}, U_h^t\right) \\ &+ m_h\left(p^t, \pi^{t-1}, U_h^t\right) - m_h\left(p^t, \pi^t, U_h^t\right) + m_h\left(p^t, \pi^t, U_h^t\right) \end{aligned} \tag{27}$$

Since our index focuses on changes in environmental quality we treat market prices as constant according to $p^{t-1} = p^t$, so that the first difference on the right-hand side of (27) becomes equal to zero. The second difference in (27) is equal to the Hicksian Equivalent Variation for a change in environmental quality

$$EV\pi_h^{t-1,t} = EV\pi_h\left(\pi^{t-1}, \pi^t\right) = m_h\left(p^t, \pi^{t-1}, U_h^t\right) - m_h\left(p^t, \pi^t, U_h^t\right) \,. \tag{28}$$

From property (23) of the money-metric utility function it follows that $EV\pi$ is positive for increases in environmental quality and negative for environmental deteriorations. It is important to find a suitable and plausible economic interpretation of this measure since we have to assess it through households interviews, i. e. we have to be able to explain it to ordinary people. From Figure 4 it can be seen that $EV\pi$ equals the amount of a hypothetical money transfer suitable to bring a consumer in the environmental situation $\pi_h^{t-1,t}$ of the former period $t-1$ to his actual utility level U_h^t. If environmental quality has improved during the last year (i. e. if $\pi^t > \pi^{t-1}$) this money transfer is positive and equals the minimum sum the consumer would accept as compensation if environmental quality were reduced now to last year's level. If environmental quality has decreased during the last year (i. e. if $\pi^t < \pi^{t-1}$) this money transfer is negative and equals the maximum amount the consumer would be willing to pay to make a restoration of last year's (higher) level of environmental quality possible. In the first case $EV\pi(> 0)$ equals his willingness to accept compensation (WTA) for a (hypothetical) reduction of actual environmental quality to its former level, while in the second case $EV\pi(< 0)$ equals his willingness to pay (WTP) for a return to the former level of environmental quality. So, $EV\pi$ can be interpreted as the money equivalent of the utility gain or loss the consumer has experienced through the change in environmental quality from period $t-1$ to period t.

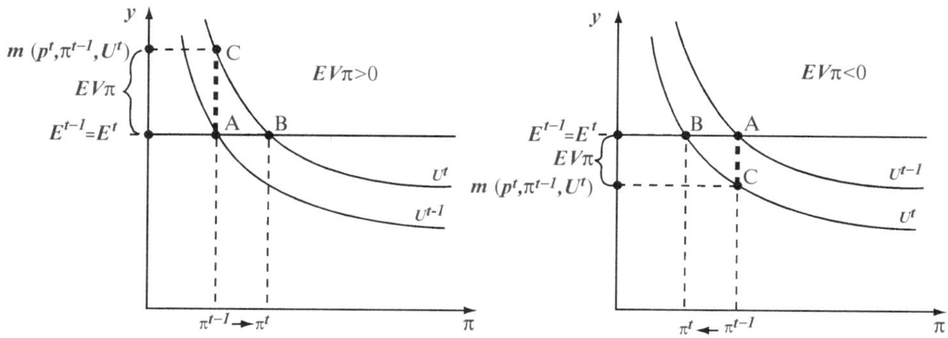

Figure 4. Willingness to accept (left hand) and willingness to pay.

Considering (26) and (28) in (24) our preference-based environmental change index becomes

$$PCX_h^{t-1,t} = \frac{E_h^t + EV\pi_h^{t-1,t}}{E_h^{t-1}} . \tag{29}$$

In this version all terms determining the index PCX can be assessed empirically: The two expenditure terms E_h^{t-1} and E_h^t are obvious and the empirical assessment of $EV\pi$ will be discussed in the next section. Since we are interested in the valuation of environmental changes only we can treat the household's expenditures for market goods as constant so that $E_h^{t-1} = E_h^t$ and our index becomes

$$PCX_h^{t-1,t} = \frac{E_h^t + EV\pi_h^{t-1,t}}{E_h^t} . \tag{30}$$

From (30) it becomes apparent that PCX is a pure environmental change index. It compares the utility in monetary terms E_h^t a consumer obtains from his market consumption only to the utility he receives from market consumption plus environmental quality change, i. e. $E_h^t + EV\pi_h^{t-1,t}$.

4.3. PROPERTIES

As a consequence of the monotonicity properties (22) and (23) of the money-metric utility function the preference-based index (30) fulfils simultaneously the Identity Axiom (15) and the Monotonicity Axiom (16) on the one hand and the Indicator Condition (20) on the other. That means that PCX meets the consistency requirements for a descriptive index measure as well as the condition for a reliable welfare measure.

It can be shown that $EV\pi$ [and, consequently, the environmental index PCX according to (30)] is strictly concave in environmental quality. Since the environmental profile π is a vector this implies that the level curves of our PCX are convex, i. e. they resemble the level curves shown in Figure 3. That means that we have decreasing marginal rates of substitution between the various theme-related sub-indices I^A, I^W, I^S etc. In other words: the relative importance of a sub-index like e.g. the water quality index I^W decreases as water quality increases relative to the quality of other environmental media like air or soil. This seems plausible from a psychological as well as from a natural science point of view as was explained in Section 3.

If we assume that household preference orderings are homothetic, as is common in most empirical studies of household behavior, PCX fulfils also the circularity condition (17), so that the overall improvement (or deterioration) of environmental quality since some base period 0 until today can be documented by linking the PCX together for all time periods between 0 and the actual period t:

$$PCX_h^{0,t} = PCX_h^{0,1} \cdot PCX_h^{1,2} \cdot \ldots \cdot PCX_h^{t-1,t} \,. \tag{31}$$

This is possible since for homothetic preferences the money-metric utility function is strictly separable in p and π on the one hand and utility U on the other:

$$m_h\left(p, \pi, U_h\right) = \hat{m}_h\left(p, \pi\right) \cdot \bar{m}_h\left(U_h\right) \tag{32}$$

This reduces PCX from (24) to

$$\overline{PCX}_h^{t-1,t} = \frac{\bar{m}_h(U_h^t)}{\bar{m}_h^{t-1}} \tag{33}$$

and implies fulfilment of the circularity condition. As mentioned above the empirical assessment of the utility people derive from environmental changes depends on stated preferences, i. e. on people's judgments regarding these changes. If the base period 0 lies back 10 years from today people cannot reasonably be expected to remember exactly what environmental quality was like in those days as compared to today. For the empirical assessment of PCX the only sensible reference point is environmental quality of last year. That means in such interviews we can only assess $PCX_h^{t-1,t}$ and if we want to compare the development of the overall-index over the years, i. e. $PCX_h^{0,1}$, $PCX_h^{0,2}$, ..., $PCX_h^{0,t}$ we have to link together the successive period indices $PCX_h^{t-1,t}$.

Until now we have discussed the individual environmental index PCX_h. Aggregation of the individual indices to a preference-based social change index $PSCX$ is analogous to the common practice in applied cost-benefit analysis. The individual Hicksian Equivalent Variations $EV\pi_h$ as well as the individual incomes are added up over all households so that we obtain the social environmental quality index as

$$PSCX^{t-1,t} = \frac{\sum_h E_h^t + \sum_h EV\pi_h^{t-1,t}}{\sum_h E_h^t} = \frac{\sum_h \left(E_h^t + EV\pi_h^{t-1,t}\right)}{\sum_h E_h^t} \,. \tag{34}$$

It follows that

$$PSCX^{t-1,t} \gtreqless 1 \quad \Leftrightarrow \quad \sum_h EV\pi_h^{t-1,t} \gtreqless 0 \,. \tag{35}$$

The sum of the individual $EV\pi$s is positive if and only if the sum of the positive $EV\pi$s (i. e. the sum of the individual $EV\pi_h^{t-1,t}$ of those, whose utility has increased as a consequence of the underlying change in environmental quality) is greater than the sum of the negative $EV\pi_h^{t-1,t}$ of those, whose utility has decreased and who would prefer to go back to the former state of the environment π^{t-1}. So, $\sum_h EV\pi_h^{t-1,t}$ can be interpreted as the monetary value of net social utility or welfare gain or loss caused by the change in environmental quality that took place during the time period to be valued (e.g. during the last year). The greater the value of the index the higher is the social welfare gain accomplished through environmental improvements. So, the preference-based social environmental change index $PSCX$ is an indicator of social satisfaction with the development of environmental quality during the period under review. In an anthropocentric world, where environmental policy is justified mainly by the preferences of man for an intact environment, such an index could be a significant measure for the success of environmental policy and for the satisfaction of people with their politicians. Therefore, it could be a useful instrument of environmental policy monitoring and a valuable complement to the existing descriptive environmental indices.

4.4. PRACTICAL ASSESSMENT

Our preference-oriented social index of environmental change $PSCX$ is based on the individual expenditures for market consumption and on the households' Equivalent Variations for the change in environmental quality. While data on household expenditures for market commodities E_h^t are directly available the Equivalent Variations $EV\pi_h$ of households for environmental changes have to be assessed through personal interviews, as explained above. Such interviews can be conducted as face-to-face interviews or as mail surveys, which is less reliable but cheaper.

As explained above the environmental Equivalent Variation $EV\pi$ can be interpreted as the monetary equivalent of the utility change induced by the change in environmental quality that took place during the period under review. If a consumer feels that environmental quality has improved during the last year his $EV\pi$ equals the minimum amount of money (WTA) that could compensate him for a return to the original state of the environment of one year ago. If environmental quality has deteriorated $EV\pi$ equals the maximum amount of money the consumer would be willing to pay (WTP) to return to the original (better) state of the environment. There are well-established techniques for the elicitation of the WTP or WTA of people for environmental changes following environmental projects or environmental accidents. The most popular assessment technique is the contingent valuation method (CVM) which is based on the construction of hypothetical markets where people reveal their preferences for environmental goods through their market behavior (for details see e.g. Ahlheim, 2003).

CVM surveys are typically conducted on a household basis. For the computation of the social index $PSCX$ one would first draw a representative household sample for which the individual household $EV\pi$s would be assessed through CVM interviews.

Then an average $EV\pi$ could be calculated for this sample. Multiplication of this average $EV\pi$ by the number of all households of a country yields an empirical approximation of the social Equivalent Variation $\sum_h EV\pi_h^{t-1,t}$. Household expenditures for market goods can also be asked during these interviews, but, of course, these data are available from household statistics as well.

For the elicitation of the $EV\pi$ one would first ask a respondent, e.g. the head of the household, if from the perspective of his household environmental quality has improved or deteriorated during the last year (one could also focus on specific aspects of environmental quality or on certain "environmental themes"). In the case of a perceived improvement one would ask e.g.: "In times like these it is very difficult to sustain the actual level of environmental quality. Imagine that we drop back to the level of environmental quality we had one year ago. What would be the minimum amount of money you would accept as a compensation for this deterioration of environmental quality so that altogether you would not feel worse off than today?" In CVM surveys it often shows that people have difficulties to think of an "adequate" value of environmental quality. Therefore, instead of this open-ended question format one often chooses a closed-ended format so that the question would be for example: "Would you agree to this deterioration if government paid you € 100 to compensate you for this loss of environmental quality?" With this elicitation format several subsamples of households are built and for each sample a different payment proposal (e.g. € 100, € 150, € 200 etc.) is made. From these data the average $EV\pi$ can be calculated. For households who state that environmental quality has dropped during the last year the analogous elicitation questions would be: "Imagine government would restore the environmental quality we had one year ago. Since this would be rather costly a surcharge on the ... tax would be necessary to finance this environmental program. What would be the maximum amount of this surcharge you would accept to regain last year's state of the environment?" The analogous closed-ended elicitation question would be: "Would you agree to this environmental program if you had to pay a surcharge of € 100 for its realization?"

In order to keep the cost of the practical assessment of a preference-based environmental index like $PSCX$ low one could add the respective $EV\pi$-questions e.g. to the questionnaire that has to be filled in anyway by the household sample chosen for the assessment of household panel data, in Germany the "Socio-Economic Panel" (GSOEP) or the Microcensus. Published on an annual basis such an index could provide a good impression of the public perception of environmental changes like e.g. a "business climate index" does for the perception of economic policy by private firms.

5. Concluding Remarks

In this paper we propose the construction and practical implementation of a preference-based environmental index as a complement to the existing descriptive environmental indices. The idea is that such an index should inform politicians as well as the public about the perception of environmental policy and the resulting change in environmental quality by common citizens. The role of such an index in society could be analogous to the role business climate indices, like e.g. the "ifo business climate index" or the "ZEW indicator of economic sentiment", play in the world of business.[6] Business climate indices inform politicians and the media on the performance of the economy as seen by private firms (i. e. by managers and shareholders) and they are taken very seriously as indicators of the actual economic situation of a country in spite of the fact that they are not based on "hard facts" but on personal judgments and expectations of private managers. Analogously, our $PSCX$ could serve as an indicator of the degree to which people agree with the actual environmental policy and development.

The $PSCX$ could be assessed annually. Like business climate indices it could be based on personal interviews with a representative random sample of private households. In order to obtain useful results it is advisable to keep the sample of households constant over time as it is common for the assessment of household panel data for household statistics like e.g. the German Socio-Economic Panel (GSOEP) or the Microcensus in Germany. Adding the questions that provide the data from which the $PSCX$ is constructed to the standard questionnaire that is sent to the households participating in a country's official panel survey would help to save costs. Therefore, the practical implementation of such an index would pose no substantial financial or organizational problems.

Summing up, a preference-based social index of environmental quality could be a valuable complement to the traditional descriptive environmental indices which are mainly based on expert knowledge. Like in other areas of public policy we experience also in the field of environmental policy a significant gap between expert opinion and the feelings of common people. This gap which should not be ignored in a democratic country could be filled by a preference-based index like the $PSCX$ proposed in this paper.

References

Ahlheim, M. 1993. *Zur Theorie rationierter Haushalte. Ein Beitrag über die Berücksichtigung limitierter staatlicher Subventionsprogramme in der Haushaltstheorie*, Heidelberg: Physica.

Ahlheim, M. 1998. "Measures of Economic Welfare", in: S. Barbera , P.J. Hammond, and C. Seidl (eds.): *Handbook of Utility Theory, Vol. 1: Principles*, Dordrecht: Kluwer Academic Publisher, 483–568.

Ahlheim, M. 2003. "Zur ökonomischen Bewertung von Umweltveränderungen", in: B. Genser (ed.): *Finanzpolitik und Umwelt*, Berlin: Duncker und Humblot, 9–71.

Allen, R. G. D. 1975. *Index Numbers in Theory and Practice*, London.

Chambers, N., C. Simmons, and M. Wackernagel. 2000. *Sharing Nature's Interest — Ecological Footprints as an Indicator of Sustainability*, London: Earthscan.

Deaton, A., and J. Muellbauer. 1980: *Economics and Consumer Behavior*, Cambridge.

Den Butter, F. A. G. 1992. "The Mirror of Cleanliness: On the Construction and Use of an Environmental Index", in: J.J. Krabbe and W.J.M. Heiman (eds.): *National Income and Nature: Externalities, Growth and Steady State*, Dordrecht: Kluwer, 49–76.

[6] The ifo business climate index (published monthly by the ifo-Institute) is formed by private business managers' assessments of their current business situations as well as their expectations of their business performances within the subsequent six months. In contrast, the ZEW indicator of economic sentiments (published monthly by the Centre for European Economic Research (ZEW)) rests on financial analysts' expectations concerning the performance of the whole economy.

Den Butter, F. A. G., and J. A. C. van der Eyden. 1998: "A Pilot Index for Environmental Policy in the Netherlands", *Energy Policy* 26(2), 95–101.

Ebert, U., and H. Welsch. 2004. "Meaningful Environmental Indices: A Social Choice Approach", *Journal of Environmental Economics and Management* 47, 270–283.

Fisher, I. 1927. *The Making of Index Numbers, A study of Their Varieties, Tests, and Reliability*, 3rd edition (reprinted in 1967), Boston: Houghton Mifflin Company.

Hope, C., and J. Parker. 1990. "Environmental Information for All - The Need for a Monthly Index", *Energy Policy* 18(4), 312–319.

Hope, C., and J. Parker. 1995. "Environmental Indices for France, Italy and the UK", *European Environment* 5, 13–19.

Inhaber, H. 1974. "Environmental Quality: Outline for a National Index for Canada", *Science* 186, 798–805.

Kang, S. M. 2002. "A Sensitivity Analysis of the Korean Composite Environmental Index", *Ecological Economics* 43, 159–174.

Markandya, A., and N. Dale. 2001. *Measuring Environmental Degradation. Developing Pressure Indicators for Europe*, Cheltenham.

OECD. 2001. *OECD Environmental Indicators. Towards Sustainable Development*, Paris.

Ott, W. R. 1978. *Environmental Indices. Theory and Practice*, Ann Arbor, Michigan: Ann Arbor Science.

Pollak, R. A. 1978. "Welfare Evaluation and the Cost of Living Index in the Household Production Model", *American Economic Review* 68, 285–299.

Rees, W. E. 1992. "Ecological Footprints and Appropriated Carrying Capacity: What Urban Economics Leaves Out", *Environment and Urbanization* 4(2), 121–130.

Rees, W. E. 2000. "Eco-footprint Analysis: Merits and Brickbats", *Ecological Economics* 32(3), 371–374.

Ten Brink, B. J. E., S. H. Hosper, and F. Colijn. 1991. "A Quantitative Method for Description and Assessment of Ecosystems: The AMOEBA-approach", *Marine Pollution Bulletin* 23, 265–270.

Wiggering, H., and F. Müller. 2004: *Umweltziele und Indikatoren. Wissenschaftliche Anforderungen an ihre Festlegung und Fallbeispiele*, Berlin.

Wheeler, B. W. 2004. "Health-related Environmental Indices and Environmental Equity in England and Wales", *Environment and Planning A* 36, 803–822.

Michael Ahlheim
Institut für Volkswirtschaftslehre
Universität Hohenheim
D-70593 Stuttgart
Germany
ahlheim@uni-hohenheim.de

Oliver Frör
Institut für Volkswirtschaftslehre
Universität Hohenheim
D-70593 Stuttgart
Germany
froer@uni-hohenheim.de

MEASURING AND EVALUATING INTERGENERATIONAL MOBILITY: EVIDENCE FROM STUDENTS' QUESTIONNAIRES

MICHELE BERNASCONI
Università dell'Insubria
VALENTINO DARDANONI
Università di Palermo

1. Introduction

Intergenerational mobility is an issue of a great theoretical and practical importance, with a very multi-faceted nature. Broadly defined, it deals with the evolution of families' socio-economic status across generations, usually traced through the male line. The transition mechanism governing the evolution may, however, be examined under several perspectives and scholars of various fields have proposed alternative approaches to the analysis of mobility. The result is that, as warned by a recent important survey of the literature, "a considerable rate of confusion confronts a newcomer to the field" (Fields and Ok, 1999, p. 557).

Part of the difficulty stems from the very same fact that social scientists coming from closely related, but separate fields, give to the central issue of finding proper ways of "measuring mobility" somewhat different purposes. In particular, while sociologists and statisticians are especially interested in measuring mobility in a pure sense and hence in addressing questions like "what makes one society more mobile than another?" or "when can a society be considered more mobile than another?" Economists are interested in judging and evaluating intergenerational mobility from a welfare-based perspective, and hence are interested in addressing questions like "when or how can a different degree of intergenerational mobility make a society better or more socially preferable than an other?"

Prais (1955), Rogoff (1953), Duncan (1966), Goldthorpe (1980) are classical references for the first perspective; Atkinson (1981), Markandya (1982), Chakravarty et al. (1985), Dardanoni (1993) started different lines within the second (which includes Gottschalk and Spolaore, 2002, as a recent contribution); Shorrocks (1978) is credited for having pioneered an even third route, known as the axiomatic approach (pursued further by, among others, Cowell, 1985, Fields and Ok, 1996, Mitra and Ok, 1998),

U. Schmidt and S. Traub (eds.), Advances in Public Economics: Utility, Choice and Welfare, 173-195.

which is somewhere between the two, in particular when certain axioms are introduced to carry specific social values.[1]

In this paper we adopt a questionnaire method to gain evidence on three basic ideas which in one way or another cross all the different approaches to the study of intergenerational mobility. The three ideas are those of: structural mobility, which broadly speaking applies to the evolution of the overall economic environment which the different generations of fathers and sons happen to live in; origin independence, which is a way to view another classical notion of mobility, known as exchange mobility, and refers to the degree of statistical independence between fathers' and sons' status in society; rank reversal, which is a more extreme way of thinking of exchange mobility, and applies to the degree to which in a society fathers' and sons' socio-economic positions reverse between generations.[2]

In Section 2, we review in some detail the three notions and formalize them as hypotheses that can be appropriately tested by the questionnaire. The presentation will maintain a level of generality to encompass the different lines of research carried forward by either the descriptive, welfaristic or axiomatic approach. We will, however, emphasize the aspects of the different notions which may be more relevant in either a pure measuring or a socially-evaluating perspective.

The same double perspective is also applied to the questionnaire study. The method of using students' responses for testing basic principles in issues concerning social measurements and ethics has some tradition in economics, especially in the area of income inequality analysis.[3] Amiel and Cowell (1992) are credited for one of the most quoted questionnaires on inequality measurement; Harrison and Seidl (1994) extend the approach to the investigation of preferential judgments for income distributions.

In Bernasconi and Dardanoni (2004) we conducted a first exploration of the method for the analysis of mobility measurement. We found a considerable rate of variations in students' responses and some unexpected evidence, referring in particular to a consistent failure of subjects to recognize social mobility along the dimension of origin independence.

In the present follow-up study we have improved the questionnaire design and extended the approach in various directions. First of all, as alluded to, the questionnaire is conducted within a frame that henceforth we will refer to as pure "measurement", which means that respondents are asked to express "value-free" judgments about intergenerational mobility, and within an "evaluation" frame, in which students are

---

[1] See Bartholomew (1996), van de Gaer et al. (2001), Formby et al. (2004), in addition to Fields and Ok (1999), for reviews and discussions of the literature.

[2] The three ideas as well as most of the literature dealing with them apply also to the other classical side of social mobility, namely intragenerational mobility (sometimes referred to as occupational mobility). In this paper, however, we don't deal with intragenerational mobility and even in the questionnaire, when we use the the term social mobility, we really mean only referring to intergenerational mobility.

[3] See Amiell (1999) for a survey; and see Moyes et al. (2002) and Cowell (2004) for collections of recent papers in the area.

explicitly asked to express their personal views about what type and what degree of mobility is better or worse for a society. The three different notions of mobility are tested using both verbal statements of the principles and numerical examples involving pairwise comparisons of hypothetical societies embodying a (theoretically) different amount of mobility. For the latter exercise, the present design introduces a new display to describe mobility in a society, which we think is more intuitive than the format based on mobility tables adopted in the previous study. Finally, as noted, this investigation extends to the issue of rank reversal, which perhaps represents the most controversial aspect of intergenerational mobility when considered in the "evaluating" perspective.

Although only a step in the application of the questionnaire method to social mobility, the evidence from the present questionnaire is more solid and provides various new and interesting insights: most notably, we find that origin independence enters positively in the evaluation of social mobility; on the contrary, rank reversal is judged as particularly negative when evaluating mobility, even if, on a pure measurement side, people view mobility increasing with reversal; structural mobility is generally valued positively, though with some ambiguities for people to fully recognize its implications.

We are aware of the criticisms that some writers attach to the questionnaire approach in social measurement and ethics (see e.g. Frohlich and Oppenheimer, 1994). These, for example, include the idea that theoretical knowledge in ethics should mainly be based on deductive reasoning and scholarly introspection, while validated through academic confrontation and consensus; the argument that questionnaire results are typically unstable and exposed to framing effects of various kinds; the point that students represent very specific samples and their views cannot be taken to reflect those of the layman; that subjects in the questionnaires lack proper (monetary) incentives to consider seriously the questions they face.

While we reject the extreme position that any scientific discourse in ethics should only be validated by the academic community (leaving especially aside any tests based on subjective perceptions), we also think that a more constructive criticism should not be ignored and is healthy for the approach. Thus, we deal with some of the above more constructive criticisms when presenting the questionnaire design and the results in Section 3, and when bringing the various themes of the paper once more together in the conclusions (Section 4).

2. Basic Issues in the Theories of Measurement and Evaluation of Intergenerational Mobility

The intergenerational mobility of a society can be described by the joint distribution $H(x, y)$ of a pair of random variables X and Y representing, respectively, fathers' and sons' *socio-economic status*. With the help of a simple framework, we now review various basic issues in the theories of measurement and evaluation of intergenerational mobility.

We use income as the relevant economic indicator. We assume that, within each generation, the income indicator can take only two values: x_l and x_h for, respectively, fathers' low and high incomes; y_l and y_h for sons' incomes in the same order. A standard way to represent the joint distribution of fathers' and sons' incomes, hence the intergenerational mobility of a society, is by means of a so called *mobility table*, taking in the present simple framework the following general form:

A general 2 × 2 *table.*

Sons' ⟶ Fathers' ↓	y_l	y_h	Fathers' margin. distribution
x_l	p_{ll}	p_{lh}	$p_{ll} + p_{lh} = p_{l.}$
x_h	p_{hl}	p_{hh}	$p_{hl} + p_{hh} = p_{h.}$
Sons' marginal distribution	$p_{hl} + p_{lh} = p_{.l}$	$p_{lh} + p_{hh} = p_{.h}$	

In the table, p_{ij} (with $i, j = h, l$) denotes the relative frequency of families in the society with father belonging to category i and son to category j. It can also be viewed as an estimate of the probability of the intergenerational transition from income status i to j. The row and column sums $p_{i.}$ and $p_{.j}$ (with $i, j = h, l$) give the frequencies of the marginal distributions of the fathers' and sons' incomes, respectively. They can also be similarly viewed as the chances for fathers and sons to be in the various income positions. Obviously, the grand total $\sum_i p_{i.} = \sum_j p_{.j}$ is equal to 1.

Mobility tables[4] can be considered from various different perspectives and, as anticipated in the introduction, there is very little agreement in the area regarding which aspects are more relevant in the analysis of economic mobility. Part of the disagreement also depends on whether we are interested in measuring or evaluating mobility.

---

[4] An alternative way often used to describe intergenerational mobility is by way of transition matrices. The cells π_{ij} of a transition matrix correspond to the cells p_{ij} of a mobility table divided by the row sums $p_{i.}$. Thus, $\pi_{ij} = p_{ij}/p_{i.}$, give directly the conditional probabilities of sons with fathers in class i to move to class j. While such type of information is particularly useful for certain reasoning about mobility (see below), transition matrices however come at a cost of a loss of information. For example, a transition matrix is necessarily stochastic, i.e. $\sum_j \pi_{ij} = 1$, which implies that, in general, one cannot induce the fathers' and sons' marginal distributions by using only the information provided by the matrix. (See Fields and Ok, 1999, for a discussion of further various types of information loss which may occur by summarizing distributional transformation by a transition matrix).

2.1. MEASUREMENT

When measuring the intergenerational mobility of a society, scholars (especially sociologists and statisticians, including classical works like Rogoff, 1953, Duncan, 1966, Goldthorpe, 1980) have often emphasized two quite different aspects of the interplay between the distributions of X and Y in a mobility table: one is *structural mobility*, the other is *exchange* or *pure mobility*. Structural mobility refers to, and is measured by, the difference between the fathers' and sons' marginal distributions $p_{i.}$ and $p_{.j}$. For example, if a country is experiencing substantial economic growth, there will be a greater chance for sons of being in the high-income status than for fathers, namely $p_{.h} > p_{h.}$. The opposite case in which $p_{.l} > p_{l.}$ can clearly occur following an economic decline; whereas in the case of no growth or no decline, it will be $p_{.h} = p_{h.}$ (or $p_{.l} = p_{l.}$), which is referred to as a situation of no structural change.

Society H of the following example 1 depicts an instance of the latter situation, whereas Society L is of the first type in which there is a higher proportion of rich sons rather than rich fathers. The example is taken from the previous questionnaire we conducted on mobility table comparisons, see Bernasconi and Dardanoni (2004). Overall, 224 subjects participated in that investigation: 113 (51%) confirmed the theoretical prediction that Society L should be regarded as more mobile than H, 69 (31%) said the opposite and 42 (19%) answered that the two tables have the same mobility or that they are not comparable. Thus, although the majority of respondents of that questionnaire were consistent with the theory, the responses were far from unanimous.

Example 1: two societies with different structural mobility.

Society H

Sons' $\longrightarrow$ Fathers' $\downarrow$	50	100	
50	0.16	0.14	0.30
100	0.14	0.56	0.70
	0.30	0.70	

Society L

Sons' $\longrightarrow$ Fathers' $\downarrow$	50	100	
50	0.27	0.43	0.70
100	0.03	0.27	0.30
	0.30	0.70	

Exchange mobility refers to the degree to which families interchange their relative position. Special cases taken as benchmarks in the literature are those of: a) perfect immobility, where both the elements p_{hl} and p_{lh} outside the main diagonal are zero; b) complete origin independence, sometimes also referred to as the case of equality of opportunities, where the sons' position is statistically independent from the fathers', that is $p_{ll} \cdot p_{hh} = p_{hl} \cdot p_{lh}$; c) perfect negative dependence, or complete reversal, where the elements p_{ll} and p_{hh} on the main diagonal are both zero.

For societies characterized by the same structural mobility, and restricting attention to 2×2 tables, the exchange mobility structure of different societies can be compared looking at their so called *odds ratio*. The odds ratio (or) for a generic 2×2 table is defined as $or = \dfrac{p_{ll}/p_{lh}}{p_{hl}/p_{hh}}$.

Hence, the odds ratio is the ratio between the odds of a son with a low-income father remaining with low income rather than moving upwards, with respect to the odds that a son with a high-income father has of becoming poor, rather than remaining rich. The odds ratio can then be considered as a measure of association between individuals of different social origin and is therefore an index of the rigidity in society. Thus, for instance, in the case b) above of complete origin independence (or equality of opportunities) $or = 1$. On the other hand, societies where fathers' and sons' incomes are positively associated have odds ratios greater than 1, with the case a) of perfect immobility characterized by an odds ratio which tends to ∞; while societies with negative association between fathers' and sons' incomes have an odds ratio below one, which tends to 0 in the case c) of perfect negative association or complete reversal.

Examples 2 and 3: examples of exchange mobility in societies with positive association.

Example 2

Society F

Sons' $\longrightarrow$ Fathers' $\downarrow$	50	100	
50	0.25	0.25	0.50
100	0.25	0.25	0.50
	0.50	0.50	

Society G

Sons' $\longrightarrow$ Fathers' $\downarrow$	50	100	
50	0.35	0.15	0.50
100	0.15	0.35	0.50
	0.50	0.50	

Example 3

Society M

Sons' $\longrightarrow$ Fathers' $\downarrow$	50	100	
50	0.21	0.49	0.70
100	0.09	0.21	0.30
	0.30	0.70	

Society O

Sons' $\longrightarrow$ Fathers' $\downarrow$	50	100	
50	0.27	0.43	0.70
100	0.03	0.27	0.30
	0.30	0.70	

From the perspective of evaluating mobility, there may be a tension between the concept of mobility as origin independence and that of reversal. However, as discussed below, this tension evaporates if one restricts the attention to tables displaying non-negative association, and this is justified by the fact that real world mobility data almost never display negative association between fathers' and sons' status. In our previous questionnaire, we tested people's attitude toward exchange mobility and origin independence, restricting the attention to table comparisons with non-negative association, like those in the two examples below.

Society F in example 2 is a very clear instance of perfect origin independence ($or = 1$): it is a *bistochastic* mobility table,[5] in which all sons have a 50% chance of being rich and a 50% chance of being poor, regardless of the conditions of their fathers. Society G shows instead the case of a strong positive association between the fathers' and sons' classes ($or = 5.4$). Thus, for those viewing social mobility as increasing with origin independence, Society F carries definitively more (exchange) mobility than Society G.

A similar prediction holds in example 3 for Society M in comparison to Society O. Indeed, Society M is also a case of perfect origin independence ($or = 1$), though it is not a bistochastic table. Society O is in turn a table with positive association ($or = 5.7$), which has in fact been constructed from Society M, by moving probability mass (in particular 6% probability mass) from the off-diagonal cells to the diagonal cells, so as to leave constant the sum of each row.

Such type of transformations are called *diagonalizing switches*. To the extent that the analysis is restricted to tables displaying non-negative association, diagonalizing switches reduce origin independence and hence social mobility.[6]

Despite the theoretical predictions, few subjects confronted with the two examples in our previous questionnaire gave responses consistent with theory: the evidence was particular disappointing with regard to example 2, with only 68 subjects out of 226 (29%) judging Society F more mobile than Society G; the evidence from example 3 was slightly better, but still far from being friendly to theory, with just less than 42% subjects (94 out of 225) giving the correct answer that Society M is more mobile than Society O.

There are various possible reasons for the failure we found. One is obviously that, despite our effort in the instructions of the previous questionnaire to describe the meaning of the numbers in the mobility tables (which to make things easier were incidentally expressed in absolute, rather than relative frequencies), people had great difficulty in dealing with the numerical examples. A related problem may be that participants found mobility tables particularly obscure. For example, subjects may have found even computing the conditional probabilities for sons' incomes very problematic, which is obviously another way through which participants may have

[5] A *bistochastic* mobility table is a table with positive entries such that both rows and columns sum to unity.

[6] Indeed, notice that Society G of example 2 can also be viewed as constructed by diagonalizing switches (of 10% of probability mass) from each of the off-diagonal cells of Society F.

ascertained the different degrees of the statistical independence between the fathers and sons' classes in the various societies.[7]

Of course, another explanation may also be that some or most people simply do not regard origin independence as a relevant attribute of social mobility. Though this may seem surprising at first, it may be less so when social mobility is considered not only from a pure measurement perspective, but also from one conducted with evaluation purposes.

2.2. EVALUATION

As anticipated in the introduction, with the term evaluating intergenerational mobility, we refer to a case in which, in addition to measuring mobility, we also wish to attach a value judgment whether a given level of mobility increases or reduces the welfare of a society.

This is a typical exercise conducted under the spirit of welfare economics. When mobility tables are considered in such a spirit, however, various differences may emerge from judgments given within a purely statistical measurement frame. In some cases the differences are intuitive and natural; in others, they may be more surprising.

For example, if one thinks of structural mobility and agrees that a society experiencing a downward movement in the marginal distribution of sons with respect to the distribution of fathers is more mobile than a society in which the marginal distributions are the same, he or she may still think that the latter, more structurally rigid society, is more preferable under a social welfare perspective. More surprisingly, however, it is the fact that the latter judgment may also apply when a greater structural mobility comes in the form of an upward movement of the sons' marginal distribution with respect to the fathers'.

To see this, consider again example 1 in which Society L has greater structural mobility than society H (with the two societies having the same odds ratios)[8]. Notice, however, that if considered in a welfare perspective, fathers' marginal distribution in Society H stochastically dominates father's marginal distribution in Society L, while sons' marginal distributions are the same. Thus, Society H is overall richer than Society L and one may declare the former socially preferable, despite its lower amount of structural mobility.

This difficulty of the welfare approach in valuing structural mobility is not so surprising, since as has long been recognized in the literature (at least since Markandya, 1982), structural mobility has exerted little appeal among scholars of the evalua-

[7] In particular, statistical independence implies that all sons, regardless of their fathers, face the same probabilities (or opportunities) of obtaining the different income levels. As pointed out in footnote 4, that is instead information directly provided by transition matrices. The questionnaire described in the present study introduces a new display which also directly provides information on conditional probabilities.

[8] More specifically, the odds ratio of Society H is 4.6, while that of Society L is 5.6. The small difference is due to the fact that all tables in this and the other examples have been constructed by a MATLAB program which takes as input the marginal distributions and the odds ratios and gives as output a mobility table. The output cell numbers are then rounded to the nearest integer.

tion approach to social mobility, who have instead focused much more narrowly on exchange mobility.

Even, however, along the latter dimension, things are not very simple. It is in particular due to Markandya (1982) having firstly shown that with the utilitarian social welfare function

$$\sum_i \sum_j V(x_i y_j) p_{ij} \tag{1}$$

we have that:

$$\partial^2 V / \partial x_i \partial y_j < 0 \quad \text{implies that diagonalizing switches decrease welfare} \tag{2}$$

$$\partial^2 V / \partial x_i \partial y_j > 0 \quad \text{implies that diagonalizing switches increase welfare} \tag{3}$$

The first condition may in particular reflect a case in which aversion to inequality in society is judged to be more important than aversion to intertemporal fluctuations of incomes within families, so that welfare diminishes moving toward a situation of perfect rigidity (where all the rich remain rich, and all the poor poor); the opposite holds under the second condition.

Example 4: negative association versus origin independence.

Society T

Sons' ⟶ Fathers' ↓	50	100	
50	0.15	0.35	0.50
100	0.35	0.15	0.50
	0.50	0.50	

Society F

Sons' ⟶ Fathers' ↓	50	100	
50	0.25	0.25	0.50
100	0.25	0.25	0.50
	0.50	0.50	

At this point, two important considerations follow. The first is that, when condition (3) applies, then a society with positive association between fathers' and sons' classes is to be judged more socially preferable than a society characterized by complete origin independence,[9] such as Society G versus F or Society O versus M, in examples 2 and 3, respectively.

The second observation is that, when diagonalizing switches decrease welfare so that origin independence is valued in society, then situations of negative association are valued even better. Example 4 presents a possible situation of this kind, in which the bistochastic Society F is compared with Society T which displays negative association (or = 0.2). In fact, Society F can be viewed as obtained by diagonalizing

[9] Obviously, the prediction holds always true only for comparisons between societies characterized by the same marginal distributions of fathers and sons.

switches (of 10% probability mass) from the cells of Society T.[10] Thus, the above argument implies that if origin independence is valued in respect to a society with positive association, then Society T should in turn be ranked better than F.

Put differently, adopting a social welfare function of the general form (1) implies that either a society with perfect immobility is the social optimum, or a society with complete reversal is the optimum, while societies characterized by origin independence (or equality of opportunity) don't appear to have a special value.

Since, however, the notion of equality of opportunity seems to appeal to many scholars, various attempts have been pursued in the literature to overcome the problem: among others, Shorrocks (1978) has simply taken as an axiom to give to origin independence the maximum of mobility (within a framework which implicitly assigns social value to mobility); Dardanoni (1993) has developed a welfare-based approach which drops symmetry of the social welfare function (1) and assigns a greater weight to those who start with a lower position in the status hierarchy; Gottschalk and Spolaore (2002) have generalized the social welfare function in (1) to allow for a form of an equality aversion specifically restricted to sons' generation, which in some cases may induce a strict preference for origin independence. However, as argued above, since no actual society is likely to display negative association between fathers' and sons' statuses, this issue is of very little practical significance.

A detailed analysis of the above lines of research is obviously beyond the purpose of the present discussion, as the point here is indeed more simple and general. In particular, on the one side, the works quoted above are relevant to indicate that it may be possible to find models which under certain conditions value origin independence;[11] on the other side, however, the social welfare function in (1) is important to show that there are also theoretically coherent arguments to sustain the opposite, namely that social optima may in fact correspond to situations of complete reversal or even of complete immobility.

The purpose of the following questionnaire is to obtain some further evidence, in addition to that already quoted from our previous study (Bernasconi and Dardanoni, 2004), of how people perceive the above various subtle issues of the multifaceted phenomenon of social mobility.[12]

---

[10] The comparison is in this respect symmetric to that of example 2.

[11] It is also important to notice some shortcomings of the approaches quoted above: for example, a difficulty of Dardanoni's (1993) model is that it is elaborated within a Markov chains approach of transition matrices and cannot always be transposed in the more general framework considered here; a problem with Gottschalk and Spolaore (2002) is that their theory requires a violation of the reduction of compound lottery axiom; in Shorrocks (1978), as noted, a social value for origin independence is simply assumed.

[12] We also emphasize that we have nevertheless restricted the discussion to a few basic principles in the literature on mobility. Other important issues in the field concern, for example, whether mobility is an absolute concept, or whether it is a concept invariant to possible alternative transformations of the status variable. A further argument of research centers around the question of how to extend some of the technical ideas, like for example the notion of odds ratios, to tables of an order greater than 2×2. A discussion and some preliminary questionnaire evidence on the above other aspects of mobility is also given in Bernasconi and Dardanoni (2004).

3. A questionnaire experiment

The present questionnaire experiment focuses both on the measurement and on the evaluation of intergenerational mobility. The study is in particular based on two questionnaires containing similar questions, but different wording so as to distinguish a pure measurement questionnaire from an evaluation questionnaire.

The questionnaires were administered in September 2004, to undergraduate students coming from different classes in economics at two Italian universities. A total of 373 subjects participated in the study: 189 in the measurement questionnaire, 184 in the evaluation questionnaire.[13]

As alluded to at various points in the paper, preparing questionnaires to test basic principles in issues concerning social measurement and ethics is not an easy task in general, and it appears particularly difficult in the context of social mobility, given the very multidimensional nature of the phenomenon. We have gained experience from our previous study, and have tried to improve on the questionnaire design in various directions.

First of all, in the present study we divide both the measurement and the evaluation questionnaires into two parts: the first part is introductory and asks participants to express their views about three general propositions regarding intergenerational mobility; the second part presents participants with seven pairs of hypothetical societies which subjects compare and rank according to their perception of mobility.

The questionnaires are introduced by a set of instructions, distributed and read aloud. The instructions have several purposes. First of all, they explain that the experiment is about "measuring" or "evaluating", depending on the questionnaire, "social mobility". Since the term "social mobility" is probably unfamiliar to most respondents, the instructions give a brief definition of what is meant by the term. The instructions in particular define social mobility as "the transition of socio-economic class within a family line, from the fathers' generation to the sons' generation".

The instructions are also explicit about the fact that intergenerational mobility is a controversial issue in the social sciences and that it is precisely the purpose of the questionnaire to understand more on the issue by directly asking what people think on the matter. They also emphasize that "university students represent a common and very suitable group to be targeted in questionnaires on subtle social issues, given the attitude that students have to think in abstract terms, reason about logical propositions, express coherent opinions, work with numerical examples". In the absence of a monetary reward, it was thought that the latter statement could somehow encourage students to take the questionnaires more seriously. In any regards, the instructions explain that the questionnaire is voluntary, personal and anonymous.

[13] One class was at the University of Pavia (129 students all participating in the measurement questionnaire) and three classes at the University of Varese (a class of 60 students also participating in the measurement questionnaire, and two classes of 130 and 54 students taking both part in the evaluation questionnaire). In the present study we aggregate the responses for each treatment, since we didn't find any systematic difference in the questionnaire evidence depending on the class or the university.

A further important innovation of the present questionnaire is that it introduces a new format to represent the intergenerational mobilities of societies for the second part of the investigation on the pairwise comparisons; and the instructions obviously explain and give details on how to interpret the displays.

In the sequel, we first give the questions and the answers on the general propositions and then move on to consider the design and to present the results on the pairwise comparisons.

3.1. PART I: GENERAL PROPOSITIONS

To help participants start thinking about social mobility and get acquainted with various possible perspectives one may look at the issue, in the first part of the questionnaire we ask respondents to state the extent to which they agree or disagree on three general propositions about intergenerational mobility. The three propositions are thought to capture some essential aspects of the three notions of intergenerational mobility outlined in Section 2, namely that of structural mobility, that of origin independence and that of rank reversal.

Table I gives the exact wording of the propositions for the two questionnaire treatments, with the distributions of responses across five types of possible answers: *a)* "strongly disagree" with the proposition; *b)* "disagree"; *c)* "neither disagree nor agree"; *e)* "agree"; *d)* "strongly agree". The last two columns of the table provide some statistical tests.

The first proposition (P1) focuses on structural mobility which is presented as a type of mobility where the sons improve their socio-economic positions with respect to the fathers. In the measurement questionnaire, it is asked whether respondents agree or disagree in defining as more mobile a society where the greater are the chances for sons to register such an improvement;[14] in the evaluation questionnaire, subjects are asked whether they are willing to use the same characterization to declare a society "the more preferable".

Both in the measurement and in the evaluation questionnaire, participants overwhelmingly *d)* "agree" or *e)* "strongly agree" with the proposition: the two responses together count in the two questionnaires for, respectively, 81% and 88% of total answers; consistently, the null hypothesis that replies *a)* "strongly disagree" or *b)* "disagree" are equally likely, is strongly rejected for both questionnaires (see the *d*-test in the table). Also notice that, for this proposition, a χ^2-test for independent samples accepts the null hypothesis that responses from the two treatments can be considered as if drawn from the same sample.[15] Thus, for this question at least, it doesn't seem to be a difference between the way respondents look at this aspect of

---

[14] Notice that while in principle structural mobility applies to both situations of socio-economic improvement as well as decline, in the proposition we only refer to the first to avoid confusion.

[15] To conduct the test, we combine responses in three cells only, namely $(a, b), (c), (d, e)$, to avoid the well-known problem of the low power of the test when some cells contain very few observations (e.g., Siegel and Castellan, 1988).

TABLE I. Three general propositions

	a) strongly disagree	b) disagree	c) neither dis- nor agree	d) agree	e) strongly agree	*d*-test	χ^2-test
			P1: Structural mobility				
	Measurement: The greater the chances are of sons to improve their socio-economic positions with respect to their fathers in a society, the greater is the amount of social mobility						
n 189	2	10	24	111	42	−10.90***	
p	0.01	0.05	0.13	0.59	0.22		
	Evaluation: The greater the chances are of sons to improve their socio-economic positions with respect to their fathers in a society, the more preferable the society is for its degree of social mobility						3.01
n 184	6	5	15	108	53	−5.63***	
p	0.03	0.01	0.08	0.59	0.29		
			P2: Origin independence				
	Measurement: The more independent are sons' and fathers' socio-economic positions in a society, the greater is the amount of social mobility						
n 189	3	35	21	112	18	−7.18***	
p	0.02	0.19	0.11	0.59	0.10		
	Evaluation: The more independent are sons' and fathers' socio-economic positions in a society, the more preferable the society is for its degree of social mobility						18.66***
n 184	6	46	44	70	18	−3.03**	
p	0.03	0.25	0.24	0.38	0.10		
			P3: Rank reversal				
	Measurement: The greater the extent to which sons' and fathers' socio-economic ranks are reversed in a society, the greater is the amount of social mobility						
n 189	12	89	48	30	10	−5.05***	
p	0.01	0.05	0.13	0.59	0.22		
	Evaluation: The greater the extent to which sons' and fathers' socio-economic ranks are reversed in a society, the more preferable the society is for its degree of social mobility						12.58**
n 184	25	105	34	17	3	8.90***	
p	0.14	0.57	0.18	0.09	0.02		

Legend: The d-test is a difference of proportion test for $H_0 : p(a+b) = p(d+e)$, based on the standard normal approximation of the binomial distribution (with the values of the test corrected for continuity; see e.g., Siegel and Castellan, 1988). The χ^2-test is for the null hypothesis that the distributions of responses in the two questionnaires can be viewed as if drawn from the same sample (the test aggregates cells $(a, b), (c), (d, e)$). Stars ***, **, *, denote in the order rejection at 0.1%, 1% and 5% significance levels.

mobility, in the sense that more mobility is largely perceived as being also a more preferable society.

The second proposition (P2) looks at origin independence: subjects are asked whether they agree or disagree that increasing the extent to which sons' socio-economic positions are independent from fathers' makes a society "more mobile" (measurement questionnaire) or "more preferable" (evaluation questionnaire).

In both treatments, the majorities *d)* "agree" or *e)* "strongly agree" with the propositions. The evidence is stronger in the measurement questionnaire, with 69% of all responses falling in either one or the the other of the two categories (the two proportions together are significantly different from those of type *a)* "strongly disagree" or *b)* "disagree" at more than 0.01% level). In the evaluation questionnaire the two patterns count for 48% of the answers against 28% who "disagree" or "strongly disagree" (with the *d*-test which rejects the hypothesis of equality of proportions at the 1% level), while 24% "neither disagree nor agree". The χ^2-test confirms that the evidence in the second questionnaire is weaker.

Proposition three (P3) is about reversal. It tests whether a greater extent of rank reversal in a society is thought to increase social mobility or to make a society more preferable. More strongly in the evaluation questionnaire, but also in the measurement questionnaire, the majorities of respondents "disagree" or "strongly disagree" with the statement: in the measurement questionnaire, the two answers account together for 53% of the total patterns versus 21% of those who "agree" or "strongly agree" (with the value of *d*-test significant at 0.1% level); in the evaluation questionnaire, responses of the two types are 73% versus only 11% of those who "agree" or "strongly agree". The evidence of the χ^2-test confirms that, despite the fact that there is clearly a similarity in the distribution of the answers from the two questionnaires, it is not possible to view the two distributions as if drawn from the same sample and that the opposition to reversal from an evaluation perspective is indeed stronger.

Following the above judgments on the general principles, it is now interesting to check whether and how subjects effectively use the principles when they face specific mobility situations.

3.2. PART II: PAIRWISE COMPARISONS OF "MOBILITY TREES"

The second part of the questionnaire tests the attitude respondents have toward the various aspects of social mobility using simple pairwise comparisons as those of the examples discussed in Section 2.

As anticipated, however, the displays used in the questionnaires are different from the theoretical format of mobility tables, also adopted in our previous experiment (Bernasconi and Dardanoni, 2004).

Indeed, as alluded to at various points in the paper, while mobility tables provide all the relevant information regarding distributional transformations possibly occurring in a society, they perhaps are not very clear for people who are not sufficiently trained. For example, one may mix up row numbers applying to fathers with column numbers referring to sons; there may be little intuition about which father generates

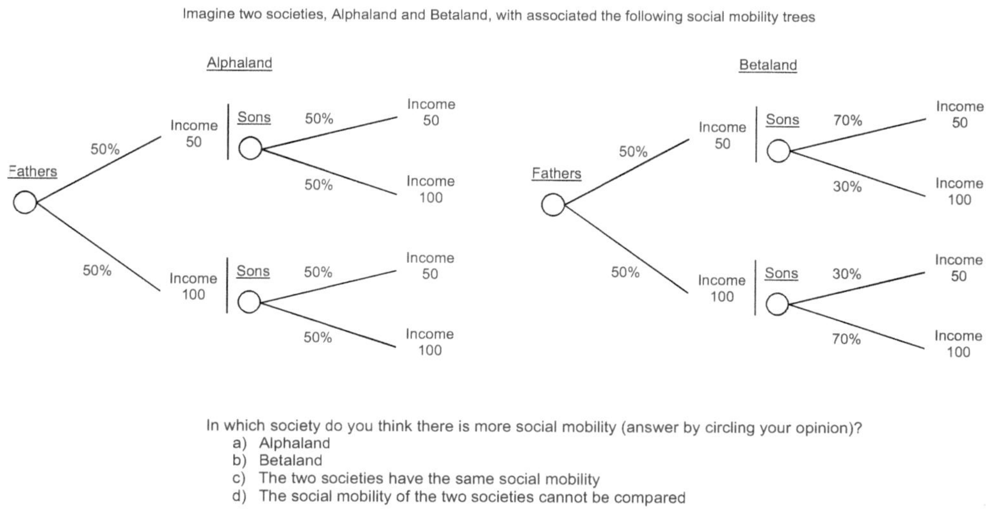

Figure 1. A typical comparison display of the measurement questionnaire. For the evaluation questionnaire the question below the mobility trees reads: "Which society according to your view stands as more preferable for its degree of social mobility?". The possible answers are the same as for the measurement questionnaire, expect for answer c) which in the evaluation questionnaire reads: "the two societies are equally preferable".

which son; some computations may not be direct, as for example those referring to the conditional probabilities for sons' incomes.

The difficulty in dealing with mobility tables may perhaps also explain the failure of subjects of our previous experiment to satisfy various predictions of the theory of mobility measurement.

In an attempt to control the problem, in the present investigation we have introduced a new display format based on *mobility trees*, which we consider more intuitive. A mobility tree presents sequentially fathers and sons' generations (see Figure 1): each member of a generation faces a node, which, depending of his family line determines his chances of obtaining a given income level. In addition, mobility trees give directly sons' conditional income probabilities, so that one can immediately ascertain the case of perfect origin independence between fathers' and sons' status in a society.[16] In particular, perfect independence obviously implies the same income probabilities for all sons' nodes regardless of fathers' income. That is for example the case of society Alphaland in the display of Figure 1. The display is in fact the tree representation of example 2 of Section 2, with Alphaland referring to the bistochastic Society F and Betaland corresponding to Society G.

[16] Mobility trees are in this sense similar to transition matrices, without however implying the loss of information about fathers' and sons' marginal distributions (see footnote 4).

TABLE II. The seven pairwise comparisons of mobility trees

	Alphaland	Betaland	Theoretical predictions
C1	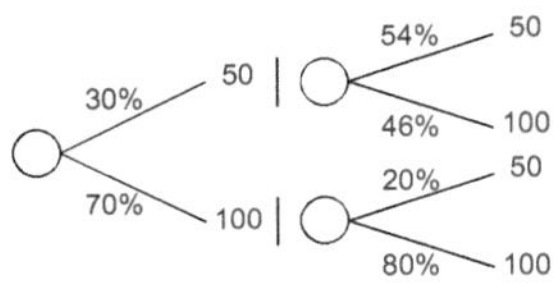	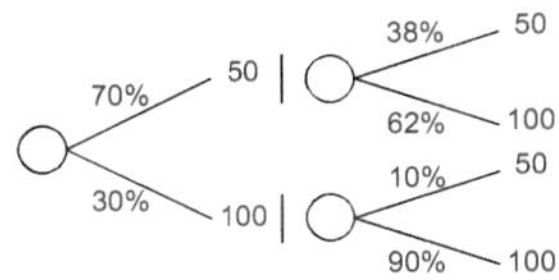	More structural mobility in B; $or(A) = 4.6$, $or(B) = 5.6$: (approximately) same origin independence and same reversal in A and B
C2	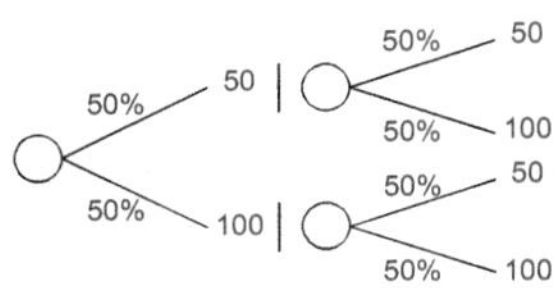	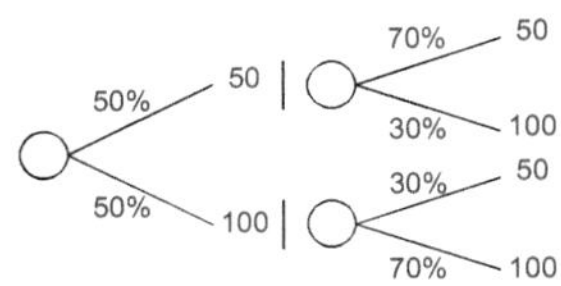	Same structural mobility in A and B; $or(A) = 1$, $or(B) = 5.4$: more origin independence and more reversal in A
C3	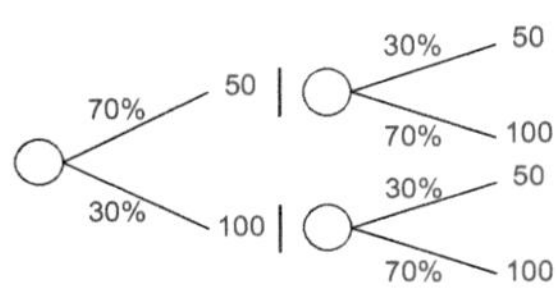	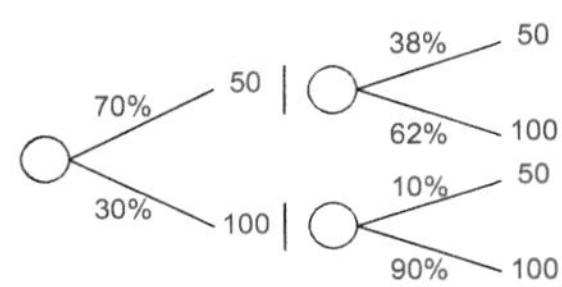	Same structural mobility in A and B; $or(A) = 1$, $or(B) = 5.7$: more origin independence and more reversal in A
C4	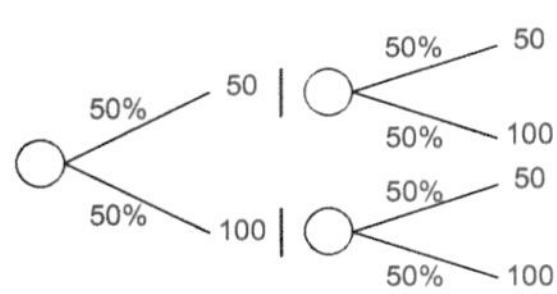	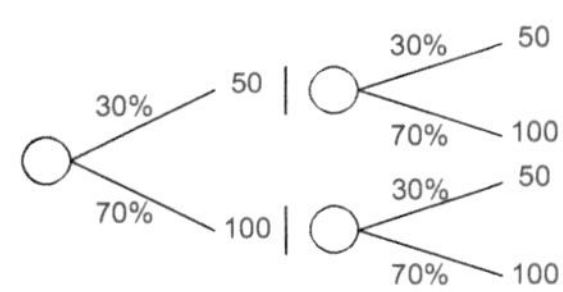	Same structural mobility in A and B; $or(A) = 1$, $or(B) = 1$: same origin independence and same reversal in A and B

Table continues.

A total of seven pairwise mobility trees are included in the present questionnaire. They are shown in Table II. The first three comparisons, C1, C2 and C3, correspond, in order, to the three examples of Section 2 also considered in our previous investigation (Bernasconi and Dardanoni, 2004). We record the following. Betaland in C1 has more structural mobility than Alphaland, while the two societies are characterized by (approximately) the same origin independence: thus, in the measurement questionnaire, Betaland should be regarded as more mobile than Alphaland; the prediction is more unsettled in the evaluation questionnaire, as in particular structural mobility is, at least theoretically, not clearly valued by the approach; in addition, fathers' marginal distribution in Alphaland stochastically dominates that of Betaland.

C2 and C3 both compare cases in which a society with perfect origin independence, namely Alphaland, is confronted with one, Betaland, with positive association: Alphaland should therefore be unambiguously considered more mobile in the measurement

TABLE II.

Continuation of Table II.

	Alphaland	Betaland	Theoretical predictions
C5	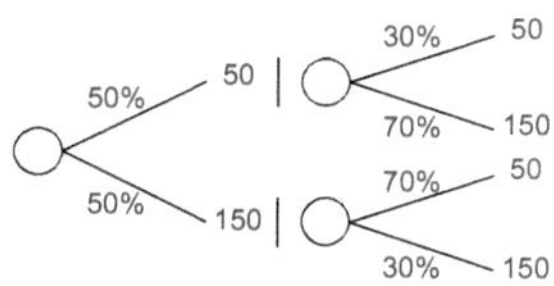	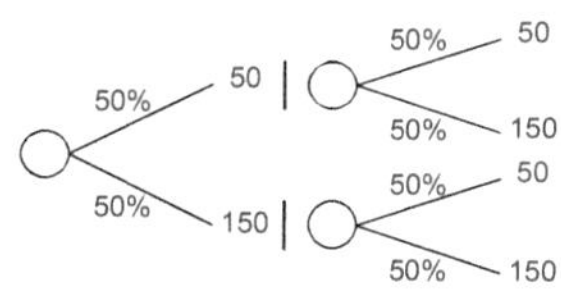	Same structural mobility in A and B; $or(A) = 0.2$, $or(B) = 1$: more origin independence in B, more reversal in A
C6	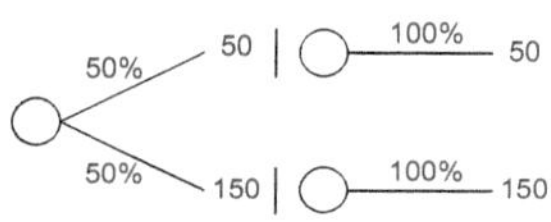	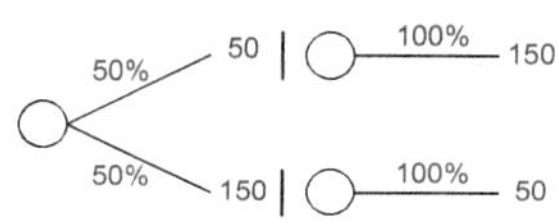	Same structural mobility in A and B; $or(A) \longrightarrow \infty$, $or(B) \longrightarrow 0$: origin independence indeterminate, more reversal in B
C7	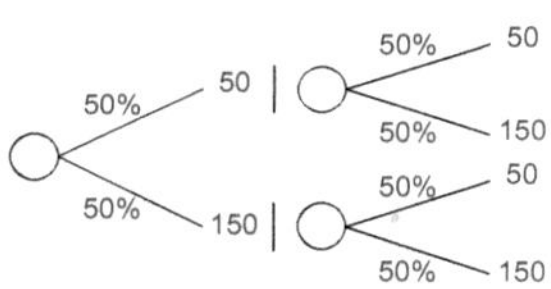	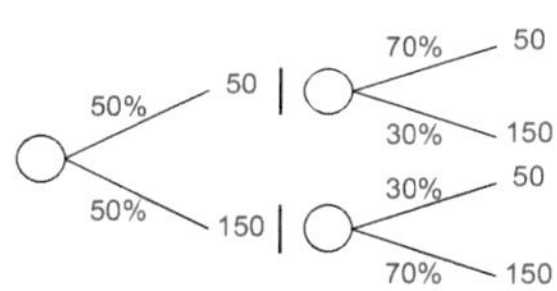	Replica of C2 (Same structural mobility in A and B; $or(A) = 1$, $or(B) = 5.4$: more origin independence and more reversal in A)

Note. In the actual questionnaires, both the order of the questions and the positions of the mobility trees are randomized across participants.

questionnaire; the same prediction applies in the evaluation questionnaire for those who value equality of opportunity and\or reversal, while the opposite might hold for those who [holding a social welfare like that in equation (1)] oppose reversal without however valuing origin independence.

The fourth comparison (C4) looks at two societies with perfect origin independence and same structural mobility, as within each society the marginal distributions of fathers and sons are the same. Still notice that both fathers' and sons' marginal distributions in Betaland stochastically dominate the corresponding distributions of Alphaland; thus, if under a pure measurement of mobility Alphaland and Betaland might be regarded as equally mobile, under an evaluation perspective the latter society might be preferred to the former.

The first four comparisons involve only societies characterized by non-negative associations between fathers' and sons' status, so that positive attitudes toward origin independence and\or reversal operate in the same direction. Comparisons 5 and 6 (C5 and C6) introduce instances of negative association where the two attitudes imply different judgments. In particular, C5 is a tree representation similar to example 4 of Section 2. A minor difference also from the other examples concerns fathers' incomes

(150 income units rather than 100 income units) which is introduced to maintain students' attention.[17] In the comparison, Betaland corresponds to a case of origin independence already met in various illustrations, while in Alphaland there is a large degree of reversal (with structural mobility being the same in the two societies). C6 presents instead the extreme situation in which a society with perfect rigidity, namely Alphaland, is compared to one with complete reversal, namely Betaland. Clearly, in the comparison the implication of origin independence is indeterminate.

The last comparison (C7) is a replica of C2 (with fathers' incomes equal to 150), introduced as a consistency check within the questionnaires. Finally notice that both the order of the comparisons and the positions of the mobility trees are randomized across participants in the two questionnaires.

Table III presents the distribution of answers to the seven comparisons. In C1, despite Betaland being the more structurally mobile society, it doesn't receive great favor in either of the two questionnaires: 46% of responses for Betaland against 38% for Alphaland in the measurement questionnaire (with the *d*-test signalling no statistical difference between the two proportions); 41% for both societies in the evaluation questionnaire. The result is somewhat surprising, given also the large support that the idea of structural mobility has received when stated verbally in Part I of the investigation (see Section 3.1). One possible explanation is that the degree to which Betaland is more mobile than Alphaland doesn't completely compensate for the fact that in Alphaland the fathers' generation is better-off than in Betaland; and it is also possible that this aspect of the comparison, which should only be relevant in an evaluation perspective, somehow spills over also on the responses to the measurement questionnaire.

The evidence from C2 is instead substantially in line with the theoretical implications of origin independence when considered against a society with positive association. The results are particularly sharp in the evaluation questionnaire, where the preferences for Alphaland are the absolute majority (56% versus 23% for Betaland, with the value of *d*-test significant at 0.1% level). The evidence is weaker in the measurement questionnaire (45% for Alphaland versus 38% for Betaland), but still in the direction of the theoretical prediction. In addition, the same patterns of answers are also confirmed for both questionnaires in the replica of C2, namely in C7.

It is interesting to contrast the evidence here with the violations of origin independence in the same basic example (referred to in Section 2.1), observed in our previous study based on mobility tables. Also observe that a similar evidence in favor of independence, even if at a lower rate, is confirmed by responses to C3. Here Alphaland is not a bistochastic society, and this may perhaps explain the weaker support. Overall, in any case, we think that responses to the three comparisons C2, C3 and C7 speak here in favor of origin independence when compared to societies with

[17] As already pointed out in footnote 13, an important issue in the literature on social mobility also concerns the extent to which mobility comparisons are unaffected by alternative transformations of the status variable. We do not consider this issue in the present study; all the predictions considered in this investigation hold generally true regardless of the specific values of the status variable.

TABLE III. Distributions of answers to the seven pairwise comparisons

	a) Alphaland	b) Betaland	c) Same / equally pref. mobility	d) not comp.	d-test	χ^2-test
Comparison 1				*Measurement*		
n 185	70	85	13	17	−1.29	
p	0.38	0.46	0.07	0.09		
				Evaluation		1.05
n 182	75	74	17	16	0.00	
p	0.41	0.41	0.09	0.09		
Comparison 2				*Measurement*		
n 189	85	72	24	8	0.96	
p	0.45	0.38	0.13	0.04		
				Evaluation		10.37**
n 184	106	42	31	5	5.18***	
p	0.56	0.23	0.17	0.03		
Comparison 3				*Measurement*		
n 189	86	75	22	6	0.89	
p	0.46	0.40	0.12	0.03		
				Evaluation		0.46
n 184	87	67	19	11	1.53	
p	0.47	0.36	0.10	0.06		
Comparison 4				*Measurement*		
n 188	50	92	24	22	−3.44**	
p	0.27	0.49	0.13	0.12		
				Evaluation		1.93
n 183	45	102	19	17	−4.62***	
p	0.25	0.56	0.10	0.09		

Table continues.

positive association, and particularly when considered from an evaluation perspective.

In C4 the responses in both questionnaires are very much in the direction of Betaland. Recall that the theories of social mobility measurement don't make any specific predictions in this comparison, since the two societies have both the same structural and same exchange mobility. Betaland is, however, an overall richer society

TABLE III.

Continuation of Table III

	a) Alphaland	b) Betaland	c) Same / equally pref. mobility	d) not comp.	d-test	χ^2-test
Comparison 5				*Measurement*		
n 180	98	57	19	6	3.21**	
p	0.54	0.32	0.11	0.03		37.05***
				Evaluation		
n 180	42	90	40	8	−4.26***	
p	0.23	0.50	0.22	0.04		
Comparison 6				*Measurement*		
n 187	36	59	70	22	−2.46**	
p	0.19	0.32	0.37	0.12		10.13**
				Evaluation		
n 180	49	32	67	32	1.78**	
p	0.27	0.18	0.37	0.18		
Comparison 7				*Measurement*		
n 184	82	72	17	7	0.40	
p	0.45	0.42	0.09	0.04		8.51*
				Evaluation		
n 182	86	55	29	12	2.69**	
p	0.47	0.30	0.16	0.07		

Legend: The d-test is for the null hypothesis that responses for Alphaland and Betaland are equally likely, that is $H_0 : p(A) = p(B)$ (critical values based on the standard normal approximation of the binomial distribution corrected for continuity). The χ^2-test is for the null hypothesis that the distributions of responses in the two questionnaires can be viewed as if drawn from the same sample (the test aggregates cells $(a), (b), (c, d)$). Stars ***, **, *, denote in the order rejection at 0.1%, 1% and 5% significance levels.

and this may well explain subjects' responses. Among other things, the evidence may also be viewed as a sign that subjects have taken the exercises seriously, in spite of the difficulty which they clearly involve.

The results from comparisons C5 and C6, including societies with negative association, are very interesting. We start by considering C5. In the measurement questionnaire a large majority of responses judge Alphaland, the society with negative association, more mobile than Betaland, which is bistochastic and entails perfect origin independence. The figures are 54% for Alphaland versus 32% for Betaland (value of d-test significant at 1% level). The opposite occurs in the evaluation questionnaire, with 50% of responses for Betaland and 23% for Alphaland (d-test significant at 0.1% level).

In C6, the society with complete reversal, Betaland, is considered more mobile than the society with perfect immobility, Alphaland, by 32% versus 19% of respondents (difference of proportions significant at 1% level); approximately opposite figures apply to the evaluation questionnaire: 27% responses preferring pure immobility against 18% favoring complete reversal. It is also important to notice that, for this comparison, in both questionnaires, the larger percentage of people answer either that the two societies are equally mobile/preferable [answers *c)*] or that they are not comparable [answers *d)*]: the two types of answers account together for 49% of responses in the first questionnaire and for 55% in the second.

Overall, we believe that answers to C5 and C6 therefore indicate that, in the evaluation questionnaire, subjects clearly oppose reversal, while they definitively value origin independence; in the pure measurement questionnaire, on the other hand, subjects seem to see mobility as increasing with rank reversal, possibly not to the extent of viewing complete reversal as the maximum of mobility, but certainly more than that necessary for perfect origin independence.

Perhaps the latter evidence is surprising when compared with the opinions expressed against reversal when stated verbally also in the measurement questionnaire (see Table I in Section 3.1). It is however possible that when giving those opinions people were thinking of social mobility as something always socially positive; while when facing the specific examples in C5 and C6 they cannot fail to recognize more social mobility going with negative association, even if they might not like it.

4. Final discussion and conclusions

In the conclusion of the investigation, the obvious question is: what have we learned from the responses people have given to the questionnaires?

The answer may not be simple: there is certainly some volatility in the data, with some inconsistencies or even contradictory pieces of evidence, as for example between certain results from Part I and Part II of the questionnaires, or between some of the present results and others quoted from our previous study (Bernasconi and Dardanoni, 2004).

We however believe that, despite some of the difficulties it raises, there are also some firm and important conclusions which can be established from the data. Perhaps the sharpest results are about the two classical interpretations one may give to the notion of exchange or pure mobility, namely that of origin independence or of reversal. In particular, in our previous investigation, conducted only on the measurement of mobility, people gave judgments substantially inconsistent with the idea that a greater positive association between fathers' and sons' incomes implies a more rigid society. In this paper we have introduced a more natural display for illustrating to subjects the idea of independence and statical association, have used questions involving situations of both positive and negative associations (reversal), and have clearly separated the issue of measurement from that of evaluating mobility.

The interesting evidence we have found is that while from a measuring perspective people see mobility as increasing with reversal, from an evaluating approach people tend to strongly oppose reversal and in fact to assign the maximum of welfare to situations of origin independence. With some qualifications, similar evidence also holds for judgments given on verbal statements of the two notions of exchange mobility.

An other interesting piece of evidence from the questionnaire concerns structural mobility. Even with regards to this principle, people's perception is only partially friendly to theories. On the one side, when stated verbally, people seem generally to agree with the idea of structural mobility from both a measurement and an evaluating perspective; on the other side, in actual numerical comparisons, there seems to be a lower capacity of subjects to give judgments consistent with the principle, with other considerations (like for example those concerning overall stochastic dominance) possibly also playing some effects. This is a piece of evidence confirmed also from our previous study. Also interesting, concerning structural mobility, is that we have found a greater homogeneity than for exchange mobility, between judgments given under either the measurement or the evaluation frame. We also recall, however, that from the latter perspective there has been up to now little attention by the theoretical literature to value structural mobility.

Some variation in the data should also be considered not surprising, as it may be the sign of a genuine difference of opinions inherent in the very multidimensional concept of social mobility. We are aware that some readers may see in the variation of the evidence only a confirmation of the shortcomings of using the questionnaire method in ethics and social measurement. While we think that constructive criticism is welcome as it encourages a better questionnaire design, we believe that it would be wrong and presumptuous for theorists to proceed without any tests of what people actually think about ethical ideas and measures developed by the scientific community.

Indeed, we should finally emphasize that there has been important achievement of the questionnaire research conducted during the last decade on inequality measurement, to remind the scientific community not only that certain theoretical conventions may not be shared by the majority of individuals; but also that people are different and hence it is natural for them to hold different views about what is important or good for society. The point may obviously be even more important in the context of social mobility, which as emphasized throughout involves intrinsically more problematic judgments than those implied by inequality comparisons.

References

Amiel, Y. 1999. "The Measurement of Income Inequality. The Subjective Approach", in J. Silber (ed.): *Handbook of Inequality Measurement*, Dordrecht: Kluwer Academic Publisher.

Amiel, Y., and F. Cowell. 1992. "Measurement of Income Inequality. Experimental Test by Questionnaire", *Journal of Public Economics* 47, 3-26.

Atkinson, A. 1981. "The Measurement of Economic Mobility", in: P. Eggelshaven, and L. van Gemerden (eds.): *Inkommens Verdeling en Openbard Financien*, Leiden: Het Spectrum.

Bartholomew, D. 1996. *The Statistical Approach to Social Measurement*, San Diego: Academic Press.

Bernasconi, M., and V. Dardanoni. 2004. "An Experimental Analysis of Social Mobility Comparisons", in: F. Cowell (ed.): *Research on Economic Inequality*, vol. 11, Amsterdam: Elsevier, 55-83.

Chakravarty, S., B. Dutta, and J.Weymark. 1985. "Ethical Indices of Income Mobility", *Social Choice and Welfare* 2, 1-21.

Cowell, F. 1985. "Measures of Distributional Change: An Axiomatic Approach", *Review of Economic Studies*, 135-151.

Dardanoni, V. 1993. "Measuring Social Mobility", *Journal of Economic Theory* 61, 372-394.

Duncan, O. 1966. "Methodological Issues in the Analysis of Economic Mobility", N. Smelser, and S. Lipsetin (eds.): *Social Structure and Mobility in Economic Development*, Chicago: Aldine, 51-97.

Fields, G., and E. Ok. 1996. "The Meaning and Measurement of Income Mobility", *Journal of Economic Theory* 71, 349-377.

Fields, G., and E. Ok. 1999. "The Measurement of Income Mobility: An Introduction to the Literature, in J. Silber (ed.): *Handbook of Inequality Measurement*, Dordrecht: Kluwer Academic Publisher, 557-596.

Formby, J., W. Smith, and B. Zheng. 2004. "Mobility Measurement, Transition Matrices and Statistical Inference", *Journal of Econometrics* 120, 181-205.

Frohlich, N., and J. Oppenheimer. 1994. "Preferences for Income Distribution and Distributive Justice: A Window of the Problems of Using Experimental Data in Economics and Ethics", *Eastern Economic Journal* 20(2), 147-155.

Godlthorpe, J., 1980, *Social Mobility and Class Structure in Modern Britain*, Oxford: Oxford University Press.

Gottschalk, P., and E. Spolaore. 2002. "On the Evaluation of Economic Mobility", *Review of Economic Studies* 69, 191-208.

Harrison, E., and C. Seidl. 1994. "Perceptional Inequality and Preferential Judgments: An Empirical Examination of Distributional Axioms", *Public Choice* 79, 61-81.

Markandya, A. 1982. "Intergenerational Exchange Mobility and Economic Welfare", *European Economic Review* 17, 307-324.

Mitra, T., and E. Ok. 1998. "The Measurement of Income Mobility: A Partial Ordering Approach", *Economic Theory* 12, 77-102.

Moyes, P., C. Seidl, and A. Shorrocks. 2002. "Inequalities: Theories, Experiments and Applications", *Journal of Economics* Supplement 9, Wien: Springer.

Prais, S. 1955. "Measuring Social Mobility", *Journal of the Royal Statistical Society* A118, 56-66.

Rogoff, N. 1953. *Recent Trends in Occupational Mobility*, Glencoe: The Free Press.

Shorrocks, A. 1978. "The Measurement of Mobility", *Econometrica* 46, 1013-1024.

Siegel, S., and N. J. Castellan. 1988. *Nonparametric Statistics for the Behavioral Sciences*, II ed., New York: McGraw-Hill.

Van de Gaer, D., E. Schokkaert, and M. Martinez. 2001. "Three Meanings of Intergenerational Mobility", *Economica* 68, 519-538.

Michele Bernasconi
Dipartimento di Economia
Università dell'Insubria
Via Ravasi 2
I-21100 Varese
Italy
michele.bernasconi@uninsubria.it

Valentino Dardanoni
Dip. Scienze Economiche, Aziendali e Finanziarie
Università degli Studi di Palermo
Viale delle Scienze (Parco D' Orleans)
I-90128 Palermo
Italy
vdardono@unipa.it

EQUITY, FISCAL EQUALIZATION, AND FISCAL MOBILITY

A Comparison of Canada and Germany for the 1995–2000 Period

STEFAN TRAUB
Universität Kiel

1. Introduction

The constitutions of many federal states involve a *categorial equity* argument, and therefore call for fiscal equalization among their member states. Categorial equity exists "when all citizens have fair access to public services that are thought to be particularly important to their opportunities in life" (Ladd and Yinger, 1994, p. 212). The categorial-equity precept can be interpreted in different ways, for example, ensuring a minimum quality of public services. In its strictest interpretation, however, categorial equity requires complete equality in service levels, "based on the view that certain public services (education, police, or fire protection, for example) are so important to a person's life chances that all citizens should have equal access to them regardless of their circumstances, or the circumstances of their community" (Ladd and Yinger, 1994, p. 217).[1]

This view is reflected, for example, in Germany's basic law, where Article 106 (3) demands that equal living conditions be preserved among the laender. Accordingly, Article 107 (2) of Germany's basic law requires for an "adequate adjustment" of fiscal capacity (per-capita tax revenue) among the laender.[2] Another typical example is Part III of Canada's Constitution Act of 1982, where it can be read that "Parliament and the legislatures, together with the government of Canada and the provincial governments, are committed to (a) promoting *equal opportunities* for the well-being of Canadians... and (c) providing essential public services of reasonable quality to all Canadians" (emphasis added). Hence, the Constitution Act specifies that "Parliament and the Government of Canada are committed to the principle of making *equalization*

[1] An alternative equity precept is *horizontal equity*, as suggested by Buchanan (1950). This notion of equity grounds on Pigou's (1929) principle of the "equal treatment of equals".

[2] Note, however, that this implies partial equalization of fiscal capacity rather than completely evening out differences in fiscal capacity according to the interpretation of the German Federal Constitutional Court.

U. Schmidt and S. Traub (eds.), Advances in Public Economics: Utility, Choice and Welfare, 197-211.

payments to ensure that provincial governments have sufficient revenues to provide reasonably *comparable levels* of public services at reasonably comparable levels of taxation" (emphasis added).

While the primary purpose of fiscal equalization may be seen in narrowing down interjurisdictional inequality for a given fiscal year, its secondary purpose, or long-run goal must be placing poorer states, provinces, or laender in a position to raise sufficient tax revenue on their own in order to fulfill the categorial equity precept. This notion of fiscal equalization considers fiscal equalization as an act of solidarity that strengthens the fiscal autonomy of lower-level jurisdictions.[3] Of course, not all differences in the abilities of the states, provinces, or laender to generate own tax revenue can be evened out, even in the long run. In particular, this applies to cost differences in the provision of infrastructure and other public goods which are caused by differing natural resource endowments.

This paper takes up the question whether fiscal equalization has been successful in reaching its goal of bringing the German laender and the Canadian provinces and territories, respectively, closer together with respect to their fiscal capacity (per-capita tax revenue). Since 1995 the formerly East German laender have been integrated into the existing fiscal equalization scheme, the laenderfinanzausgleich.[4] Therefore, we consider the *fiscal mobility* of the laender and the Canadian provinces and territories, respectively, during the 1995-2000 time period. By fiscal mobility we mean the development of the fiscal capacity of a land or province both in relation to its own initial fiscal capacity and in relation to the other laenders' or provinces' fiscal capacity. The strong resemblance between the terms fiscal mobility and income mobility as used in dynamic income distribution analysis is intended. In fact, our basic idea is to apply a method of income mobility measurement that was recently developed by Van Kerm (2001) to interjurisdictional inequality instead of interindividual inequality. From a methodological point of view, this seems to be justified since considerations of interjurisdictional inequality do not involve any "organic" concept of state. Ultimately, the recipient of equalization is the individual citizen who has joined a group of individuals in a particular member state of the federation. Thus, the reduction of interjurisdictional inequality is used here only as a vehicle to reduce interindividual inequality (compare, Mieszkowski and Musgrave, 1999). Van Kerm's (2001) method has the advantage that decompositions of income mobility and fiscal mobility, respectively, into its "structural" and "exchange" components are easily obtained.[5]

Our main result is that, although there has been large fiscal mobility in both countries, inequality among the laender and the provinces and territories, respectively, has risen. The increase in interjurisdictional inequality was more pronounced in Germany than in Canada. The decomposition of the mobility measure into its

[3] Compare Hidien (1999) who criticized that fiscal equalization has often been overburdened (by economists) with efficiency and regional policy goals.

[4] We use the term laenderfinanzausgleich in a generic sense, including all three steps of the currently applied fiscal equalization scheme.

[5] A similar method has independently been developed by Ruiz-Castillo (2001).

different components shows that fiscal mobility was manly due to growth (increased average fiscal capacity). Thus, fiscal equalization was not successful in reaching its long-run goals.

The paper is organized as follows. In the next section, we review Van Kerm's (2001) approach to the measurement and decomposition of income inequality. Section 3 briefly summarizes the main features of the Canadian and the German equalization programs. In Section 4, we presented our results concerning the fiscal mobility of the Canadian provinces and territories, and the German laender. Section 5 concludes the paper.

2. Decomposing Fiscal Mobility

Since Van Kerm's (2001) approach to the decomposition of income mobility is relatively new, we give a detailed review of his approach, applied here to jurisdictions instead of individuals. The notion of *fiscal capacity* is central to fiscal equalization and to our measurement of fiscal mobility. The fiscal capacity of a jurisdiction is defined as its total tax revenue at a given fiscal year divided by population size, that is, its per-capita tax revenue. Mobility is observed between two fiscal years, the base period, $t = 0$, and the final period, $t = 1$. The federation consists of $i = 1, \ldots, n$ provinces and territories, or laender. For any time period $t \in \{0, 1\}$, $f_i^k \in \mathbb{R}_+$ denotes the fiscal capacity of jurisdiction i, and $f_i = (f_i^0, f_i^1)$ denotes its profile of fiscal capacity over the two periods of time. The marginal distribution of fiscal capacity at each period is given by the vector $f^k = (f_1^k, \ldots, f_n^k)$, and all profiles of fiscal capacity are collected in the matrix $\mathbf{f} = (f^0, f^1) \in \mathbb{R}_+^{2n}$. A mobility index $M \ : \ \mathbb{R}_+^{2n} \to \mathbb{R}$ assigns a real numbered value to any $\mathbf{f} \in \mathbb{R}_+^{2n}$, measuring the level of mobility while moving from f^0 to f^1.

According to Van Kerm (2001), $M(\mathbf{f})$ can be decomposed into two basic components: a *structural* component and an *exchange* component.[6] The former component measures the change in the marginal distribution of fiscal capacity (as could be measured by its moments), while the latter captures the mobility which is associated with a re-ordering of the jurisdictions according to their fiscal capacity. Even if the marginal distributions of fiscal capacity stay the same over the two time periods, jurisdictions may not keep their relative position of fiscal capacity. Thus, the structural mobility component is the share of overall mobility that can be explained solely by changes in the distribution of fiscal capacity where it is assumed that all provinces or laender keep their original position in the distribution, while the exchange mobility component is the share of overall mobility that is solely due to the re-ordering of jurisdictions within a given distribution of fiscal capacity. Van Kerm (2001) further refines the decomposition of (fiscal) mobility by decomposing the structural component into a *growth* term and a *dispersion* term. As the name suggests, the growth term refers to the share of structural mobility that is due to growth of fiscal capacity (an increase

[6] Van Kerm (2001) attributes the distinction between exchange and structural mobility to Markandya (1982).

in the mean). Correspondingly, the dispersion term captures a change in the degree of inequality in the distribution of fiscal capacity.

In order to achieve the decomposition of fiscal mobility into its three components, the movement from f^0 to f^1 can be decomposed into three sequences $f^0 \to f^\alpha$, $f^\alpha \to f^\beta$, and $f^\beta \to f^1$, where any sequence involves only one of the components. For example, if the ordering of the components is growth, followed by dispersion and exchange, the decomposition is given by

$$\begin{aligned} M(\mathbf{f}) &= \underbrace{\{M(f^0, f^\alpha) - M(f^0, f^0)\}}_{\text{growth}} + \underbrace{\{M(f^0, f^\beta) - M(f^0, f^\alpha)\}}_{\text{dispersion}} \\ &\quad + \underbrace{\{M(f^0, f^1) - M(f^0, f^\beta)\}}_{\text{exchange}}, \end{aligned} \tag{1}$$

where f^α is obtained by multiplying f^0 with the ratio of the mean of the final period distribution of fiscal capacity to the base period distribution of fiscal capacity, $f^\alpha = \frac{\mu(f^1)}{\mu(f^0)} f^0$, f^β is obtained by a permutation π of the final period distribution of fiscal capacity in such a way that the jurisdictions keep their original positions of fiscal capacity, $f^\beta = \pi f^1$, and the exchange effect is introduced simply by re-ordering the jurisdictions in the order of the final period.

A shortcoming of this approach is that the values obtained for the different components depend upon the sequence chosen to introduce the components. To clarify this, consider the following example: set $f^0 = (3, 2)$ and $f^1 = (4, 5)$.[7] There are possible $3! = 6$ sequences:

$$\begin{array}{lllllll}
a) & (3,2) & \xrightarrow{\text{growth}} (5.4, 3.6) & \xrightarrow{\text{dispersion}} (5,4) & \xrightarrow{\text{exchange}} & (4,5) \\
b) & (3,2) & \xrightarrow{\text{growth}} (5.4, 3.6) & \xrightarrow{\text{exchange}} (3.6, 5.4) & \xrightarrow{\text{dispersion}} & (4,5) \\
c) & (3,2) & \xrightarrow{\text{dispersion}} (2.8, 2.2) & \xrightarrow{\text{growth}} (5,4) & \xrightarrow{\text{exchange}} & (4,5) \\
d) & (3,2) & \xrightarrow{\text{dispersion}} (2.8, 2.2) & \xrightarrow{\text{exchange}} (2.2, 2.8) & \xrightarrow{\text{growth}} & (4,5) \\
e) & (3,2) & \xrightarrow{\text{exchange}} (2,3) & \xrightarrow{\text{growth}} (3.6, 5.4) & \xrightarrow{\text{dispersion}} & (4,5) \\
f) & (3,2) & \xrightarrow{\text{exchange}} (2,3) & \xrightarrow{\text{dispersion}} (2.2, 2.8) & \xrightarrow{\text{growth}} & (4,5)\,.
\end{array}$$

Obviously, for example, the growth component in case a), $M_a^G((3,2),(4,5)) = M((5.4, 3.6), (3, 2)) - M((3,2),(3,2))$, will, in general, not be the same as the growth component as determined by sequence f) $M_f^G((3,2),(4,5)) = M((3,2),(4,5)) - M((3,2),(2.2, 2.8))$. In order to get around this problem of path dependence, Van Kerm (2001) suggests to employ the Shapley value method which is well known from

[7] For a graphical representation of different possible component sequences see Van Kerm (2001).

cooperative game theory to determine the *average* total effect of each component.[8] Let $M^j(\mathbf{f})$ denote the total effect of component j, $j \in \{G, D, E\}$, and $M^{j,s}(\mathbf{f})$ denote the marginal effect of component j in sequence s, $s \in S$, where S is the set of all possible sequences, then the contribution of component f is given by[9]

$$M^j(\mathbf{f}) = \frac{1}{3!} \sum_{s \in S} M^{j,s}(\mathbf{f}) \,. \tag{2}$$

Finally, a mobility measure needs to be chosen. Many mobility measure have been proposed in the literature, but only two of them are able to capture all the effects which are of interest for us, namely the Fields and Ok (1996) index, which is given by

$$M_{FO96}(\mathbf{f}) = \frac{1}{n} \sum_{i=1}^{n} |f_i^1 - f_i^0| \,, \tag{3}$$

and the Fields and Ok (1999) index, which is given by

$$M_{FO99}(\mathbf{f}) = \frac{1}{n} \sum_{i=1}^{n} | \log(f_i^1) - \log(f_i^0)| \,. \tag{4}$$

These two indices are neither *ordinal in units* (which would imply rank sensitivity), nor *intertemporal scale invariant* (which would imply relativity).[10] Since they are based on the rank or rank correlations, indices which are ordinal in units would attribute all mobility to exchange. Intertemporal scale invariant, or relative indices would not be able to capture the growth component.[11]

3. Fiscal Equalization in Canada and Germany

3.1. THE CANADIAN EQUALIZATION PROGRAM

Canada is comprised of 10 provinces and 3 territories. Since some of the necessary data for Nunavut, a former part of the Northwest Territories, have not been recorded before 2000, we treat Nunavut and the Northwest Territories as an aggregate. There are three major transfer programs: the equalization program, territorial formula financing (TFF), and the Canada Health and Social Transfer (CHST).

The equalization program is intended for reducing disparities among *provinces*. It provides vertical unconditional transfers to provinces with below-than-average fiscal

[8] See Shorrocks (1999), Chantreuil and Trannoy (1999), and Rongve (1999) for a detailed discussion.

[9] Note that Van Kerm (2001) also distinguishes between non-hierarchical and hierarchical structures. A hierarchical structure would be given, if we were differentiating between structural and exchange components at the top level and between growth and dispersion at the second level. Then a different formula would apply. See also Shorrocks (1999).

[10] See Table 1 in Van Kerm (2001).

[11] A property that all sensible mobility indices share is *normalization*, that is, $M(f, f) = 0$.

capacity. Equalization payments are calculated according to a formula laid down in "The Federal-Provincial Fiscal Arrangements Act". Provinces with a fiscal capacity (ability to raise revenue) below a *standard amount* are entitled to equalization transfers from the federal government to bring their tax revenues up to that standard amount. The fiscal capacity of a province is calculated as the per-capita yields of more than 30 revenue sources (including natural resource royalties etc.) that would result if it applied national average tax rates to standardized tax bases. Standardized tax bases and tax rates for these revenue sources are defined in the representative tax system (RTS). The standard amount is determined by the average fiscal capacity of the five provinces Quebec, Ontario, Manitoba, Saskatchewan, and British Columbia. Equalization payments are subject to "floor" and "ceiling" provisions. Floor provisions protect provinces against too large year-to-year declines in their payments. Entitlements may not decrease by more than 5% to 15%, depending on the relative shortfall with respect to the standard amount. Ceiling provisions control the year-to-year growth in equalization. If entitlements grow at a higher rate than the GNP, entitlements are reduced by an equal per-capita amount.

TFF is an annual unconditional transfer from the federal government to the territorial governments (including Nunavut). It is determined through a formula based on a "gap-filling" principle, that is, it takes into account the difference between the expenditure needs and the revenue means of territorial governments. The difference is paid out as a cash payment. Expenditure needs are represented by the formula's Gross Expenditure Base reflecting the *provinces* expenditure pressures. The Gross Expenditure Base is indexed to move in line with growth in provincial spending, and it is also adjusted for territorial population growth relative to Canada as a whole. A territory's ability to raise revenue is measures by estimating the revenue a territory would have at its disposal if it exercised a tax effort similar to that in other parts of Canada, adjusted to recognize the special circumstances in the North (dense settlement of population, economic activity lags behind).

The CHST is a federal transfer program that came into effect as of 1996–97, replacing its predecessors, the Established Programs Financing (EPF), and the Canada Assistance Plan (CAP). It goes to all provinces and territories and is used to fund health care, post-secondary education, social assistance and social services. Like the EPF, the CHST provides the provinces and territories with both cash payments and tax transfers. Tax transfers were introduced in the 1960's when the federal government offered provinces contracting-out arrangements for some federal-provincial programs, such as hospital care and social welfare. Only Quebec chose to use these arrangements. Under the arrangements, the federal government reduced ("abated") its personal income tax rate by 13.5 percentage points while Quebec increased its personal income taxes by an equivalent amount. Quebec continues to receive the value of these extra tax points through its own income tax system, while other provinces receive the corresponding amounts in cash. Note that the Quebec abatement has no net impact on federal transfers, Quebec's own receipts, and other provinces' receipts. Under CHST, total cash transfers are limited to a certain amount (in 2001–02 the cash floor was 15,500 mill. Canadian $). The cash component is determined residually

TABLE I. Volume of the Canadian equalization program 1995–2000

Fiscal year	1995–96	1996–97	1997–98	1998–99	1999–00	2000–01
CHST[a,b]	29,882	26,900	25,295	25,833	29,979	31,986
Cash[a]	18,476	14,850	12,500	12,500	14,500	15,500
Tax transfer[a]	11,406	12,050	12,795	13,333	15,479	16,468
Equalization[a]	8,759	8,789	8,987	8,750	10,770	10,828
TFF[a]	1,180	1,135	1,138	1,137	1,320	1,436
Total[a,c]	38,984	35,932	34,508	34,807	40,797	42,912
per capita[d]	1,318	1,212	1,151	1,150	1,338	1,395
Own tax revenues[a]	130,086	137,778	143,263	149,826	155,560	165,744
Equalization ratio[e]	29.97	26.08	24.09	23.23	26.23	25.89

Table notes. Data sources: Statistics Canada, Tables 051–0001 and 385–0002; Department of Finance.

[a] Mill. Canadian $.

[b] In 1995–96: CAP and EPF.

[c] Equalization associated with tax transfers under CHST appears in both the equalization and the CHST figures. Totals are adjusted to avoid double counting.

[d] Canadian $ per capita.

[e] Ratio of total equalization payments/tax transfers and own tax revenues as a percentage.

as the difference between a jurisdiction's entitlement (based on its population share) and its equalized notional tax yield. The notional tax yield of a province or territory is defined as 13.5 personal income tax points and 1 corporate income tax point. Since the provinces and territories exhibit different potential to generate tax revenue given the transferred tax points, the value of the tax transfer is equalized according to the above mentioned five-province average.

Table I reports the volume of the Canadian Equalization Program for the fiscal years 1995–96 to 2000–01.[12] The three major programs involved a per-capita transfer from the federal government to provinces and territories of some 1,300 Canadian $ in 1995. After a decline in the meantime, the per-capita transfer reached roughly 1,400 Canadian $ in 2000. As can be taken from the last row of the table, the ratio between total transfers and the provinces' and territories' own tax revenues amounted to between 23% and 30%.

3.2. THE LAENDERFINANZAUSGLEICH

Since its reunification in 1990, Germany is a federation of 16 laender. Germany's fiscal constitution is set down in Articles 104a to 115 of its constitution. Moreover, the fiscal constitution includes several federal laws of which the fiscal equalization law

[12] Note that a Canadian fiscal year runs from April to March of the following year.

("Finanzausgleichsgesetz") from 1993 is most important as it contains all relevant regulations as to the present intergovernmental transfer system at the state level. The "Finanzausgleichsgesetz" came into effect as of January 1995. It is part of a bundle of laws dealing with fiscal consequences of the German reunification. Virtually, tax legislation is concentrated at the federal level, while the laender as a whole have a right of co-determination as far as taxes are concerned that are, at least partly, due to the laender. Thus, in contrast to Canada, tax rates for all significant taxes such as personal and corporate income tax, VAT, and consumption taxes are uniform within the federal territory. In fact, creating uniformity of taxing conditions is one of the main objectives of the German fiscal constitution.

Germany's tax system is a blend of unshared and shared taxes. Unshared taxes, as the name suggests, are assigned exclusively to one of the three governmental layers (federal government, laender, municipalities). Typical unshared taxes are mineral oil tax, a federal tax; motor vehicle tax, a state tax; and trade earnings tax, a municipal tax. Shared taxes are assigned to and then divided among at least two of the governmental layers according to legally determined percentages. There are four shared taxes: personal and corporate income taxes, VAT, and interest withholding tax. In 2000 the laender received 42.5% of personal income tax, 50% of corporate income tax, 45.9% of VAT, and 44% of interest withholding tax.[13] Among the laender taxes are distributed according to their local returns. The principle of residence allots pay-as-you-go taxes such as wages tax, a part of personal income tax, to the state where the tax payer lives. Corporate income tax is distributed among the laender according to the principle of business premises.

Fiscal equalization takes place in three steps. The first step is VAT-equalization ("Umsatzsteuer-Vorwegausgleich"). 75% of the total VAT receipts flow into the laender according to their number of inhabitants. The remainder is due to those laender whose per-capita tax revenues reach less than 92% of the average per-capita tax revenues (fiscal capacity) of all laender. In the second step (horizontal fiscal equalization), those laender who have less than 95% of the average fiscal capacity, including about half of the tax returns of their municipalities, receive transfers from those laender who have more than 100% until they reach the 95% threshold exactly. Rich laender pay funds into the equalization pot according to a rather complicated progressive scheme. In order to save space, we omit details. It is important to be aware of the fact, however, that the marginal burden of rich states can reach more than 80%. Note that the number of inhabitants of the city-states Berlin, Bremen, and Hamburg is multiplied by 1.35 in order to calculate their fiscal capacities. Moreover, in order to calculate the per-capita tax revenues of the municipalities, their number of inhabitants is adjusted: The first 5,000 inhabitants receive a weight of 1.0, the next 15,000 inhabitants receive a weight of 1.1 and so on. Conditional and unconditional federal grants make up the final step of fiscal equalization in Germany. After collection of federal grants, all laender have at least 99.5% of the average fiscal capacity.

[13] These percentages are adjusted on a regular basis in order to keep the vertical fiscal balance, that is, the ratio of tax revenue and spending.

TABLE II. Volume of the laenderfinanzausgleich 1995–2000

Fiscal year	1995	1996	1997	1998	1999	2000
VAT-equalization[a]	14,723	16,777	16,211	17,593	19,465	22,064
Horizontal equalization[a]	11,195	12,229	11,997	13,534	14,602	16,275
Federal grants[a]	25,072	25,150	25,235	25,654	25,841	26,091
Total[a]	50,990	54,156	53,443	56,718	59,908	64,430
per capita[b]	625	661	651	692	730	784
Own tax revenues[a,c]	277,725	281,216	278,371	290,308	304,888	311,286
Equalization ratio[d]	18.36	19.26	19.20	19.54	19.65	20.70

Table note. Data source: Bundesfinanzministerium (2001).
[a]Million deutschmarks.
[b]Deutschmarks per capita.
[c]Tax revenues from own sources and shared taxes less 25% of VAT.
[d]Ratio of total equalization payments and own tax revenues as a percentage.

Table II lists the relevant figures for the German laender as a whole. The laenders' own tax revenue plus shared taxes except for VAT forms the base of assessment for VAT-equalization. VAT-equalization redistributes up to 25% of the laenders' VAT share to the laender with less-than-average tax revenue; the volume (contributions made by the rich laender) of VAT-equalization amounted to 11 billion deutschmarks in 1995 and to 16 billion deutschmarks in 2000. In order to determine the volume of the horizontal equalization step, about 50% of the municipalities' tax revenue is added to the total tax revenue of the laender, taking into account the above mentioned population weights. Horizontal fiscal equalization came up to 11 billion deutschmarks in 1995 and 16 billion deutschmarks in 2000. Finally, the laender collect conditional and unconditional grants, which amounted to 25 billion deutschmarks in 1995 and 26 billion deutschmarks in 2000. All in all, the volume of the laenderfinanzsausgleich amounted to 48 billion deutschmarks in 1995 and 64 billion deutschmarks in 2000, or, in per capita terms, 625 deutschmarks and 784 deutschmarks, respectively. Most of these transfers went to the East German laender. The equalization ratio was 18.36% in 1995 and it increased to 20.70% in 2000.

Due to the different tax and fiscal equalization systems the figures stated in Tables I and II cannot be compared directly. In contrast to a Canadian province or territory, a German land hardly has the possibility to generate additional tax revenue by setting own tax rates or imposing new taxes. Moreover, the Canadian equalization program redistributes funds from the federal government to provinces and territories, that is, the equalization system is vertical, while more than 50% of the volume of the German laenderfinanzausgleich is due to horizontal redistribution among the laender. It is interesting to see, however, that the average per-capita transfers in Canada were more than twice as much as the average per-capita transfers in Germany in any year of

TABLE III. Per capita fiscal capacities of the Canadian provinces and territories

Province/Territory	1995		2000	
	Fiscal capacity	Rank	Fiscal capacity	Rank
British Columbia	5,434	1	5,526	4
Alberta	5,394	2	6,431	1
Saskatchewan	4,815	3	5,876	3
Quebec	4,511	4	5,982	2
Northwest-Territories	4,401	5	4,406	8
Manitoba	4,365	6	5,184	5
New Brunswick	4,032	7	4,410	7
Ontario	3,955	8	5,070	6
Prince Edward Island	3,724	9	4,150	9
Newfoundland	3,604	10	4,141	10
Yukon	3,432	11	3,931	11
Nova Scotia	3,141	12	3,792	12

Table note. All figures in Canadian $. Northwest-Territories including Nunavut.

the 1995–2000 period (a deutschmark was worth about 0.73 Canadian $ on average).

4. Fiscal Mobility in Canada and Germany

Tables III and IV list the fiscal capacities (in per capita terms) and the associated rank places of the Canadian provinces and territories and the German laender, respectively. As can be taken from Table III, the four least off provinces and territories Prince Edward Island, Newfoundland, Yukon, and Nova Scotia, were not able to improve on their 1995 rank place, though their fiscal capacities increased. Ontario and Quebec won 2 rank places. The big loosers were British Columbia and the Northwest territories loosing 3 rank places each.

In Germany, only Berlin was able to improve distinctly on its 1995 rank place by 3 positions. The rank places of the other laender did not change by more than one position. Hamburg clearly outperformed the other laender, exhibiting a fiscal capacity in per-capita terms more than 20% larger than Hesse following on the second place. The five East German laender Brandburg, Saxony, Mecklenburg-Vorpommern, Saxony-Anhalt, and Thuringia formed the group of the least off laender in both years; their tax revenues hardly changed.

In Table V, we have collected some statistics concerning the distribution of fiscal capacities in both countries. In Canada, the mean fiscal capacity in per-capita terms rose by some 16%. The increase in both the coefficient of variation and the Gini coefficient by more than 5% indicates that fiscal inequality rose slightly within the 1995–2000 period. Germany's average fiscal capacity increased by about 11%. The figures for both the coefficient of variation and the Gini coefficient are much higher

TABLE IV. Per capita fiscal capacities of the German laender

Land	1995		2000	
	Fiscal capacity	Rank	Fiscal capacity	Rank
Hamburg	4,920	1	6,177	1
Hesse	4,017	2	5,136	2
Baden-Wuerttemberg	3,944	3	4,591	3
North-Rhine Westphalia	3,910	4	4,402	5
Bavaria	3,899	5	4,583	4
Bremen	3,895	6	4,139	6
Schleswig-Holstein	3,734	7	3,890	8
Rhineland-Palatinate	3,540	8	3,877	9
Lower-Saxony	3,489	9	3,725	10
Berlin	3,447	10	3,904	7
Saarland	3,217	11	3,487	11
Brandenburg	2,519	12	2,478	12
Saxony	2,419	13	2,393	14
Mecklenburg-Vorpommern	2,329	14	2,420	13
Saxony-Anhalt	2,282	15	2,284	16
Thuringia	2,275	16	2,306	15

Table note. All figures in deutschmarks.

TABLE V. Distributional statistics

Measure	1995	2000	Relative change (%)
	Canada		
Mean fiscal capacity (CND$)	4,234	4,908	15.92
Coefficient of variation	.1650	.1740	5.46
Gini coefficient	.1019	.1073	5.26
	Germany		
Mean fiscal capacity (DM)	3,365	3,737	11.05
Coefficient of variation	.2266	.2945	30.00
Gini coefficient	.1330	.1741	30.91

than those obtained for Canada. Moreover, the increase of both inequality measures by 30% shows that the gap between the "have" and the "have-nots" laender widened drastically as compared to Canada. This increase in the degree of inequality was mainly due to the poor performance of the East German laender which were not able to keep up with growth in the rest of the country (see Table II).

Following the 41st annual Premiers' Conference in August 2000, the Canadian

TABLE VI. Decomposition of fiscal mobility

Factor	M_{FO96}		M_{FO99}	
	Absolute	Relative	Absolute	Relative
	Canada			
Exchange	105.07	15.59	.0225	15.39
Growth	522.38	77.49	.1128	77.10
Dispersion	46.63	6.92	.0110	7.51
Total	674.08	100.00	.1463	100.00
	Germany			
Exchange	18.93	4.98	.0060	6.64
Growth	257.08	67.58	.0613	67.80
Dispersion	104.42	27.45	.0231	25.56
Total	380.43	100.00	.0905	100.00

Intergovernmental Conference Secretariate released a note expressing the Premiers' deepest concern about the "current and growing" horizontal fiscal imbalances among the provinces and territories. Though the claim that inequality among the provinces and territories has increased is confirmed by our analysis, Canada's concerns seem almost diminutive as compared to Germany's.

In Table VI we present decompositions of the Fields and Ok income mobility indices into the "exchange", "growth", and "dispersion" factors. Fiscal mobility was much higher in Canada than in Germany. In both countries fiscal mobility was mainly due to growth (77% in Canada, 68% in Germany), that is, an increase in the mean fiscal capacities. There is, however, an important difference between Canada and Germany. In Canada, the exchange component contributed to 16% of total fiscal mobility which means that some provinces and territories changed their rank places in the distribution of fiscal capacities. The dispersion factor did not play an important role as it contributed to only 7% of overall mobility. In contrast to this, Germany exhibited less exchange and more dispersion.

Table VII lists the figures for the fiscal mobility required to erase all interjurisdictional inequality. In order to compute these numbers, we assumed that every jurisdiction had the mean fiscal capacity of the year 2000 of the respective country. Since all provinces and territories and laender, respectively, have the same hypothetical fiscal capacity in 2000 now, the exchange component assumes a value of zero. In fact, exchange is neither intended nor desired by fiscal equalization. If jurisdictions switch their rank places due to fiscal equalization, this obviously creates strong negative incentives both for rich and poor jurisdictions. Moreover, rich jurisdictions will legitimately argue that the degree of fiscal equalization is too high.

Table VII shows that actual total fiscal mobility was too small in both countries. The fiscal mobility necessary to erase inequality among Canada's provinces and

TABLE VII. Fiscal mobility required to erase interjurisdictional inequality

Factor	M_{FO96}		M_{FO99}	
	Absolute	Relative	Absolute	Relative
		Canada		
Exchange	.00	.00	.0000	.00
Growth	465.32	55.22	.1013	52.25
Dispersion	377.34	44.78	.0926	47.75
Total	824.66	100.00	.1939	100.00
		Germany		
Exchange	.00	.00	.0000	.00
Growth	185.56	28.88	.0521	26.24
Dispersion	457.05	71.12	.1464	73.76
Total	642.62	100.00	.1985	100.00

territories completely is about 22% higher than actual fiscal mobility. As was to be expected, this figure is much higher for Germany. In order to place all laender in the same position, a fiscal mobility 69% higher than actual fiscal mobility would have been necessary. Consequently, the growth component looses relative importance, while the dispersion factor gains strongly. Again, there are important differences between Canada and Germany. In Canada, the growth factor still is more important than the dispersion factor. This does not come as a surprise as inequality rose only by some 5% in the time period considered. For Germany the picture is different. Here, the dispersion factor contributes more than 70% of total fiscal mobility.

5. Summary and Conclusion

The constitutions of Canada and Germany involve a categorial equity argument, and therefore call for fiscal equalization among their member provinces and territories and laender, respectively. In this paper, we have argued that the long-run goal of fiscal equalization must be placing poorer states, provinces, or laender in a position to raise sufficient tax revenue on their own in order to fulfill the categorial equity precept. Fiscal equalization is considered as an act of solidarity that strengthens fiscal autonomy and therefore keeps federalism alive.

In order to assess the success of the Canadian and German equalization programs regarding their long-run goals, we applied a method of income mobility measurement developed by Van Kerm (2001) to interjurisdictional inequality instead of interindividual inequality. Fiscal mobility as measured by the development of the per-capita fiscal capacities of Canada's provinces and territories and Germany's laender, respectively, was decomposed into its "growth", "exchange", and "dispersion" components.

Though there was a high degree of fiscal mobility in both countries in the 1995–2000 period, our results suggest that both equalization programs failed to reach their long-run goal of reducing interjurisdictional inequality. Fiscal mobility was mainly due to growth of mean fiscal capacities. Interjurisdictional inequality, however, rose by 5% in Canada and by more than 30% in Germany. Computing the degree of fiscal mobility necessary to erase all interjurisdictional inequality showed that the dispersion factor should have been much higher in both absolute terms and relative terms. The relative better performance of Canada's equalization program may be explained by two major factors. First, in per capita terms, CHST, equalization, and TFF involved much higher transfers than the laenderfinanzausgleich. Second, Canadian provinces and territories have more freedom and flexibility in generating own tax revenues than their German counterparts. This may have two interpretations: either the level of fiscal equalization must be further increased, or structural reasons, including those which can not be overcome by transfer payments, have forestalled fiscal equalization from being successful.

It is hardly conceivable, however, that the richer German laender will agree on further increasing the degree of horizontal fiscal equalization, since a group of them already successfully appealed to the German Federal Constitutional Court, resulting in the Constitutional Court's order to reorganize the laenderfinanzausgleich and to limit the marginal burden of the richer laender. Given the restrictions of the Maastricht treaty, it is also unlikely that more funds can be transferred from the federal government's household to the households of the laender. The laenderfinanzausgleich in its present form seems to be overcharged by the large financial burden caused by integrating the East German laender into the equalization program. More freedom and flexibility for the laender to generate their own tax revenues could possibly relieve the problem of growing interjurisdictional inequality.

On the occasion of the 41st annual Premiers' Conference in August 2000, the Premiers called on the federal government of Canada to "strengthen its commitment to the Equalization Program so that the Program meets its constitutionally mandated objectives". In particular, the Premiers suggested to remove the ceiling on equalization payments and to escalate equalization payments in an appropriate manner. As in Germany, there is an ongoing debate on the "right" implementation of equalization. Couchrene (1998), for example, suggested to replace the five-provinces standard by a national-average standard. For 1996, he estimated a national average of 5,200 Canadian $ as compared to a five-province standard of 5,093 Canadian dollars, implying an increase of equalization payments by 1,3 billion Canadian $ (3.6% of total equalization payments).

The results presented in this paper are, of course, subject to limitations. First, a time period of six years is too short to draw reliable conclusions about the future development of fiscal mobility in Canada and Germany. Thus, our observations regarding the development of fiscal capacities should be understood as tendencies only. Second, we did not take into account negative incentive effects that could possibly have foiled the success of the equalization programs. Though there exists already some literature on strategical responses of lower-level jurisdictions to fiscal equalization (see, for example, Chernick, 2000, Ebert and Meyer, 1999, Baretti et al., 2000) this is clearly an understudied domain.

Acknowledgements

This research was financially supported by the European Commission under TMR contract no. ERBFMRXCT98-0248.

References

Baretti, C., B. Huber, and K. Lichtblau. 2000. *A Tax on Tax Revenue: The Incentive Effects of Equalizing Transfers. Evidence from Germany*, CES-ifo Working Paper 333, München: CES-ifo.
Buchanan, J. M. 1950. "Federalism and Fiscal Equity", *American Economic Review* 40, 583–599.
Chantreuil, F., and A. Trannoy. 1999. *Inequality Decomposition Values: The Trade-Off between Marginality and Consistency*, Discussion Paper DP 9924, THEMA, Université de Cergy-Pontoise.
Chernick, H. 2000. "Federal Grants and Social Welfare Spending: Do State Respones Matter?", *National Tax Journal* 53, 143–168.
Courchene, T. J. 1998. *Renegotiating Equalization: National Polity, Federal State, International Economy*, Toronto: C. D. Howe Institute.
Ebert, W., and S. Meyer. 1999. "Die Anreizwirkungen des Finanzausgleichs", *Wirtschaftsdienst* 79, 106–114.
Fields, G. S., and E. A. Ok. 1996. "The Meaning and Measurement of Income Mobility", *Journal of Economic Theory* 71, 349–377.
Fields, G. S., and E. A. Ok. 1999. "Measuring Movement of Incomes", *Economica* 66, 455–471.
Hiddien, J. W. 1999. *Der bundesstaatliche Finanzausgleich in Deutschland. Geschichtliche und staatsrechtliche Grundlagen*, Baden-Baden: Nomos.
Ladd, H. F., and J. Yinger. 1994. "The Case for Equalizing Aid", *National Tax Journal* 47, 211–224.
Markandya, A. 1982. "Intergenerational Exchange Mobility and Economic Welfare", *European Economic Review* 17, 307–324.
Mieszkowski, P., and R. A. Musgrave. 1999. "Federalism, Grants, and Fiscal Equalization", *National Tax Journal* 52, 239–260.
Pigou, A. C. 1929. *A Study in Public Finance*, London: Macmillan.
Rongve, I. 1999. *A Shapley Decomposition of Inequality Indices by Income Source*, Discussion Paper 59, Department of Economics, University of Regina, Canada.
Ruiz-Castillo, J. 2001. *The Measurement of Structural and Exchange Income Mobility*, Mimeo, Universidad Carlos III de Madrid, Spain.
Shorrocks, A. F. 1999. *Decomposition Procedures for Distributional Analysis: A Unified Framework Based on the Shapley Value*, Mimeo, University of Essex, Colchester, UK.
Van Kerm, P. 2001. *What Lies Behind Income Mobility? Reranking and Distributional Change in Belgium, Germany and the USA*, Mimeo, CEPS/INSTEAD, Luxemburg.

Stefan Traub
Institut für Volkwirtschaftslehre
Universität Kiel
24098 Kiel
Germany
traub@bwl.uni-kiel.de

COMPARING THEORIES: WHAT ARE WE LOOKING FOR?

JOHN HEY
Universities of York & Bari

1. Introduction

Two recent papers, Harless and Camerer (1994) and Hey and Orme (1994), were both addressed to the same question: which is the 'best' theory of decision making under risk? A second question that both addressed was: are any of the new generalizations of Expected Utility theory (EU) *significantly better* than EU (in some appropriate sense)? These are important questions: much theoretical effort has been expended in trying to produce a 'better' story of decision making under risk than that apparently provided by EU. What has been the purpose of this effort? Surely to improve the *predictive power* and *descriptive validity* of economics. These, of course, are competing objectives in general: other things being equal, the greater the predictive power of a theory, the lower the descriptive validity of that theory. However, the purpose of 'better' theory is to make other things *not* equal. Nevertheless, there generally (and as it happens in the context of recent theories of decision making under risk, specifically) is the need to make some judgement of the appropriate trade-off between predictive power and descriptive validity: simply because if one theory was better in *both* predictive power and descriptive ability than a second, the second would simply be discarded — it would be dominated by the first.

Unfortunately, discarding dominated theories does not lead — in the area of decision making under risk — to a uniquely dominating theory. To discriminate amongst the remaining theories one therefore needs to do three things:

1. Decide on an appropriate measure of the predictive success of any theory
2. Decide on an appropriate measure of the predictive power of a theory
3. Decide on an appropriate way of trading-off the one against the other.

Selten (1991) gives one possible set of answers to these questions; two recent papers Harless and Camerer (1994) and Hey and Orme (1994) give two interpretations of another. The purpose of this present paper is to try and shed light on their relative merits, as well as providing a general framework for the analysis of such questions.

Selten (1991) suggests:

U. Schmidt and S. Traub (eds.), Advances in Public Economics: Utility, Choice and Welfare, 213-234.

1. that we measure the predictive success of a theory as *the proportion of observations* in some given data set *consistent with that theory*
2. that we measure the predictive power of the theory by the *proportion of all possible observations* on that same data set *that are consistent with* (or predicted by) *that theory*
3. that the appropriate trade-off is simply given by the difference between these two proportions.

An illustration and application is given in Hey (1998). The main problem with this approach is that it leaves unresolved the key issue of the question of the meaning and interpretation of those observations *inconsistent* with the theory. Observations *consistent* with the theory are easy to interpret; but observations inconsistent with a theory are not so easy. A hardline approach requires us to interpret such observations as *refutations* of the theory — if we observe something inconsistent with a theory then that theory must be wrong. Unfortunately, if we proceed on this basis then we must conclude that *all* theories are wrong — since none predict *all* the observations on any given data set (unless we restrict the data set enormously). Selten's approach recognizes this and therefore does not give a theory a rating of minus infinity if any inconsistent observations are noted; instead it treats all observations consistent with a theory the same (positive) weight and all observations inconsistent with a theory the same (finite and negative) weight. As Selten remarks: "A hit is a hit and a miss is a miss". I am not sure that all would agree. For instance, suppose on a set of 10 Pairwise Choice questions, that the only responses consistent with Expected Utility theory are *either* all Left *or* all Right, then according to Selten both 'LLLLLLLLLL' and 'RRRRRRRRRR' are consistent with EU, whilst anything else, for example 'LRRRRRRRRR' and 'LRLRLRLRLR' are inconsistent with EU. However, many others would want to qualify this, saying that 'LRRRRRRRRR' is somehow *nearer* to EU than is 'LRLRLRLRLR'. Selten's measure does not allow such discrimination. In contrast the approach used by Harless and Camerer (1994) and Hey and Orme (1994) does.

A further disagreement might be over Selten's suggested measure of the predictive power of a theory — which is effectively measuring what might be termed the *parsimony* of the theory. Is this really measured by the *proportion of the possible observations* on that same data set *that are consistent with* (or predicted by) *that theory*? As I shall argue, this depends upon what we are going to use our measure for — in other words, upon what we are going to use our analysis of the comparative ranking of the various theories for. Presumably this depends upon the application on which we are going to employ our 'best' or 'better' theories. It also depends upon the way that we are going to 'fit' our data to the various theories. As I shall show, the Selten measure of parsimony is very close to that used by Harless and Camerer — and this, in turn, is related to the way that they fit the data to the theories. Let me look at these two lines of argument in detail, beginning with the use to which we are going to put our analysis.

This all depends on the way we 'do' economics. If the economics we are 'doing' is a straight exercise in theory then one makes some assumptions about the objective functions of the various economic agents and then one explores the implications. Whether the theorist assumes the decision makers are EU maximizers or whether they are assumed to have some other objective function is in some sense irrelevant to what the theorist is doing — since the theorist can be argued to be simply exploring the implications of certain assumptions. So for the purpose of the exercise of straight economic theory the question of which is the 'best' theory of decision making under risk is irrelevant. But, of course, the exercise of straight theory is not the ultimate objective of economics — that must surely be the prediction of economic behavior in a variety of contexts. Here we use the theory that the theorists have developed. But the way we use it must depend upon the context: we make assumptions about the economic agents in the context under study and then employ the relevant theory. We might then investigate whether the assumptions are valid and whether we might employ alternative or stronger assumptions. Clearly, in general, the stronger assumptions that we make the stronger the predictions that we can make — though, at the same time it is equally clear that the stronger the assumptions we make the more likely it is that these assumptions are incorrect. So we collect some relevant information about the particular context in which we are interested. For example, when predicting demand, we assume a particular form for the consumers' utility function(s), test whether that particular form appears to be consistent with the data, and (if relevant, which it almost always is) estimate any relevant parameters. *Occasionally* we may be able (or may have) to predict without any data at all, but such circumstances are unusual.

The context will determine what exactly it is that we are trying to predict — usually the aggregate behavior of a group of individuals. However, given current economic methodology, much of microeconomic theory is a story about *individual* behavior, so one needs to decide how one is going to solve the aggregation problem. Is it better to think of the group as represented by some representative individual and hence predict on the basis of that representative individual? Or is it better to work on the assumption that different people within the group are different, try to discover how many people are of each possible type and predict on the basis of such a characterization? In general the second of these two approaches will work better if indeed different people in the group are different, though it could be the case that aggregation over the individuals averages out the individual responses in such a way that the aggregate looks as if it is behaving as though all the individuals were of a particular type. But the conditions for this to be so are likely to be strong — though much depends upon the context. Indeed there are contexts where the 'representative agent' model must be doomed to failure unless all people are identical: for example, consider the problem of predicting a group's choice in a pairwise choice problem (given information about the group's choices on earlier pairwise choice problems): the 'representative agent' model must necessarily predict that all the group would choose one or the other choice, whereas if there is a distribution of types, some will choose one option, others will choose the other.[1]

---

[1] Unless, of course, there is some stochastic element in behavior. On this, see later.

These two different interpretations lead to two different ways of assessing how well various models fit the data. Of course, if the data set consists solely of aggregate data then there is no alternative but to fit the models to the aggregate data. But if one has individual data then one can implement both approaches. Let us suppose that that is the case. One wants to see how well the various theories fit the data. Occasionally a theory has no parameters — Expected Value Maximization is an example of this — in which case there is no fitting to be done (unless one needs to estimate some error parameter). With other theories parameters are involved — which means that the appropriate parameters need to be chosen in some fashion to fit the theory to the data. Consider, as an example, the case of Expected Utility theory — which posits the maximization of the expected value of some utility function. Unless one assumes that all agents are identical — and thus have the same utility function — then the 'parameters' that need to be chosen are the parameters that define the utility functions over the relevant domain. This can be done in general — or it could be done in a number of ways specifically for the data set under consideration. In order to explain what I mean by this, I need to give a specific example. This can obviously be generalized but it is difficult to make my point in a general context.

Suppose for example that the data set at hand is the set of responses of a set of I individuals, $i = 1, ..., I$, to a series of J pairwise choice questions, $j = 1, .., J$. Let the choice on question j by individual i be denoted by C_{ij} and suppose this can take one of two values L_j or R_j. The data set, therefore, consists of the ixj matrix $\mathbf{C} = C_{ij}, i = 1, .., I, j = 1, ..J$. Suppose further that individual i is an Expected Utility maximizer with utility function $u_i(.)$, then the individual's responses to the J questions can be either described by the value of $u_i(.)$ at the set of outcomes involved in the J pairwise choice questions, or the actual set of responses by the individual on the J questions. Note that the former imply the latter but the converse is not true. One could therefore argue that the former characterization is more primitive in some appropriate sense.

Suppose, in addition to the data, one has a set of theories each of which is an attempt to explain the data. How might one fit the data to this set of theories? In general there are lots of ways of doing this — depending upon what restrictions, or assumptions, one imposes on the fitting process. Clearly the fewer the restrictions one places on the fitting process, the better that the fit is likely to be but the more 'parameters' one needs to estimate. Thus, if one is going to penalize the 'goodness of fit' of the data to the set of theories for the number of 'parameters' involved in the fitting, those fits with fewer restrictions are going to be penalized more heavily. One has a classic trade-off problem — which cannot be resolved in general but only in specific cases.

2. Ways of Fitting the Data to the Set of Theories

Let me list a partial set of the ways that one may 'fit' the data to the set of theories:

S1. One can assume that the behavior of all agents in the data set is consistent with one particular theory (for example, Expected Utility theory) and that they all have exactly the same preference function (for example, in the case of Expected Utility theory, they all have the same (Neumann-Morgenstern) utility function.

S2. One can assume that the behavior of all agents in the data set is consistent with one particular theory (for example, Expected Utility theory) but that different agents (potentially) have different preference functions (for example, in the case of EU theory, different agents (potentially) have different (Neumann-Morgenstern) utility functions).

S3. One can assume that different agents behave in accordance with different theories but that all those whose behavior is consistent with one particular theory share the same preference function relevant for that theory.

S4. One can assume that different agents behave in accordance with different theories and that agents whose behavior is consistent with one particular theory may have differing preference functions (relevant for that theory).

As an empirical fact, one quickly discovers that, however few restrictions one imposes on the fitting method (unless the restrictions are so few that the whole exercise becomes meaningless), one is *unable to fit the data exactly*. What does one do? The obvious response — both for the economist and the econometrician — is to incorporate some story of *errors* into the fitting process. In the context of the majority of the currently popular theories of decision making under risk, this 'error' or noise term can very readily be interpreted as genuine error on the part of the decision maker.[2] So one needs a story of these errors — or at least, a stochastic specification of the errors. As I shall demonstrate, the choice of error story may limit what one can do in terms of fitting the data to the set of theories.

3. Error Specifications

Let me concentrate on the two error stories proposed in the papers cited above: Harless and Camerer (1994) and Hey and Orme (1994). The first of these papers simply assumes that there is a probability θ that the agent will make a mistake[3] on any pairwise choice question — and that *this probability does not depend upon the nature of the pairwise choice question* itself. One can go further, as Harless and Camerer (1994) do and assume that θ is constant across all questions and indeed across all subjects, but this, of course, is not necessary. Again this depends upon how many restrictions one wishes to impose on the fitting and upon the resulting effect upon the goodness of fit. But one could adopt any of the following:

[2] There are theories of stochastic preference, see Loomes and Sugden (1995) and Carbone (1997b) and of stochastic choice with deterministic preference, see Hey and Carbone (1995) but here I shall concentrate on the mainstream literature which is a story of deterministic choice and deterministic preference. In this story 'noise' must be error.

[3] By 'make a mistake' I mean that the agents say that he or she prefers the left (right) hand choice when in fact he or she prefers the right (left) hand choice.

CP1. There is a probability θ_{ij} that subject i makes a mistake on question j.
CP2. There is a probability θ_i that subject i makes a mistake on *each* question.
CP3. There is a probability θ_j that *each* subject makes a mistake on question j.
CP4. There is a probability θ that *each* subject makes a mistake on *each* question.

I ignore, for the time being, the issue of the *identifiability* of these various models, issues which could be very severe, particularly for the first of these. Let me call these error specifications, respectively, CP1, CP2, CP3 and CP4, where CP stands for Constant Probability.

The story proposed in Hey and Orme (1994) is quite different. It goes back to the primitive of the preference functional $V(.)$ implied by the theory: according to a theory with preferences given by $V(.)$, L_j is preferred to R_j if and only if $V(L_j) > V(R_j)$, that is, if and only if $V(L_j) - V(R_j) > 0$. However, to accommodate the empirical 'fact' that agents make errors when choosing, Hey and Orme (1994) interpret this as *measurement error*, suggesting that actual decisions are taken on the basis of whether $V(L_j) - V(R_j) + \epsilon > 0$ where ϵ is a *measurement error*. Obviously to make this operational one needs to specify the distribution of ϵ: it is fairly natural to specify its mean as being zero (assuming no left or right bias in the agent's answers) and possibly reasonably acceptable to assume that it has a normal distribution (appealing to the Central Limit Theorem). The magnitude of the error variance σ^2 can therefore be taken as a measure of the magnitude of the error spread: the larger is σ the greater in general will be the measurement error. Originally, Hey and Orme (1994) assumed that σ^2 was not dependent on the specific pairwise choice question, and I shall continue to work with that as a maintained hypothesis.[4] Nevertheless, there are still a variety of formulations that one could adopt:

WN1. That for subject i on question j the error variance is σ^2_{ij}.
WN2. That for subject i on *each* question the error variance is σ^2_i.
WN3. That for *each* subject on question j the error variance is σ^2_j.
WN4. That for *each* subject on *each* question the error variance is σ.

Again I ignore, for the time being, the issue of identifiability. I call these error specifications WN1, WN2, WN3 and WN4, where WN stands for White Noise (papers which have explored this type of specification extensively include Carbone and Hey, 1994, and Carbone and Hey, 1995, in addition to earlier references).

4. Describing True Preferences

In *principle* one can fit any of the model specifications combined with any of the error specifications, though we see that sometimes this is not possible. Sometimes this is because of a type of identification problem. Partly this depends on how we intend to describe the 'true' preferences, as defined by the specific preference functionals specified by the theory or theories in question. Let me return to that specification

[4] Though see Hey (1995) which suggests that specifying it as dependent on the questions might well improve the fit.

and illustrate with the case of Expected Utility theory. A *particular* EU preference function is defined by the underlying Neumann-Morgenstern utility function. This *might* be describable by a particular functional form, for example, linear, or constant absolute risk averse, or constant relative risk averse or it might not. Of course, one can always fit using a particular restricted functional form and the resulting saving in numbers of parameters to estimate may compensate for the worsening in the goodness of fit. An alternative is to specify the function at all possible values of its argument — but there may well be an infinite number of these, most being unidentifiable in any particular context. The best one can hope for, given that the pairwise choice questions must have been defined over a particular set of final outcomes, is to fit the function at those outcomes. Suppose there are L of these final outcomes, $O_l, l = 1, ..., L$. Then, at best, one can fit the function by estimating the value of $U(O_l)$ at the L values. Let me call this specification of the underlying true preferences as the specification of the underlying *True Values*. Now, as I have remarked before, any set of L values for $U(O_l)$ implies a particular set of responses on the J questions — for example: $L_1 L_2 R_3....L_J$; let me call this specification of the underlying true preferences as the specification of the underlying *True Responses*. Of course, these will be context specific, but then so will be the set of underlying True Values. Note crucially that it does not follow that a different set of $U(O_l)$ implies a different set of responses on the J questions; that is, it does not follow that a different set of underlying True Values implies a different set of underlying True Responses: there may be several sets of $U(O_l)$ consistent with any given set of responses to the J questions. Of course, in the context of a particular set of questions, knowledge of the sets of $U(O_l)$ consistent with a given set of answers does not increase the amount of knowledge gained from that data set; it just seems that it does.[5] In other words knowledge of the underlying *True Values* does not imply any extra knowledge — in a particular context — to knowing the underlying *True Responses*.

The above discussion has assumed that agents do not make mistakes. The evidence, however, would appear to contradict this. Of course, if agents do make mistakes then the way we specify their true preferences, combined with the way that we specify that they make mistakes, now has crucial and important significance. Consider a particular pairwise choice question and suppose that an agent's true preference is for L_j. Let $\mathbf{a}(L_j)$ denote the set of parameter values of the underlying true preference functional which would give this particular preference. The CP error specifications would give that the probability of the agent choosing R_j as $\theta_{(ij)}$ *irrespective of the actual value of the parameters* within the set $\mathbf{a}(L_j)$. In contrast the WN error specifications would imply that the probability of the agent choosing R_j is dependent upon the particular value of the parameters (within, of course, the set $\mathbf{a}(L_j)$). This implies that one

[5] An interesting question is whether one can use the information gained from a particular set of questions to predict choice in some choice problem outside the original data set. The answer is that one could if it were the case that all sets of underlying true values consistent with a given set of responses implied a particular response on the new choice problem. This is unlikely to be the case but if it were then the information about the new choice problem would also have been implicit in the original responses.

can not use the WN error specification combined with underlying true preferences specified through the underlying True *Responses* — the reason simply being that, under the WN approach, the probability of making a mistake depends upon the underlying True Values and not just upon the underlying True Responses. However, and in contrast, one *can* use the CP error specifications with the underlying true preferences specified through the underlying *True Values* — though the implication is, as I will demonstrate, that the data does not allow us to discriminate between all underlying true values consistent with the estimated underlying True Responses. The reason for this is that the CP error specification identifies first the underlying True Responses and hence secondly but not uniquely the underlying True Values (the lack of uniqueness stemming from the fact that there is a *set* of underlying True Values consistent with any given underlying True Responses).

Given that one cannot use the WN error specification with the underlying true preferences specified through the underlying True Responses, but that one *can* use the CP error specification with the underlying true preferences specified through the underlying True Values, one might well be tempted to ask the question: why specify underlying true preferences through the underlying True Responses? Is there any advantage to doing so? The answer is: not really, at least when one understands what is the implication. There are some savings in computational effort — but these simply reflect the nature of the problem. For example, when using the CP error specification with the underlying true preferences specified through the underlying True Values, one discovers that the likelihood function (the thing we are trying to maximize — see later) is a *step function* when graphed as a function of the underlying True Values. This simply reflects the fact that this error specification does not distinguish between all values of the underlying True Values — indeed it *cannot* distinguish between those which imply the same set of observed responses, but only between those which imply different observed responses. The fact that the likelihood function is a step function creates computational and econometric problems — but these simply reflect the essentially *economic* nature of the problem in the first instance. Hence the difference between specifying the underlying true preferences through the underlying True Values or through the underlying True Responses is essentially cosmetic. This eliminates one apparent difference between the two papers under examination Harless and Camerer (1994) and Hey and Orme (1994). I shall work with whichever is most convenient. However, the aggregation problem should be kept in mind: although several agents may have the same underlying True Responses they may well *not* have the same underlying True Values.

Notwithstanding these theoretical considerations it remains the case that these computational difficulties are sufficiently important to shape the nature of the test that I wish to undertake. Ideally, I want a data set on which I can implement several of the above specifications. The problem is in implementing the CP error specification on data sets in which the number of questions J is at all large. If one characterizes the problem in terms of the underlying True Responses, there is an interesting problem in determining the composition of the set of responses consistent with any particular theory. I have discussed this elsewhere (Hey, 1998) and will not rehearse the arguments

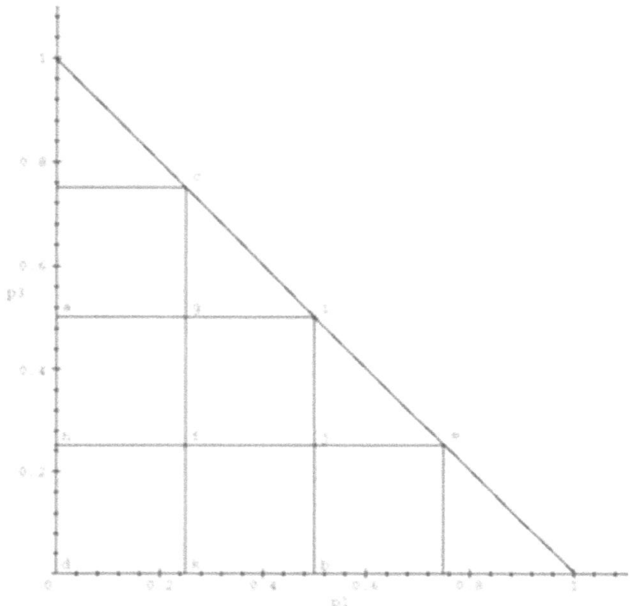

Figure 1. The risky choices in the two experiments.

here. Suffice it to say that for J at all large the number of possible responses 2^J is extremely large and the identification of the subset consistent with any given theory becomes a difficult task — particularly if the number of underlying True Values is itself large. Of course, one can carry out the fitting in the latter space, but if one is using the CP error specification this requires finding the maximum of a step function in a high-dimensioned space. And there is no guarantee that the function (the likelihood function) is everywhere concave in some appropriate sense.[6] There are also complications if one wants to fit across *all* subjects.

If one is to employ one of the specifications in which agents are assumed to be different (at least partially) then one needs a reasonable amount of data for each subject. That is, one requires J to be reasonably large. This conflicts with the requirement of the paragraph above. I compromised by carrying out an experiment with $J = 15$. I also carried out a complete ranking experiment. The next section gives the details. The idea was to fit using both the CP error specification and the WN error specification so that the two could be compared.

[6] There is also the problem that one does not know where the next step is going to be, nor the width of it, which means that one could well miss the maximum. Indeed, with the algorithms currently in use — I have elsewhere used a Simulated Annealing program written in GAUSS by E.G. Tsionas — there is no guarantee that the maximum will be found.

5. The Experiments

I undertook two experiments — a Pairwise Choice experiment with J reasonably large (to be precise $J = 15$) and a Complete Ranking experiment. The Complete Ranking experiment was linked to the Pairwise Choice experiment in a sense that will be described shortly - but they were otherwise carried out completely independently of each other. Both involved gambles involving three final outcomes, which for the moment I shall refer to as x_1, x_2 and x_3 where these are indexed in such a way[7] that $x_1 \prec x_2 \prec x_3$ where $\prec$ denotes 'less preferred than'. A specific risky prospect is now described by the three numbers p_1, p_2 and p_3 where p_i denotes the probability that the outcome will be x_i $(i = 1, 2, 3)$. Note, however, that these three numbers must sum to unity — which means that any risky prospect can be described by just two of these three numbers. Take p_1 and p_3 — respectively the probability of the worst outcome and the probability of the best outcome. Now employ the expositional device known as the Marschak-Machina Triangle — with p_3 on the vertical axis and p_1 on the horizontal axis. See Figure 1. Each point within the Triangle represents some risky prospect; each of those on one of the sides of the Triangle is a prospect involving just two of the three outcomes; and those at the vertices of the Triangle are certainties (involving just one of the three outcomes). The 11 prospects I used in the Complete Ranking experiment are the 11 points labelled a through k on this triangle. It will be noted that they all involve probabilities which are multiples of one-quarter. This was for a number of reasons, not least that, given the way we displayed the risky choices (see the Appendix containing the instructions for the Complete Ranking experiment), the probabilities were immediately and obviously discernible. In the Pairwise Choice experiment I used the same 11 basic prospects and presented to the subjects all possible pairs involving these 11 prospects subject to the proviso that neither prospect in the pair dominated (in the first-degree sense) the other. There were 15 such pairs: specifically $ac, hc, hg, hi, fi, dc, dg, di, df, dj, de, ki, kj, ke$ and be. The reason why I omitted pairs in which one prospect dominated the other was that previous experimental evidence suggested that subjects virtually never chose the dominated prospect — in which case such questions would be uninformative. As it happened I observed surprisingly frequent violations of dominance on the Complete Ranking experiment. This suggests that subjects avoid violating dominance when dominance is obvious, but not necessarily otherwise — a view that has been gaining credence recently.

The Pairwise Choice experiment, with the 15 pairwise choices noted above, was carried out at *EXEC*[8] in York in 1995. The three outcomes were $x_1 = £0$, $x_2 = £300$ and $x_3 = £500$. I tried to recruit 250 subjects (the publicity material mentioned this number) but in the end I managed to recruit just 222.[9] To motivate the subjects,

[7] We actually used amounts of money increasing in magnitude, so we are assuming that all our subjects preferred more money to less.

[8] The Centre for Experimental Economics at the University of York

[9] In a sense this number is irrelevant (as long as one gets 'enough' subjects — whatever that means) as long as it does not affect the choice made by the subjects.

I used the following payment mechanism: after all 222 subjects had completed the experiment, all 222 were invited to a lecture room at a particular time. Each subject had a numbered cloakroom ticket identifying them; these tickets were put in a box and one selected at random. The subject with that number came to the front of the lecture theater and drew at random one number from the set of integers 1 through 15. That particular subject's earlier-stated preferred choice on that particularly-numbered pairwise choice question was then played out for real — and the subject paid accordingly. As it happened the subject was paid £300[10] — if the outcome had been £0 then the whole procedure would have been repeated from the beginning.[11]

The Complete Ranking experiment was carried out (with the permission and very helpful cooperation of the conference organizers to whom I am most grateful) at the Seventh World Congress of the Econometric Society in Tokyo, Japan, in 1995. In the participants' conference packs there was included a single sheet inviting them to participate in this experiment; this invitation is reproduced in the Appendix. Anyone wishing to participate in the experiment — which involved simply ranking in order of preference the 11 basic prospects — had to hand in their ranking at the beginning of a lecture session at which I gave one invited paper (and Vince Crawford another). The experiment was played out at the end of the two lectures. Specifically, one of the answers was picked at random; the person concerned came to the front of the lecture room; then two of the 11 prospects were drawn at random by this person — and the one highest in that person's previously-stated ranking was played out for real.

In this experiment, the outcomes were denominated in American dollars: $x_1 = \$0, x_2 = \$200$ and $x_3 = \$1000$. Again the technique was deliberately to use large amounts of money and to pay off just one subject; my previous caveats apply.[12] It should also be noted that the middle outcome in the Complete Ranking experiment was chosen much closer to the worst outcome than in the Pairwise Choice experiment; this was because we had seriously misjudged the degree of risk aversion displayed by the subjects in the York experiment.

[10] For those interested in such things,the winning subject was one who had approached me at the beginning of the meeting — having found some other subject's cloakroom ticket and having the honesty to say so. Clearly there is a reward for honesty!

[11] An extended footnote is necessary at this stage. First, we should admit that playing the whole procedure repeatedly until someone had won something, slightly distorts the incentive mechanism — but since a different subject would (almost certainly) be chosen on each repetition the distortion is very slight. Second, although we could argue that this payment mechanism does give a strong incentive for honest reporting, in that *if* a particular subject is chosen and *if* a particular question is selected, then that subject will want (*ex post*) to have given his or her true preference on that question, the incentives might not be so strong as viewed from an *ex ante* perspective — given that the chance of being selected is so low. But ultimately, of course, this is an empirical issue: it would be interesting to explore the relative efficiency of using this procedure, as compared with using payoffs of one-tenth of these but paying off 10 subjects, or using payoffs one-hundredth of these, but paying off 100 subjects.

[12] Again, for those who like to know such things: the winner was a Russian academic and his winnings were $1000 - equivalent to approximately twice his annual salary! Proof that there is a God?!

TABLE I. Various possible specifications

Error/Model	Error parameter	S1	S2	S3	S4
CP1	θ_{ij}	13	1	14	1
CP2	θ_i	3	A	4	B
CP3	θ_j	23	2	24	2
CP4	θ	3	C	4	6
WN1	σ_{ij}	13	1	14	1
WN2	σ_i	3	D	4	E
WN3	σ_j	23	2	24	2
WN4	σ	3	5	4	5

6. Analyzing the Results

If I was to fit all four models (S1 through to S4) specified above in conjunction with all the eight error specifications discussed above (CP1 through to CP4 and WN1 through to WN4) I would have to fit 32 different models to the data. Many of these can be discarded however. See Table I; the following numbers refer to the entries in that table.

1. First, given the data set consisting of the results of the two experiments described above, the rows CP1 and WN1, involving the fitting of a different error parameter (either θ or σ) for each subject and for each question, cannot be implemented — the parameters are not identifiable, since questions were not repeated.
2. Harless and Camerer (1994) would argue that we should also exclude rows CP2 and WN2 since "... allowing error rates to be choice-dependent can lead to nonsensical results" (p. 1261).
3. I would argue that we should exclude column S1 since the notion that all subjects in our experiment had exactly identical tastes is manifestly absurd.
4. I would also go further and exclude column S3 on the argument that if we are prepared to accept that different agents may have different preference functionals it is then odd to argue that all those with the same functional should also have the same tastes within that functional.
5. I would eliminate the remainder of the WN4 row on the grounds that the empirical evidence obtained from the estimation of the WN2 row is that the error variances clearly vary considerably from subject to subject.
6. Finally I would eliminate column S4 combined with row CP4: if subjects really are as different as implied by S4 it is highly unlikely that they are identical in the way indicated by CP4.

As far as columns are concerned this leaves us with two — S2 and S4, effectively the representative agent model and the varied agent model. A comparison of the fitting for the two columns enables us to see which of these two stories appears to be the better. Generally we are left with specifications A through E, as follows:

Specification A: [S2,CP2] All subjects have the same preference functional but different (CP) error parameters. This is particularly simple to fit: for each subject we find the 'nearest' set of consistent responses (consistent with a particular theory) to the observed responses (nearest in the sense of the smallest number of mistakes between the consistent responses and the observed responses). We then add up the log-likelihoods across all subjects, theory by theory, correct them for degrees of freedom (as described below) and choose that preference functional for which the corrected log-likelihood is maximized.

Specification B: [S4, CP2] Different subjects have different preference functionals and different (CP) error parameters. We follow the procedure described above, but then work subject by subject, rather than preference functional by preference functional: for each subject we find the preference functional for which the corrected log-likelihood is maximized (corrected in the manner described below) and then aggregate the corrected log-likelihoods over all subjects. Because the correction procedure is different from that in Specification A (see below) there is no guarantee that this Specification does worse or better than Specification A.

Specification C: [S2, CP4] This is the original Harless and Camerer specification: all subjects have the same preference functional and the (CP) error is constant across subjects. We calculate the log-likelihood *across all subjects*, preference functional by preference functional, correct them for degrees of freedom and then aggregate.

Specification D: [S2,WN2] All subjects have the same preference functional but they have different (WN) error parameters. This is similar to Specification A except that we use the WN error specification. We work preference functional by preference functional, aggregating the maximized log-likelihoods across all subjects, correcting them for degrees of freedom and then choose that preference functional for which the corrected log-likelihood is maximized. Because the correction factor is the same as in Specification E, this is *bound* to do no better than Specification E. Nevertheless, it is interesting to see how much worse it performs.

Specification E: [S4, WN2] This is the original Hey and Orme specification: different subjects (may) have different preference functionals with differing (WN) error parameters. We follow the procedure described above, but then work subject by subject, rather than preference functional by preference functional: for each subject we find the preference functional for which the corrected log-likelihood is maximized (corrected in the manner described below) and then aggregate the corrected log-likelihoods over all subjects.

There are some interesting estimation problems involved with the CP stories: as described in the original paper Harless and Camerer (1994) the fitting problem is one of finding the proportion of subjects in the sample with underlying true responses of each type consistent with any one theory. This is the case when the error parameter θ is assumed to be constant across both questions and subjects. In this case, the interpretation as to what is implied for any particular subject is that one is estimating the probabilities that the subject's underlying true responses are each of the allowable ones: the overall fitted proportions are the weighted average of these probabilities, averaged over all observed responses. In contrast, when one assumes that the error parameter, θ_i, varies across subjects (but not across questions) then the maximum likelihood estimator of θ_i is the minimized proportion of mistakes (across all questions for that particular subject). So fitting this story is equivalent to finding, for each subject, the response consistent with the appropriate theory closest to the subject's actual response — closest in the sense of the smallest number of errors implied by the actual response if that consistent response were indeed the subject's underlying true response. In this case the maximized log-likelihood is simply the maximum of $ln[\theta_i^j(1-\theta_i)^{(J-j)}]$ where J is the total number of questions and j the number of incorrect responses given the underlying true consistent response. This maximized likelihood is achieved when $\theta_i = j/J$ and takes the value $jln(j) + (J-j)ln(J-j) - Jln(J)$.

7. Correcting for Degrees of Freedom

It is clear that different specifications involve different numbers of estimated parameters. Clearly also it is the case that the more parameters involved in the fitting of a particular specification, the better that specification will fit. Goodness of fit is measured by the maximized log-likelihood for that specification. One therefore needs a way of 'correcting' the maximized log-likelihood for the number of parameters involved in the fitting.

This is a familiar problem in econometrics; there are a number of recommended solutions — none obviously superior to all others. I therefore simply adopt one of the more familiar ones — namely the Aikake Criterion.[13] This involves maximizing $2ln[L(\hat{\alpha})] - 2k/T$ where $L(\hat{\alpha})$ is the maximized likelihood, T the number of observations and k the number of parameters involved in the fitting. Given that, in the comparisons I will be carrying out, the number of observations T will be constant, this is equivalent to maximizing $ln[L(\hat{\alpha})] - k$. In other words, we simply correct the maximized log-likelihood by subtracting from it the number of parameters involved in its fitting. Let me know turn to consideration of the number of parameters involved in the fitting of the various specifications.

I need two bits of notation. Denote by M_k the number of consistent responses under theory k. This obviously varies from theory to theory (preference functional to preference functional) and clearly also depends upon the specific questions asked in the experiment.

[13] For a Monte-Carlo investigation of the efficiency of this criterion, see Carbone and Hey (1994) and Carbone (1997a).

Let me also denote by N_k the number of underlying true values required under theory k. Again this will vary across theories and will depend upon the specific questions in the experiment. In the context of my two experiments — with just 3 outcomes — then N is *zero* for the Risk Neutral preference functional (as there are no parameters involved with it), N is *one* for the Expected Utility functional — since the utility of two of the three outcomes are normalized (to zero and unity) leaving just one utility value to be determined. As we shall see later, N is *two* for all the other theories under consideration — as the fitting involves just one utility value (as in Expected Utility theory) and one other parameter.

I can now specify the number of parameters involved with each specification and hence summarize my procedure for ranking and comparing the various specifications. Let LL^*_{ik} denote the maximized log-likelihood function for subject i on theory k if the specification allows us to fit subject by subject. If not, use LL^*_k to denote the maximized log-likelihood across all subjects. Then it works as follows:

Specification A: [S2,CP2] All subjects have the same preference functional but different (CP) error parameters. Then, for each preference functional, we estimate the proportion of subjects with each of the M_k true responses — thus giving us $(M_k - 1)$ parameters to estimate (because these M_k proportions must sum to one — and, *for each subject* i, estimate that subject's error parameter θ_i. We then choose that preference functional for which the following expression is maximized:

$$\max_{k=1}^{K} \left(\sum_{i=1}^{I} [LL^*_{ik} - 1]) - [M_k - 1]\right)$$

Specification B: [S4, CP2] Different subjects have different preference functionals and different (CP) error parameters. Because we are now effectively fitting subject by subject it is better if we fit the N_k true values. We thus get as our maximized corrected log-likelihood:

$$\sum_{i=1}^{I} \max_{k=1}^{K} [LL^*_{ik} - N_k - 1]$$

Specification C: [S2, CP4] This is the original Harless and Camerer specification: all subjects have the same preference functional and the (CP) error is constant across subjects We are therefore fitting $M_k - 1$ proportions (the final one being determined by the fact that they must sum to unity) and one error parameter. We thus get:

$$\max_{k=1}^{K} [LL^*_k - M_k]$$

Specification D: [S2,WN2] All subjects have the same preference functional but they have different (WN) error parameters. So for each subject we need, for preference functional k, to fit N_k values and one error parameter σ_i. We thus get:

$$\max_{k=1}^{K} \sum_{i=1}^{I} [LL_{ik}^* - N_k - 1]$$

Specification E: [S4, WN2] This is the original Hey and Orme specification: different subjects (may) have different preference functionals with differing (WN) error parameters. The story is the same as Specification D, though the aggregation and maximization are done in reversed orders. Thus the expression below is bound to be higher than that for Specification D above. We have:

$$\sum_{i=1}^{I} \max_{k=1}^{K} [LL_{ik}^* - N_k - 1]$$

8. Full and Overfull Correction

There is one *caveat* that needs to be made to the above discussion: it assumes that different subjects respond differently. If, however, they do not not, then one could argue that the correction is excessive. If one has j subjects all with the same response, then under all specifications other than Specification C, one could argue that having fitted one of these j subjects then the other $j-1$ are also fitted by the same parameter values — one does need to repeat the correction. However, one does need to repeat the maximized log-likelihood as the other $j-1$ subjects are genuine observations. This is the procedure followed in the tables below: under the 'full correction' only one set of corrections is implemented for multiple (repeat) observations. The 'overfull corrections' carry out a correction for each subject, irrespective of whether they have the same experimental responses as other subjects. I would argue that the *Full Correction* is the correct procedure.

9. CP Errors in the Complete Ranking Experiment

Given that Harless and Camerer introduced their error story in the context of Pairwise Choice experiments, and given that, to the best of my knowledge, this story has not been extended to the Complete Ranking context, I must make the extension myself. Whilst I have consulted with David Harless over this, I cannot be sure that this meets with his approval.

Consider a ranking of two objects, and suppose the true ranking is '12'. If the subject states this, there is no error; if he or she instead reports '21', then there is one error. Consider now three objects, and suppose '123' is the true ranking. Then '132' or '213' could be considered as one mistake — just one item in the wrong position — and '321' could be considered two mistakes. Such considerations lead to the following story.

TABLE II. Log-likelihoods for Specification A

Preference Functional Fitted	Pairwise Choice Correction			Complete Ranking Correction		
	None	Full	Overfull	None	Full	Overfull
rn	-2010	-2090	-2232	-1272	-1336	-1397
eu	-675	-760	-902	-848	-917	-978
da	-615	-723	-865	-690	-782	-843
pr	-578	-693	-835	-592	-679	-780
rp	-640	-766	-908	-556	-666	-727
rq	-584	-729	-871	-462	-591	-652
wu	-594	-721	-863	-519	-630	-691

TABLE III. Log-Likelihoods for Specification B

Pairwise Choice Correction			Complete Ranking Correction		
None	Full	Overfull	None	Full	Overfull
-554	-744	-1035	-353	-527	-618

Suppose there are Z objects to rank and suppose the true ranking is $x_1x_2\ldots x_Z$ but the reported ranking is $y_1y_2\ldots y_Z$ then one could argue that the 'number of mistakes' made is $\sum_{z=1}^{Z}|x_z - y_z|/2$. This is the measure I used. In keeping with the spirit of the CP approach I assumed that (under the CP specifications) the probability of making any one of such mistakes was a constant (independent of the context).

10. Preference Functionals Fitted

In addition to the models already discussed (Risk Neutrality and Expected Utility) I fitted five other functionals: Disappointment Aversion (**da**); Prospective Reference (**pr**); Rank dependent with the Power weighting function (**rp**); Rank dependent with the Quiggin weighting function (**rq**); and Weighted Utility (**wu**). Details of these can be found in Hey (1997). All the generalizations of Expected Utility theory (**da**, **pr**, **rp**, **rq** and **wu**) involve one parameter extra to EU in the context of these experiments: **da** has Gul's β parameter; **pr** has Viscusi's λ parameter; **rp** and **rq** have the weighting function's γ parameter; and **wu** has the w weighting parameter.

TABLE IV. 'Best' Models under Specification B

Preference Functional	Pairwise Choice	Complete Ranking
rn	10.00	44.00
eu	165.00	22.00
da	4.50	4.67
pr	18.75	8.67
rp	4.92	17.00
rq	11.92	17.50
wu	6.92	11.17

TABLE V. Log-Likelihoods for Specification C

Preference	Pairwise Choice			Complete Ranking		
Functional	Correction			Correction		
Fitted	None	Full	Overfull	None	Full	Overfull
rn	-2065	-2066	-2066	-1746	-1747	-1747
eu	-985	-992	-992	-1348	-1354	-1354
da	-982	-1010	-1010	-1237	-1266	-1266
pr	-977	-1011	-1011	-1167	-1231	-1231
rp	-972	-1019	-1019	-1140	-1187	-1187
rq	-973	-1039	-1039	-1057	-1123	-1123
wu	-976	-1024	-1024	-1115	-1161	-1163

11. Results

Let me discuss the results specification by specification first. Begin with Specification A in Table II. If one judges, as I have argued one should, on the basis of the Fully Corrected Log-Likelihood, then Prospective Reference theory (**pr**) emerges as the 'best' functional on the Pairwise Choice experiment, and Rank dependent with the Quiggin weighting function (**rq**) on the Complete Ranking experiment. This echoes earlier findings. Expected Utility theory does not do particularly well — as a Representative Agent model — and neither does Disappointment Aversion theory especially in the Complete Ranking experiment.

Specification B is summarized in Table III. Details of the 'best' model are given in Table IV, which specifies the number of subjects for whom a particular model was 'best' in terms of the Corrected Log-Likelihood.[14] It may be of interest to note that

[14] When k models tied for 'best' under this criterion, each was given a score of $1/k$.

TABLE VI. Log-Likelihoods for Specification D

Preference Functional Fitted	Pairwise Choice Correction			Complete Ranking Correction		
	None	Full	Overfull	None	Full	Overfull
rn	-2145	-2225	-2367	-963	-1027	-1088
eu	-613	-773	-1057	-408	-536	-658
da	-527	-767	-1193	-340	-532	-715
pr	-467	-707	-1133	-266	-458	-641
rp	-516	-756	-1182	-298	-490	-673
rq	-518	-758	-1184	-257	-449	-632
wu	-500	-740	-1166	-250	-442	-625

TABLE VII. Log-Likelihoods for Specification E

Pairwise Choice Correction			Complete Ranking Correction		
None	Full	Overfull	None	Full	Overfull
-429	-625	-938	-200	-377	-466

Risk Neutrality comes best for 10 subjects on the PC experiment and best for 44 on the CR experiment. Corresponding figures for EU are 165 (PC) and 22 (CR), whilst a top-level functional (one of **da**, **pr**, **rp** , **rq** or **wu**) came best for just 47 subjects on PC and 59 subjects on CR. (Recall there were 222 subjects on the PC experiment and 125 on the CR experiment.) Prospective Reference theory (**pr**) did particularly well on the PC experiment and the Rank Dependent models on the CR experiment. It is interesting to note that Specification B does marginally worse than Specification A on the Pairwise Choice experiment, though marginally better on the Complete Ranking experiment.

Specification C is summarized in Table V. This is the original Harless and Camerer specification. It performs considerably worse than Specifications A and B — indicating that the constant-across-all-subjects error hypothesis looks highly suspect — as one might imagine. For the record, EU does 'best' for the PC experiment and Weighted Utility (**wu**) for the CR experiment. But one should not attach too much weight to these remarks.

Specification D is summarized in Table VI. Remember that this is bound to do worse than Specification E — but the difference is not too large. From Table VI it

TABLE VIII. 'Best' Models under Specification E

Preference Functional	Pairwise Choice	Complete Ranking
rn	13	42
eu	131	25
da	13	9
pr	32	7
rp	6	16
rq	17	10
wu	10	16

can be seen that Prospective Reference theory (**pr**) does 'best' on the PC data and Weighted Utility on the CR data.

Finally, specification E is summarized in Table VII. The breakdown of 'best' models is summarized in Table VIII. It can be seen that Risk Neutrality and Expected Utility theory do rather well.

An overall summary is provided in Table IX. It is particularly clear from this that Specification C (the original Harless and Camerer specification) does rather badly. The 'best' specification appears to be that of Specification E — the original Hey and Orme specification. I suspect that this is the combined incidence of two effect, first a possibly better error specification[15] and partly and perhaps more importantly, because Specification C embodies the Representative Agent model which seems to be seriously misleading.[16] The evidence of this paper must surely be that people *are* different.

12. Conclusions

Two methods of assessing and comparing theories have been referred to in this paper: the Selten method and the Harless/Camerer/Hey/Orme (HCHO) method. Both penalize the 'goodness of fit'[17] of theories through some measure of the parsimony of the theory. The Selten penalization turns out to be effectively the same[18] as that of HCHO in the context of the Harless and Camerer method of fitting the data to the theories (Specification C). This penalization is effectively the number of parameters

[15] Though elsewhere (Carbone and Hey, 1997) I provide direct evidence to compare the WN error specification with the CP error specification, from which it is not clear that either can be regarded as *generally* superior.

[16] It may be interesting to 'translate' the maximized log-likelihoods into probabilities for individual subjects on individual questions. On the Pairwise Choice experiment the LL figure of -625 for Specification E is equivalent to a probability on average of 0.829 on each question for each subject of observing what was observed given the fitted model. In contrast, the LL figure of -992 for Specification C is equivalent to a probability of 0.742.

[17] Here measured by the Maximized Log-Likelihood.

[18] Compare the penalization used in this paper with that in Hey (1998).

TABLE IX. Overall Summary of Log-Likelihoods

Specification	Pairwise Choice			Complete Ranking		
	Correction			Correction		
	None	Full	Overfull	None	Full	Overfull
A	-578	-693	-835	-462	-591	-652
B	-554	-744	-1035	-353	-527	-618
C	-972	-992	-992	-1057	-1123	-1123
D	-467	-707	-1133	-250	-442	-625
E	-429	-625	-938	-200	-377	-466

involved with the fitting of the specification — and is familiar to econometricians. In other specifications it needs to be modified appropriately. But it is not *this* that distinguishes Selten from HCHO. Rather it is in the measurement of 'goodness of fit' or predictive success: Selten ("A miss is a miss and a hit is a hit") counts all observations consistent with a theory as successes and all those inconsistent as failures. In contrast HCHO measure how bad misses are — near misses being better for a theory than distant misses. This requires a stochastic specification (which, of course, Selten's does not) and allows the use of the Maximized Log-Likelihood as the measure of predictive success. The stochastic specification differs between Constant Probability and White Noise. A peripheral question answered in this paper concerns which of the two is empirically best, but the major finding is that one can view both Harless and Camerer and Hey and Orme as two attempts to answer the same question within the same basic framework. This paper has made clear what that framework is.

Fundamentally the issue at the heart of this paper boils down to the question of the best (corrected) fit — which is a essentially empirical question. As it happens, with the data set that we have, it appears to be the case that the Representative Agent model performs particularly badly — with the conclusion being that it is better to treat different people as different. Doing otherwise leads to worse predictions — notwithstanding the improved parsimony.

And finally, as far as the 'Best' theory of decision making under risk is concerned, our analysis tells us that we should not discard Expected Utility theory. Nor should we discard *all* the many new theories — some are 'best' for some subjects — though there are some theories which look of increasingly minor interest.

Acknowledgements

I am grateful to a number of people whose thoughts and ideas have influenced the development of this paper, particularly Bob Sugden and Enrica Carbone.

References

Carbone, E. 1997a. "Investigation of Stochastic Preference Theory Using Experimental Data", *Economics Letters* 57, 305–311.

Carbone, E. 1997b. "Discriminating between Preference Functionals: A Monte Carlo Study", *Journal of Risk and Uncertainty* 15, 29–54.

Carbone, E., and J. D. Hey. 1994. "Discriminating Between Preference Functionals. A Preliminary Monte Carlo Study", *Journal of Risk and Uncertainty* 8, 223–24.

Carbone, E., and J. D. Hey. 1995. "A Comparison of the Estimates of EU and Non-EU Preference Functionals Using Data from Pairwise Choice and Complete Ranking Experiments", *Geneva Papers on Risk and Insurance Theory* 21, 111–133.

Harless, D. W., and C. F. Camerer. 1994. "The Predictive Utility of Generalized Expected Utility Theories", *Econometrica* 62, 1251–1290.

Hey, J. D. 1995. "Experimental Investigations of Errors in Decision-Making Under Risk", *European Economic Review* 39, 633–640.

Hey, J. D. 1997. "Experiments and the Economics of Individual Decision Making", in: D. M . Kreps and K. F. Wallis (eds.): *Advances in Economics and Econometrics*, Cambridge University Press, 171–205.

Hey, J. D. 1998. "An Application of Selten's Measure of Predictive Success", *Mathematical Social Sciences* 35, 1–16.

Hey, J. D., and E. Carbone. 1995. "Stochastic Choice with Deterministic Preferences. An Experimental Investigation", *Economics Letters* 47, 161–167.

Hey, J. D., and C. D. Orme. 1994. "Investigating Generalizations of Expected Utility Theory Using Experimental Data", *Econometrica* 62, 1291–1326.

Loomes, G. C., and R. Sugden. 1995. "Incorporating a Stochastic Element into Decision Theory", *European Economic Review* 39, 641–648.

Selten, R. 1991. "Properties of a Measure of Predictive Success", *Mathematical Social Sciences* 21, 153–167.

John D. Hey
Dipartimento di Scienze Economiche
Universita degli Studi di Bari
Via Camillo Rosalba 53
I-70124 Bari
Italy
jdh1@york.ac.uk

OVERBIDDING IN FIRST PRICE PRIVATE VALUE AUCTIONS REVISITED: IMPLICATIONS OF A MULTI-UNIT AUCTIONS EXPERIMENT

VERONIKA GRIMM
Universidad de Alicante
DIRK ENGELMANN
Royal Holloway

1. Introduction

One of the to date most intense debates in experimental economics has evolved from a series of papers by Cox, Roberson and Smith (1982) and Cox, Smith and Walker (1983a, 1983b, 1985, 1988) on bidding behavior in single-unit first-price sealed-bid auctions. In several laboratory experiments they observe persistent overbidding of the risk neutral Nash equilibrium (RNNE) strategies, which they argue to be due to risk aversion of the bidders. They show that data of various experiments fit a model of bidders that exhibit constant relative risk aversion (CRRA) and demonstrate that the data yield rather similar estimates of the bidders' average degree of CRRA.

Their conclusion has been criticized by Harrison (1989) who argues that due to the low cost of deviation from RNNE behavior in the experimental settings of Cox, Smith, and Walker, the results cannot be considered significant evidence for risk aversion of the bidders (the so-called "flat maximum critique").

In the subsequent debate, several authors came up with evidence against the CRRA hypothesis and suggested different possible explanations for the observed behavior. In the present paper, we investigate the consistency of the different hypotheses with data obtained from a multi-unit discriminatory auction experiment. Before we do so, let us give an overview over the debate that has been going on up to now.

Kagel and Roth (1992, p. 1379) state that " [...] risk aversion cannot be the only factor and may well not be the most important factor behind bidding above the risk neutral Nash equilibrium found so often in first-price private value auctions." They provide evidence for other possible explanations:

U. Schmidt and S. Traub (eds.), Advances in Public Economics: Utility, Choice and Welfare, 235-254.

First, they note that overbidding of the (dominant) optimal strategy is also observed in second-price sealed-bid auctions, where it cannot be explained by risk aversion.[1] Second, they mention that Cox, Smith and Walker (1985) themselves find evidence against the CRRA hypothesis in an experiment where they pay the subjects one time in money and the second time in lottery tickets. In the second series of experiments the overbidding of RNNE theoretically should disappear, but it does not, which leads Cox, Smith and Walker to reject the empirical adequacy of the lottery technique, rather than revising their hypothesis. Third, they refer to an experiment on multiple unit discriminatory auctions (Cox, Smith and Walker, 1984) where bids are found to be significantly lower than the RNNE prediction.

Friedman (1992), on the other hand, notes that asymmetric costs of deviation from RNNE would be needed in order to explain the observed "misbehavior" as a consequence of payoff function flatness. Since, however, in most of the relevant experimental studies the loss function is almost symmetric, Harrison's argument cannot be sufficient to explain the observed deviations.

Goeree, Holt and Palfrey (2000) take this point into account and compare behavior of subjects in two different first-price sealed-bid auctions that have the same equilibria but differ with respect to the curvature of the loss function. Inspired by the long lasting debate, they compare several competing explanations for overbidding of RNNE observed also in their data:

1. Constant relative risk aversion.
2. Misperception of the probability distribution over outcomes (rank dependent utility).
3. Joy of winning or a myopic (per auction) joy of being in the money.

In their estimations, Goeree, Holt and Palfrey find that risk aversion and misperception of probabilities both yield a good fit of their data, whereas the joy of winning hypothesis is still reasonable but does significantly worse. Their estimated degree of CRRA, moreover, coincides with many other studies in the literature.

In this paper, we contrast those findings with data from multi-unit auction experiments where two bidders compete for two units of a homogenous good. In our analysis we focus on a discriminatory auction and use results from a Vickrey and a uniform-price auction as benchmarks.[2]

In the discriminatory auction data, we observe a high degree of bid spreading, which can be explained neither by risk aversion,[3] nor by misperception of probabilities. A myopic joy of winning seems to fit these data better. Moreover, it is consistent with some subjects' statements in the post-experimental questionnaire: that they used the first bid to ensure getting a unit and the second one for making money. This leads us

[1] See studies by Kagel, Harstad and Levin (1987) and Kagel and Levin (1990). The same evidence is found in a multi-unit setting by Engelmann and Grimm (2004).

[2] We present a detailed analysis of the other auction formats in Engelmann and Grimm (2004).

[3] Decreasing absolute risk aversion can yield unequal bids, but would imply bids above the RNNE for *both* units which we do not observe.

to a last point that is in sharp contrast to the risk aversion hypothesis: the majority of lower bids (58%, without any discernible time trend) are below the RNNE prediction.

The paper is organized as follows: In Section 2 we introduce the model, derive the RNNE of the game and discuss the implications of the three different alternative hypotheses on equilibrium bidding behavior. The experimental design is presented in Section 3. In Section 4 we report the experimental results and, in Section 5, we contrast them with the three different hypotheses that might explain deviations from RNNE behavior. Section 6 concludes.

2. Theoretical Background and Hypotheses

We investigate bidding behavior in independent private value discriminatory auctions (DA) with two bidders and two indivisible identical objects for sale. In this format, the two highest bids win a unit each and the respective prices equal these bids. Each bidder i, $i = 1, 2$, demands at most two units and places the same value v_i on each of the two units. The bidders' valuations are drawn independently from the uniform distribution on the interval $[0, V]$.

2.1. RISK NEUTRALITY

We start our theoretical analysis by deriving the Risk Neutral Nash equilibrium (RNNE) of the auction. An important observation in order to derive the optimal strategy is that with flat demand a bidder places the same bid on both units.[4] To see this, suppose the other bidder placed two different bids. Then, in order to win one unit, a bidder has to overbid only the other bidder's lower bid and in order to get two units both his bids have to exceed the other bidder's higher bid. Therefore, a bid on the first unit solves the optimal trade-off between the probability of winning (against the other bidder's lower bid) and profit in this case. Now observe that the probability of winning the second unit is even lower (one has to overbid the other bidder's higher bid) and therefore, the optimal trade-off for the second unit cannot be solved at a lower bid.[5] Thus, both bids will be equal since by definition the bid for the second unit cannot be higher than the bid for the first unit. If the other bidder chooses identical bids, the argument is even more obvious, since the trade-off is the same for both units.

Suppose that there exists a symmetric and increasing equilibrium and denote by $b(\cdot)$ and $b^{-1}(\cdot)$ the equilibrium strategy and its inverse function, respectively. Given that the other bidder bids $b(\cdot)$, a bidder with value v on each unit bids

$$\arg\max_{\beta} F(b^{-1}(\beta))[v - \beta], \tag{1}$$

[4] See Lebrun and Tremblay (2003) for a formal proof of this fact for much more general demand functions.

[5] "First unit" ("second unit") always refers to the unit on which the bidder places the higher (lower) bid.

where $F(\cdot)$ is the distribution function of the bidders' values. In the case of uniformly distributed valuations on $[0, V]$ it holds that $F(b^{-1}(\beta)) = \frac{b^{-1}(\beta)}{V}$ and the equilibrium bid functions are

$$b_1(v) = b_2(v) = \frac{1}{2}v, \tag{2}$$

where $b_1(v)$ ($b_2(v)$) is the bid on the first (second) unit.

2.2. RISK AVERSION

The most prominent explanation of overbidding in single-unit first price auctions is risk aversion. Thus, in this section we consider the effect of risk aversion on the optimal strategies in our setting.

First, note that a standard result from single-unit auction theory is that (symmetric) risk aversion of any type increases bids above the RNNE level. Thus, independent of the type of risk aversion we assume, we should expect subjects to bid more than half their valuation (the RNNE bid) on any of the two units.[6]

Now consider the case that bidders exhibit constant absolute risk aversion (CARA). Then, a bidder's bids would still be equal, although at a higher level. The reason is the same as under risk neutrality. In order to be able to employ the above argument, it is, however, important to note that under CARA a bidder's wealth does not affect his degree of risk aversion. Then, if a bidder faces the same probability of winning for his first and his second bid, the optimal tradeoff between a higher probability of winning and a higher profit in case of winning is solved by the same bid.[7]

If absolute risk aversion is increasing in wealth[8] optimal bids on the two units will still be equal. A bidder facing two equal bids would have an incentive to bid higher on the second unit he bids for, because given he obtained the first one, he will be "more risk averse". However, since bidding higher on the second unit is not possible (the bid would turn into the first unit bid), he will bid the same on both units. Note also that increasing absolute risk aversion would make the bids increase over time (i. e. from one auction to the next as long as he makes a profit on the first), depending on the wealth already accumulated by the bidders.

Now consider a bidder with decreasing absolute risk aversion (e. g. constant relative risk aversion (CRRA), which is most often assumed in the literature we referred to). Under decreasing absolute risk aversion, a bidder who has already won one unit will exhibit a lower degree of risk aversion due to his higher wealth. Therefore, if the other player would place equal bids, a bidder would like to bid lower on the second unit. We should therefore expect to observe bid spreading to some extent.

Solving for the equilibrium of the discriminatory auction with bidders that have a CRRA utility function seems to be untractable. Thus, we try to shed light on the

[6] See Krishna (2002), Maskin and Riley (1984).

[7] This argument applies if the other bidder places identical bids, which hence holds in equilibrium. Otherwise, we get, as in the case of risk neutrality, that the second-unit bid should be higher than the first-unit bid, which naturally cannot hold.

[8] This is not very plausible in many situations.

behavior of risk averse agents by the following considerations: We simplify the problem by assuming that a bidder decides about his bids sequentially. That is, he first chooses a first-unit bid, ignoring that he will also place a second-unit bid and then he decides on the optimal second-unit bid, conditional on having won with his first-unit bid.

The coefficient of relative risk aversion usually estimated is about 0.5 (see Goeree, Holt, and Palfrey, 2000). This corresponds to a utility function $U(x) = 2x^{\frac{1}{2}}$. Now consider the case that bidder 2 bids according to the simple linear bid functions $d_1(v) = k_1 v$ and $d_2(v) = k_2 v$ with $k_2 \leq k_1$. For ease of notation assume here that $V = 1$, hence that valuations are uniformly distributed on [0,1]. Then the distribution functions of bidder 2's bids are $F_1(z) = \frac{z}{k_1}$, and $F_2(z) = \frac{z}{k_2}$, for $z < k_1$ and $z < k_2$, respectively, and 1 otherwise. Consider first the case that bidder 1's bids are smaller than k_2. His second unit bid is only relevant if he already wins with his first unit bid. Bidder 1's first-unit bid has to maximize the utility that can be obtained by winning the first unit.

$$\begin{aligned} U(b_1, v) &= 2(v - b_1)^{\frac{1}{2}} P(b_1 > k_2 v_2) = \frac{2b_1}{k_2} (v - b_1)^{\frac{1}{2}}, \\ U'(b_1, v) &= 0 \Leftrightarrow b_1 = \frac{2}{3} v. \end{aligned}$$

If $\frac{2}{3}v > k_2$, then $b_1 = k_2$. Hence, as long as bidder 2's second-unit bid is a simple linear function of his valuation, bidder 1's first unit bid is independent of the precise form of bidder 2's bidding function (except for large valuations, because the bid can then be capped at k_2 which becomes relevant if the other bidder bids relatively low). Conditional on bidder 1's first unit bid being higher than bidder 2's second-unit bid, bidder 2's first-unit bid is uniformly distributed on the interval $[0, \frac{k_1}{k_2} b_1]$, so for any $b_2 < b_1$ we get for the conditional probability $P(b_2 > k_1 v_2) = \frac{b_2}{k}$ with $k := \frac{k_1}{k_2} b_1$.

Given the first-unit bid, the second-unit bid should maximize

$$\begin{aligned} U(b_2, v) &= 2(2v - b_1 - b_2)^{\frac{1}{2}} P(b_2 > k_1 v_2) + 2(v - b_1)^{\frac{1}{2}} (1 - P(b_2 > k_1 v_2)) \\ &= 2\left(\frac{4}{3}v - b_2\right)^{\frac{1}{2}} \frac{b_2}{k} + 2\left(\frac{1}{3}v\right)^{\frac{1}{2}} \left(1 - \frac{b_2}{k}\right), \\ U'(b_2, v) &= 0 \quad \Leftrightarrow \quad b_2 = \left(\frac{22}{27} - \frac{2\sqrt{13}}{27}\right) v \approx 0.5477v, \end{aligned}$$

discarding the second solution which implies $b_2 > v$.

Hence, if a bidder with a degree of constant relative risk aversion of 0.5 bids against a bidder whose bids are given by any simple linear bid functions $b_1^2 = k_1 v$ and $b_2^2 = k_2 v$ his optimal bids would then be $b_1 = \frac{2}{3}v$ and $b_2 \approx 0.55v$ where b_1 and b_2 are capped at k_2 for large v (b_2 is really capped by k_1, but since it is also constrained to be no larger than b_1, it is in fact capped at k_2.)

The resulting bid spread is quite substantial (about 24% of the RNNE equilibrium bid), but the average equilibrium spread for two risk averse bidders would be smaller.

First, since the other bidder's maximal second unit bid is smaller than his maximal first-unit bid, the first-unit bids are capped at the maximum second-unit bid, which lowers the bid-spread. Second, notice that simultaneous maximization would imply that at least for low values of k_2, b_1 and b_2 would be larger than k_2, enabling the bidder to win *both units* with a high probability. This would clearly reduce the average bid spread.

Hence, for reasonable degrees of risk-aversion we should expect bid-spreads clearly lower than 25% of the RNNE bid for low valuations and lower to no bid spreads for high valuations. Note, however, that this should be coupled with substantial overbidding on both units.[9]

Summarizing, the important observations are (1) that all bids placed by any risk averse bidder should be above the RNNE bids, (2) under risk neutrality, constant, or increasing absolute risk aversion bids on both units should be equal (and in the latter case they should increase over time, depending on the wealth already accumulated by the bidder), and (3) under decreasing absolute risk aversion (e. g. CRRA) bids might be different across units and should decrease over time (i. e. over the course of several auctions) depending on the wealth already accumulated by the bidder.

2.3. MISPERCEPTION OF PROBABILITY OUTCOMES

Some skepticism concerning the CRRA hypothesis may arise from the fact that experimental evidence from lottery choice experiments often suggests that subjects do not even behave consistent with expected utility theory. Thus, several authors have proposed (and tested) models of probability misperception to explain upwards deviations from the RNNE bids in first price auctions. Goeree, Holt, and Palfrey (2000) propose a model of rank dependent utility, where bidders maximize expected utility, but misperceive probabilities. They estimate the parameters of a "S"-shaped probability weighting function proposed by Prelec (1998),

$$w(p) = \exp\left(-\beta\left(-\ln(p)\right)^{\alpha}\right) \tag{3}$$

Subjects behaving according to this function will overestimate the probabilities close to 0, but will underweight probabilities close to 1. This can explain why subjects are willing to bet on gains if the probability of winning is low (this would imply lower bids on the second unit) while they shy away from doing so when in fact the probability of winning is high (which would lead to higher bids on the first unit).[10]

---

9 Furthermore, according to Rabin (2000) and Rabin and Thaler (2001) risk aversion on such small stakes cannot be reconciled with the maximization of the expected utility of wealth. (According to Cox and Sadiraj, 2001, however, it is consistent with the maximization of the expected utility of income). The fact that the small gains from winning the first unit should cause substantially smaller second-unit bids appears to be a good illustration that small stakes risk-aversion is not very plausible in the first place. While we observe even larger bid-spreads, it appears counterintuitive that they result from a dramatic decrease in risk aversion due to a such a small income gain.

10 The parameters that Goeree, Holt, and Palfrey estimate do actually not correspond to an S-shaped function, but closely to a quadratic function. This corresponds to risk aversion. According

Misperception of probabilities, however, does not destroy equal bidding as an equilibrium. If the other bidder places two equal bids, the probability to win the first and the second unit if one places two identical bids are the same. Hence while misperception of probabilities can lead to higher or lower bids, it would have the same effect on both bids and hence as long as the other bidder places two equal bids, the best reply always consists of two equal bids.

If, however, the other bidder places two different bids, this might imply bid spreading. If the probability weighting function is S-shaped, and in particular the density is convex, this would mean that if the probability to win is very small, then the perceived $H(b)/h(b)$ [where H (h) is the distribution (density) of the other's bid] is larger, which implies a lower optimal bid. On the other hand, if the probability to win is very large, then the perceived $H(b)/h(b)$ is smaller, implying a larger optimal bid. This can lead to the optimal first and second unit bids being different if the other bidder places different bids. Since the probability to win with the first unit is higher than with the second unit, the distorted perception of the probabilities would bias the second-unit bid down relative to the first-unit bid. Unless the perception of probabilities is dramatically distorted, the effect would, however, not be very large, even if the other bidder's bids are very different. Hence a possible bidspread in equilibrium would be small. In particular, they would be limited for large valuations because the first-unit bid need never be higher than the maximum of the other bidder's second unit bid. Furthermore, the argument above has additional implications. If the valuation is high, and hence the probability to win either of the units is high, both bids should be higher than the RNNE. On the other hand, if the valuation is low, and hence the probability to win either of the units is low, both bids should be below the RNNE.[11] Finally, if bidders are risk neutral and learn over time, bids should converge to RNNE bids.

We summarize that under misperception of probabilities (1) bidding the same on both units is still an equilibrium, (2) depending on the shape of the probability weighting function and the distribution of values, equilibria with moderate bid spreading might exist, (3) whether bids are above or below RNNE bids depends on the shape of the probability weighting function and (4) if bidders are risk neutral and learn over time, bids should converge to RNNE bids.

2.4. JOY OF WINNING

Cox, Smith, and Walker (1983b, 1988) and Goeree, Holt, and Palfrey (2000) suggest as an alternative explanation for overbidding in first-price auctions a model, where bidders receive a utility from the event of winning the auction. A pure joy of winning model (without incorporating risk aversion) explains overbidding in single-unit first-

to the authors, this does not come as a surprise, because single unit auctions cannot discriminate between nonlinear utility and nonlinear probability weighting.

[11] If the probability weighting function is not S-shaped, but for example as estimated by Goeree, Holt, and Palfrey, quadratic, bids could be above the RNNE throughout. A quadratic probability weighting function would, however, not be distinguishable from risk aversion and hence the problems that occur for risk aversion as explanation would apply as well.

price auctions, although (according to Goeree, Holt, and Palfrey) not as good as the previous two explanations. In a multiple unit setting, joy of winning has further implications on the structure of bids which allows us to distinguish it better from the previous two alternatives.

Suppose that the additional utility from winning the auction is proportional to the observed valuation, so that a bidder with valuation v who is bidding (b_1, b_2) has expected utility

$$U(b_1, b_2, v) = H_2(b_1)(vw - b_1) + H_1(b_2)(v - b_2), \tag{4}$$

where $H_1(\cdot)$ ($H_2(\cdot)$) denotes the distribution of the other bidder's higher (lower) bid, and $w > 1$ models the joy of winning.[12] For w big enough it can be shown that bidders always bid higher on the first unit than on the second one, and also that the second unit bid is above RNNE.

Moreover, joy of winning as modelled above could also explain overbidding in second-price auctions (as observed in Kagel, Harstad, and Levin (1987), Kagel and Levin (1990), and Engelmann and Grimm (2004)), which the alternative models suggested above can not.[13]

Summarizing, joy of winning would imply (1) extreme bid spreading if the parameter w is big, (2) higher than RNNE bids on both units, and (3) no adjustments of bids over time since joy of winning as introduced here is a myopic concept in the sense that there is always a joy of winning at least one unit in each auction.[14]

2.5. HYPOTHESES FROM THE THEORY

Table I summarizes the predictions that follow from the alternative explanations.

3. Experimental Design

In each auction two units of a homogeneous object were auctioned off among two bidders with flat demand for two units. The bidders' private valuations for both units were drawn independently in each auction from the same uniform distribution on $[0, 100]$ experimental currency units (ECU).[15] The bidders were undergraduate students from Humboldt University Berlin, the University of Zürich, and the ETH Zürich. Pairs of bidders were randomly formed and each of the nine pairs played ten auctions.

---

[12] Note that in this formulation winning a second unit does not yield additional joy.

[13] In this case, however, we would require winning to also yield joy if the monetary gain is negative, which might appear less plausible.

[14] In particular, since subjects get the result they aim for, namely almost always a positive profit and occasionally a large profit, reinforcement learning would not lead to a decrease in bid spreading in spite of it generating sub-optimal profits.

[15] Valuations were in fact drawn from the set of integers in [0,100] and also bids were restricted to integers. This does not, however, influence the predictions.

TABLE I. Hypotheses from the different theories

	First unit bid	Second unit bid	Bid spreads	Bids over time
RNNE	$\frac{1}{2}v$	$\frac{1}{2}v$	no	const.
CARA	$> \frac{1}{2}v$	$> \frac{1}{2}v$	no	const.
CRRA	$> \frac{1}{2}v$	$> \frac{1}{2}v$	moderate	decreasing
Probability misperception	(?)	(?)	no / moderate for certain distribution and weighting functions	converging to RNNE
Joy of winning & risk neutrality	$> \frac{1}{2}v$	$> \frac{1}{2}v$	possibly large	const.

Subjects were placed at isolated computer terminals, so that they could not determine whom they formed a pair with. Then the instructions (see Appendix A.1 for the translation) were read aloud. Before the start of a sequence of ten auctions, subjects played three dry runs, where they knew that their partner was simulated by a pre-programmed strategy. This strategy and the valuations of the subjects in the three dry runs were chosen in such a way that it was likely that each subject was exposed to winning 0 units in one auction, 1 unit in another and 2 units in the third. The pre-programmed strategy did not reflect any characteristics of the equilibrium and the subjects were explicitly advised that they should not see this strategy as an example of a good or a bad strategy (because they only observed the bids, they could not really copy the programmed strategy in any case).

The auctions were run in a straightforward way, i. e. both bidders simultaneously placed two bids. Subjects were informed that the order of the bids was irrelevant. After each auction bidders were informed about all four bids, as well as the resulting allocation, their own gains or losses and their aggregate profits.

The experimental software was developed in zTree (Fischbacher, 1999). The sessions lasted for about 30 minutes. At the end of each session, experimental currency units were exchanged in real currency at a rate of DM 0.04 (Berlin) or CHF 0.04 (Zürich) per ECU. In addition subjects received DM 5 (Berlin) or CHF10 (Zürich) as show-up fee.[16] Average total payoffs were 270 ECU. This resulted in average earnings (including show-up fees) of DM 14.79 (about EURO 7.56) in Berlin and CHF 21.68 (about EURO 14.09) in Zuerich.

[16] In order to relate the earnings, the exchange rates are 1 CHF = 0.65 Euro and 1 DM = 0.51 Euro. Cost of living is higher in Zurich, which justified the higher returns. The higher show-up fee in Zurich is based on a longer average commute to the laboratory than in Berlin.

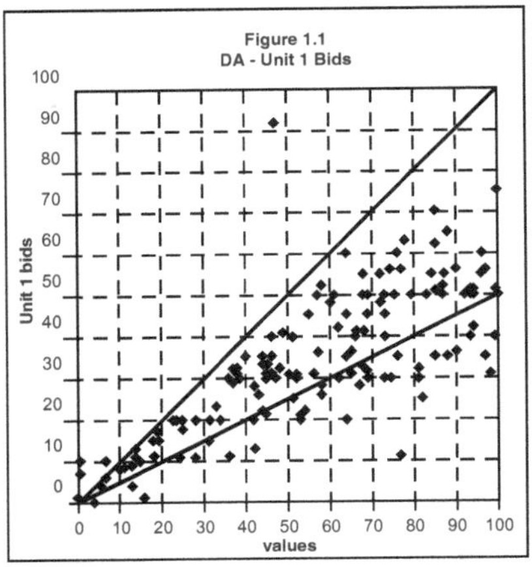

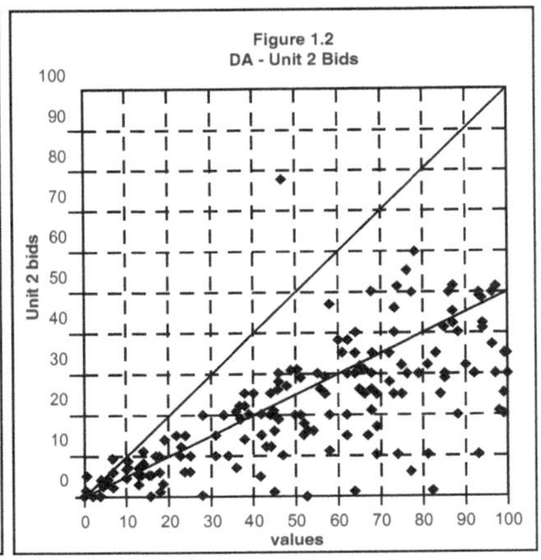

Figure 1. Scatter Diagrams.

4. The Data

In this section, we first summarize the results from the experiment before in Section 5 we contrast the data with the hypotheses derived in Section 2. Throughout our discussion of the experimental results, we use non-parametric Mann-Whitney tests for comparisons between treatments. These are always based on aggregate data per pair. The aggregate is computed over all periods. For comparisons between the first five and the second five auctions, as well as for comparisons with equilibrium predictions, we use non-parametric Wilcoxon signed-rank tests, because the data are paired. Again the tests are based on aggregate data per pair.

4.1. A FIRST LOOK AT THE DATA

The scatter diagrams in Figure 1 provide a first impression of the behavior of the bidders. "unit1 bids" refers to the (weakly) higher, and "unit2 bids" to the (weakly) lower bid of a bidder. According to the RNNE prediction, in a discriminatory auction the bidders should place equal bids ($b_1 = b_2 = \frac{1}{2}v$) on both units. However, as the scatter diagrams show, subjects placed substantially different bids on unit 1 and unit 2. The first unit bids seem to be well above the RNNE prediction, whereas the second unit bids are mostly below that level. According to Wilcoxon signed-rank tests, first-unit bids were significantly higher ($p = 0.021$) than the RNNE bid (average difference 5.48 ECU). The average second-unit bid is 3.73 ECU smaller than the RNNE equilibrium bid ($p = 0.139$).

As can also be seen in Figure 1, except for one subject in one auction, we observed overbidding of the valuation only for very small valuations and to a very small degree. It seems that it is obvious to bidders in DA that overbidding is dominated.

4.2. ESTIMATION OF BID FUNCTIONS FOR THE FIRST AND THE SECOND UNIT

Our initial observations are supported by estimating first-unit (b_1) and second-unit (b_2) bid functions that are linear in the valuation, i. e.

$$b_i = \alpha_i + \beta_i v. \tag{5}$$

Over all subjects, in a regression of the higher bid (with robust standard errors taking the dependence of observations within each pair into account) the coefficient for the valuation is $\beta_1 = 0.516$ (see Table II), which is close to the equilibrium value of 0.5, while it is substantially smaller in a regression of the lower bid ($\beta_2 = 0.379$). Combined with estimated constants of $\alpha_1 = 4.706$ and $\alpha_2 = 2.25$ this is consistent with first-unit bids substantially above the RNNE and second-unit bids below the RNNE. In bid functions estimated for individual subjects, β_1 is within 10% deviation of the equilibrium prediction only for 7 out of 18 subjects. For β_2, this is the case for only 5 subjects (see Table II).

4.3. BID SPREADING

The above results suggest that bids on the first and the second unit were rather different, contrary to the RNNE prediction. Table III contrasts the observed bid spreading with the bidspreads observed by Engelmann and Grimm (2004) in two other multiple unit sealed auction formats: the Vickrey-Auction (VA), where it is a bidder's dominant strategy to bid his true value on both units (i. e. we expect no bid spreading) and the Uniform-Price Sealed-Bid Auction (UPS) (where we expect up to 100% bid spreading).

We observe that in the discriminatory auction in only 12% of cases the bids were exactly equal and in only 15% (including the 12% equal bids) the difference was smaller than 10% of the risk-neutral equilibrium bid (i. e. 5% of the valuation, see Table III). More than half of these nearly equal bids (12 out of 21) were submitted by only two subjects (8 by subject 16 and 4 by subject 13, see Table II for their estimated bid functions). 49% of the bid spreads were larger than or equal to 40% of the equilibrium bid. The aggregate bid spread is 37%. This corresponds, for example, to bids of 21 and 30 for a valuation of 50 where the risk-neutral equilibrium bids would be 25.

According to Kolmogorov-Smirnov tests, the hypothesis that both, the higher and the lower bids in DA (relative to RNNE bids) are drawn from the same distribution, can be rejected at the 5%-level for 12 out of 18 bidders.

In comparison, in the Vickrey auction (VA) the aggregate bid spread is 13% (see Engelmann and Grimm, 2004) and the hypothesis that both, the higher and the

TABLE II. Parameter estimates for the bidding functions

Bidder	α_1	β_1	α_2	β_2
1	6.608	0.533	4.601	0.468
2	0.512	0.612	-1.072	0.493
3	0.113	0.602	2.261	0.244
4	14.481	0.299	5.354	0.343
5	8.881	0.479	3.704	0.459
6	6.630	0.744	5.638	0.667
7	14.534	0.227	16.453	-0.071
8	10.647	0.462	10.693	0.220
9	5.434	0.573	2.973	0.401
10	7.205	0.532	1.715	0.519
11	6.829	0.593	0.353	0.306
12	2.090	0.749	2.777	0.408
13	4.753	0.328	4.858	0.252
14	6.165	0.355	2.068	0.334
15	3.572	0.549	4.463	0.326
16	1.781	0.537	0.163	0.511
17	-1.587	0.406	-1.679	0.157
18	3.002	0.449	-1.438	0.354
all	4.706	0.516	2.250	0.379

TABLE III. Share of bid pairs that are exactly equal, where the difference is smaller than 10, or larger than 40 percent of the RNNE bids

Maxbid-minbid	UPS	VA	DA
$= 0$	18%	49%	12%
$<$ 10% RNNE	34%	62%	15%
$\geq$ 40% RNNE	33%	14%	49%

lower bid are drawn from the same distribution can be rejected for only 4 out of 20 bidders at the 5% level. Hence, bid spreading (relative to equilibrium bids) was clearly more prominent in DA than in VA, which is also confirmed by a Mann-Whitney test ($p = 0.0025$). Recall that in both auctions RNNE bids on both units are equal.

In UPS, the aggregate bid spread is 41% (see Engelmann and Grimm, 2004) and the hypothesis that both, the higher and the lower bid are drawn from the same distribution can be rejected for 13 out of 20 bidders at the 5% level. Hence

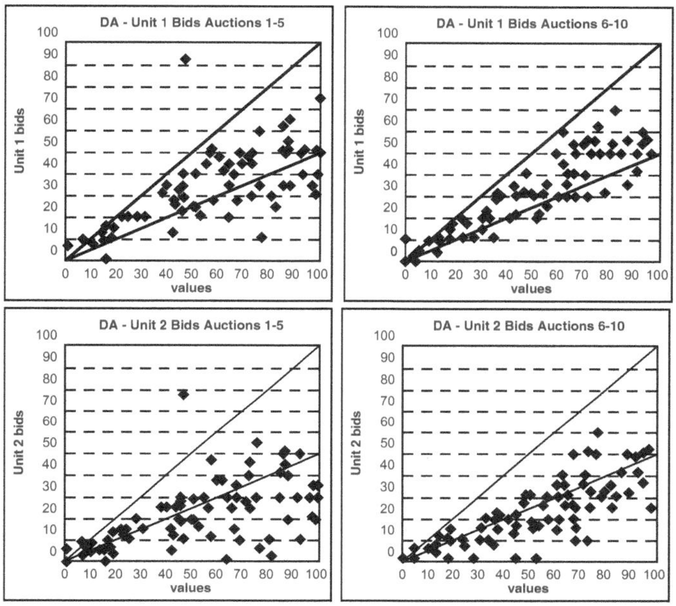

Figure 2. Scatter Diagrams for the first and the second five periods.

bid-spreading was of the same order in UPS as in DA. Bid spreading (relative to equilibrium bids) was indeed indistinguishable from that in DA (Mann-Whitney test, $p = 0.807$). This is surprising, since in UPS extreme bid spreading is predicted by equilibrium analysis, whereas in DA it is not.

To summarize, bid spreading in DA is much larger than in VA, although it should be zero in both auction formats, and is similar to that in UPS, where it is predicted to be large.

4.4. TIME TRENDS

A linear regression of the bidspread yields, over all subjects and periods (with robust standard errors) a negative coefficient (-0.05) for period, which is, however, not significantly smaller than 0 ($p = 0.83$). Hence, on average the bidspread decreased over time, but the effect is very small and insignificant. Indeed, the aggregate bid spread is 38% in periods 1 to 5 and 36% in periods 6 to 10. Moreover, the aggregate bid spread increased from the first to the second half of the experiment in five pairs, but decreased in only four.

The first- and second-unit bids by themselves do not exhibit any clear time trends either. Indeed, aggregating over all pairs and either all bids in the first five periods or all bids in the second five periods (see, as an illustration, Figure 2), the first-unit bids amount to 1.22 times the RNNE bid in both the early and the late periods, while the second-unit bids amount to 0.83 times the RNNE bids in periods 1–5, and to 0.86 times the RNNE bids in periods 6–10. The pattern is also highly heterogenous across pairs. First-unit bids relative to the RNNE increase in five pairs from the first five to the last five auctions, and decrease in four. With respect to second-unit bids, the result is just the opposite.[17] In particular, there is no discernible trend towards lower bids that would be implied by decreasing absolute risk aversion.

5. Comparative Performance of the Suggested Explanations

In this section we discuss the performance of the different theories with respect to organizing our data.

5.1. RISK AVERSION — CANNOT BE ALL THAT MATTERS

While in single-unit first-price auction experiments risk aversion seems to explain the observed behavior considerably well, it cannot be a satisfactory explanation of our multiple-unit auction data. Several of the observed and significant patterns are not consistent with risk aversion:

1. *Low second-unit bids.* Bids on the second unit are lower than the RNNE bid. This is clearly inconsistent with the risk aversion hypothesis. Under any kind of risk aversion, the other bidder's first-unit bid is higher than the RNNE bid. Thus, it is even harder for a bidder to obtain the second unit. The lower probability of winning the second unit (due to the high first-unit bid of the opponent) together with risk aversion should yield second-unit bids that are considerably higher than the RNNE bids.
2. *Extreme bidspreads.* We observe extreme bidspreads in the discriminatory auction. Recall that bidspreads in DA are of the same order as in UPS (where bidspreading should occur in equilibrium) and significantly higher than in VA (where bids should be equal in equilibrium). While the bidspreads are significantly smaller in VA than in DA, they are still present and in this auction format they cannot possibly be explained by risk aversion. Therefore, although mild bidspreading in DA could be explained by decreasing absolute risk aversion, there must still be another motivation for the observed behavior.
3. *No significant time trends.* As shown in Section 2, only decreasing absolute risk aversion could possibly be consistent with a positive bid spread. However, this would also imply that bids should decrease over time, depending on the wealth accumulated by a bidder. Since we do not observe this, decreasing absolute risk aversion would have to be highly myopic, i. e. bidders would be required to consider the utility of income and this for each auction separately. To see most clearly that

[17] Note that these results are unlikely to follow from different draws of valuations in the different auctions, because the aggregate valuations across all pairs and all of either the first or the last five auctions increases by only about 2% from the former to the latter.

decreasing absolute risk aversion does not work as an explanation, consider the frequent case (32% of the bid pairs) that a bidder places a first-unit bid above the RNNE and a second-unit bid below the RNNE. Apart from the fact that this would require risk aversion to decrease so dramatically that it is actually turned into risk seeking, it further implies, that in all future auctions, both bids should be below the RNNE (as long as the bidder is successful with at least one bid in the current auction), which we clearly do not observe.

To summarize, risk aversion is only a viable explanation for the observed bid-spreads if absolute risk aversion is decreasing and stronger than usually estimated. On the other hand, this would imply that both bids are substantially higher than the RNNE and decrease over time, neither of which we observe.

5.2. MISPERCEPTION OF PROBABILITIES

While misperception of probabilities can explain overbidding in single-unit first-price auctions (Goeree, Holt, and Palfrey estimate a concave probability weighting function), it also fails to explain our multi-unit auction data because it is not consistent with the following aspects:

1. *Bid spreads.* Misperception of probabilities does not eliminate equal bidding as equilibrium. Moreover, while misperception of probabilities might also be consistent with mild bid-spreading, the distortion would have to be dramatic to explain the large spreads that we observe. Furthermore, this would have additional implications not consistent with our data.
2. *No learning.* In case bidders misperceive probabilities, they should notice that they do so during the course of the experiment. Therefore, over time one should expect bids to get closer to the RNNE prediction. This, however, cannot be observed in our data. The problem could be that subjects played too few rounds in order to be able to learn.

Thus, although it may well be that subjects misperceive probabilities, this can definitely not be the only driving force behind the observed behavior. The data are not consistent with any of the unambiguous predictions implied by this model, that is, small bidspreads and convergence over time.

Still, among the models discussed in Section 2, misperception of probabilities is the only one that could possibly explain lower than RNNE bids (which we observed on the second unit). However, for low valuations we should then also observe first-unit bids below the RNNE, which we clearly do not.

Finally, in the postexperimental questionaire some subjects state that they placed "a high secure bid and a lower bid that could yield a higher profit". This suggests that they *willingly* bid rather low on the second unit and did not misperceive the probability of winning.

5.3. JOY OF WINNING

Joy of winning does not perfectly explain the data, but does considerably better than the alternatives discussed above. As already mentioned, some statements in the post-experimental questionnaires suggest that bidders wanted to secure one unit by placing a high bid on the first one, while they aimed at realizing a high profit by placing a low bid on the second. This seems to describe a (highly myopic) joy of being successful in each single auction, which is consistent with the "Joy of Winning" models that have been discussed in Section 2. This explanation is consistent with the following main aspects of out data:

1. *Bid spreading.* Those models indeed could predict extreme bid spreading as observed in the data, if the additional utility received from winning at least one unit is sufficiently high.
2. *Overbidding in Vickrey and uniform-price auctions.* Joy of winning is the only among the discussed models that could also explain the often observed overbidding of the valuation in auction formats where the equilibrium first unit bid equals the valuation (VA and UPS). This is sometimes interpreted as a bidding error. It does, however, not disappear even if it is explained to bidders why they should not overbid (see Kagel and Levin, 2001), and it is persistent across almost all experiments on those auctions.
   Already Kagel and Roth (1992) made the point that bidders also overbid in auctions where risk aversion plays no role and concluded that there must be something different from risk aversion driving this behavior. Given that bidders run the risk of paying a price higher than their valuation, the joy seems to be present even if winning could imply monetary losses.[18]
3. *No learning* Finally, the model could also explain why subjects did not revise their behavior in the course of the auction. Actually, they rather get reinforced by frequently winning one unit and occasionally making a large profit on the second one.

The only feature of the data that could not be explained by a "Joy of Winning plus Risk Neutrality" hypothesis (but neither by the other theories discussed above in isolation) is that second unit bids are frequently below the RNNE bid. Hence, a combination with either risk seeking behavior or misperception of probabilities (in the sense that the probability of receiving the second unit is overestimated) would get further in explaining our results. However, in order to fit our data as equilibrium, either of these effects would have to be very strong, because due to first-unit bids well above RNNE bids, the probability of getting a second unit is rather low which should imply rather high second-unit bids.

---

[18] Possibly bidders have a distorted view of the game in the sense that they realize that overbidding increases both the probability of winning a unit and the probability of making a loss, without realizing that the additional units are *exactly* won when they result in monetary losses. If this is the case then the joy of winning would not have to be so strong as to compensate actual monetary losses (which seems unlikely in the first place) but only bias the perceived trade-off between higher chances to win a unit and higher risks of a monetary loss in favor of the first.

The data of auction experiments in general strongly suggest that bidders aim at being "successful" on each single occasion. Our data strengthen this point, since they exclude alternative explanations that usually cannot be well distinguished on the basis of data from single-unit auction experiments. A possible explanation for the observed behavior might combine a joy of winning (high first-unit bid) with a joy of gambling (low second-unit bids). Hence our bidders would act like people who buy insurance (against the risk of having zero profit) while at the same time buying lottery tickets.

6. Overbidding in First-Price Auctions Revisited

At a first glance the observed bidding behavior in our multi-unit auction experiments looks more or less consistent with the well known phenomenon of overbidding in first-price single-unit auctions. However, as we have shown, it can be explained neither by risk aversion nor by misperception of probabilities, which are the two most prominent hypotheses in the literature on overbidding in single-unit first-price auctions. The fact that in our data the majority of second-unit bids is below the RNNE is clearly inconsistent with risk aversion. Furthermore, the observed bidspreads are of a magnitude that is inconsistent with misperception of probabilities and reasonable degrees of risk aversion. Since an explanatory model should be consistent across different auction formats (e. g. not only be valid for single-unit auctions), the data from our multi-unit auction experiments raise doubts about the explanatory adequacy of risk aversion and misperception of probabilities for overbidding in single-unit auctions.

A further insight from our multi-unit auctions for the interpretation of behavior in single-unit auctions follows from the comparison between risk aversion and misperception of probabilities. In contrast to our auctions, in a single-unit setting the two explanations are usually not distinguishable. Goeree, Holt and Palfrey (2000) study single-unit auctions with asymmetric loss functions, which also allows them to compare these two hypotheses. They find that they perform equally well and better than a joy of winning model. In our setting, however, this order seems to be reversed and, moreover, the first two models perform quite differently.

The behavioral pattern observed in our experiment seems to be caused by a myopic "joy of winning", which leads subjects to increase the probability of acquiring at least one unit in each auction at the expense of expected profits. This has a lower distorting effect in the other auction mechanisms we mentioned in Section 4 (UPS and VA), since the probability of acquiring at least one unit (without making losses) is maximized by bidding the valuation on the first unit, consistent with equilibrium behavior. However, in those auction formats some bidders even risk a loss in order to further increase the probability of winning one unit. Again, a joy of winning hypothesis is the only one that could explain the observed behavior.[19]

[19] An interesting conclusion from this observation is that auction formats where everyone obtains something in equilibrium are likely to raise rather low revenues. The effect is the stronger, the more the auction permits the bidders to ensure their opponents winning a unit, i. e. open auctions, where a bidder can do this by dropping out immediately. Sealed bid formats, in contrast, maintain a certain

For a complete explanation of our data, several reasons have to come together. Our analysis suggests that in any such combination joy of winning would play a prominent role, because no possible combination of the other models can explain the observed behavior, in particular the bidspreading, in a satisfactory way. On the other hand, the observed underbidding on the second unit, which looks like risk-seeking behavior, implies that joy of winning alone cannot provide a complete explanation. The data could be explained by combining joy of winning with either risk prone behavior or with joy of gambling, which could be due to the low stakes in an experiment, or with misperception of probabilities.

A somewhat puzzling observation is that the bidders in all auction experiments appear to be driven by a highly myopic (per auction) desire to win. While such a myopic joy of winning does not appear so surprising in a single-unit auction since it would just suggest that a bidder likes to win as many auctions as possible, it is interesting that in our auction it appears to apply just to win one unit per auction. Hence bidders appear to want to win something in each auction, but not necessarily all the available units.[20]

To conclude, reevaluating the hypotheses that have been suggested for the explanation of the common behavioral pattern in single-unit auctions has cast significant doubt on the performance of the usual suspects. Further experimental research on multi-unit auctions may substantially improve our understanding of the behavior in single-unit auctions, because hypotheses that imply only subtle differences in single-unit auctions can have substantially different implications in multi-unit auctions, making the latter a more powerful tool to discriminate among them.

Appendix

A.1. INSTRUCTIONS (ORIGINAL INSTRUCTIONS WERE IN GERMAN)

Please read these instructions carefully. If there is anything you do not understand, please raise your hand. We will then answer your questions privately. The instructions are identical for all participants.

In the course of the experiment you will participate in 10 auctions. In each auction you and another bidder will bid for two units of a fictitious good. This other bidder will be the same in each auction. Each unit that you acquire will be sold to the experimenters for your private resale value v. Before each auction this value *per unit*, v, will be randomly drawn independently for each bidder from the interval $0 \leq v \leq 100$ ECU (Experimental Currency Unit). Any number between 0 and 100 is equally probable. The private resale values of different bidders are independent. *In each auction any unit that you acquire will have the same value for you. This value will be drawn anew before each auction.*

extent of uncertainty about winning a unit and therefore trigger more aggressive behavior. This is consistent with findings in Engelmann and Grimm (2004), where sealed bid formats yield significantly higher revenues than open auctions.

[20] Joy of winning might in some cases be driven by an aversion against zero-profits. While such a myopic zero-profit aversion might explain our data for DA, it is not a viable explanation for the overbidding in UPS and VA, since a dislike for zero-profits is hardly strong enough to risk negative profits.

Before each auction you will be informed about your resale value *per unit*, v. Each participant will be informed only about his or her own resale value, but not about the other bidder's resale value.

Subsequently, you have to make your bids b_1 and b_2. You enter your bids in the designated fields (one each for the first and the second unit) and click the field *OK*.

The two highest bids win the units. Hence you will win one unit if one of your bids is among the highest two units and you obtain both units if both your bids are higher than those of the other bidder. If because of identical bids the highest bids are not uniquely determined, then the buyers will be chosen randomly.

If you win a unit then you pay the amount you have bid for this unit. Your profit per unit that you obtain amounts thus to your resale value minus the bid you have won the unit for. If you do not win any unit then you will not obtain anything and also not pay anything, hence your profit is 0.

Note that you can make losses as well. It is always possible, however, to bid in such a way that you can prevent losses for sure.

You will make your decision via the computer terminal. You will not get to know the names and code numbers of the other participants. Thus all decisions remain confidential.

One ECU corresponds to 0,04 DM. You will obtain an initial endowment of 5 DM. If you make losses in an auction these will be deducted from your previous gains (or from your initial endowment). You will receive your final profit in cash at the end of the experiment. The other participants will not get to know your profits.

If there is something you have not understood, please raise your hand. We will then answer your questions privately.

Acknowledgements

We thank Bob Sherman as well as seminar participants at Nottingham for helpful comments and suggestions. Financial Support by the Deutsche Forschungsgemeinschaft, through SFB 373 ("Quantifikation und Simulation Ökonomischer Prozesse"), Humboldt-Universität zu Berlin, and through grant number EN459/1-1 is gratefully acknowledged. Part of this research was conducted while Dirk Engelmann visited the Institute for Empirical Research in Economics, University of Zurich. The hospitality of this institution is gratefully acknowledged.

References

Cox, J. C., B. Roberson, and V. L. Smith. 1982. "Theory and Behavior of Single Object Auctions", in: V. L. Smith (ed.): *Research in Experimental Economics*, Vol. 2, Greenwich, CT: JAI Press, 1–44.

Cox, J. C., and V. Sadiraj. 2001. *Risk Aversion and Expected-Utility Theory: Coherence for Small- and Large-Stakes Games*, Working Paper, University of Arizona.

Cox, J. C., V. L. Smith, and J. M. Walker. 1983a. "Tests of a Heterogenous Bidder's Theory of First Price Auctions", *Economics Letters 12*, 207–212.

Cox, J. C., V. L. Smith, and J. M. Walker. 1983b. "A Test that Discriminates Between Two Models of the Dutch-First Auction Non-isomorphism", *Journal of Economic Behavior and Organization* 4, 205–219.

Cox, J. C., V. L. Smith, and J. M. Walker. 1984. "Theory and Behavior of Multiple Unit Discriminative Auctions", *Journal of Finance* 39, 983–1010.

Cox, J. C., V. L. Smith, and J. M. Walker. 1985. "Experimental Development of Sealed-Bid Auction Theory:Calibrating Controls for Risk Aversion", *American Economic Review: Papers and Proceedings* 75, 160–165.

Cox, J. C., V. L. Smith, and J. M. Walker. 1988. "Theory and Individual Behavior of First-Price Auctions", *Journal of Risk and Uncertainty* 1, 61–99.

Engelmann, D., and V. Grimm. 2004. *Bidding Behavior in Multi-Unit Auctions — An Experimental Investigation and some Theoretical Insights*, Working Paper, University of Alicante.

Fischbacher, U. 1999. *Z-Tree: Zurich Toolbox for Readymade Economic Experiments*, Working paper No. 21, Institute for Empirical Research in Economics, University of Zurich.

Friedman, D. 1992. "Theory and Misbehavior of First-Price Auctions: Comment", *American Economic Review* 82, 1374–1378.

Goeree, J. K., C. A. Holt, and T. R. Palfrey. 2000. *Quantal Response Equilibrium and Overbidding in Private Value Auctions*, Working Paper, California Institute of Technology.

Harrison, G. W. 1989. "Theory and Misbehavior of First-Price Auctions", *American Economic Review* 79, 749–762.

Kagel, J. H., R. M. Harstad, and D. Levin. 1987. "Information Impact and Allocation Rules in Auctions with Affiliated Private Values: A Laboratory Study", *Econometrica* 55, 1275–1304.

Kagel, J. H., and D. Levin. 1990. *Independent Private Value Auctions: Bidder Behavior in First-, Second- and Third-Price Auctions with Varying Numbers of Bidders*, mimeo, University of Houston.

Kagel, J. H., and D. Levin. 2001. "Behavior in Multi-Unit Demand Auctions: Experiments with Uniform Price and Dynamic Auctions", *Econometrica* 69, 413 – 454.

Kagel, J. H., and A. E. Roth. 1992. "Theory and Misbehavior of First-Price Auctions: Comment", *American Economic Review* 82, 1379–1391.

Krishna, V. 2002. *Auction Theory*, Academic Press.

Lebrun, B., and M. C. Tremblay. 2003. "Multi-Unit Pay-Your-Bid Auction with One-Dimensional Multi-Unit Demands", *International Economic Review* 44, 1135–1172.

Maskin, E., and J. Riley. 1984. "Optimal Auctions with Risk Averse Buyers", *Econometrica* 52, 1473–1518.

Prelec, D. 1998. "The Probability Weighting Function", *Econometrica* 66, 497–527.

Rabin, M. 2000. "Risk Aversion and Expected-Utility Theory: A Calibration Theorem", *Econometrica* 68, 1281–1292.

Rabin, M., and R. H. Thaler. 2001. "Anomalies: Risk Aversion", *Journal of Economic Perspectives* 15, 219–232.

Veronika Grimm
Departamento de Fundamentos del Análisis Económico
Universidad de Alicante
Campus San Vicente
E-03071 Alicante
Spain
grimm@merlin.fae.ua.es

Dirk Engelmann
Department of Economics
Royal Holloway, University of London
Egham, Surrey TW20 0EX
United Kingdom
dirk.engelmann@rhul.ac.uk

MODELLING JUDGMENTAL FORECASTS UNDER TABULAR AND GRAPHICAL DATA PRESENTATION FORMATS

OTWIN BECKER
Universität Heidelberg

JOHANNES LEITNER
Universität Graz

ULRIKE LEOPOLD–WILDBURGER
Universität Graz

1. Introduction

The accuracy of statistical time series forecasts is a critical factor for the situation-specific application of a model. Makridakis and Hibon (1979) were the first to empirically explore the performance of various statistical models in forecasting competitions on a data set of thousands of real time series. It was found inter alia that simple procedures, such as exponential smoothing, perform equivalently to sophisticated models (Makridakis and Hibon, 2000) — a result supported by many other authors. Although statistical models were the initial interest of forecasting competitions probably the most common forecasting approach was incorporated soon: judgmental forecasting. Judgmental forecasts are based on subjective eyeballing of the past realizations of the time series without the support of statistical procedures — a technique which seems to be inferior to statistical procedures at first glance. Lawrence et al. (1985) applied 111 real-life time series of the Makridakis forecasting competition (Makridakis et al., 1982) in a forecasting experiment and compared the accuracy of judgmental forecasts to statistical models. Judgmental forecasts were at least as accurate as statistical models, and in some cases even superior to them.[1] The authors also identified the influence of data presentation formats on the accuracy: Forecasts of time series presented in tables significantly outperformed graphs for annual time series (long run). They also found table forecasts to be more robust, i.e. smaller standard deviations of the forecasting errors. The authors attribute the differences to the inability of tabular forecasters to

[1] However, not all authors conclude superiority of judgmental over statistical methods. See Webby and O'Connor (1996) for an extensive review.

U. Schmidt and S. Traub (eds.), Advances in Public Economics: Utility, Choice and Welfare, 255-266.

recognize short-term trends for the most recent realizations. In a direct experimental comparison of data presentation formats on forecasting accuracy, Harvey and Bolger (1996) tested the forecasts of trended and untrended time series with different noise levels. They find a slight advantage of untrended time series in tabular format, but a clear superiority for the graphical format in all other cases.

Unlike the mentioned studies, the main focus of the present paper is not forecasting accuracy but the modelling of judgmental forecasts of a tabularly and graphically presented time series. In prior experimental setups for the analysis of expectation formation mechanisms the effects of data presentation formats have been widely ignored. Schmalensee (1976) tested the forecasts of subjects on compatibility with the adaptive and the extrapolative models with a chart of a time series. Dwyer et al. (1993) demonstrated that subjects rationally forecast a graphically presented random walk. For instance, Brennscheidt (1993), Hey (1994), Beckman and Downs (1997) tested various models on judgmental forecasts of time series presented in both formats simultaneously. Hey allowed his subjects to switch between formats according to their own convenience. Hence, potential format effects were completely lost in the results.

In our experiment, tabular and graphical forecasts of a time series are collected from student subjects. We apply a simple scheme-oriented explanation model, the bounds and likelihood heuristic, for the explanation of the subjects' average forecasts. The heuristic was successfully tested on a sample of about 600 subjects in various experimental versions by Becker et al. (2004a, 2004b) and Becker and Leopold-Wildburger (2000), whereas all these experiments were exclusively based on charts. The primary question is now the extent to which tabular and graphical supported forecasts differ and whether they can be explained — on average — by the heuristic. It is hypothesized that that tabular and graphical supported forecasts are both based on forecasting schemes. It is our motivation to verify whether the rationale of the heuristic explains the forecasts, i.e. that the average forecasts of both groups follow the same scheme. The performance of the bounds&likelihood heuristic will be compared to the rational expectations hypothesis REH.

2. The Experiment

Academic subjects made judgmental forecasts of a time series x_t over 42 periods. The subjects were not provided with any additional information, help from statistical models or any contextual information. The time series was unlabelled. The only utilizable information were the past realizations of x_t. The time series is a realization of the stochastic difference equation

$$x_t = x_{t-1} - INT(\frac{1}{2} \cdot x_{t-2}) + u_t \tag{1}$$

with the endogenous variable x_t and the white noise u_t. The variable u_t is uniformly distributed in the interval [1,6]. All values of x_t and the subjects' forecasts are integer. The forecasts were limited to the interval [0,30]. The start value $x_1 = 7$ was given to the subjects in the first period. No history of realizations was presented to the subjects

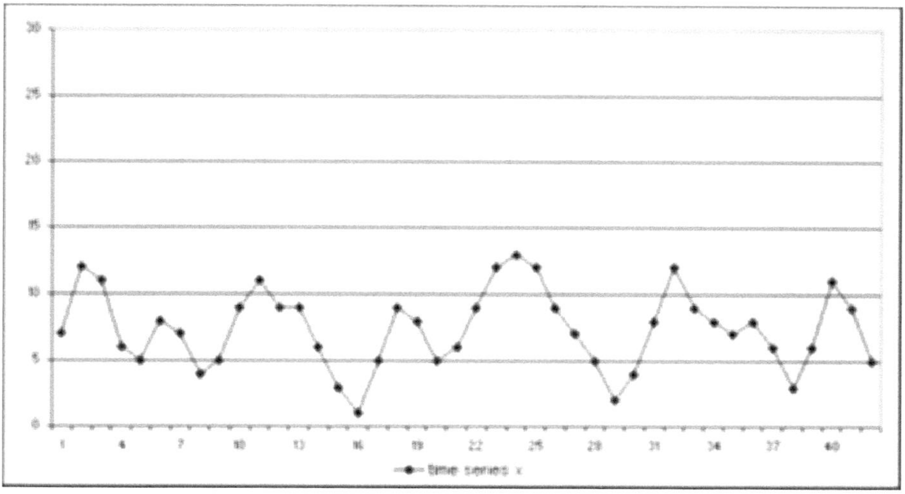

Figure 1. The time series in the graphical presentation format.

1	2	3	4	5	6	7	8	9	10	11	12	13	14	15	16	17	18	19	20	21	22	23	24	25
7	12	11	6	5	8	7	5	4	9	11	9	9	6	3	1	5	9	8	5	6	9	12	13	12

Figure 2. The time series in the tabular presentation format.

in the first period. Based on this, subjects made their forecast f_2 and were then informed about the true realization of x_2. Hence, the information set of the subjects for the forecast of period $t+1$ only consisted of all past values ($\Omega_t = \{x_t, x_{t-1}, \ldots x_1\}$). The experiment was carried out in two versions. The introductions and information given to the subjects, the payment function and the experimental procedure were the same in both versions. The main difference was the presentation format of the time series: In the graphical versions, the values of x_t and f_t were presented in a chart, in the tabular version in a table. Figure 1 and Figure 2 show the time series x_t as it was presented to the subjects in both versions.

The tabular experiment was carried out with paper and pencil, the graphical version with computers. In the tabular version, subjects were handed out a table with 42 columns and three rows.[2] The periods were numbered in the first row. The realizations of the time series were inserted in the second row, the subject's own forecasts in the third row. On the handout, the first column of the second row had the value 7. All other fields of the second and third row were empty. When all subjects had made their forecasts, they were informed about the true value verbally and noted

[2] We know from our database of experimental results that no significant differences between computerized and paper-based settings exist. The differences reported here can accordingly be ascribed only to the data presentation format.

it in the table. Then the next forecast was made, and this was repeated for all 42 periods.

The experiments were conducted at the Department of Statistics and Operations Research, University of Graz. Altogether 102 undergraduate subjects participated voluntarily, 72 in the graphical and 30 in the tabular version. The subjects were recruited from undergraduate courses of business administration. They were given a significant financial incentive to forecast the time series accurately. They were paid 60 Cents for an exact forecast, a forecast error of one (two) unit(s) was rewarded with 40 (20) Cents. This simple payment scheme corresponds to a function of absolute forecast errors that is cut off to zero at the value of three. The average payments in the graphical (tabular) version of the experiment were 9.2 (8) Euros at an average duration of about 30 minutes.

3. Two Explanation Models

3.1. THE BOUNDS AND LIKELIHOOD HEURISTIC

The bounds and likelihood heuristic (b&l heuristic) by Becker and Leopold-Wildburger (1996, 2000) models average forecasts. It is assumed that two features of the time series are essential for the forecasts: the average variation and the turning points. The average absolute variations of the time series $b_t = \frac{1}{t-1}\sum_{j=2}^{t}|x_j - x_{j-1}|$ are the bounds for the predicted change based on the actual time series value x_t. The maximum predicted change is supposed to be in the interval [-b_t, b_t]. The actually predicted change depends on the likelihood that x_t is a turning point. For $x_t > x_{t-1}$, an upswing case, $l_{t(peak)}$ is the probability that x_t is a local maximum. The total number of local minima observed so far (N_t) and the number of local minima $\leq x_t$ (n_t) are considered. If all local maxima are below x_t, i.e. $n_t = N_t$, it is very likely to be a turning point. For a downswing case ($x_t < x_{t-1}$), the total number of local minima (M_t) and the number of local minima $\geq x_t$ are considered for the calculation of $l_{t(trough)}$. This is shown in equation (2).

$$\begin{aligned} l_{t(peak)} &= \frac{1+n_t}{2+N_t} \\ l_{t(trough)} &= \frac{1+m_t}{2+M_t} \end{aligned} \tag{2}$$

In the case of no change ($x_t = x_{t-1}$), it is assumed that the upswing and downswing cases are combined linearly. At a high level of the time series, subjects will forecast a downswing; at a low level, an upswing. Based on these assumptions, the values of the heuristic $f_{t,b\&l}$ are described by equation (3).

$$f_{t+1,b\&l} = \begin{cases} x_t + b_t(1 - 2l_{t(peak)}) & for\ x_t > x_{t-1} \\ x_t + b_t(l_{t(trough)} - l_{t(peak)}) & for\ x_t = x_{t-1} \\ x_t - b_t(1 - 2l_{t(trough)}) & for\ x_t < x_{t-1} \end{cases} \tag{3}$$

3.2. THE RATIONAL EXPECTATIONS HYPOTHESIS

The rational expectations hypothesis (REH) suggests that agents form their expectations consistent with economic theory. They should derive their forecasts from the true economic model that generates the variable to be forecasted. The subjective distributions about future realizations should be the same as the actual distributions, conditional on the available information set (Muth, 1961). The information set of a rational forecaster contains the true model and its parameters and all the realizations of the time series observed so far. The knowledge of the true model (1) that generated the experimentally applied time series allows the calculation of the values of rational expectations. In our experiment, the REH values can simply be calculated by replacing u_t in (1) with its expected value 3.5:

$$f_{t,REH} = x_{t-1} - INT(\frac{1}{2} \cdot x_{t-2}) + 3.5 \tag{4}$$

With these values it can be tested whether the rational expectations hypothesis gives a valid explanation of the subjects' average forecasts.

4. Results

In this section we analyze the forecasts of the subjects. The differences between the tabular and graphical forecasts are explored on the collective and the individual level. The performance of the b&l-heuristic and the REH in explaining the subjects' average forecasts will be tested.[3]

4.1. THE FORECASTS OF THE SUBJECTS

The first crucial question for the modelling of average forecasts is whether the distributions of the forecasts in both groups differ, and if so, what reasons for these differences can be assigned. In each of the 36 considered periods a Kolmogorov-Smirnov test was performed to test for differences in the distributions of the individual forecasts. In 29 periods, graphical and tabular forecasts do not differ significantly at the 99%-level of significance. The remaining seven periods (8, 11, 23, 32, 36, 40 and 41) are local extrema or periods before/after local extrema. The graphical group overestimates the time series especially in periods of local maxima. A possible explanation for the overestimation bias is the presentation of the time series in the lower half of the chart (see Figure 1). Both groups were told that the realizations of the time series are within the interval [0,30] but only the graphical group was permanently aware of this fact by the scale of the ordinate. Despite the cyclical structure of the time series, the graph group could expect the time series to reach higher values than the local

[3] In both experimental versions, the first six periods serve as a phase for familiarization and practice. Hence, periods 1 to 6 are not taken into account within the statistical analysis and only periods 7–42 are considered.

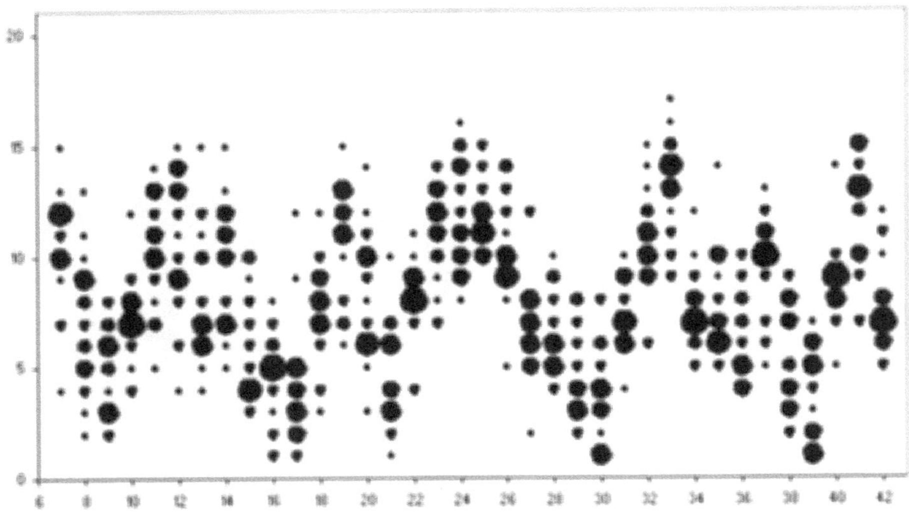

Figure 3. The distribution of the forecasts in the graphical presentation format.

maxima observed so far. The local minima are less relevant since they occur close to the abscissa of the chart. In the tabular experiment, subjects need longer to notice the low level of the time series (see Figure 5). The subjects forecast much higher values in the first periods, which explains the large deviation in period 8. There are indications for systematic differences between the forecasts of both groups in these seven periods, but the small sample does not allow the test for significance. In Figures 3 and 4, the frequencies of forecasted values are represented by circles of different sizes.

The differences in the individual and collective forecasts of both groups are analyzed by their forecasting errors. The collective forecasts f_t^{avg} are calculated as arithmetic means of the forecasts in each period. The error measurement categories are reported in Table I. At values of 0.808 (graphical) and 0.886 (tabular) the Theil's U of both average forecasts are below the critical value of 1. Consequently, both groups outperform the naive random walk forecasts. The MdAPE, MSE and the MAE consistently favor the graphical group, but the ME is lower for the tabular forecasts. The latter implies that the graphical group overestimates the time series. More detailed insight into the structure of the forecasting errors can be brought by a decomposition of the MSE (see Theil, 1966)

$$MSE = \frac{1}{T}\sum_{t=7}^{T}(x_t - f_t)^2 = (\overline{x} - \overline{f})^2 + (SD_x - SD_f)^2 + 2(1 - r_{xf})SD_x SD_f \qquad (5)$$

where $\overline{x}$ is the arithmetic mean of the time series x_t, $\overline{f}$ is the arithmetic mean of the corresponding forecasts f_t, SD_x and SD_f are their standard deviations and r_{xf} denotes the correlation between the time series and the forecasts. In Table I, the MSE components are reported. As expected from the mean error, the deviation from $\overline{x}$ is

TABLE I. Accuracy of the average individual forecasts (***$p < .001$)

Forecasts	Individual Forecasts		Average Forecasts	
Format	Graph	Table	Graph	Table
MdAPE	26.136%	32.86%	21.407%	25.556%
ME	0.684	0.506	0.694	0.539
MAE	2.360	2.740	1.856	2.021
MSE	8.820	12.594	4.73	5.689
Theils' U	1.093	1.305	0.808	0.886
$(\overline{x} - \overline{f})^2$	0.483	0.426	0.481	0.291
$(SD_x - SD_f)^2$	0.078	0.219	0.096	0.283
r_{xf}	0.604	0.447***	0.731	0.639

larger in the graphical group, but its standard deviation is lower and its correlation coefficient is higher. The $\overline{f}$ of the tabular forecasts is closer to $\overline{x}$, which compensates their lower correlation and worse accordance with the standard deviation of x_t. Despite the reported differences, according to a Wilcoxon signed rank test of the forecast errors of both groups, the differences are not significant (z=-1.384, p=0.166). Thus, neither the distributions nor the forecasting errors of average forecasts of both groups differ significantly.

The same measurement categories are applied to the forecasts of the individuals.

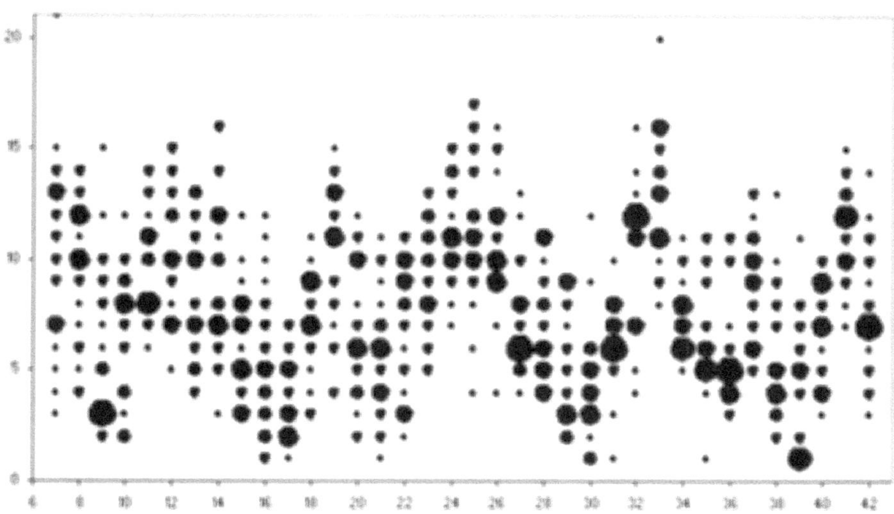

Figure 4. The distribution of the forecasts in the tabular presentation format.

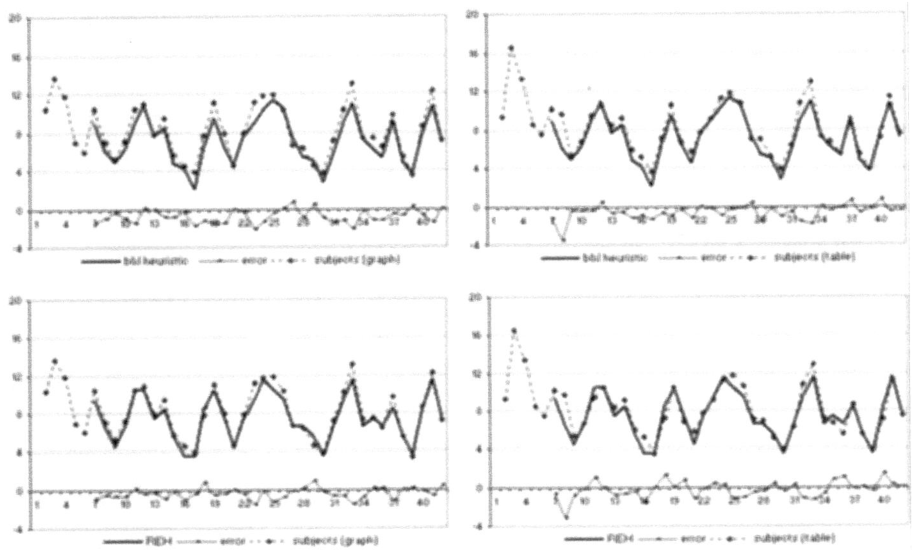

Figure 5. The subjects' average forecasts compared to REH and b&l.

The average/median measures of all individuals in both groups are presented in Table I. MSE, Theil's U and MAE are lower in the graphical group, but the ME is higher. Furthermore, the same conclusions as for the individuals can be drawn from the MSE components. The individuals in the graphical version overestimate the time series, the standard deviations of their forecasts are closer to the actual standard deviations and their forecasts show a significant higher correlation (Mann-Whitney U Test, $p < .001$) to the actual values.

It can be concluded that there are some significant differences between the individual forecasts which can be attributed to the correlation of the forecasts. However, the distributions of the individual forecasts and their averages do not differ significantly. These results are the basis for the modelling of average forecasts reported in the next section. Another interesting observation is that the combination of the forecasts of both groups results in much higher forecasting accuracy. The arithmetic mean of 30 tabular subjects has a Theil's U of 0.886 while the average individual Theil's U is at 1.305, far above the critical value of 1. Thus, by combining 30 forecasts with a simple arithmetic mean the accuracy can be improved substantially.

4.2. MODELLING AVERAGE FORECASTS

The main interest of the analysis is the extent to which average forecasts of both groups can be explained by the b&l heuristic and the REH. We estimate a simple linear regression with the average forecast as a predicted variable and the two models

TABLE II. Regression results for both models

Model	Format	Periods	α	β	R^2	DW
b&l	Graph	7–42	0.479 (0.368)	1.046 (0.049)	0.931	1.811
		7–25	0.704 (0.505)	1.034 (0.068)	0.936	1.831
		25–42	0.247 (0.542)	1.58 (0.071)	0.933	1.824
	Table	7–42	1.079 (0.41)	0.94 (0.054)	0.898	1.822
		7–25	1.725 (0.609)	0.609 (0.081)	0.878	1.940
		25–42	0.478 (0.536)	1.000 (0.070)	0.927	1.917
REH	Graph	7–42	-0.146 (0.309)	1.078 (0.039)	0.957	1.902
		7–25	0.585 (0.406)	0.988 (0.051)	0.959	2.271
		25–42	-0.960 (0.406)	1.181 (0.052)	0.970	1.646
	Table	7–42	0.755 (0.504)	0.938 (0.064)	0.864	1.471
		7–25	1.861 (0.714)	0.803 (0.090)	0.833	1.679
		25–42	-0.475 (0.626)	1.091 (0.080)	0.921	1.407

as predictors:

$$f_t^{avg} = \alpha + \beta f_{t,\theta} \qquad \text{with } \theta = b\&l, REH. \tag{6}$$

Both models are tested over the forecasting horizon of periods 7–42. The results are presented in Table II. The most important result is that the heuristic explains 93.1% of the variance of the average forecast in the graphical version and only slightly less (89.9%) in the tabular version. While the heuristic performs worse than the REH in the graphical version, it outperforms rational expectations in the tabular version (89.9% vs. 86.4%). These results hold at lower autocorrelation of the residuals for both b&l estimates as indicated by the Durbin-Watson statistics. While the estimated slope coefficients in the tabular experiment are not significantly different from 1, the intercepts are significantly larger than 0. This is a drawback compared to the graphical version. In order to test potential learning processes and the time invariance of these results, a half split analysis is performed and further regressions are estimated by considering periods 7–24 and 25–42. The results reported in Table II support the conclusions from the analysis of the total subset. The coefficients of determination hardly vary with the exception of REH in the tabular version in which it increases from 83.3% to 92.1%. The heuristic explains the average behavior of the subjects over the whole considered time horizon. Figure 5 shows the average forecasts of the subjects f_t^{avg} and the two models in the two experimental versions.

These results demonstrate that the b&l-heuristic explains the average forecasts of the subjects very well in both experimental versions. The rationale of the bounds and likelihoods can be applied to tabularly presented time series, since there are no remarkable differences between the tabular and the graphical average forecasts. The heuristic explains the forecasts to the same degree as the REH. This is a remarkable fact since the REH works with strong assumptions: It assumes the knowledge of the true model, whereas the heuristic is only based on the gestalts characteristics of the time series. Furthermore this means that the efficiency of the scheme-oriented forecasting procedure is remarkably high.

5. Summary and Conclusion

In this study we reported on a forecasting experiment with the first application of the bounds and likelihood heuristic on judgmental forecasts of a tabularly presented time series. The average forecasting behavior of the subjects can be explained surprisingly well by the heuristic. A comparison with an experiment in graphical format shows hardly any performance differences. It was also shown that the heuristic performs equivalently to the REH.

This result can be attributed to the fact that no significant differences in the distributions of the two samples could be found. Why is this the case? The psychological background of the bounds&likelihood heuristic is the schema-theory. This psychological theory explains human behavior with the application of categorical rules that are used to interpret the environment. New information is processed according to how it fits into this schema. Schemes are not only used to interpret, but also to predict future events in our environment. In both presentation formats, the only source of information is the history of past realizations of the time series. Based on these values, the past experience is transferred to the forecast of the next situation. The presentation format does not affect the schemes, on average. However, some significant differences on the individual level are observed. Future research will therefore focus on the explanation of individual behavior.

Acknowledgements

This work was supported by the project P 17156–N12 of the FWF (Austrian Science Foundation).

References

Becker, O., J. Leitner, and U. Leopold-Wildburger. 2004a. *Expectation Formation in a Complex Information Environment*, Working Paper of the European University Institute Fiesole.

Becker, O., J. Leitner, and U. Leopold-Wildburger. 2004b. *Modelling Expectation Formation Involving Several Sources of Information*, Working Paper of the European University Institute Fiesole.

Becker, O., and U. Leopold-Wildburger. 1996. "The Bounds and Likelihood-procedure — A Simulation Study Concerning the Efficiency of Visual Forecasting Techniques", *Central European Journal of Operations Research and Economics* 4, 223–229.

Becker, O., and U. Leopold-Wildburger. 2000. "Erwartungsbildung und Prognose — Ergebnisse einer experimentellen Studie", *Austrian Journal of Statistics* 29, 7–16.

Beckman, S. R., and D. Downs. 1997. "Forecasters as Imperfect Information Processors: Experimental and Survey Evidence", *Journal of Economic Behavior and Organization* 32, 89–100.

Brennscheidt, G. 1993. *Predicitve Behavior — An Experimental Study*, Lecture Notes in Economics and Mathematical Systems, Vol. 403, Berlin: Springer.

Dwyer, G. P., A. W. Williams, R. C. Battalio, and T. I. Mason. 1993. "Tests of Rational Expectations in a Stark Setting" ,*The Economic Journal* 103, 586–601.

Harvey, N., and F. Bolger. 1996. "Graphs versus Tables: Effects of Data Presentation Format on Judgemental Forecasting", *International Journal of Forecasting* 12, 119–137.

Hey, J. D. 1994. "Expectations Formation: Rational or Adaptive or... ?", *Journal of Economic Behavior and Organization* 25, 329–349.

Lawrence, M. J., R. H. Edmundson, and M. J. O'Connor. 1985. "An Examination of the Accuracy of Judgmental Extrapolation of Time Series", *International Journal of Forecasting* 1, 25–35.

Makridakis, S., A. Andersen, R. Carbone, R. Fildes, M. Hibon, R. Lewandowski, J. Newton, E. Parzen, and R. Winkler. 1982. "The Accuracy of Extrapolative (Times Series) Methods: The Results of a Forecasting Competition", *Journal of Forecasting* 1, 111–153.

Makridakis, S., and M. Hibon. 1979. "Accuracy of Forecasting: An Empirical Investigation (with Discussion)", *Journal of the Royal Statistical Society A* 142, 97-145.

Makridakis, S., and M. Hibon. 2000. "The M3-Competition: Results, Conclusions and Implications", *International Journal of Forecasting* 16, 451–476.

Muth, J.F. 1961. "Rational Expectations and the Theory of Price Movements", *Econometrica* 29, 315–335.

Schmalensee, R. 1976. "An Experimental Study of Expectation Formation", *Econometrica* 44, 17–41.

Theil, H. 1966. *Applied Economic Forecasting*, Chicago: Rand McNally.

Webby, R., and M. O'Connor. 1996. "Judgemental and Statistical Time Series Forecasting: A Review of the Literature", *International Journal of Forecasting* 12, 91–118.

Otwin Becker
Universität Heidelberg
Tannenweg 21a
D-69190 Walldorf
Germany
o.becker.walldorf@t-online.de

Johannes Leitner
Institut für Statistik und Operations Research
Universität Graz
Universitätsstraße 15/E3

A-8010 Graz
Austria
johannesleitner@gmx.de

Ulrike Leopold-Wildburger
Institut für Statistik und Operations Research
Universität Graz
Universitätsstraße 15/E3
A-8010 Graz
Austria
ulrike.leopold@uni-graz.at

UNDERSTANDING CONJUNCTION FALLACIES: AN EVIDENCE THEORY MODEL OF REPRESENTATIVENESS

HANS WOLFGANG BRACHINGER
University of Fribourg

1. Introduction

Ever since Tversky and Kahneman started their *heuristics-and-biases* research program on judgment under uncertainty 30 years ago it is well-known that people apparently fail to reason probabilistically in experimental contexts. The best known failure is the *conjunction fallacy*, in which people violate one of the most fundamental laws of probability theory, the so-called *conjunction rule*: The basic axioms of probability imply that the probability of a conjunction, $P(A\&B)$, cannot exceed the probabilities of its constituents, $P(A)$ and $P(B)$. The most famous experiment used to demonstrate the conjunction fallacy is the well-known Linda problem introduced by Tversky and Kahneman (1982).

In the classical version of the *Linda problem*, subjects are provided with the following personality sketch E of a fictitious individual named Linda (Tversky and Kahneman, 1982, 1983).

> E: Linda is 31 years old, single, outspoken and very bright. She majored in philosophy. As a student, she was deeply concerned with issues of discrimination and social justice, and also participated in anti-nuclear demonstrations.

Then, the subjects are asked to rank 8 different statements associated with that personality sketch according to their probability, using 1 for the most probable and 8 for the least probable. Three of the 8 statements are the following:

> F: Linda is active in the feminist movement.
>
> T: Linda is a bank teller.
>
> $T\&F$: Linda is a bank teller and is active in the feminist movement.

The description of Linda is constructed to be representative of an active feminist (F) and unrepresentative of a bank teller (T).

Tversky and Kahneman (1982) have reported that systematic violations of the conjunction rule were observed in both between-subjects and within-subjects designs, and this irrespective of the level of statistical sophistication of the subjects. Hertwig

U. Schmidt and S. Traub (eds.), Advances in Public Economics: Utility, Choice and Welfare, 267-288.

and Chase (1998) reviewed a sample of 17 conditions in 10 studies in which the proportion of conjunction violations in this probability ranking representation of the Linda problem was examined and found a median of 87%. Similar experiments with the same type of findings have been reported in many other experimental studies.

Tversky and Kahneman suggested that the peoples' "fallacious behaviour" is often mediated by so-called *judgmental heuristics*. They argue, e.g., that the *representativeness heuristic* can make a conjunction appear more probable because it is more representative than one of its constituents. These heuristics have been heavily criticized by Gigerenzer (1996) as being far "too vague to count as explanations". According to Gigerenzer they "lack theoretical specification". The focus should be the construction of detailed models of cognitive processes that explain when and why fallacious behaviors appear or disappear.

On basis of their thesis "that human minds resolve the uncertainty in the Linda problem by intelligent semantic inferences", Hertwig and Gigerenzer (1999) have shown that people infer nonmathematical meanings of the polysemous term "probability" in the classic Linda problem. They provide evidence that, in fact, people use the representativeness heuristic when judging the "probability" of the different statements.

In this paper, first, a detailed description of the representativeness heuristic as it has been introduced by Tversky and Kahneman (1983) is given. On the basis of that description a suitable mathematical framework for modelling the representativeness heuristic is developed. Within that framework the question arises how, for a given mental model, its "degree of representativeness" can be assessed. In the next chapter, it is shown that this question can perfectly be treated within the framework developed using a concept well-known from the Mathematical Theory of Evidence (cf. Dempster 1967, 1968; and Shafer, 1976). Then certain evidence theory operations which are necessary to argue within the representativeness framework are presented. These operations outline a kind of rationality principle according to which one has to act within the mathematical framework proposed. In the final chapter it is shown that this mathematical framework is well-suited to explain the "fallacious" behavior of the people in the Linda problem.

2. Mathematical Framework of Representativeness

The basic idea of Tversky and Kahnemann (1983) is that people base their intuitive predictions and judgments of probability on the relation of similarity or "representativeness" between the given evidence and possible outcomes. For them, "representativeness is an assessment of the degree of correspondence between a sample and a population, an instance and a category, an act and an actor or, more generally, between an outcome and a model. The model may refer to a person, a coin, or the world economy, and the respective outcomes could be marital status, a sequence of heads and tails, or the current price of gold. Representativeness can be investigated empirically by asking people, for example, which of two sequences of heads and tails is more representative of a fair coin or which of two professions is more representative of a given personality" (Tversky and Kahnemann, 1983, pp. 295–296). Tversky and Kahnemann further argue that this relation differs from other notions of proximity in that it is distinctly *directional*, because "it is natural to describe a sample as more or less representative of its parent distribution".

Additionally, Tversky and Kahnemann (1983, p. 296) emphasize that representativeness is reducible to similarity

> when the model and the outcomes are described in the same terms ... Representativeness, however, is not always reducible to similarity; it can also reflect causal and correlational beliefs ... Thus, an outcome is representative of a model if the salient features match or if the model has a propensity to produce the outcome.

This original characterization of the representativeness heuristic shows that there are four basic notional constituents of this heuristic: These are *outcome*, *models*, *directional relation from outcome towards models*, and *degree of correspondence between outcome and models.* For the specification of a mathematical framework of representativeness these constituents have to be specified in a suitable manner. By a *model* Tversky and Kahnemann understand a mental model, such as a prototype or a schema in relation to which information is commonly stored and processed (Tversky and Kahnemann, 1983, p. 295). The first constituent of our representativeness framework therefore is a (finite) set Θ of mental models. It is assumed that the true model is contained in Θ.

Tversky and Kahnemann do not say much about what their general comprehension of an "outcome" is. Obviously, for them an outcome is something which can be described. Therefore, every *outcome* is characterized by a certain description. Every description is a piece of information or evidence relative to a certain question. In general, every such piece of information allows for different interpretations. Let these interpretations be represented by the elements ω of a (finite) set Ω. The second constituent of our representativeness framework therefore is a set Ω of possible interpretations ω of a given description. It is assumed that exactly one of these interpretations is correct.

With respect to the interesting question, in general, the given description can be interpreted in different ways, i.e., it is uncertain which of the interpretations $\omega \in \Omega$ of the description is the correct one. Uncertainty about the correct interpretation of the given description can be modelled by a subjective probability distribution P over Ω: $P(\omega)$ gives the probability that ω is the correct interpretation of the given description. The subjective probability distribution P over Ω constitutes a third component of our representativeness framework.

Furthermore, in general, a given description is imprecise, i.e., for any interpretation $\omega \in \Omega$ several mental models may be true. Imprecision of the given description can be modelled by a multivalued mapping

$$\Gamma : \{ \Omega \rightarrow 2^{\Theta} \omega \mapsto \Gamma(\omega)$$

which, for any interpretation $\omega \in \Omega$, restricts the possibly true models to some subset $\Gamma(\omega) \subseteq \Theta$. $\Gamma(\omega)$ contains the true model with $P(\omega)$. This mapping constitutes a forth component of our representativeness framework. This constituent covers the directional relation from the outcome, described by its set of interpretations, towards models which is a distinctive feature of the representativeness heuristic.

Summing up, a suitable framework for investigating the representativeness heuristic is given by the quadruple

$$\mathcal{H} = (\Omega, P, \Gamma, \Theta), \tag{1}$$

where, for a given question, Ω is a set of possible interpretations of the description of a given outcome, P is a (subjective) probability measure over Ω, Γ a multivalued mapping from Ω into Θ, and Θ a set of admissible mental models.

The representativeness heuristic is used to compare a given outcome with a set of mental models. More specifically, the representativeness heuristic is used to evaluate the degree to which that outcome is representative of a mental model, it is used to assess the degree of correspondence between an outcome and a model. Thereby, obviously, the outcome is given and fixed, and the degree of representativeness varies over subsets of mental models. Now, the problem arises how that "degree of representativeness" for a (certain subset of) mental model(s) can be assessed? What is a suitable measure? A suitable measure can be found by resorting to a well-known concept of the mathematical Theory of Evidence.

3. Representativeness Heuristic

Mathematical structures of the form $\mathcal{H} = (\Omega, P, \Gamma, \Theta)$ have been introduced by Dempster (1967, 1968). These structures can be given different interpretations. A new interpretation has been developed in section 2 where such structures are interpreted as representativeness framework. This interpretation can be regarded as a special case of the *hint interpretation* of these structures developed by Kohlas (1990). A concise introduction to the Theory of Hints can be found in Kohlas and Monney (1994). A more sophisticated treatment is given in the monograph by Kohlas and Monney (1995).

3.1. HINT INTERPRETATION

The hint interpretation of quadruples of the form $\mathcal{H} = (\Omega, P, \Gamma, \Theta)$ starts with "a certain precise question, whose answer is unknown, has to be studied and the elements θ of Θ represent the possible answers to the question. This means that exactly one of the $\theta \in \Theta$ is the correct answer, but it is unknown which one. However there is some information or evidence available relative to this question. This information allows for several, distinct interpretations, depending on some unknown circumstances and these interpretations are represented by the elements $\omega \in \Omega$. This means that there is exactly one correct interpretation ω in Ω, but again it is unknown which one. Not all interpretations are equally likely and the probabilities $p(\omega)$ describe these different likelihoods. If $\omega \in \Omega$ is the correct interpretation, then the unknown answer θ is known to be in the subset $\Gamma(\omega)$ of Θ. Such a piece of information is called a *hint* (Kohlas and Monney, 1994). The advantage of the hint interpretation of quadruples of the form $\mathcal{H} = (\Omega, P, \Gamma, \Theta)$ is that it gives a specific and clear sense the important notions introduced by Dempster.

A hint is a quadruple of the form (1) where, for a given question, Ω is a (nonempty finite) set of possible interpretations of a given information, P is a probability measure over Ω, Θ is a (nonempty finite) set of possible answers to the question, called *frame of discernment*, and Γ is a multivalued mapping from Ω into Θ. For any interpretation $\omega \in \Omega$, the subset $\Gamma(\omega)$ of Θ is called the *focal set* of this interpretation. The focal set of an interpretation ω represents the restriction of Θ to all answers to the given question which are possible if this interpretation is the correct one. For any interpretation ω in Ω, the value $P(\omega)$ represents the probability that ω is the correct interpretation. Finally, a hint with frame of discernment Θ is called a hint *relative* to Θ.

Example 1 (cf. Brachinger and Monney, 2002) Suppose that Connie is taking a night train to Paris on a late Sunday evening. In the train, she finds a piece of a Sunday newspaper announcing a strike on the Paris metro for Monday. Unfortunately, the date of the newspaper is illegible, so that she is unsure whether indeed this newspaper is from this Sunday or from a previous Sunday. So the question is "Will there be a strike upon her arrival in Paris on Monday morning?" Obviously, the piece of paper is a hint relative to the frame of discernment $\Theta = \{s, \bar{s}\}$, where s means that there will be a strike and $\bar{s}$ means that there will be no strike. The first interpretation of the hint, ω_1, is that the newspaper is from this Sunday. Under this interpretation, there will be a strike and so $\Gamma(\omega_1) = \{s\}$. A second interpretation of the hint, ω_2, is that the newspaper is from a previous Sunday. Under this second interpretation, there may or may not be a strike and so $\Gamma(\omega_2) = \Theta$. The probability assigned to ω_1 and ω_2, respectively, depends on the way the piece of newspaper looks like: if it clean and fresh, the probability of ω_1 will be larger than if it is crumpled and dirty. $\diamond$

For illustration purposes, let us consider the three most elementary general types of hints which will be important for explaining the Linda fallacy in section 5.

Example 2 (Vacuous hint) A hint $\mathcal{V} = (\Omega, P, \Gamma, \Theta)$ such that $\Gamma(\omega) = \Theta$ for all $\omega \in \Omega$ is called *vacuous* because it does not contain any information whatsoever about Θ, i.e. no interpretation permits to restrict the set of all possible answers Θ. Integrating such a hint in a given knowledge-base clearly does not change the support of any hypothesis concerning the frame Θ. $\diamond$

Example 3 (Precise hint) A hint $\mathcal{H}$ is called *precise* when all its focal sets are singletons, i.e. one-element subsets of Θ. Obviously, for precise hints the probability measure P defined on Ω is carried over to Θ by the function Γ in the classical way. This indicates that probability theory can be viewed as a special case of the theory of hints. $\diamond$

Example 4 (Simple hint) A hint $\mathcal{H} = (\Omega, P, \Gamma, \Theta)$ is called *simple* when, for every $\omega \in \Omega$, $\Gamma(\omega)$ is either equal to Θ or to a strict subset F of Θ. In particular, if $\Omega = \{\omega_1, \omega_2\}$ with $P(\omega_1) = p$ and $P(\omega_2) = 1 - p$ and $\Gamma(\omega_1) = F$ and $\Gamma(\omega_2) = \Theta$,

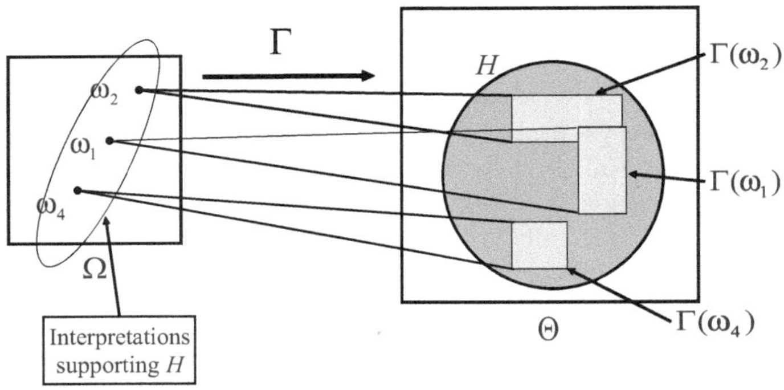

Figure 1. Support or representativeness function.

then ω_1 is called the *supporting* interpretation and ω_2 the *vacuous* interpretation of the simple hint. ◊

3.2. SUPPORT FUNCTION

In the hint interpretation of quadruples of the form (1) the problem is that the correct answer to the given question is unknown. The goal is to evaluate hypotheses about it in the light of the information available represented in general by a collection of several different hints. Of course, a hypothesis is a subset H of Θ. The most important tool for the evaluation of a hypothesis H is the *degree of support* of H, which is defined by

$$sp(H) = P(\{\omega \in \Omega : \Gamma(\omega) \subseteq H\}), \tag{2}$$

i.e. by the probability that one of those interpretations is true which restrict the answers to the given question to a subset of H. For each hypothesis H, $sp(H)$ represents the strength according to which the given evidence supports the hypothesis H.

Since $sp(H)$ is defined for all subsets H of Θ, definition (2) generates the so-called *support function*

$$sp : \{ 2^{\Theta} \longrightarrow [0,1] H \longmapsto P(\{\omega \in \Omega : \Gamma(\omega) \subseteq H\}). \tag{3}$$

The concept of a support function is represented in Figure 1.

$$sp(H) := \sum \{P(\omega) : \Gamma(\omega) \subseteq H\} = P(\omega_1) + P(\omega_2) + P(\omega_4)$$

Example 5 (Precise hint) For precise hints $\mathcal{H}$ where all the focal sets are singletons the support function represents an ordinary probability distribution on Θ, i.e.

$$sp(H) = \sum \{sp(\theta) : \theta \in H\} \tag{4}$$

for all $H \subseteq \Theta$. This, once more, indicates that probability theory can be viewed as a special case of the theory of hints. $\diamondsuit$

To avoid a possible misunderstanding, it is important to mention that the degree of support (2) is different from the notion of a support used by Shafer (1976). The degree of support (2) has nothing to do with the degree of support introduced by Tversky and Koehler (1994).

3.3. REPRESENTATIVENESS FUNCTION

In the representativeness interpretation of quadruples of the form (1) one has an analogous problem as in the hint interpretation. In the representativeness interpretation, mental models θ have to be evaluated by the degree to which a given outcome is representative of them. Here the problem is that is it unknown if a certain mental model is correct. The goal is to evaluate a mental model in the light of the given outcome represented by a description, e.g. of a certain person. Of course, a metal model is an element of Θ.

Now, analogously to the hint interpretation, it appears natural to evaluate a set $T \subseteq \Theta$ of mental models by the probability that one of those interpretations $\omega \in \Omega$ is true which restrict the possibly true models to the subset T or, in the case of a single model θ to the subset $\{\theta\}$. Therefore, in the representativeness interpretation of quadruples of the form 1, the *degree of representativeness* of a certain mental model can, in a very natural form, be defined by

$$rp\,(T) = P(\{\omega \in \Omega : \Gamma(\omega) \subseteq T\}), \tag{5}$$

For each set T of mental models, $rp\,(T)$ represents the degree according to which a given outcome is representative of them.

Since $rp(T)$ is defined for all subsets T of Θ, definition (5) generates the so-called *representativeness function*

$$rp : \{\, 2^{\Theta} \longrightarrow [0,1] T \longmapsto P(\{\omega \in \Omega : \Gamma(\omega) \subseteq T\}). \tag{6}$$

For a given representativeness structure $\mathcal{H} = (\Omega, P, \Gamma, \Theta)$ this function will be called the *induced representativeness function.*

Now, the mathematical structure of the form $\mathcal{H} = (\Omega, P, \Gamma, \Theta)$ together with its induced representativeness function rp can serve as a mathematical model of representativeness. In the sequel, every quadruple of that form together with its induced representativeness function will be called *representativeness heuristic* or, for short, *R-heuristic.* The notions of a *frame of discernment* and a *focal set* will be used in the same sense a as in the hint interpretation of forms (1).

4. Operations on Representativeness Heuristics

To argue within a representativeness framework and, finally, to explain the fallacious behavior in conjunction problems like the Linda problem within that structure it is necessary to sketch some evidence theory operations. This is done within the R-heuristic interpretation of structures of the form (1).

4.1. COMBINATION OF R-HEURISTICS RELATIVE TO THE SAME QUESTIONS

In general, given a certain question, there are several R-heuristics relative to the same question, i.e. relative to the same frame of discernment Θ. The problem is then how to combine these R-heuristics to obtain one single R-heuristic relative to Θ. The basic operation to combine R-heuristics is *Dempster's rule of combination.* For the sake of simplicity, we only consider the case where two R-heuristics have to be combined. The generalization to more than two R-heuristics is then straightforward (see Kohlas and Monney, 1995).

Suppose there are two R-heuristics $\mathcal{H}_1$ and $\mathcal{H}_2$ both relative to the same fixed frame Θ, i.e., $\mathcal{H}_1 = (\Omega_1, P_1, \Gamma_1, \Theta)$ and $\mathcal{H}_2 = (\Omega_2, P_2, \Gamma_2, \Theta)$. Consider the product set $\Omega_1 \times \Omega_2$ of all pairs of interpretations (ω_1, ω_2) with $\omega_1 \in \Omega_1$ and $\omega_2 \in \Omega_2$. If, for any such pair (ω_1, ω_2), the respective focal sets are not compatible, i.e. if the intersection $\Gamma_1(\omega_1) \cap \Gamma_2(\omega_2)$ is empty, then the pair (ω_1, ω_2) is called *contradictory* because it is impossible that both, ω_1 and ω_2, are correct interpretations of the information that generated $\mathcal{H}_1$ and $\mathcal{H}_2$, respectively. Let

$$C = \{(\omega_1, \omega_2) \in \Omega_1 \times \Omega_2 : \Gamma_1(\omega_1) \cap \Gamma_2(\omega_2) = \emptyset\}$$

denote the set of contradictory pairs of interpretations. Thus, from the two R-heuristics, we have learned that the correct pair of interpretations must be in the set

$$\begin{aligned} \Omega &= \{(\omega_1, \omega_2) \in \Omega_1 \times \Omega_2 : \ \Gamma_1(\omega_1) \cap \Gamma_2(\omega_2) \neq \emptyset\} \\ &= (\Omega_1 \times \Omega_2) - C. \end{aligned}$$

Of course, this information should be used when combining the two R-heuristics. This is done as follows. Assuming stochastic independence of the probability measures P_1 and P_2, the initial probability measure on $\Omega_1 \times \Omega_2$ is the product measure $P_1 P_2$. But, since it is known that the correct pair of interpretations is in Ω, this product measure must be conditioned on Ω. Since the probability of the contradictory set C is

$$k = \sum \{P_1(\omega_1) P_2(\omega_2) : \ \Gamma_1(\omega_1) \cap \Gamma_2(\omega_2) = \emptyset\}, \tag{7}$$

this leads to the new probability space (Ω, P) where

$$P(\omega_1, \omega_2) = \frac{P_1(\omega_1) P_2(\omega_2)}{1-k} \tag{8}$$

for all $(\omega_1, \omega_2) \in \Omega$. Moreover, if $(\omega_1, \omega_2) \in \Omega$ is the correct pair of interpretations, then the correct answer to the given question must be in the set

$$\Gamma(\omega_1, \omega_2) = \Gamma_1(\omega_1) \cap \Gamma_2(\omega_2). \tag{9}$$

The combination of the R-heuristics $\mathcal{H}_1$ and $\mathcal{H}_2$ is then defined as the R-heuristic

$$\mathcal{H}_1 \oplus \mathcal{H}_2 = (\Omega, P, \Gamma, \Theta). \tag{10}$$

This procedure to obtain the combined R-heuristic is called *Dempster's rule of combination.* The combined R-heuristic $\mathcal{H}_1 \oplus \mathcal{H}_2$ represents the information about the given question generated by pooling the two R-heuristics $\mathcal{H}_1$ and $\mathcal{H}_2$. Note that the vacuous R-heuristic $\mathcal{V}$ is the neutral element with respect to Dempster's rule, i.e.

$$\mathcal{H}_1 \oplus \mathcal{V} = \mathcal{H}_1 \tag{11}$$

for every R-heuristic $\mathcal{H}_1$ relative to Θ. It can be proved that the combination of R-heuristics by Dempster's rule is both commutative and associative (see Kohlas and Monney, 1995).

4.2. COMBINATION OF R-HEURISTICS RELATIVE TO DIFFERENT QUESTIONS

It has been shown above how two R-heuristics relative to the same question can be combined. Imagine now there are two R-heuristics $\mathcal{H}_1$ and $\mathcal{H}_2$ relative to two different questions and these two questions together should simultaneously be considered as a *compound question.* To use the two R-heuristics as pieces of information relative to the compound question, each of them has to be extended such that the extension is a R-heuristic relative to the compound question.

The extension of a R-heuristic begins by extending its frame. Suppose Θ_1 and Θ_2 are the two frames representing the set of all possible answers to two different questions. If we consider the two questions together as a compound question, then it is clear that all pairs of answers (θ_1, θ_2) where $\theta_1 \in \Theta_1$ and $\theta_2 \in \Theta_2$ are the possible answers to this compound question. Therefore, any R-heuristic bearing information relative to the compound question has $\Theta_1 \times \Theta_2$ as frame of discernment.

Let

$$\mathcal{H}_1 = (\Omega_1, P_1, \Gamma_1, \Theta_1)$$

be the R-heuristic relative to the first question and

$$\mathcal{H}_2 = (\Omega_2, P_2, \Gamma_2, \Theta_2)$$

be the R-heuristic relative to the second question. Since, by definition, the frame Θ_2 contains the correct answer to the second question, no information is either gained or lost by replacing each focal set $\Gamma_1(\omega_1)$ of $\mathcal{H}_1$ by its *cylindrical extension*

$$\Gamma_1(\omega_1)' = \Gamma_1(\omega_1) \times \Theta_2.$$

This leads to the *vacuously extended* R-heuristic

$$\mathcal{H}_1 \uparrow \Theta_1 \times \Theta_2 = (\Omega_1, P_1, \Gamma_1', \Theta_1 \times \Theta_2).$$

With respect to Θ_1, this R-heuristic conveys exactly the same information as $\mathcal{H}_1$, but, unlike $\mathcal{H}_1$, it is a R-heuristic relative to the compound frame $\Theta_1 \times \Theta_2$. Similarly, the R-heuristic $\mathcal{H}_2$ can be vacuously extended to the compound frame $\Theta_1 \times \Theta_2$, which leads to the R-heuristic

$$\mathcal{H}_2 \uparrow \Theta_1 \times \Theta_2 = (\Omega_2, P_2, \Gamma_2', \Theta_1 \times \Theta_2),$$

where

$$\Gamma_2'(\omega_2) = \Theta_1 \times \Gamma_2(\omega_2)$$

for all $\omega_2 \in \Omega_2$. Since they are now defined over the same frame $\Theta_1 \times \Theta_2$, the two extended R-heuristics can be combined by Dempster's rule of combination as described in the previous section, which results in the combined R-heuristic

$$\mathcal{H} = (\mathcal{H}_1 \uparrow \Theta_1 \times \Theta_2) \oplus (\mathcal{H}_2 \uparrow \Theta_1 \times \Theta_2).$$

4.3. RESTRICTION OF R-HEURISTICS

In a system of R-heuristics relative to different frames, these R-heuristics can be extended to a common frame and then combined by Dempster's rule. However, often one is interested in a specific question represented by a particular frame. In this case it suffices to coarsen or restrict the combined R-heuristic to the smaller frame. This operation is called *restriction* or *projection* of a R-heuristic. Suppose that $\mathcal{H} = (\Omega, P, \Gamma, \Theta)$ is a R-heuristic relative to a frame $\Theta = \Theta_1 \times \Theta_2$ and we want to calculate the degree of support of a hypothesis H pertaining to the question represented by the frame Θ_1, i.e. $H \subseteq \Theta_1$. Then it is convenient to consider the R-heuristic $\mathcal{H} \downarrow \Theta_1$ obtained by replacing the focal sets $\Gamma(\omega)$ by their projections on Θ_1, i.e.

$$\mathcal{H} \downarrow \Theta_1 = (\Omega, P, \Gamma', \Theta_1) \tag{12}$$

where

$$\Gamma'(\omega) = \{\theta_1 \in \Theta_1 : \text{ there exists } \ \theta_2 \in \Theta_2 \ \text{ such that } \ (\theta_1, \theta_2) \in \Gamma(\omega)\}. \tag{13}$$

4.4. RATIONALITY PRINCIPLE

The combination and restriction operations pointed out above outline a kind of *rationality principle* according to which one has to act within mathematical structures of the form (1). This holds, of course, independently of the kind of semantic interpretation of such structures.

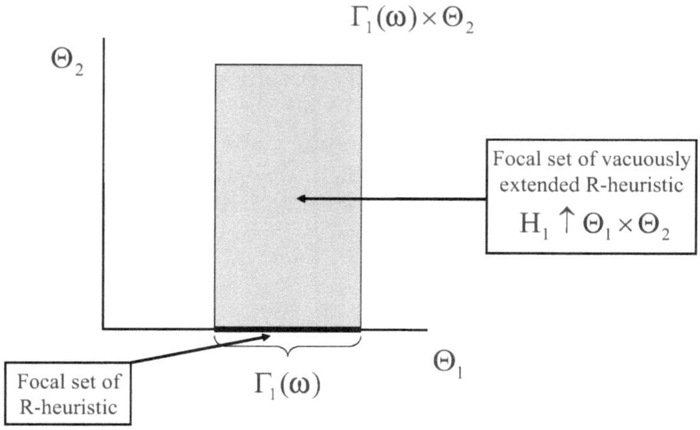

Figure 2. Restriction of a R-heuristic.

When a certain question has to be treated then, in general, several R-heuristics pertaining to different frames are available. Then, for treating the given question, a *first rationality axiom* requires that the overall information these R-heuristics convey has to be exploited. The overall information they generate is represented by their combination which is carried out after they all have been vacuously extended to a common frame. Then a *second rationality axiom* requires that this combined R-heuristic is restricted to the frame of interest. The resulting R-heuristic, finally, has then to be used to judge hypotheses about the question of interest.

Note that computation in this procedure rapidly tends to be complicated and difficult to handle. In fact, it is well known that Dempster's rule is computationally complex. However, so-called local computational procedures can be applied to reduce the complexity of the problem (Kohlas and Monney, 1995; and Shenoy and Shafer, 1990).

It should noted that working with R-heuristics when confronted with a conjunction problem of the Linda kind is, in principle, by no means "fallacious". Fallacious behavior occurs when one of the two rationality axioms above is violated. We will see in the next section that this is exactly what usually happens when Linda type problems are treated.

5. Explanations of the Linda Fallacy

Let us now come back to the conjunction fallacy in the Linda problem presented in section 1. In the following section, different explanations of this fallacy based on the concept of R-heuristics are presented. Essentially, these explanations follow those in Brachinger and Monney (2002).

In their original paper, Tversky and Kahneman (1983, p. 296) differentiate between three cases of representativeness. A first case, where representativeness is "reducible to similarity". This was the case when model and outcome are described in the same terms. Further below they point out that "representativeness ... is not always reducible to similarity; it can also reflect causal and correlational beliefs". All three of these cases are conceivable in the Linda problem. Therefore, the first three of the following four explanations of the Linda fallacy go along these lines and deal with the cases where the compound model $T\&F$ is treated by R-heuristics covering similarity of T and F, causal relationship, as well as correlational beliefs between T and F, in turn.

5.1. EXPLANATION 1

Regarding the question whether or not Linda is a bank teller, the frame of discernment obviously is $\Theta_1 = \{T, \overline{T}\}$, where T means that Linda is a bank teller and $\overline{T}$ denotes the negation of T. The description E does not contain any information about Θ_1 and so, with respect to Θ_1, the unique interpretation of E is ω_0 = "everything is possible". Therefore, the question whether Linda is a bank teller can be regarded on the basis of the vacuous R-heuristic

$$\mathcal{H}_0 = (\{\omega_0\}, P_0, \Gamma_0, \Theta_1) \tag{14}$$

with $P_0(\omega_0) = 1$ and $\Gamma_0(\omega_0) = \Theta_1$. Since the unique focal set Θ_1 is not included in $\{T\}$, it follows that the degree of representativeness of T is zero, i.e. $rp_0(T) = 0$ if rp_0 denotes the representativeness function associated with the R-heuristic $\mathcal{H}_0$.

Regarding the question whether Linda is a feminist, the frame of discernment is obviously $\Theta_2 = \{F, \overline{F}\}$ where F means that Linda is active in the feminist movement and $\overline{F}$ denotes the negation of F. The description E contains much information supporting F. Therefore, one interpretation, ω_{11}, is that Linda is indeed a feminist. As there is no evidence for Linda not being a feminist, a second interpretation, ω_{12}, is that, with respect to Θ_2, "everything is possible". Hence the correspondence Γ_1 from $\Omega_1 = \{\omega_{11}, \omega_{12}\}$ into Θ_2 is given by $\Gamma_1(\omega_{11}) = \{F\}$ and $\Gamma_1(\omega_{12}) = \Theta_2$. The subjective probability that ω_{11} is the correct interpretation should be high, say $P_1(\omega_{11}) = p$ with $p > 0.5$. The R-heuristic

$$\mathcal{H}_1 = (\Omega_1, P_1, \Gamma_1, \Theta_2) \tag{15}$$

representing the information relative to Θ_2 that is contained in E is a simple R-heuristic. If rp_1 denotes its representativeness function, then the degree of representativeness of F is $rp_1(F) = p$.

When treating the compound question, subjects are forced to address the sub-question whether Linda is a bank teller because T is part of the compound question. In order to do this, they refer to their general knowledge base, which allows them to retrieve a subjective prior probability q that a woman looking like Linda is a bank teller. Now, in the spirit of Hertwig and Gigerenzer's argument that people try to draw relevance-preserving inferences (cf. Hertwig and Gigerenzer, 1999, p. 297f), they think that, of course, this probability will be very low because the description of Linda is not "representative" of a bank teller at all. But, according to this argument this probability will not be zero either, because otherwise the question would be irrelevant.

In other words, on the basis of the relevance preserving maxim, when treating the compound question, subjects refer a precise R-heuristic

$$\mathcal{H}_2 = (\Omega_2, P_2, \Gamma_2, \Theta_1) \tag{16}$$

relative to Θ_1 characterized by the two interpretations ω_{21} ("bank teller") and ω_{22} ("not bank teller"), $\Omega_2 = \{\omega_{21}, \omega_{22}\}$, with the corresponding probabilities $P_2(\omega_{21}) = q$ and $P_2(\omega_{22}) = 1 - q$. This R-heuristic covers the degree of "similarity" to a bank teller that the people concede to Linda. The focal sets of this R-heuristic are given by $\Gamma_2(\omega_{21}) = \{T\}$ and $\Gamma_2(\omega_{22}) = \{\overline{T}\}$. If rp_2 denotes the representativeness function of the R-heuristic $\mathcal{H}_2$, then the degree of representativeness of T is $rp_2(T) = q$.

For treating the compound question whether Linda is a feminist bank teller, the two R-heuristics $\mathcal{H}_1$ and $\mathcal{H}_2$ have to be combined. As these R-heuristics are R-heuristics relative to different frames of discernment, they have to be extended to the frame $\Theta_1 \times \Theta_2$ before they are combined. The extension procedure described in subsection 4.2 leads to the R-heuristics $\mathcal{H}_1 \uparrow \Theta_1 \times \Theta_2$ and $\mathcal{H}_2 \uparrow \Theta_1 \times \Theta_2$. The extended R-heuristic $\mathcal{H}_1 \uparrow \Theta_1 \times \Theta_2$ conveys the information about $\Theta_2 = \{F, \overline{F}\}$ that is contained in E, but expressed with respect to the compound question represented by $\Theta_1 \times \Theta_2$. Similarly, the extended R-heuristic $\mathcal{H}_2 \uparrow \Theta_1 \times \Theta_2$ conveys the information about $\Theta_1 = \{T, \overline{T}\}$ that is contained in E, but expressed with respect to the compound question represented by $\Theta_1 \times \Theta_2$. The focal sets of $\mathcal{H}_1 \uparrow \Theta_1 \times \Theta_2$ are

$$\begin{aligned} \Gamma_1'(\omega_{11}) &= \Theta_1 \times \{F\} \\ \Gamma_1'(\omega_{12}) &= \Theta_1 \times \Theta_2 \end{aligned} \tag{17}$$

whereas the focal sets of $\mathcal{H}_2 \uparrow \Theta_1 \times \Theta_2$ are

$$\begin{aligned} \Gamma_2'(\omega_{21}) &= \{T\} \times \Theta_2 \\ \Gamma_2'(\omega_{22}) &= \{\overline{T}\} \times \Theta_2. \end{aligned}$$

Now, the extended R-heuristics $\mathcal{H}_1 \uparrow \Theta_1 \times \Theta_2$ and $\mathcal{H}_2 \uparrow \Theta_1 \times \Theta_2$, can be combined by Dempster's rule, which leads to the combined R-heuristic

$$\mathcal{H}_3 = (\Omega, P, \Gamma, \Theta_1 \times \Theta_2) := (\mathcal{H}_1 \uparrow \Theta_1 \times \Theta_2) \oplus (\mathcal{H}_2 \uparrow \Theta_1 \times \Theta_2) \tag{18}$$

conveying the overall information about the compound question that is contained in E. Thereby, $\Omega = \Omega_1 \times \Omega_2$ and

$$\begin{aligned} P(\omega_{11}, \omega_{21}) &= pq & P(\omega_{11}, \omega_{22}) &= p(1-q) \\ P(\omega_{12}, \omega_{21}) &= (1-p)q & P(\omega_{12}, \omega_{22}) &= (1-p)(1-q). \end{aligned}$$

Furthermore, Γ is given by

$$\begin{aligned} \Gamma(\omega_{11}, \omega_{21}) = \Gamma_1'(\omega_{11}) \cap \Gamma_2'(\omega_{21}) &= (\Theta_1 \times \{F\}) \cap (\{T\} \times \Theta_2) = \{(T, F)\} \\ \Gamma(\omega_{11}, \omega_{22}) = \Gamma_1'(\omega_{11}) \cap \Gamma_2'(\omega_{22}) &= (\Theta_1 \times \{F\}) \cap (\{\overline{T}\} \times \Theta_2) = \{(\overline{T}, F)\} \end{aligned}$$

and

$$\begin{aligned}\Gamma(\omega_{12},\omega_{21}) = \Gamma_1'(\omega_{12}) \cap \Gamma_2'(\omega_{21}) &= (\Theta_1 \times \Theta_2) \cap (\{T\} \times \Theta_2) = \{T\} \times \Theta_2 \\ \Gamma(\omega_{12},\omega_{22}) = \Gamma_1'(\omega_{12}) \cap \Gamma_2'(\omega_{22}) &= (\Theta_1 \times \Theta_2) \cap (\{\overline{T}\} \times \Theta_2) = \{\overline{T}\} \times \Theta_2.\end{aligned}$$

If rp_3 denotes the representativeness function of $\mathcal{H}_3$, then

$$rp_3(T,F) = P(\{(\omega_1,\omega_2) \in \Omega : \Gamma(\omega_1,\omega_2) \subseteq \{(T,F)\}\}) = P(\omega_{11},\omega_{21}) = pq$$

because $\Gamma(\omega_{11},\omega_{21})$ is the only focal set that is included in the mental model $H = \{(T,F)\}$ indicating that T and F go together. Since

$$0 = rp_0(T) < rp_3(T,F) = pq < p, \tag{19}$$

i.e. since the degree of representativeness of T is strictly smaller than the degree of representativeness of (T,F), we have found an explanation of the conjunction fallacy in the Linda problem. It should be noted that equation (19) holds for any non-zero base-rate q for a woman looking like Linda being a bank teller, even if it is very low.

5.2. EXPLANATION 2

In this second explanation of the Linda conjunction fallacy, it is still assumed that the evidence E induces a vacuous R-heuristic $\mathcal{H}_0$ on $\Theta_1 = \{T,\overline{T}\}$, thereby expressing that E does not convey any information about whether or not Linda is a bank teller. It is also still assumed that the R-heuristic $\mathcal{H}_1$ defined in the previous subsection represents the evidence about $\Theta_2 = \{F,\overline{F}\}$ induced by E. Recall that $\mathcal{H}_1$ supports the hypothesis that Linda is a feminist to the fairly large degree p.

Above, it was mentioned that according to Tversky and Kahneman representativeness can also reflect causal or correlational beliefs. In that spirit, in the following explanations of the Linda fallacy it is assumed that when dealing with the compound model $T\&F$, subjects use their general knowledge to retrieve additional information about the relation between the concepts of "bank teller" and "feminist". The result of this *retrieval process* is a model of the relational evidence between these two concepts expressed in the form of a so-called *relational R-heuristic*

$$\mathcal{R} = (\Omega_2, P_2, \Gamma_2, \Theta_1 \times \Theta_2) \tag{20}$$

over the frame

$$\Theta = \Theta_1 \times \Theta_2$$

for the compound question. Thereby, the set of interpretations Ω_2, the probability measure P_2 on Ω_2 and the multivalued mapping Γ_2 of the relational R-heuristic $\mathcal{R}$ are not the same same as in equation (16). These constituents will be precisely defined in the different models presented below.

In section 4.4 two rationality axioms for dealing with R-heuristics have been introduced. When treating a representativeness problem where several R-heuristics are used, the first rationality axiom requires that the overall information these R-heuristics convey has te be exploited. The overall information they generate is represented by their combination which is carried out after they all have been vacuously extended to a common frame. In particular, this extended R-heuristic has to be used to evaluate the compound hypothesis (T, F).

To do this, first the two R-heuristics $\mathcal{H}_0$ and $\mathcal{H}_1$ coming from the evidence E have to be vacuously extended to $\Theta_1 \times \Theta_2$, which yields the R-heuristics $\mathcal{H}_0 \uparrow \Theta_1 \times \Theta_2$ and $\mathcal{H}_1 \uparrow \Theta_1 \times \Theta_2$. Then these R-heuristics have to be combined and the result itself has to be combined with the relational R-heuristic $\mathcal{R}$, which results in the combined R-heuristic

$$\mathcal{H}_3 = (\mathcal{H}_0 \uparrow \Theta_1 \times \Theta_2) \oplus (\mathcal{H}_1 \uparrow \Theta_1 \times \Theta_2) \oplus \mathcal{R}. \tag{21}$$

Since $\mathcal{H}_0 \uparrow \Theta_1 \times \Theta_2$ is vacuous, it can simply be discarded in the combination (21), so that

$$\mathcal{H}_3 = (\mathcal{H}_1 \uparrow \Theta_1 \times \Theta_2) \oplus \mathcal{R}. \tag{22}$$

Note that the set Ω of interpretations, the probability measure P on Ω, as well as the multivalued mapping Γ of this R-heuristic are not yet specified and depend on the specification of $\mathcal{R}$.

If rp_3 denotes the representativeness function of $\mathcal{H}_3$, then, in the light of all the information available, the mental model (T, F) is evaluated by its degree of representativeness $rp_3(T, F)$. The idea is that this degree of representativeness is then compared with the degree of representativeness $rp_0(T) = 0$ of the mental model "bank teller". Note that this mental model is evaluated with respect to the vacuous R-heuristic $\mathcal{H}_0$ representing the information relative to Θ_1 conveyed by E. In the following, three different relational R-heuristics $\mathcal{R}$ will be considered and each of them will lead to a combined R-heuristic $\mathcal{H}_3$ assigning a positive degree of representativeness to the compound mental model (T, F). Since

$$0 = rp_0(T) < rp_3(T, F), \tag{23}$$

each of these three different models explains the conjunction fallacy in the Linda problem.

5.2.1. *Relational R-heuristic $\mathcal{R}_1$*

Under this first "relational" approach it is assumed that the subjects, when confronted with the compound question, acknowledge the *possible existence* of some feminist bank tellers. So, under a first interpretation ω_{21} of the information retrieved when confronted with the compound question, the relation between Θ_1 and Θ_2 is given by the subset $\Gamma_2(\omega_{21}) = \{(T, F)\}$. This interpretation is assumed to be true with a small positive probability $P_2(\omega_{21}) = q$. Furthermore, under a second interpretation ω_{22}, which is correct with probability $P_2(\omega_{22}) = 1 - q$, nothing can be inferred about the relation between Θ_1 and Θ_2, i.e $\Gamma_2(\omega_{22}) = \Theta$. With $\Omega_2 = \{\omega_{21}, \omega_{22}\}$, the relational R-heuristic $\mathcal{R}$ in equation (20) is well defined. This relational R-heuristic $\mathcal{R}_1$ covers in a certain sense the "correlational beliefs" of the subjects.

With the R-heuristic $\mathcal{H}_1 \uparrow \Theta_1 \times \Theta_2$ defined in the previous subsection, we are ready to specify the constituents Ω, P and Γ of the combined R-heuristic $\mathcal{H}_3$ in (22). The multivalued mapping Γ is given by

$$\begin{aligned}\Gamma(\omega_{11}, \omega_{21}) &= (\Theta_1 \times \{F\}) \cap (\{(T, F)\}) = \{(T, F)\} \\ \Gamma(\omega_{11}, \omega_{22}) &= (\Theta_1 \times \{F\}) \cap (\Theta_1 \times \Theta_2) = \Theta_1 \times \{F\}\end{aligned}$$

and

$$\begin{aligned}\Gamma(\omega_{12}, \omega_{21}) &= (\Theta_1 \times \Theta_2) \cap (\{(T, F)\}) = \{(T, F)\} \\ \Gamma(\omega_{12}, \omega_{22}) &= (\Theta_1 \times \Theta_2) \cap (\Theta_1 \times \Theta_2) = \Theta_1 \times \Theta_2,\end{aligned}$$

which shows that, in this case, the application of Dempster's rule of combination does not require any conditioning. Therefore, $\Omega = \Omega_1 \times \Omega_2$, and the probability distribution P is given by

$$\begin{array}{ll} P(\omega_{11}, \omega_{21}) = pq & P(\omega_{11}, \omega_{22}) = p(1-q) \\ P(\omega_{12}, \omega_{21}) = (1-p)q & P(\omega_{12}, \omega_{22}) = (1-p)(1-q). \end{array}$$

If rp_3 denotes the representativeness function of $\mathcal{H}_3$, then we obviously have

$$rp_3(T, F) = P(\{(\omega_{11}, \omega_{21}), (\omega_{12}, \omega_{21})\}) = pq + (1-p)q = q.$$

Since q is non-zero, equation (23) holds. Therefore, this reasoning explains the conjunction fallacy.

5.2.2. *Relational R-heuristic* $\mathcal{R}_2$

Under this second "relational" approach it is assumed that, given the description E of Linda and confronted with the compound question, the subjects consider the *implication* that a person being a feminist is a bank teller. In other words, it is assumed that the subjects use some "causal belief" on this implication. Because of the "negative" evidence E, first, subjects comes the implication to mind that a person being a feminist is not a bank teller. According to the basic rules of logic this implication is represented by the subset $\{(\overline{T}, F), (T, \overline{F}), (\overline{T}, \overline{F})\}$ of $\Omega = \Omega_1 \times \Omega_2$.

Therefore, a first interpretation ω_{21} of the causal belief retrieved when confronted with the compound question is characterized by the subset

$$\Gamma_2(\omega_{21}) = \{(\overline{T}, F), (T, \overline{F}), (\overline{T}, \overline{F})\}.$$

Of course, if q denotes the probability of this interpretation, i.e.

$$P_2(\omega_{21}) = q,$$

then q will be large in general, but strictly smaller than 1.

However, the interesting *implication* is that a person being a feminist (surprisingly) is a bank teller. According to the basic rules of logic this implication is represented by the subset $\{(T,F),(T,\overline{F}),(\overline{T},\overline{F})\}$ of $\Omega = \Omega_1 \times \Omega_2$. So, a second interpretation ω_{22} of the causal belief retrieved when confronted with the compound question is characterized by the subset

$$\Gamma_2(\omega_{22}) = \{(T,F),(T,\overline{F}),(\overline{T},\overline{F})\}.$$

Of course, the probability of this second interpretation is

$$P_2(\omega_{22}) = 1 - P_2(\omega_{21}) = 1 - q.$$

Note that $1-q$ is small but positive in general. With $\Omega_2 = \{\omega_{21},\omega_{22}\}$, this completely defines the relational R-heuristic $\mathcal{R}_2$. This relational R-heuristic covers in a certain sense the "correlational beliefs" of the subjects.

Now, once more, we are ready to specify the constituents Ω, P and Γ of the combined R-heuristic $\mathcal{H}_3$ in (22). The multivalued mapping Γ is given by

$$\begin{aligned}\Gamma(\omega_{11},\omega_{21}) &= (\Theta_1 \times \{F\}) \cap \Gamma_2(\omega_{21}) = \{(\overline{T},F)\}\\ \Gamma(\omega_{11},\omega_{22}) &= (\Theta_1 \times \{F\}) \cap \Gamma_2(\omega_{22}) = \{(T,F)\}\end{aligned}$$

and

$$\begin{aligned}\Gamma(\omega_{12},\omega_{21}) &= (\Theta_1 \times \Theta_2) \cap \Gamma_2(\omega_{21}) = \Gamma_2(\omega_{21})\\ \Gamma(\omega_{12},\omega_{22}) &= (\Theta_1 \times \Theta_2) \cap \Gamma_2(\omega_{22}) = \Gamma_2(\omega_{22}),\end{aligned}$$

which shows that, also in this case, the application of Dempster's rule of combination does not require any conditioning. Therefore, $\Omega = \Omega_1 \times \Omega_2$, and the probability distribution P is given by

$$\begin{aligned}P(\omega_{11},\omega_{21}) &= pq & P(\omega_{11},\omega_{22}) &= p(1-q)\\ P(\omega_{12},\omega_{21}) &= (1-p)q & P(\omega_{12},\omega_{22}) &= (1-p)(1-q).\end{aligned}$$

If, once more, rp_3 denotes the representativeness function of $\mathcal{H}_3$, then we obviously have

$$sp_3(T,F) = P(\omega_{11},\omega_{22}) = p(1-q).$$

Since both p and $1-q$ are non-zero, equation (23) holds. Therefore, also this reasoning explains the conjunction fallacy.

5.2.3. *Relational R-heuristic* $\mathcal{R}_3$

In the literature, several researchers argue (cf. Hertwig and Gigerenzer, 1999, p. 297) that participants interpret the model T, i.e. Linda is a bank teller, to mean $(T,\overline{F})$, i.e. Linda is bank teller and is not active in the feminist movement. This argument preserves Hertwig and Gigerenzer's relevance maxim by making the description E of Linda relevant to deciding between $T\&F$ and $T\&\overline{F}$.

Under this third "relational" approach it is assumed that the subjects, when confronted with the compound question, simply consider the set of all four *combinations* which are logically possible. Given this approach, there are four different interpretations of the information given by the description E and retrieved from general knowledge,

$$\Omega_2 = \{\omega_{21}, \omega_{22}, \omega_{23}, \omega_{24}\}.$$

Under the first interpretation ω_{21}, subjects assume that a woman is a feminist if and only if she is a bank teller, which means that this information is characterized by the subset $\Gamma_2(\omega_{21}) = \{(T, F)\}$. Under the second interpretation ω_{22}, they assume that a woman is not a feminist if and only if she is a bank teller, which means that this information is characterized by the subset $\Gamma_2(\omega_{22}) = \{(T, \overline{F})\}$. The focal sets of the remaining two interpretations are, analogously, defined as

$$\Gamma_2(\omega_{23}) = \{(\overline{T}, F)\} \qquad \Gamma_2(\omega_{24}) = \{(\overline{T}, \overline{F})\}.$$

To completely specify the relational R-heuristic $\mathcal{R}_3$, assume now that the subjective probabilities of these interpretations are given by

$$P_2(\omega_{21}) = q_1 \quad P_2(\omega_{22}) = q_2 \quad P_2(\omega_{23}) = q_3 \quad P_2(\omega_{24}) = q_4\ . \tag{24}$$

Thereby it is, e.g., reasonable to assume that the subjects assign a larger probability to ω_{24} than to ω_{21} because it is more likely that a given woman is neither a bank teller nor a feminist than she is a feminist bank teller. But the following argument holds independently of any particular specification of these probabilities as long as the probability q_1 is nonzero. Note that the relational R-heuristic $\mathcal{R}_3$ is precise in this case.

For the specification of the combined R-heuristic $\mathcal{H}_3$ one has to investigate all the intersections $\Gamma_1(\omega_{1i}) \cap \Gamma_2(\omega_{2j})$. This investigation shows that

$$\begin{aligned}\Gamma_1(\omega_{11}) \cap \Gamma_2(\omega_{22}) &= (\Theta_1 \times \{F\}) \cap \{(T, \overline{F})\} = \emptyset \\ \Gamma_1(\omega_{11}) \cap \Gamma_2(\omega_{24}) &= (\Theta_1 \times \{F\}) \cap \{(\overline{T}, \overline{F})\} = \emptyset,\end{aligned}$$

i.e., in this case, the combination leads to two contradictory pairs of interpretations. It can easily been shown that the remaining intersections are nonempty. Hence, the set of all contradictory pairs of interpretations is given by

$$C = \{(\omega_{11}, \omega_{22}), (\omega_{11}, \omega_{24})\} \tag{25}$$

and

$$\begin{aligned}\Omega = \{&(\omega_{11}, \omega_{21}), (\omega_{11}, \omega_{23}), (\omega_{12}, \omega_{21}) \\ &(\omega_{12}, \omega_{22}), (\omega_{12}, \omega_{23}), (\omega_{12}, \omega_{24})\}\,.\end{aligned} \tag{26}$$

Specification of the mapping Γ of the combined R-heuristic $\mathcal{H}_3$ leads, among others, to

$$\begin{aligned}\Gamma(\omega_{11}, \omega_{21}) &= (\Theta_1 \times \{F\}) \cap \{(T, F)\} = \{(T, F)\} \\ \Gamma(\omega_{12}, \omega_{21}) &= (\Theta_1 \times \Theta_2) \cap \{(T, F)\} = \{(T, F)\}.\end{aligned}$$

In fact, the interpretations $(\omega_{11}, \omega_{21})$ and $(\omega_{12}, \omega_{21})$ are the only interpretations in Ω representative for the model $H = \{(T, F)\}$.

Since the probability of the contradictory set C is

$$k = pq_2 + pq_4 = p(q_2 + q_4)$$

it follows from (24) that

$$P(\omega_{11}, \omega_{21}) = \frac{pq_1}{1 - p(q_2 + q_4)},$$

and

$$P(\omega_{12}, \omega_{21}) = \frac{(1-p)q_1}{1 - p(q_2 + q_4)}.$$

Now, obviously the degree of representativeness of (T, F) is given by

$$\begin{aligned} rp_3(T, F) &= P(\omega_{11}, \omega_{21}) + P(\omega_{12}, \omega_{21}) \\ &= \frac{pq_1}{1 - p(q_2 + q_4)} + \frac{(1-p)q_1}{1 - p(q_2 + q_4)} \\ &= \frac{q_1}{1 - p(q_2 + q_4)}. \end{aligned}$$

Since this degree of representativeness is positive as long as q_1 is positive we have a further explanation of the conjunction fallacy (23). In other words, as long as in this third "relational" approach the subjects, when asked for ranking $T\&F$, believe that the combination (T, F) is possible they commit the conjunction fallacy.

Note that the first explanation of the conjunction fallacy presented in subsection 5.1 can *mathematically* also be seen as resulting from the combination of $\mathcal{H}_1 \uparrow \Theta_1 \times \Theta_2$ with a relational R-heuristic $\mathcal{R}$. Indeed, the extension of the R-heuristic $\mathcal{H}_2$ in equation (16) to the frame $\Theta = \Theta_1 \times \Theta_2$ can be considered as as relational R-heuristic $\mathcal{R}$ representing the result of the retrieval process by the base-rate q that a given woman is a bank teller. In this way, all explanations presented in this paper have the same mathematical structure, although the nature of the retrieved information is different in explanation 1 and explanation 2.

6. Fallacy or Intelligent Inference?

The starting point of this paper was the fact that even "highly sophisticated respondents" (Tversky and Kahneman, 1983, p. 298) like the author and his collaborators felt a strong tendency to violate the conjunction rule when confronted with the Linda problem. Though convinced by the basic rules of probability hurting the conjunction rule had a high degree of attractiveness. Why?

We agree with Gigerenzer's critique "that content-blind norms overlook the intelligent ways in which humans deal with uncertainty, namely, the human capacity for semantic and pragmatic inferences" (Hertwig and Gigerenzer, 2002, p. 276). We also agree with their position that the term probability is polysemous and "'probable' cannot be reduced to mathematical probability" (Hertwig and Gigerenzer, 2002, p. 277). Finally, we share their opinion that Tversky and Kahneman's heuristics are far "too vague to count as explanations".

However, Hertwig and Gigerenzer (1999) have shown that people infer nonmathematical meanings of the polysemous term "probability" in the classic Linda problem and they provide evidence that, in fact, people use something like the representativeness heuristic when judging the "probability" of the different statements. As they do not further specify what people might understand by some of the expressions they used in Study 1 (cf. Hertwig and Gigerenzer, 1999, p. 281, Exhibit 1), the use of the representativeness heuristic may play an even more important role.

We have shown that a mathematical structure which is well-known from evidence based reasoning can more or less directly be used to model the representativeness heuristic. This model takes into account all the essential characteristics of this heuristic described by Tversky and Kahneman. At the same time, it takes into account the conversational rationality "maxim of quantity" propagated by Hertwig and Gigerenzer. This model shows that it is by no means irrational to work with the representativeness heuristic even if this, quite often, leads to violations of the conjunction rule. Above all, it reveals where the main point in the Linda problem lies.

According to the rationality principle formulated in section 4.4, for treating a given question, e.g. ranking different statements, simultaneously all the information available or retrieved for a certain set of statements has to be used to treat each and every single statements. This principle can easily be formalized within the framework proposed. Intentionally, Linda type problems are constructed such that some information is only used for a certain statement but disregarded when treating others. Subjects use some retrievable information only when they are forced to. The fallacious behavior in the Linda problem is not fallacious because the content-blind conjunction rule is not obeyed but because subjects use some pieces of information in a "biased" way.

This becomes evident when one scrutinizes the different approaches to explain the Linda fallacy presented in the last paragraph. In all of these approaches, for treating the question if Linda is a bank teller only the information presented in E is taken into consideration. For treating the compound question $T\&F$, some additional information is referred to which is neglected when treating the bank teller question alone. Arguing within our formal approach 5.2, for evaluating the model "bank teller", on the basis of the evidence provided by E, only the vacuous R-heuristic $\mathcal{H}_0$ is used. Whereas for evaluating the compound model $T\&F$, "bank teller" and "feminist", the R-heuristic $\mathcal{H}_3$ resulting from the combination of $\mathcal{H}_1 \uparrow \Theta_1 \times \Theta_2$ with a certain relational R-heuristic $\mathcal{R}$ is used.

In general, for treating different particular questions, subjects tend to use different pieces of information: they use only those pieces of information which appear directly relevant or they are forced to use. This "biased" use of information is the main problem. Linda type problems show that it is easy to seduce subjects to use the information available or retrievable in such a biased way. They have to be taught, first, to collect all the relevant information they dispose of and, then, to treat all the particular questions on the basis of that, in a subjective sense, full information. In the representativeness framework developed in this paper, it can easily be shown that the conjunction fallacy immediately disappears when the full information available, i.e., when the R-heuristic $\mathcal{H}_3$ is used to evaluate both hypotheses T and (T, F).

Acknowledgements

I am grateful to Elitza Ouzounova for her critical comments on an earlier draft of this paper, and Daniel Suter for his very helpful editorial support.

References

Bar-Hillel, M. 1973. "On the Subjective Probability of Compound Events", *Organizational Behavior and Human Performance* 9, 396-406.

Birnbaum, M.H. 1983. "Base Rate in Bayesian Inference: Signal Detection Analysis of the Cab Problem", *American Journal of Psychology* 96, 85-94.

Brachinger, H.W., and P.-A. Monney 2003. "The Conjunction Fallacy: Explanations of the Linda Problem by the Theory of Hints", *International Journal of Intelligent Systems* 18, 75-91.

De Finetti, B. 1974. *Theory of Probability*, New York: Wiley.

Dempster, A. 1967. "Upper and Lower Probability Induced by a Multivalued Mapping", *Annals of Mathematical Statistics* 38, 325-339.

Dempster, A. 1968. "A Generalization of Bayesian Inference", *Journal of the Royal Statistical Society, Series B* 3, 205-247.

Gigerenzer, G. 1991. "How to Make Cognitive Illusion Disappear: Beyond "Heuristics and Biases", in: W. Stroebe and M. Hewstone (eds.): *European Review of Social Psychology*, Chichester: Wiley.

Gigerenzer, G. 1994. "Why the Distinction between Single-Event Probability and Frequencies is Relevant for Psychology (and vice versa)", in: G. Wright, and P. Ayton (Eds.): "Subjective Probability", New York, Wiley.

Gigerenzer, G. 1996. "On Narrow Norms and Vague Heuristics: A Reply to Kahneman and Tversky (1996)", *Psychological Review* 103, 592-596.

Gigerenzer, G., U. Hoffrage, and H. Kleinbölting. 1991. "Probabilistic Mental Models: A Brunswikian Theory of Confidence", *Psychological Review* 98, 509-528.

Gigerenzer, G., and D.J. Murray. 1987. *Cognition as Intuitive Statistics*, Hillsdale, NJ: Erlbaum.

Hertwig, R., and G. Gigerenzer. 1999. "The Conjunction Fallacy Revisited: How Intelligent Inferences Look Like Reasoning Errors", *Journal of Behavioral Decision Making* 12, 275-305.

Kahneman, D., P. Slovic, and A. Tversky. 1982. *Judgment under Uncertainty: Heuristics and Biases*, Cambridge: Cambridge University Press.

Kahneman, D., and A. Tversky. 1996. "On the Reality of Cognitive Illusions", *Psychological Review* 103, 582-591.

Kohlas, J., and P.A. Monney. 1994. "Theory of Evidence - A Survey of its Mathematical Foundations, Applications and Computational Aspects", *Zeitschrift für Operations Research* 39, 35-68.

Kohlas, J., and P.A. Monney. 1995. *A Mathematical Theory of Hints. An Approach to the Dempster-Shafer Theory of Evidence*, Berlin: Springer.

Krantz, D., C. Jepson, Z. Kunda, and R. Nisbett. 1983. "The Use of Statistical Heuristics in Everyday Inductive Reasoning", *Psychological Review* 90, 339-363.

Nisbett, R., and L. Ross. 1980. *Human Inference: Strategies and Shortcomings of Social Judgment*, Englewood Cliffs: Prentice-Hall.

Pollard, P. 1982. "Human Reasoning: Some Possible Effects of Availability", *Cognition* 12, 65-96.

Shafer, G. 1976. *A Mathematical Theory of Evidence*, Princeton: Princeton University Press.

Shafer, G. 1986. "Probability Judgment in Artificial Intelligence", in: L.N. Kanal, and J.F. Lemmer: *Uncertainty in Artificial Intelligence*, Amsterdam: North-Holland.

Shafer, G., and A. Tversky. 1985. "Languages and Designs for Probability Judgment", *Cognitive Science* 9, 309-339.

Shenoy, P., and G. Shafer. 1990. "Axioms for Probability and Belief Functions Propagation", in: R.D. Shachter et al. (eds): *Uncertainty in Artificial Intelligence* 4, Amsterdam: North Holland.

Tversky, A., and D.J. Koehler. 1994. "Support Theory: A Nonextensional Representation of Subjective Probability", *Psychological Review* 101(4), 547-567.

Tversky, A., and D. Kahneman. 1982. "Judgments of and by Representativeness", in: D. Kahneman, P. Slovic, and A. Tversky (eds.): *Judgment under Uncertainty: Heuristics and Biases*, Cambrige: Cambridge University Press.

Tversky, A., and D. Kahneman. 1983. "Extensional Versus Intuitive Reasoning: The Conjunction Fallacy in Probability Judgment", *Psychological Review* 91, 293-315.

Hans Wolfgang Brachinger
Department of Quantitative Economics
University of Fribourg
Beauregard 13
CH-1700 Fribourg
Switzerland
HansWolfgang.Brachinger@unifr.ch

THE RISKLESS UTILITY MAPPING OF EXPECTED UTILITY AND ALL THEORIES IMPOSING THE DOMINANCE PRINCIPLE: ITS INABILITY TO INCLUDE LOANS, COMMITMENTS EVEN WITH FULLY DESCRIBED DECISION TREES

ROBIN POPE*
*University of Bonn***

1. Introduction

Let EU denote the set of axiomatised versions of the expected utility (and game) theory. Let EU+ denote the set of non-EU theories imposing the dominance principle, namely a preference for first order stochastically dominant distributions of outcomes. Let NM utility denote the mapping from outcomes into utilities employed in EU and EU+. Von Neumann and Morgenstern, declared that NM utility has the unappealing and unrealistic feature that it excludes secondary satisfactions (risk attitude) but reported that they had encountered a contradiction in going beyond EU and including them and so left this task to future researchers (1947, pp626-32).

But by the early 1950s some dissented and claimed that NM utility is already general enough, or generalisable, to include secondary satisfactions. The paper finds that no matter whether risk attitude involves emotional or financial instances of secondary satisfactions, and no matter how fully the decision situation and associated decision trees are specified with regard to commitment, NM utility excludes secondary satisfactions.

The paper thus confirms the von Neumann-Morgenstern interpretation of NM utility as excluding secondary satisfactions and as normatively unappealing. The paper shows how a stages by a *degree-of-knowledge-ahead* framework overcomes the contradiction that prevented von Neumann and Morgenstern from including secondary satisfactions. It shows how to build models that avoid the implausible dominance principle and consistently incorporate those secondary satisfactions that do and should enter serious personal and corporate decisions.

---

* I thank Will Baumol, Kjell Hausken, David Kelsey, Roman Krzysztofowicz, Stefan Markowski, Harry Markowitz, Adrian Pagan, Norman Roberts Paul Samuelson, Rakesh Sarin and Reinhard Selten for comments and discussions, Rafael Dreyer for proofing.

U. Schmidt and S. Traub (eds.), Advances in Public Economics: Utility, Choice and Welfare, 289-327.

1.1 THE DOMINANCE PRINCIPLE

In this paper an act, a prospect, a strategy, a gamble and a lottery have the English language denotation and neutral connotation of a prospect.[1] But we shall mainly use the shortest of these three, act. For simplicity, we let the likelihood of distinct outcomes at a given time be denoted by probabilities of those outcomes. We let these probabilities obey the Kolmogorov axioms, and be common knowledge to all relevant parties. Under EU, axiomatised expected utility theory, an act is simply a probability distribution over outcomes. This is likewise the case under the dominance principle, and thus under EU+, the set of decision theories imposing the dominance principle. After background understanding has been built up, we shall discuss an act's component theoretical entities, the concepts of a probability and the concept of an outcome, and whether such a simple concept of an act is adequate for rational choice. Then we are in a position to appraise whether the dominance principle is plausible or reasonable in either a descriptive or normative decision theory.

Praise has been heaped on the dominance principle, and there is reluctance to deviate from it in generalizing EU, resulting in EU+ comprising most of the generalizations of EU. If a principle did not impose restrictions on how acts appraised, it would not be a principle. But the first two of its three restrictions listed below are typically left implicit. Leaving them implicit, unrecognized, instead of critically evaluating them has contributed to acceptance of the dominance principle.

(i) The outcome space partitions into a set of mutually exclusive entitities we may term outcomes that exhaust the outcome space, with each outcome inherently uni-dimensional with respect to time and attributes. Inherently unidimensional here means that each outcome can be mapped into a different real number on the real number line.

Comment on (i) This restriction does not preclude the outcomes having each multiple dimensions with respect to time and attributes within each time segment, but does preclude those multiple dimensions having a lack of substitutablility between them. If each outcome has a flow dimension of distinct time periods, and in each time period say a value for its colour and weight, there must be a rule for combining the colour and weight attributes into a unidimensional index (that corresponds to a real number.) That

[1] *Ie* we follow Savage in disregarding normal English usage (under which an act, unlike a prospect, gamble or lottery) involves choice, and therefore shall engage where needed for clarity) in the redundancy for normal English language usage, of talking about choosing an act. We do not follow Savage in lending to the word act the connotation that we are restricted to the notion of subjective, as distinct from object, probabilities.

combining rule could for instance be a simple addition of a number attributed to its colour and a number attributed to its weight in each period, *ie* a simple addition of four numbers. In the typical description of the dominance principle in EU and EU+, the outcomes already have this inherently uni-dimensional quality since the outcomes are simply timewise dimensionless money amounts. We shall see as the paper progresses that the timewise inherently dimensionless character of the outcome space bears on the inherent implausibility of the dominance principle.

(ii) The decision maker can and does make a preference ordering of the outcomes from worst to best independently of *knowing ahead* which act she will choose, and thus independently of her *degree of knowledge ahead* of which outcome will occur and thus of any implications of going through a period after choosing before learning the outcome. The few decision scientists today who do realise that the principle imposes this restriction, impose the restriction in the manner of Friedman and Savage (1948), namely by evaluating each outcome as if it were certain.

Illustration of (ii) Let the outcomes be monetary amounts of 0€, 10€, 20€, 50€, and 80€, and the chooser preferentially orders them from the lowest, 0€ to the highest 80€.

(iii) The decision maker invariably prefers and chooses stochastically dominant acts where for any pair of acts A and B, act A is said to stochastically dominate act B if act A has no lower preference ordered outcome with a higher probability of occurring than does act B, and at least one higher preference ordered outcome with a higher probability of occurring than does act B.

Illustration of (iii) If act R has a 0.7 probability of 50€ and a 0.3 probability of 0€, while act VR has merely a 0.6 probability of 50€, and a 0.4 probability of 0€, then the lower preference ordered outcome is 0€, and the higher preference ordered outcome is 50€. Since relative to act VR, act R has a lower probability for the lower preference ranked outcome and a higher probability of the higher preference ranked outcome, act R stochastically dominates act VR. If acts R and VR comprise the choice set, the chooser prefers and chooses R.

With this sort of illustration, the dominance principle seems plausible, indeed to vast numbers of decision scientists, a necessary feature of any rational choice theory. But as we shall see, the plausibility and apparent rationality of the principle stems from selecting a very peculiar and restricted example to appraise it. We shall see that the dominance principle's constraint (ii), that preferences for outcomes (and thus indirectly for acts) be ordered independent of knowledge ahead is implausible and unreasonable. We shall see that in conjunction with constraint (i), it precludes any of the multiple periods of an outcome flow occurring before all risk is passed, and thereby excludes all the phenomena of interest to economists and other decision scientists connected to choice under risk.

To begin assessing the objections to this principle and to move toward a scientific understanding of the constraints it imposes and thus an understanding of EU itself, we need first to address a methodological issue. This is the issue of why what may be termed the black box approach to decision theory is incompatible with the specification, understanding, appraisal and empirical testing of EU or indeed any decision theory.

1.2 EU: INTUITION VERSUS THE BLACK BOX

Preferences are ordinal if they can be ordered sequentially in value. If in addition the differences between preferences can be specified quantitatively to denote differences in preference intensity, the ordering is cardinal. Under EU, the approach initiated in Marschak (1950) has been to specify a set of ordinal preference ordering over acts and other preference orderings that together imply what Harsanyi (1977) termed the expected utility property, namely that people choose as if they possessed a cardinal utility index for each outcome that was unique apart from origin and scale, and probability weighted an act's outcomes to form an overall value of an act. Baumol (1951) coined for this index whose expectation is maximised the name Neumann-Morgenstern utility,[2] shortened to NM utility in this paper. This maps *into* a utility index and for simplicity (we shall assume is a real number) *from* what is called a domain of outcomes, *eg* Samuelson (1952, p677), or a domain of classes of outcome or states, termed events, *eg* von Neumann and Morgenstern (1944, 1947, 1953 and 1972).

If we leave NM utility uninterpreted, we can treat as a black box *why* people choose. We can attempt, as Hicks advocated in his influential 1956 book, to take a preferences only approach and make "no claim, no pretense to be able to look inside their [the choosers'] heads". If we seek to avoid entirely the mental, the introspective processes of choice, then we leave also in the black box of unanswerable questions, whether there is anything plausible or rational about any decision theory including EU, and also about any of its axioms. This leaves EU with axioms but not a justification.[3]

---

[2] Baumol (1951, p61). See also Savage (1954, p98).

[3] Sen (1993, 2002, p124, footnote 5), in arguing that EU is unjustifiable and of the need to go into the black box, reports that later Hicks had doubts about the wisdom of his earlier advocacy of the preferences only approach.

A justification of EU must rest on the theory itself being plausible, reasonable. The plausibility of a theory can be argued (i) to be itself directly *intuitively* plausible, reasonable, or (ii) to ensue because all its (so far noticed) implications are *intuitively* plausible, reasonable, or by (iii) to ensue because it is derivable from a set of axioms, every one of which is *intuitively* plausible, reasonable. When choice is such a black box, we cannot intuit, and thus cannot comment on whether NM utility has normatively desirable properties like including the chooser's risk attitude since even the meaning of risk attitude is uninterpretable when the whole concept of the NM mapping is itself "an uninterpretable technical artifact".

Those advocating the black box approach to the reasoning steps of a chooser with NM utility ("an uninterpretable technical artifact") test EU and in testing it are unwittingly violating their own black box approach. When choice is such a black box, we cannot even scientifically specify the outcome space of any decision theory. To scientifically specify a theory's outcomes space, we need to know enough about what happens inside the black box of people's heads to know that the attributes of the outcome space that we (the external scientists) have specified are attributes relevant to choosers. Otherwise we cannot connect what the chooser perceives to be acts involving distributions over outcomes with what the scientists perceives as acts. When choice is such a black box therefore, we cannot test whether anyone obeys EU. (Nor can we test whether anyone obeys any of its standard rank dependent generalisations or any of the many other theories that employ NM utility.) Thus when those advocating the black box approach to the reasoning steps of a chooser with NM utility ("an uninterpretable technical artifact") test EU and EU+, they are unwittingly violating their own black box approach.

Examples of efforts to test EU and its generalisation within generic utility theory while at least partially restricting the tests of this class to its black box revealed preferences features include Chechile and Cooke (1997), and Chechile and Luce (1999). These investigations found that context dependent non-black box explicitly cognitive models of "looking inside the chooser's head" worked better. But there is a myriad of problems when even the scientists themselves are keeping the mental analysis implicitly underlying a theory in a black box. As Stefan Traub, Christian Seidl, Ulrich Schmidt and Peter Grösche (1999) skilfully demonstrate, when so many of the (mentally implied) probability equivalences do not exist in the Chechile and Cooke experimental set-up, it cannot afford a robust test of even the partially black box variant of EU (and the entire class of generic utility). We throw away a great deal of our understanding of EU while we try in vain to look at choices as a black box, and throw away vast amounts of potential observations for testing it.

There is an easier way to understand and test EU and related theories if we repudiate the black box approach, especially since, as already demonstrated, we can never fully and consistently implement the black box anyway. The easier way is to retain the original approach of Bernoulli: interpret NM utility as an introspective index of satisfactions. The original approach is in *eg* Ramsey (1926, 1950), von Neumann and Morgenstern (1944, 1947, 1953 and 1972), Friedman and Savage (1948), Allais (1952, 1979b), Harsanyi (1983, 1986), Dyer and Sarin (1979a, 1979b and 1982), Sarin (1982), Schoemaker (1982), Drummond, O'Brien, Stoddart and Torrance (1997), and Richardson (2001).

The original approach of going inside the black box and introspecting is that adopted in this paper. Under it we can discuss consistently whether NM utility has plausible descriptive and normative properties. We can ask whether NM utility includes secondary satisfactions. We can ask whether NM utility is identical to classical utility, which measures intensity of preference under certainty — when classical utility is restricted, as is NM utility, to denote a cardinal index of the value of a set of outcomes which is univariate and unique apart from scale and origin.[4]

NM utility applies to both risky and riskless situations. The mere fact that NM utility applies in risky situations is not of course a guarantee that it differs from classical utility. Indeed the traditional interpretation has been that NM utility is a riskless classical utility index devoid of consideration of secondary satisfactions, and that any aversion of an EU decision maker to fair bets stems from the interaction of (i) the probability weights used to add up the different NM utilities into an overall value of the risky act with (ii) the chooser having a concave "as if certain" NM utility mapping, concavity that results in lower outcomes mapping into a disproportionately high utility numbers relative to the utility numbers into which the higher outcomes map.

But nowadays the normative appeal of EU importantly stems from a new view of the *supposed* role of risk in making NM utility distinct from classical utility because it includes secondary satisfactions, *eg* the *Journal of Economic Literature* survey of EU, Schoemaker (1982, p 535). The American Economic Association takes measures to ensure that its *Journal of Economic Literature* surveys represent mainstream expert thinking. Hence it is reasonable to conclude that the mainstream view in 1983 was that NM utility includes secondary satisfaction, and there is little evidence of any change in mainstream understanding since.

Many (maybe all) of those endorsing the new mainstream view are innocent of their disagreement with early and later distinguished contributors to EU such as Ramsey (1926), von Neumann and Morgenstern (1944, 1947, 1953 and 1972), Friedman and Savage (1948), Marschak (1950), Allais (1952, 1979b), Marschak and Radner (1972) and Harsanyi (1983). This paper investigates four distinctions between NM and classical utility with respect to risk which surfaced in the 1950s and that underlie this new mainstream view that NM includes secondary satisfactions. The first concerns how utilities are measured, *eg* Ellsberg (1954) Schoemaker (1982),

[4] Paul A. Samuelson 1983, pp510-512, Jeffrey 1983, pp35-38 and Harsanyi 1986, pp31-41.

investigated in parts 5 and 6. The second distinction concerns whether the outcomes of NM utility could be elaborated to include risk attitude, *eg* Samuelson (1952), investigated in parts 7 and 8. The third distinction arises out of a confusion of NM utility with buyer or consumer utility in supply-demand analysis, investigated in part 9. The fourth distinction concerns the chooser's use of a full description of the whole gambling situation (decision tree) to decide, *eg* Luce and Raiffa (1957), investigated in parts 10 to 14. Supposed differences between classical and NM utility which are unrelated to risk (and measurement under risk) are not being contested in this paper. For a review of these non risk factors, see *eg* Fishburn (1970, 1976, 1988 and 1989).

2. Secondary Satisfactions (Risk Attitude) in a Utility Index

Many different phrases have been used to denote secondary satisfactions (risk attitude). Perhaps the most traditional is a (specific) utility of gambling. Histories of the numerous phrases used for this concept and the problems with each are in Pope (1996/7 and 2001). The phrase secondary satisfactions is more neutral in its connotations than is the (specific) utility of gambling that has denigratory and frivolous connotations. The phrase secondary satisfactions is less prone to misconstrual than is the phrase risk attitude which went through a change in denotation in the early 1950s as described later.

Before we can shed much light on the disagreement between scientists who endorse the traditional interpretation of NM utility as including secondary satisfactions and those who disagree, we need to elucidate the concept itself. Two alternative definitions of the concept are in Pope (1984, 1995). When risk includes the border case of risk reduced to zero (certainty), both alternatives partition the set of sources of satisfaction identically between those that involve risk attitude and those that exclude it. Primary satisfactions are those derived from the outcome independent of its risk. Secondary satisfactions are those derived from the risk in the outcome.

Risk concerns the chooser's *degree of knowledge ahead of the outcome.* The probability of a particular outcome denotes the *degree of knowledge ahead* of that particular outcome. The dominance principle's restriction (ii) precludes it from incorporating *degree of knowledge ahead* in the ordering of outcomes (and hence also in the specification of outcomes). EU and EU+ embed the dominance principle. So we might conclude the paper here, we have simply rediscovered what was long ago understood. But it is illuminating to track the loss in understanding since the mid twentieth century, and in tracking it, we shall go further.

3. The Traditional Riskless Interpretation of NM Utility

In 1926 Ramsey described the NM utility index as one in which tastes are independent of beliefs, that is, as an index excluding secondary satisfactions.[5] Savage dates this sort of classical notion of utility back to the 17th century, to the inventors of EU, the Swiss mathematicians Daniel Bernoulli and his cousin Gabriel Cramer, Savage (1954, pp91-93).

Classical utility maps from the outcome domain into a univariate cardinal index of preference intensity in the form of a positive affine (EU) or a ratio scale. It may also be multi-attribute (but reducible to a univariate scale under EU). See *eg* S.S. Stevens (1946). In the classical utility mapping, at the point of choice, each outcome is treated *as if* it were a certainty, each event *as if* it were a constant in the language of Savage (1954) — an event that is bound to happen no matter which state of the world eventuates. In this context, Samuelson applies the adjective "certain" to prizes, income-situations, outcomes, while Savage applies the adjective constant to events and states. That is under the classical utility mapping each outcome is treated *as if* at the point of evaluation that outcome or event were known. A classical utility function is therefore like a demand function when a demand function traces out quantities demanded *as if* many different prices are each in turn hypothesised to be known with certainty to be the prevailing price. Note that when a classical utility mapping is used in a risky choice theory such as EU with each outcome of a risky act treated *as if* it were a certainty, this is counterfactual, the actual outcomes, events are risky at the time point in which the chooser is evaluating them.

In giving NM utility a distinctive name in 1951, Baumol was seeking to denigrate it precisely because it is a riskless classical cardinal utility index. For Baumol had answered "No" to the two questions he then posed about decision makers:

Question 1: Must they have cardinal as distinct from merely ordinal preferences (*ie* must they have a notion of intensity, of how much more, they prefer one item to another?

Question 2: Must they evaluate outcomes ignoring secondary satisfactions?

---

[5] This is a paraphrase of a section of Ramsey's 1926 lecture given in Marschak and Radner (1972, pp16, 20 and 419). Ramsey's own wording for this restriction on (what later came to be termed) NM utility is in the somewhat abstruse terminology of Wittgenstein's theory of propositions, namely that it be confined to "ethically neutral propositions":

> "... propositions ... used as conditions in the options offered ... may be such that their truth or falsity is an object of desire to the subject ... propositions for which the propositions for which this is nto the case ... we shall call ethically neutral", Ramsey (1926, 1950, p177)

In responding to Baumol (1951) and other critics, advocates of EU accordingly saw themselves as having to defend the fact that as a classical utility index, NM had two defects:

1. it was cardinal and
2. it omitted secondary satisfactions.

As discussed later, von Neumann and Morgenstern were embarrassed that NM utility was riskless and added a 1947 appendix to expand on the earlier explanation of how elusive and impossible they had found the task that they had originally set themselves. This had been the task of constructing a utility index that incorporated secondary satisfactions.

By contrast, the growing number of enthusiasts for EU in the late 1940s and early 1950s commented openly and without embarrassment on the riskless nature of NM utility. Savage and Friedman for instance, claimed that von Neumann and Morgenstern's axiomatisation of EU implies that people evaluate outcomes or events as if they were certain

> In choosing among alternatives ... *whether or not these alternatives involve risk*, a consumer ... behaves as if (his or her) ... preferences could be completely described by a function attaching a numerical value — to be designated "utility" — to alternatives each of which is regarded as *certain*.
>
> [Friedman and Savage (1948, p282, emphasis added)]

The same point is made in Friedman and Savage (1952, p471). The alternative axiomatisations of EU devised at this time have the same explicitly riskless mapping for NM utility. The NM domain is restricted explicitly to certain outcomes, to constant events, *eg* Marschak (1950 p115), Samuelson (1952, p671) and Savage (1954, pp25-26). The explicit statements that the domain is riskless are accompanied with supportive comments of the fact that the riskless classical NM utility mapping precludes the pleasure or (specific) utility of gambling, *eg* Samuelson (1952, p677).

In the 19th and early 20th century Marshall had argued that the utility of gambling sometimes helped in business via an adventurous spirit, and sometimes hindered via engendering feverish speculation, Marshall (1920, p 843). Canaan (1926) had focussed on the utility of gambling helping trade, chastising the cautious as timid. Ramsey by contrast had argued that the utility of gambling should not be a consideration in serious decisions, Ramsey (1926, 1950).

Ramsey's opposition to incorporating the utility of gambling was what attracted the attention of EU advocates in the early 1950s. This related to the fact that EU advocates were then mingling in the Rand circle. To this circle Norman Dalkey had introduced the recently re-issued volume of Ramsey's lectures and papers posthumously edited by Ronald Braithwaite.[6] With their focuson Ramsey and not

---

[6] I am indebted to Ken Arrow for passing this information on to me.

on Marshall or Canaan, EU advocates, instead of being embarrassed at the fact that the riskless NM utility omitted the pleasure or (specific) utility of gambling, argued that this omission was an advantage in normative, if not descriptive, decision theory. For further details, see Pope (1996/7).

4. The Cardinal Nature of NM Utility

It was embarrassing in the 1940s and 1950s for converts to EU that NM utility exhibits that second feature of classical utility: it is cardinal. The alternative axiomatisations to those of von Neumann and Morgenstern developed in the early 1950s, *eg* by Marschak, Samuelson and Savage, were for a period thought by some to have the advantage of avoiding the cardinal NM index. In due course it came to be generally recognised that even axiomatisations of EU that make no explicit mention of the NM utility index, nevertheless imply that decision makers choose as if maximizing the expectation of their NM utility index, an index that is cardinal and unique (other than origin and scale). See *eg* Samuelson (1983, pp 510-512).

The embarrassment at NM utility being cardinal related to the ordinal revolution. This ordinal revolution was ushered in part by a belief that the introspective methods previously used to estimate and interpret classical cardinal utility were "unscientific" if not altogether meaningless. An ordinalist goal was to eliminate from economics and decision theory the concept utility and any thing else that involved as Hicks later put it, looking inside people's heads. Hicks and Allen (1934) had been influential in persuading many economists that an ordinalist preferences only approach could explain market phenomena under certainty without introspection, merely from how choosers ordered alternatives. On the historical details, see Walsh (1996, pp34-38). This work also traces how a desire to avoid addressing ethical redistributional issues attracted influential economists such as Robbins to object to the interpsonal comparative use of cardinal utilities and assisted in ushering in ordinalism and the preferences only approach. But through the work of Sen (1970, 1982), Sonnenschein (1973) and others, it was later discovered that exceedingly little of market analysis, even under certainty, can be accomplished under ordinalism and preferences only.

But in the early 1950s, the limits of ordinalism had yet to be discovered. Ordinalism seemed to have abolished the need for introspective cardinal utility under certainty and EU seemed to many a step backwards with its cardinal introspective NM utility. In this atmosphere of the 1920s to 1950s, attempts were made to make NM utility seem scientific despite being cardinal. The attempts were to introduce the more respectable preferences only or revealed choice ways of estimating the NM cardinal utility index. Ramsey, Bruno de Finetti, von Neumann and Morgenstern began this process.

Rossi (1994) however emphasises that de Finetti stood outside the growing absurdity of attempting to do decision science excluding the decision maker and deeming the discipline more scientific as a consequence of these efforts. It should also be mentioned that some of Morgenstern's Viennese co-scientists (including Werner Leinfellner) and other scholars of the Vienna Circle Institute such as Friederich Stadtler claim that Morgenstern himself like many logical positivists had no opposition to, but rather endorsed, introspection.[7] In accord with this perception, Morgenstern's move in enticing von Neumann to axiomatise EU and proffer the standard gamble technique for measuring NM utility was apparently undertaken not to convince themselves, but to convince economists of the value of game theory (whose payoffs are cardinal.) Von Neumann was allegedly happy for these to continue to be simply money amounts as in his earlier game theory work and saw no need to replace them with utilities.[8]

Ramsey, de Finetti, von Neumann and Morgenstern in effect proposed that the classical Bernoullian or NM utility index be estimated from choices between sure and risky events regarding which the chooser was indifferent (willing to exchange one for the other). For instance the von Neumann and Morgenstern estimation method (1947, 1953 and 1972, p18, footnote 2), now known as certainty equivalent version of the standard gamble technique, was to ask people to choose sure acts equivalent to risky ones. Then assuming that people obey EU, inferred their NM utility index from their answers, and argued that so estimating the classical riskless Bernoullian or NM utility index had two advantages over the earlier method of asking people to *directly* intuitively estimate their utility index:

1. the observed choices were "reproducible" phenomena, and
2. while not eliminating the disparaged act of intuition, it at least made the intuitive estimate of preference intensity *in*direct.[9]

Whether people's observed choices turn out to be more reproducibly consistent than people's introspections is of course an empirical question, as Ellsberg (1954) notes, and one that, so far as this author knows, has yet to be investigated. Having the intuition indirect resulted in many decision scientists making a false distinction between information gained from "objective" hypothetical choices and from intuition. The false distinction arises from overlooking the fact that unless people use their conscious minds to choose, *ie* use their intuition, we have no grounds for even determining whether the person actually decided on the act, and if decided, whether using EU. No ordinalist, to this author's knowledge, has expounded on this matter.

---

[7] Walsh 1996, pp181-3, offers evidence for instance of logical positivist Ayers endorsing introspection.

[8] I am indebted to Reinhard Selten for this information. He stresses that he has not seen written documentation of the claim, but heard it in a lecture given by Thomas Kuhn. This author has not checked with Kuhn to vet the information herself.

[9] These two scientists also hopefully pointed out that as there had been advances in measurement estimation in the physical sciences, so yet better estimation methods for NM might be discovered in the future.

The obvious mental theory for EU is that the introspection involves the traditional cardinal NM intensity of preference function itself as postulated by Bernoulli and by numerous scientists since, including Allais and Harsanyi. According to this account choosers mentally calculate the EU property, introspectively attaching to each outcome a utility (which is a cardinal measure of preference intensity) and then aggregate these utilities by probability weights. As von Neumann and Morgenstern implied in the appendix that they added in 1947 to the 1944 edition of their book, it is implausible that decision makers use this riskless NM utility since it requires them to ignore their secondary satisfactions.

In discussing their proposed technique for estimating such NM utility, von Neumann and Morgenstern seemed to be so keen to meet ordinalist objections that they failed to mention that they had:

1. no solution to the ordinalist objection to indirectly bringing in introspective cardinal utilities, and
2. no solution to the problem that they deemed it implausible that people really obey EU.[10]

When people do not obey EU, using the von Neumann and Morgenstern standard gamble technique fails to uncover the chooser's *real* utility. Instead the data are contaminated through EU's omission of secondary satisfactions, the data generate pseudo NM utility functions. This contamination has been extreme — and gone largely un-noticed — in the extensive subsequent use of the technique, a matter discussed later in the paper.

Baumol's conversion to EU is testimony to the perceived uncritical acclaim of the ordinalist "preferences only" approach that decision scientists of that generation conferred on measurement techniques that avoided direct reference to introspection on cardinal utilities.[11] Baumol's conversion essay in the *Economic Journal* is titled "The Cardinal Utility Which Is Ordinal", Baumol re-labels the embarrassing cardinal NM utility index as an acceptable ordinal one because: "It is *not* the purpose of the Neumann-Morgenstern utility index to set up any sort of measure of introspective pleasure intensity", Baumol (1958, p665).

How a person should make the hypothetical choices obeying EU without introspection on preference intensity, neither Baumol nor others adopting this stance elucidated. This ordinalist preferences only approach left how a chooser was

---

10 Ramsey, at least according to Braithwaite's reproduction of his lecture notes, similarly omitted mentioning this, and was similarly excessive in giving the impression of uncontentious objectivity and accuracy in the measures of utility obtained from his probability equivalence version of the standard gamble technique.

11 On further details, and effects of logical positivism, see Pope (1983), Walsh (1996) and Pope (1996/7).

supposed to apply EU vague and obscure, and thus left obscure the fact that the measure assumed that choosers ignore secondary satisfactions. The leaving of these matters vague is was in striking contrast to the precision about how choosers should introspect, evaluate and attach utilities to be found in the earlier (Ramsey, Friedman and Savage, Marschak and Samuelson) interpretations of NM utility reported in part 2 above, namely by thinking of each outcome "as if certain" or independent of the probabilities.

5. NM Utility as Operationally Distinct

Von Neumann and Morgenstern's suggestion of measuring utility via the certainty equivalent standard gamble technique differed as explained in part 4 from what were then the normal ways of measuring it. To an operationist this different estimation method *defines* a different utility index from a classical utility index estimated by asking people to introspect on their riskless intensity of preference. Operationist sentiments are to be found in *eg* Strotz (1953). Savage (1954) made elliptical comments in the operationist direction in conjunction with his distress that von Neumann and Morgenstern were unable to agree with him on rationality of NM utility when it excludes risk attitude, secondary satisfactions. He is close to seeing the role of risky acts in von Neumann and Morgenstern and Ramsey's standard gamble techniques as not merely offering a different way of measuring the old utility concept, but of creating a new utility concept.

> "It seems mystical ... to talk about [utility] apart from probability and having done so, doubly mystical to postulate that this undefined quantity serves as utility", Savage (1954, p94)
>
> The probability-less idea of utility in economics has been completely discredited in the eyes of almost all economists ... by Pareto", Savage (1954, p96)

Savage is here close to fusing objects (risky options) that can be used to estimate a utility index with the concept being estimated. Pareto would not have agreed with Savage's appeal to his work on ordinal utility as discrediting cardinal utility. For it was Pareto who observed that ordinal utility suffices for rationally deciding among some probability less (*ie* certain) options, but that classical cardinal utility is required for rationally deciding among other probability less (certain) options, *eg* options concerning government income redistribution, Allais (1979a, p510).

In the same year Ellsberg (1954) more explicitly than Savage, criticised von Neumann and Morgenstern for being insufficiently operationist. Ellsberg argued that von Neumann and Morgenstern were mistaken in describing their measurement proposal as a more respectable method of estimating the riskless classical utility index. Ellsberg quoted operationist Bridgman's view that different operations only define the same concept if "they give, within experimental error, the same numerical results in the domain in which the two sets of operations may be both applied", Ellsberg (1954, p548). Von Neumann and Morgenstern's error, according to

Ellsberg is to perceive their proposal of measuring utility via the certainty equivalence version of the standard gamble as merely a technique for *estimating* NM utility, when in fact, according to Ellsberg, their proposal *defines* NM utility.

Ellsberg, like Bridgman, has here confused methods of estimating a concept with the concept itself. While concepts are not entirely independent of ways of estimating or measuring them, they are somewhat independent.[12] There is, for instance, more than one way to measure a person's height in centimetres: (i) estimate that person's difference in height from someone whose height you know; (ii) measure that person's with a ruler; (iii) estimate that person's height from his known weight and fatness *etc.* Not all these ways are equally accurate, nor are all available in all circumstances. But notwithstanding all the possible differences in how the height in centimetres is obtained, all estimate the same concept. Ellsberg, like Bridgman, had committed the operationist fallacy.

In any case, Ellsberg's argument does not stand. EU itself does not say how NM utility is to be measured, nor do any of the axiomatisations of the procedure suggested to date. All methods applicable to estimating NM utility are applicable to estimating the identical construct when it is instead called classical utility. (And of course, whatever the index is called, the problems with each particular estimation method remain. Changing the name of the utility index does not mitigate or worsen any of these problems.)

6. The Operationist Fallacy of Risk Attitude as in NM Utility

Schoemaker and many others writing in the late 1970s and early 1980s extol Ellsberg and others who in the 1950s put the above operationist case for distinguishing between NM and classical utility.[13] Not aware that Ellsberg's reasoning was faulty, because operationism itself is fallacious, such scientists have presumed that Ellsberg was pointing to a real difference between the classical and NM concepts of utility. Schoemaker presumed that what Ellsberg was saying was that NM utility was not riskless, but included secondary satisfactions — (relative) risk attitude.[14]

---

[12] For a critique of operationalism, see *eg* Peter Caws (1959).

[13] This does not mean that everyone agreed with Ellsberg. Paul Samuelson for instance told me that he did not feel this paper helped understanding forward. But those who differed with Ellsberg do not appear to have put their disagreement in print to influence a wider circle and the next generation

[14] That NM includes risk attitude is in *eg* Dyer and Sarin 1982, Camacho 1979, p216 and 1983, p364 Bernard 1984, p97, Krzysztofowicz 1983 (but not Krzysztofowicz 1987 and 1990), Fishburn 1988 and 1989, Watson and Buede 1987.

This is a misconstrual of what Ellsberg said. Ellsberg is explicit that NM utility excludes secondary satisfactions — *ie* risk attitude — which he denotes by the words the utility of gambling (1954, p537, p543).[15] But by the 1970s the words utility of gambling had largely dropped out of usage making it hard for Schoemaker and others to realise that Ellsberg said this. Indeed inspection of Luce and Raiffa (1957) reveals that even by the later 1950s, the fact that risk attitude and utility of gambling were synonyms had been largely lost.

In von Neumann and Morgenstern (1944, 1947, 1953 and 1972) and general usage, the words utility of gambling (secondary satisfactions) referred to sources of welfare excluded under EU. Just as Christianity more readily eclipsed paganism by having a feast of Christmas at the time of a big Pagan feast, so Friedman and Savage (1948) proposed that the concept of the utility of gambling be eclipsed and EU better accepted by the words utility of gambling being given a new meaning for something that EU includes, namely the effect of the concavity of its "as if certain" NM utility function in rendering the value of an actuarially fair risky act inferior to a sure act whose outcome was the expectation of the actuarially fair act. This effect is indirect, via the probability weights used to aggregate the different possible "as if certain" NM utilities of the actuarially fair act into its overall value. The Friedman-Savage proposal to change the denotation of the words utility of gambling did not take hold.

One reason for this name change not taking hold was two years later, in his conversion to EU, Marschak (1950) proposed a related name change, and thereby inadvertently, the eclipse of the original concept of risk aversion. Hitherto risk aversion had denoted a negative secondary satisfaction, namely a systematic dislike of deviation from central tendency measured *eg* by range, mean deviation, variance. Friedman and Savage (1948) had claimed such a dislike was included in EU, and criticized Marschak (1937) and Tintner (1942) for thinking that EU was too narrow because it excluded this negative satisfaction. Marschak thought that the Friedman and Savage (1948) criticism of him was just and converted to EU. Marschak thus thought he was merely re-expressing the concept of risk aversion, when he in fact re-defined it to mean the concavity of its "as if certain" NM utility function. It was only later, notably with Schneeweiß (1967, 1968a, 1968b, 1972a and 1972b) accompanied by a pair of *Review of Economic Studies* papers, Borch (1969) and Feldstein (1969) that it became generally acknowledged among decision theorists that Marschak (1937) and Tintner (1942) had been correct, *ie* that Friedman and Savage (1948) had made statistical / mathematical errors in concluding that this negative secondary satisfaction of a dislike of systematic deviations from central tendency was included in EU.

---

[15] In an earlier critique of operationism and of the new view that NM utility included risk attitude, Pope 1983, this author incorrectly inferred that Ellsberg's views were as indicated in Schoemaker 1982, Pope 1983.

The confusing proposal of Marschack for this name change and eclipse of the concept of a dislike of deviations from central tendency however was by then too firmly entrenched for it to be reversed by these revelations that it entered via an error. It had by then become enshrined in the Arrow-Pratt risk aversion measures. Its continued usage will have contributed to Schoemaker and others misunderstanding what Ellsberg said about NM utility. If risk averse is in EU, it is understandable to think it is in its NM utility. But concave "as if certain" NM utility, is as Marschak explained in language adopted from Friedman and Savage (1948), "as if certain". The error of Friedman and Savage (1948) and of Marschak (1950) was not that of thinking that risk aversion was in NM utility. They were clear and precise and correct in understanding that it lay outside this "as if certain" mapping. Their error had merely been to think that this sort of systematic negative secondary satisfaction could be included in EU indirectly in how the utility numbers impacted with the aggregation probability weights in forming the overall value of a risky act.

An "as if certain" mapping excludes all secondary satisfactions (all aspects of risk attitude), except in the boundary case of certainty. In that boundary case of certainty, it sometimes includes illusory secondary satisfactions, as illustrated later in the paper. To understand that NM utility excludes all secondary satisfactions (all aspects of risk attitude), examine the EU property, *ie* the property that the utility of a risky act equates to its expected utility.

If for a risky act A there are two possible mutually exclusive outcomes, Y_i, i=1,2 occurring with probability p_i, and for sure acts B and C the outcomes are Y_1 and Y_2 respectively, then by the expected utility property:

$$\mathrm{V(A)} = \mathrm{U}(p_1, Y_1, p_2, Y_2) = p_1\mathrm{U}(Y_1) + p_2\mathrm{U}(Y_2), \quad (1)$$
$$\mathrm{V(B)} = \mathrm{U}(Y_1) \quad (2)$$
$$\mathrm{V(C)} = \mathrm{U}(Y_2) \quad (3)$$

Suppose now that the utility function U(Y) also includes risk attitude. From a comparison of (1) with (2) and (3), secondary satisfactions (risk attitude) cannot not enter the mapping from outcomes into utility numbers. The utility number U(Y_1) is identical under certainty in equation (2) and under risk in equation (1). Likewise the utility number U(Y_2) is identical under certainty in equation (3) and under risk in equation (1). If the mapping U(Y) includes secondary satisfactions (risk attitude), then the outcome space$Y$ itself must include sources of utility derived from Y denoting an *uncertain* money income. EU includes the sure acts A and B in its conceivable choice set where p_1=1, p_2=0, or vice-versa, hence Y must also include sources of utility derived from Y denoting certain money income, in which case V=U(Y). Further, the outcome space Y is uni-dimensional, there being only one Y symbol — hence Y must refer to sources of utility derived from certain and uncertain money income indiscriminately. But this assumes that U simultaneously includes and does not include risk attitude, for there is not a unique separation of the uncertain situation into probabilities and Y's.

It follows that the function $U(Y)$ includes only strength of preference for the consequences under certainty, as explained by Friedman and Savage in their 1948 statement on this function quoted earlier, and largely reproduced in different (constant acts) terminology in Savage (1954).[16] Thus Schoemaker is not correct in thinking that classical and NM utility differ in this respect.

7. Conflating Outcomes with their Utility Sources

The conflation of sources of utility from an outcome with the specification of the outcome itself has led some to propose that all that is required to incorporate secondary satisfactions within EU is to "elaborate" the outcomes to include the sources of these secondary satisfactions.[17] To see that such elaborations give rise to contradictions, take Harry Markowitz's delightful birthday gift example.

> "The assumption that, if outcome A is better than outcome B, then it is also better than having a 50-50 chance of A or B is not always true of human preferences. I may prefer to receive [a tie] for my birthday rather than [socks],[18] yet I may insist on not revealing my preferences so that I may be "surprised" when my birthday arrives. ...
>
> "The expected utility rule can be extended to incorporate considerations such as surprise, ... We could attach a different utility to asking for socks and getting them than is attached to wondering whether socks or ties are forthcoming and being pleasantly surprised to find the latter. ...
>
> "By thus elaborating the set of outcomes we can remove the differences between human preferences and the expected utility maxim."
>
> Markowitz (1959 pp225-6)

Harry Markowitz prefers the stochastically dominated option of a 50/50 chance of getting ties or socks by not revealing to his wife Barbara his preference for a tie, over the guarantee of a tie by revealing this preference beforehand, but thereby depriving himself of wonder and surprise.[19] Let us denote his outcome space Y

---

[16] The constant acts terminology, unbeknowns to Savage, is only identical to choice under certainty in the absence of secondary satisfactions stemming from certainty effects, a class of effects that Savage himself overlooked, and led to the irrationality in his sure-thing principle for clarifying preferences for a chooser unsure of his preference ordering of acts (Pope 1991a, 2004).

[17] Similar elaboration proposals are made with respect to other factors currently excluded under the expected utility procedure, *eg* the choice set dependent utilities highlighted in Black (1986) and Sen (1993, 2002). Such proposed elaborations would give rise to analogous contradictions to those traced in this paper.

[18] The preferences have been transposed to accord with those of Markowitz (1969, p226).

[19] With probability dependent utilities from outcomes, there must be a violation of stochastic dominance if the choice set is sufficiently restricted, though this is not widely recognised.

comprising individual outcomes denoted by lower case letters or strings of letters, y = s, es, ... , his NM utility mapping $\mathrm{U}^{\mathrm{NM}}(Y)$ and his individual NM utilities $\mathrm{U}^{\mathrm{NM}}(y)$. Under EU, his preference for t, the outcome of a tie, over s, the outcome of socks, can be stated as:

$$\mathrm{U}^{\mathrm{NM}}(t) > \mathrm{U}^{\mathrm{NM}}(s), \tag{4}$$

and his preference for the 50/50 chance of either can be stated as

$$0.5\mathrm{U}^{\mathrm{NM}}(t) + 0.5\mathrm{U}^{\mathrm{NM}}(s) > \mathrm{U}^{\mathrm{NM}}(t). \tag{5}$$

But (4) and (5) combined imply a violation of stochastic dominance, imply inadmissible preferences under EU. Markowitz proposed that he could avoid this preference for a dominated act and remain within EU were he to elaborate on the birthday gift outcome of a tie which he prefers over the alternative socks to include the wonder (beforehand) and the pleasant surprise (on learning the outcome is a tie), and similarly with the socks outcome, except that in that case the surprise is unpleasant.

SIMPLE OUTCOMES
t tie
s socks

In formulating his elaborated outcomes implicitly Harry Markowitz has as it were divided his future *epistemically*. He has divided his future *epistemically* from the point of having to make a decision (on whether to let his wife Barbara know his gift preference). He has divided this future into two mutually exclusive and exhaustive time periods demarcating the progress in his knowledge of it — demarcating the stages in, the evolution of, his *knowledge ahead*:

(i) $0 \leq t < K$, *a risky period of positive duration* when he will have made his decision but will not know its outcome, since he only learns this at $t = K$, a period which may be termed the ***pre-outcome period***;

and

(ii) $t \geq K$, *a risk-free period* when he will know the outcome of his decision, a period which may be termed the ***outcome period.***

Under EU every outcome must be condensable to a time-wise indecomposable entity. Each outcome enters the axioms and the expected utility property in this atemporal form. What therefore Harry Markowitz does is to *aggregate* the segment of his anticipated satisfactions before the risk has resolved, that of wonder in the pre-outcome period, when his *degree of knowledge ahead of the outcome* is limited. He has aggregated this segment of his elaborated outcome, with his anticipated satisfactions after the risk has resolved. After the risk is resolved, he anticipates his satisfactions from having a tie or socks, and also whether, as a consequence of having merely previously a limited knowledge ahead, he also anticipates the satisfactions of a surprise, pleasant if the outcome is better than what might have been, unpleasant if worse than what might have been.

TABLE 1. Example of elaborated "outcomes" with utilities

	pre-outcome period *utility*		*outcome period*
st sure of tie	know tie will come 20		tie that had known would come
ss sure of socks come	know socks will come 10		socks that had known would
et extra with tie	wonder 40	then	tie+ pleasant surprise
es extra with socks	wonder 20	then	socks+ *un*pleasant surprise

It would seem that Harry Markowitz has solved his dominance violation; for now with appropriate utility numbers attached to *st*, *ss*, *et* and *es* such as those of Table 1, his preferred 50/50 risky act stochastically dominates choosing a tie for sure.

Elaborating outcomes to include the effects of the chooser's *degree of knowledge ahead* of the act readily creates muddles and largely precludes using the outcomes space in a risky choice theory. For examples of the difficulties, see Pope (2004). Moreover, whiles the outcome of EU can contain many chronologically distinct time periods, none should occur before all risk is past, Samuelson (1952). Only Samuelson did not assess how his own elaborated outcomes proposal (made in the same paper) would introduce outcome segments prior to when all risk is past. He had not noticed this because he had not analysed when his instance of a secondary satisfaction, suspense, would occur. Suspense, like Markowitz's instance of wonder, is a secondary satisfaction that the chooser anticipates reaping *before* the outcome is known.

Rather than simply reporting the verdict of Samuelson that under EU the outcome must begin after all risk is past, it is instructive to prove that such is the case. There are many ways of showing the contradictions introduced into the dominance principle if there are outcome segments occurring before all risk is past. Below is one method with a *Reductio ad Absurdum* line of reasoning in the case of EU. We initially assume that the elaborations with an outcome segment prior to when all risk is past conform to EU and so denote the NM mapping. Let Markowitz prefer a 70% chance of getting a tie and a 30% chance of socks, to a 50% chance of getting either. Then under EU with the elaborated "outcomes" and the notation of the above, we can write this preference as

$$0.5\mathrm{U}^{\mathrm{NM}}(et) + 0.5\mathrm{U}^{\mathrm{NM}}(es) < 0.7\mathrm{U}^{\mathrm{NM}}(et) + 0.3\mathrm{U}^{\mathrm{NM}}(es). \quad (6)$$

Under EU we can add to both sides of (6)

$$0.3\mathrm{U}^{\mathrm{NM}}(et) - 0.3\mathrm{U}^{\mathrm{NM}}(es) \tag{7}$$

yielding

$$0.8\mathrm{U}^{\mathrm{NM}}(et) + 0.2\mathrm{U}^{\mathrm{NM}}(es) < 1\mathrm{U}^{\mathrm{NM}}(et) \tag{8}$$

The problem with the right hand side of (8) is that it is a contradiction in terms. Markowitz cannot possibly have the wonder and surprise of this elaborated outcome *et* if sure of a tie. The number 1 preceding $\mathrm{U}^{\mathrm{NM}}(et)$ (usually left implicit) denotes full knowledge ahead of the outcome at the point of choice — excluding anticipating wondering what the outcome will be, and also excluding anticipating later being either pleasantly or unpleasantly surprised. Our initial assumption that such elaborations permit NM utilities $\mathrm{U}^{\mathrm{NM}}(et)$ and $\mathrm{U}^{\mathrm{NM}}(es)$ is disproved.

Like contradictions arise if instead of wonder and surprise, receipt of a desired loan is the elaborated "outcome" when the simple outcomes of the act of investing in a project are that her net profits make her wealthy or a pauper in a decision situation with features 1 and 2.

Feature 1: The investor gets the loan with which she boosts her consumption in the pre-outcome period if her loan default risk rate (her probability of being a pauper and unable to repay the loan) is under 16.7%, is rejected for a loan if her probability of nil returns from her project and being unable to repay is greater than 16.7 %.

Feature 2: the investor's two acts are investment projects with respectively a 0.7 and a 0.6 probability of her selected act yielding her net profits that make her wealthy rather than a pauper.

TABLE 2. Outcomes elaborated with loans obtained

		pre-outcome period		*outcome period*
sw	simply well-off from net profits	no loan		well-off from net profits
sp	simply pauper from net profits	no loan		pauper from net profits
lw	loan and well-off from net profits	loan	then	well-off from net profits + loan repaid
lp	loan and pauper from net profits	loan	then	pauper from net profits + loan not repaid

If EU permitted such an elaboration, we could express the investor's preference for the 0.7 probability over the 0.6 probability of having a loan and being well-off and otherwise having the loan and being a pauper as:

$$0.7\mathrm{U}^{\mathrm{NM}}(lw) + 0.3\mathrm{U}^{\mathrm{NM}}(lp) > 0.6\mathrm{U}^{\mathrm{NM}}(lw) + (0.4)\mathrm{U}^{\mathrm{NM}}(lp) \tag{9}$$

Under EU we can add to both sides of (9)

$$0.6\mathrm{U}^{\mathrm{NM}}(lp) - 0.6\mathrm{U}^{\mathrm{NM}}(lw) \tag{10}$$

yielding

$$0.9\mathrm{U}^{\mathrm{NM}}(lp) + 0.1\mathrm{U}^{\mathrm{NM}}(lw) > \mathrm{U}^{\mathrm{NM}}(lp) \tag{11}$$

The right hand side of (11) — a guarantee of being a pauper in the outcome period with having obtained a loan for the pre-outcome period— contradicts feature 1, that the investor gets a loan if and only if the probability of her being a pauper is less than 20%, and more fundamentally is inconsistent with the concept of a loan: the transfer of funds is only a loan if there is a positive possibility of its being repaid.[20] Our initial assumption that such elaborations permit NM utilities $\mathrm{U}^{\mathrm{NM}}(lw)$ and $\mathrm{U}^{\mathrm{NM}}(lp)$ is thus disproved. In addition, readers may notice that a like contradiction holds in (9) since the maximum default risk rate for obtaining a loan is less than her default risk rate of 30% on its left hand side, and less than her default risk rate of 40% on its right hand side.

8. Conflating Causes and Effects

The wonder and surprise or the house/loan elaborated "outcomes" proposals in fact amount to replacing the outcomes by their utility sources (or consequences) based on degrees of *knowledge ahead.* To avoid EU running into the contradictions demonstrated in part 7, Markowitz (1994) advocates that the use of elaborated "outcomes" be restricted to subsets of the probability distribution function with constant levels of secondary satisfactions. For instance in the birthday gift example, the elaborated "outcomes" would seem to be compatible with EU if EU were restricted to the subset of the probability distribution functions within which the change in probabilities does not significantly affect the level of secondary satisfactions derived from the wondering and surprise. Again in the loan example the elaborated "outcomes" might seem to be compatible with EU if EU were restricted to subsets of the probability distribution function within which loan size, repayment cost and loan eligibility are the same.

Such restrictions might seem to allow EU to operate over limited domains. For instance, in the above birthday gift example EU could remain plausible between 50/50 and 70/30 mix in favour of ties if over this segment of the probability distribution domain the amounts of secondary satisfactions derived from wonder and pleasant/unpleasant surprises are the same. EU might only seem to be operational over a null domain if instead people's secondary satisfactions derived

---

[20] The above is an alternative proof to the accounts of the incompatibility of the redefined "outcomes" with the distinctive features of the expected utility procedure in Pope (1984, pp261-2, 1988, 1991b, pp130-132 and 2000).

from wonder and surprise utility varies discernibly with each change in the ties/socks probability mix.

Again in the above loan example there is a segment of the probability distribution domain above the 16.7% probability of a loan default risk (through being a pauper). It might seem that EU could operate in this probability range since it was postulated that above this probability mix the housing loan is completely unavailable. There would also be another segment of the probability distribution domain above this cut-off probability mix in which it might seem that EU could operate since in the above example above this mix the loan is available at a constant interest rate. EU might only seem to be operational over a null domain set if instead people are offered a different housing loan interest rate for each change in the pauper/well-off probability mix. For practical normative purposes in modelling contingent loans and other secondary satisfactions, therefore, theories that can incorporate secondary satisfactions over the full range of probabilities are required.

These conclusions however would be fallacious. These conclusions ignore constraint (i) of the dominance principle and EU that outcomes be defined *independent of knowledge ahead.* As demonstrated earlier, in accord with Samuelson's insight (1952), this limits the outcome space to a time sequence of periods that begin after all risk is passed. But wonder is experienced before that, so has to be excluded, and so too is the loan, and so has to be excluded. To this author's knowledge, loans are never used to explain EU and the dominance principle, and the failure to use serious inter-temporal issues in vetting EU, EU+ and the dominance principle, is part of the reason for contentment with NM utility. Loans are nowadays used applying EU — but not with a check on whether such applications are consistent with the dominance principle and with EU.[21]

We also need to address a robust oral tradition that EU cannot include emotional secondary satisfactions, but that it can include any material and financial ones such as a loan.

9. Mistaking Utility in Supply-Demand Analysis for NM Utility

There are two different utility functions, 1 that of demand theory and 2 that of decision and game theory. There is a widespread notion that these are identical, that both map from the same outcome space into utilities. This is incorrect. The outcomes space of the utility function in (typical) demand theory excludes price (costs) since the budget / production costs, enter as separate constraints. In such analysis, lesson 1 is never mix up supply and demand, and it is an error in even talking about supply side factors such as loan availability and cost when mapping outcomes into utility. By contrast in decision and game theory, the outcomes

[21] A seminal early paper in this regard is Joseph Stigliz and A. Weiss 1981

include all the chooser's direct costs and the indirect (opportunity) costs / budget constraints enter the determination of what is an available act. The outcomes space that maps into NM utility thus includes not just *emotional* but also financial / material primary sources of positive and negative satisfactions.

10. Misconceiving Commitment in Extensive Form Games as EU Compatible

Some scientists who admit that EU cannot include emotional instances of secondary satisfactions like wonder are reluctant to conclude similarly for anything material or financial like a loan. Commitment is temporal. It involves agreeing to do something in the future, and if fulfilling that commitment involves a degree of *knowledge ahead* of the outcome on the part of any decision maker or other relevant party, then that commitment involves secondary satisfactions and lies outside EU and the dominance principle.

While therefore game theory is realistic in its current practice of modelling the secondary satisfactions of such commitment and its benefits, once commitment is modeled, any use of expectations and mixed strategies is within EU. Rather, game theory's realistic modeling of commitment violates that EU axiomatic base. That EU axiomatic base, as Savage (1954) and others have noted, requires acts (strategies) to be specified independently of *knowledge ahead*, in particular, independent of *knowledge ahead* of which act the decision maker will choose — and thus independent of loan acceptance or any other any act of commitment being known even to the chooser himself, let alone to any other player.

In accepting a loan now the borrower contingently commits to later repay. Contingent commitments involves knowledge ahead of the possibility of repaying, something that cannot be gauged from each outcome alone, only from the probability distribution of outcomes, only from *knowledge ahead*. Satisfactions from loans therefore lie outside EU

An alternative way of showing that EU excludes taking into consideration accepting a loan is to recall Samuelson's statements (1952), that EU's axioms require the outcomes to be exclusively *after* all risk is passed. But the effect of a loan is in general *before* the risk is passed. In the simplest risky cases, the loan is consumed or used in the pre-outcome period — *before* the risk is passed — and then contingently repaid in the post-outcome period — after the risk is passed. Having outcomes after all risk is passed also excludes investments not coupled with loans in that investments involve expenditures during the pre-outcome period before all risk is passed and the profitability known.[22]

---

[22] This as Walsh (1994) discerns, is what led Keynes to divide aggregate output into consumption production (riskless in his theory) and investment (risky), and led Walsh (1994) to identify the stages of knowledge ahead framework of Pope (1983) as the counterpart of Joan Robinson's contributions in tracing out the real time implications under certainty of Keynesian investment.

11. A Fully Described Decision Situation for use in a Game Theoretic Tree

Many decision scientists simply believe that by more fully describing the situation EU can include consideration of receiving a loan and all other instances of material secondary satisfactions. This for instance is a way of interpreting passages such as the below (other than as claiming that risk attitude is in the mapping from outcomes into utilities (a false account as a glance at equations (1) to (3) above demonstrates):

> EU is "justified [precisely because] the resulting [NM utility] function will incorporate the subject's attitude towards the whole gambling situation ... not only how the subject feels about the alternative ... outcomes", Luce and Raiffa 1957, p21 re-arranged.

Of course the decision situation can be ever more fully described. We can enlarge on the details in either decision theory with a single player our investor (leaving all others who interact with her in the category of random, choice set constraints) or with three players, our investor, her potential banker and a random player (nature). Let us do the latter, with enough details for every reader to compute for investor and banker the mapping from outcomes into an index of satisfactions when:

a) constrained by EU, termed (as throughout this paper), NM utilities, and

b) actual *ie* unconstrained by EU, and distinguished from 1 by being termed utils (not utilities)

Only for one of the two players in our scenario, do NM utilities and utils coincide — only for the banker (who for the sake of brevity is unrealistically modelled as suffering no planning problems from lending with merely contingent repayment).

Let us call our investor player I and her banker and potential lender player B. To differentiate the acts in the choice sets and decisions of the two parties, let us term the chooser's acts projects, and the banker's acts loans. Let the sequence of moves and nature's probabilities of its move be as in Figure 1, and the following be the case:

1 Our investor I and her banker B know the objective probabilities of all the projects available to our investor in her choice set, have common knowledge of all subsequent events, and know that each has such common knowledge.

2 There are two chronological time periods from the point of choice of our investor, denoted by subscripts 1 and 2. For neither player are satisfactions flows divided into smaller time segments than these two periods.

3 Our investor I is free to accept or reject loans available from her banker and repays any loan accepted if and only if her net project profits in period 2 are non-zero, repaying principal plus interest due up to what is payable out of her period 2 profits.

4 Our investor's potential banker B has 20€ cash at the time of choice which he must invest by lending part or whole to our investor, and placing the balance of

the 20€ in a safe project of his own. This safe project has a guaranteed net profit of zero. Loan regulations fix the interest charge at 20%, and give borrowers a choice between a small loan of 10€ and a big loan of 20€.

5 Each player has in each period a perishable endowment of consumable items that is between players and time periods non-transferable and that is consumed in the period it is acquired. Each player consumes an additional positive or negative amount of consumables purchased with C_i, i=1,2, their positive or negative cash flow in €. For our investor, in period 1, C_1 is the positive flow of any loan L received and in period 2, C_2 is the positive flow of any received net profits P minus the negative flow of any loan repayment R. For her banker, in period 1, C_1=0, and in period 2, C_2 is the positive flow of any received net profits P.

6 Each player has a zero time preference rate, and a piecewise linear, overall concave "as if certain" mapping from C_i, i=1,2 into a cardinal satisfactions index of utils U_i in each time period with respect to C.

For our investor I, this mapping is

$$U_i(C_i) = \begin{cases} 2C_i, C_i \leq 20 \\ 20 + C_i, C_i \geq 20 \end{cases} \tag{12}$$

For our her banker B, this mapping is,

$$U_i(C_i) = \begin{cases} 2C_i, C_i \leq 2 \\ 3 + \mathit{1/2}C_i, C_i \geq 2 \end{cases} \tag{13}$$

7 Each player has a zero time preference rate, and U, total utils from consumption additional to that from endowments in the two periods, of

$$\mathrm{U} = \mathrm{U}_1(C_1) + \mathrm{U}_2(C_2) \tag{14}$$

8 Each player chooses the act which maximises the expectation of equation (16), E[U], expected utils.

Then the bottom pair of rows of the Table in Figure 1 depicts respectively the outcomes under each possibility for our investor I and her banker B, while the upper pair of rows depicts respectively utils under each possibility of our investor I and her banker B. Note that the break-even likelihood of repayment that makes issuing a loan more attractive than not lending is in the case of the small loan, at a loan default risk x_s of just over 16%,

$$-20x_s + 4(1 - x_s) = 0 \rightarrow = 4/24 = 0.167 \tag{15}$$

The break-even likelihood of repayment that makes issuing a loan more attractive than not lending is in the case of the big loan, at a lower loan default risk x_b of just over 11%,

$$-40x_{\mathrm{b}} + 5(1 - x_{\mathrm{b}}) = 0 \rightarrow = 5/45 = 0.111 \tag{16}$$

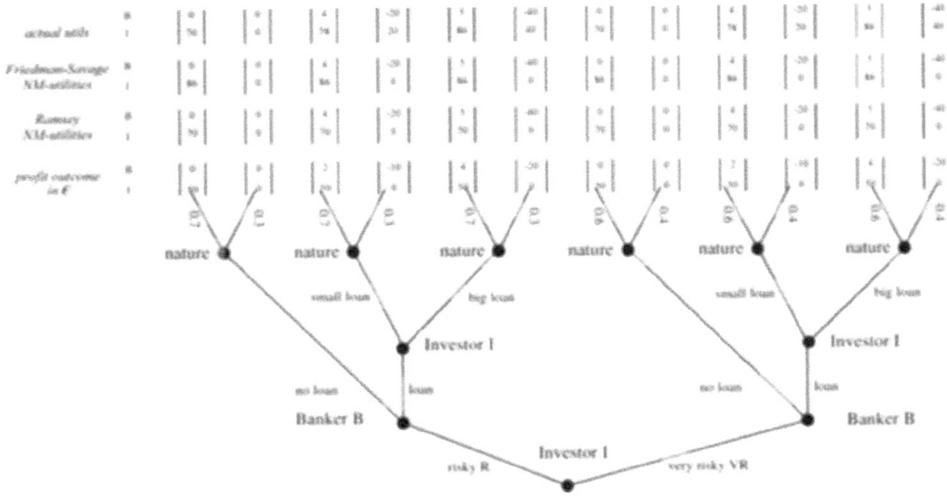

Figure 1. Game Theoretic Tree — The Conflict between our Investor's NM Utilities and her Actual Utils

(i) The outcome for investor I is net project profits in period 2

(ii) The outcome for banker B is net profits in period 2 on any loan issued

(iii) The profit outcome of the investor determines the profit outcome of the banker in the event that the banker lends since this determines whether he is repaid for the loan

(iv) NM and actual utilities are identical if and only if the player reaps zero secondary satisfactions (satisfactions from *knowledge ahead based* causes), as in the case of B, the banker, but not in the case of I, the project investor if she anticipates a loan. This asymmetry is because no commitment (*knowledge ahead*) is required of the banker in making a loan. By contrast, commitment is required of the borrower, in contracting to (contingently) repay

(v) The Friedman-Savage evaluation of outcomes as if certain implies evaluating each act by the Friedman-Savage NM utilities in its far right and far left branches. The Ramsey evaluation of outcomes independent of risk requires evaluating each act by its Ramsey NM utilities in its far left pair of branches. In this particular choice set these implausible procedures do not alter our investor's choice from that obtained by using actual utils and the reasonable branch, namely for each act the far left branch since she correctly anticipates the banker's decision not to lend. When the choice set is enlarged, this is no longer the case.

The inverse relation between loan size and loan default risk of our banker is replicated in the marketplace where it is in part due to lenders having a concave as if certain utility function for cash as in our example, in part due to factors outside our model.[23]

From figure 1 it can be seen our investor's banker has a negative expected utils from offering any sized loan under both her projects, he will choose not to issue her a loan. Our investor anticipates this, that neither of her projects meets his default requirements for even the small loan. Under neither act R nor act VR does she anticipate any secondary satisfactions from a loan. Her only anticipated satisfactions

[23] Factors outside our model also yielding this inverse relation include the borrower's negative satisfactions due to planning difficulties under risk and problems of dishonest borrowers when there is lack of common knowledge of the project investors' outcome.

are primary ones from each her two acts. The expected value of her risky act R is therefore a 70/30 mix of her actual utils in the first two columns of figure 1, the no loan columns of this act, namely $E[U(C_i)]=7*70= 49$. The expected value of her very risky act VR is therefore a 60/40 mix of her actual utils in the seventh and eighth columns of figure 1, the no loan columns of this act, namely $E[U(C_i)] = .6(70) = 42$. She chooses her stochastically dominating act R.

12. NM Utilities in our Fully Described Decision Situation

Both our investor and banker might seem to be obeying EU in that each party values each act as a probability weighted sum of its anticipated utils, and in *this* choice set chooses the stochastically dominant act, as would players obeying EU. This however is a peculiarity of the *particular* choice set, as will be seen in the next part of the paper where under a different choice set our investor makes a non-EU choice.

To obey EU as distinct from making a choice that merely in some choice sets coincides with EU, each party must also obey the NM utility mapping rules for all acts in all conceivable choice sets. Those NM mapping rules, shared in essentials by all theories within the EU+ class, must accord with the dominance principle set down in part 1 of this paper. Under the dominance principle's constraint, those NM mapping rules, (i) exclude *knowledge ahead* entering the specification of the outcome space, and thus exclude loans being part of the individual outcomes, and under that principle's constraint (ii), limit the sources of satisfactions that the chooser takes into account in mapping from outcomes into utilities to primary ones, and thus exclude any secondary source of satisfaction such as a loan.

In part 2 we discussed the recognition of Ramsey, von Neumann and Morgenstern, and Friedman and Savage that NM utility is riskless. As a riskless mapping, it restricts all of our investor's outcomes under all her conceivable acts to having an identical utility number regardless of whether under a particular act that outcome is risky (maybe so risky as to preclude her banker issuing a loan), or completely certain. The issue is therefore which way to adjust our banker's actual utils with a big small and no loan to all be the identical NM utility number to yield the identical utility under each of her two possible net profit outcomes.

It might seem that there is only one way of imposing this identity. But in fact there are two ways. On why there are no other feasible accounts of EU, see Pope (2004). The focus on lotteries instead of on serious decisions involving loans and the attempted flight from introspection into the preferences only approach have been two of the factors hampering scientists from realising that the Ramsey and

Friedman-Savage interpretations of how to implement the EU property are distinct, and that each involves a gulf between EU and reasonable decision making procedures.[24]

One way is that of Ramsey (1926, 1950), that each outcome be evaluated independent of secondary satisfactions, in which case under EU, our investor ignores any loan from her banker, the lower row in the third tier of Figure 1. The EU identity is preserved, but branches of the tree involving either the small or the big loan, the NM utilities understate actual satisfactions relative to those in the no loan branches.

The other way of adjusting each net profit outcome to have an identical utility with a zero, small and big capital input to yield the identical utility number is to evaluate each outcome as under classical utility, under certainty, or as Friedman and Savage (1948) put it, "as if certain". For the zero net profit outcome in period 2, Friedman-Savage NM utilities are computed as if certain at the time of choice, in which case our investor's banker will decide on no loan, and thus our investor is deemed to reap zero utils in period 1 (as well as none in the following period). Hence, regardless of whether this zero net profit outcome of period 2 is or is not preceded by a loan in period 1, Friedman-Savage NM utilities for our investor are calculated as zero. These erroneous attributions for the hypothetical cases of a loan are in columns 4, 6 and 10, 12 in the lower row of the second pair of rows in figure 1.

For the 50€ net profit outcome in period 2, Friedman-Savage NM utilities computed as if certain at the time of choice, mean that our investor computes these utilities as if her potential banker were to face a zero risk of zero net profits and that she will have available to her the optimal sized loan, namely the big one. Under this way of conforming to the EU restriction that our investor's utility from a 50€ net profit outcome be identical no matter how risky the embedding act, illusory loans or illusorily large loans will be attributed in those situations in which the risk of default associated with the outcome is too high for our investor's potential banker to offer the big loan. These erroneous attributions are shown in the odd numbered columns in the lower row of the second pair of rows in Figure 1, and cause our investor to overestimate the value of acts R and VR.

---

[24] I am indebted to Ken Arrow and Roy Radner for the information that scientists had not noticed the difference, and hence sometimes switched from one interpretation to the other (as can be seen from a comparison of Marschak (1950) with Marschak and Radner (1972) regarding the two as denoting an identical interpretation. For readers interested in a choice set where the Ramsey and Friedman-Savage versions of NM utilities yield different choices, see Pope (2004).

Note that the Friedman-Savage way of evaluating each outcome as if certain means that our investor calculates contrary to the postulated cause-effect chains of Figure 1. She combines for each act a no loan branch for the zero outcome with the big loan branch for the 50€ net profit outcome. This is despite the fact that in the cause effect chains of the scenario when her banker chooses dictate that loan size is in reality the same for both ensuing branches. It is thus sheer chance that in this particular choice set, such an implausible procedure of ignoring the actual cause-effect chains yields the same outcome as our investor's own reasonable procedure.[25] Since our investor is reasonable and anticipates no loan (due to neither project having a low enough loan default risk, the branches of the tree with the erroneous NM utility attributions with a loan under both the Ramsey and the Friedman-Savage way are irrelevant to her evaluations of acts R and VR and neither results in an implausible choice.

13. The Game Tree's Four Tiers at Each End Point

For each player, the game theoretic tree here presented thus has four tiers at each end-point, instead of the normal single tier of pay-offs (utilities). The first three tiers of payoffs are the:

1 actual utils
2 Friedman-Savage NM "as if certain" NM utilities
3 Ramsey independent of risk NM utilities

The fourth tier contains the outcomes. These are normally omitted under EU and game theory based on it, since as Harsanyi (1974) observes, under EU there is a one-to-one correspondence between sure acts, outcomes and their utilities. This one-to-one correspondence can be seen in comparing tier 4 with EU tiers 2 and 3. It also holds in the case of our investor's potential banker for tier 1. This one-to-one correspondence between sure acts, outcomes and their utilities is missing from the non EU tier 1 for our investor, broken by her secondary satisfactions in those cases in which the outcome in period 2 is preceded by a loan in period 1.

Our investor anticipates a loan (and thus reaping the secondary satisfactions from it) because she anticipates how her banker's *degree of knowledge ahead* of the distribution of her *chosen* project's profits determines her loan. Her loan is a secondary satisfaction since knowledge ahead of the chosen act causes the *effect* of obtaining or being refused the loan. The discrepancies between our investor's utils

---

[25] Our investor is reasonable and anticipates no loan (due to her not having a low enough loan default risk). Hence the branches of the tree with the Friedman-Savage "as if certain" erroneous utility attributions for zero profits with a loan are irrelevant to our investor's evaluations of acts R and VR, and from a 50€ net profit the the Friedman-Savage "as if certain" NM utilities overestimate the better outcome of each act by an identical amount and this also, in this particular choice set, does not cause an implausible choice.

under tiers 1, 2 and 3 indicate that in alternative choice sets, one of which is analysed in the next part of the paper, choices will differ depending on whether in forming an expectation player 1 uses her actual levels of satisfaction, *ie* uses tier 1, or whether she uses one of the EU constrained utilities, those tier 2 or those of tier 3. The discrepancies between tiers 2 and 3 indicate that there will be choice sets in which the two ways of imposing the EU constraint of identical utilities from outcomes under risk and certainty yield two different implied EU choices.

By contrast, our investor's banker's decision, taken after *already knowing which act our investor has chosen*, involves no secondary satisfactions *per se*. His net profits under each state of nature can be specified independently of his own or anybody else's *knowledge ahead*. Thus in our scenario the banker's actual utilities stand in a one-to-one correspondence with his net profit outcomes, and are identical as regards his actual utils and his utilities under EU constraints in both tiers 2 and tier 3.

14. An Enlarged Choice set

EU was devised to justify mixed strategies in game theory, Selten (2001). To be a justification, a decision maker obeying EU must not only make the plausible choice in the above situation in which choice of the statistically dominating risky act R *happens* to be the plausible choice over very risk act VR. A decision maker obeying EU must also give the plausible choice in every other conceivable choice set. Numerous of these conceivable choice sets involve player 1 choosing a stochastically dominated act in order to get a capital input form player 2 (analogous to a loan), something that EU precludes. Figure 2 depicts two extra branches added to the tree when two other acts, LR, less risky, with a 0.9 probability of 30€, otherwise nil, and UR, ultra risky, with a .45 probability of 80€, otherwise nil, are added to the choice set. For each player, its fourth pair of rows denotes these possible outcomes and their associated probabilities, while its top pair of rows denotes actual utils under each possibility of each act.

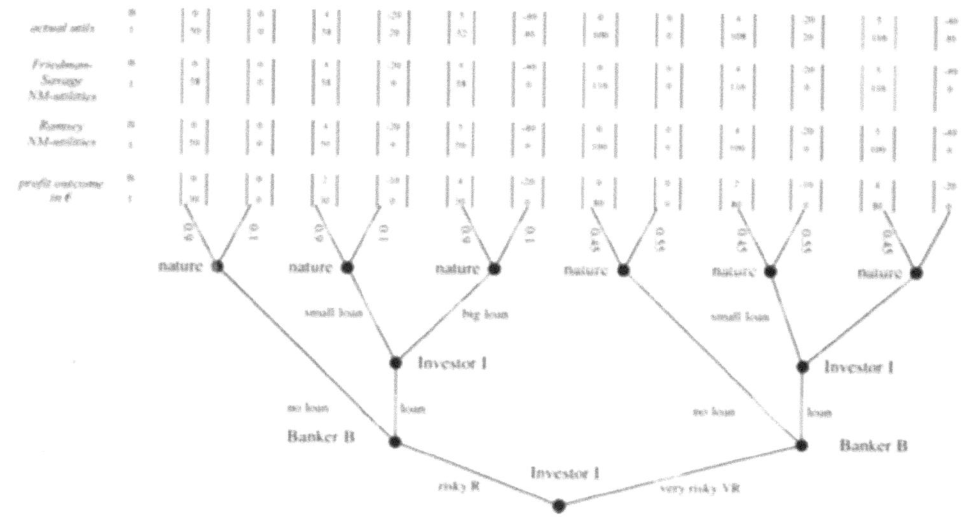

Figure 2. Extra branches of the Tree if Acts LR and UR are available.

Note: Of player 1's four acts LR has under its middle branch the highest expected actual utils, is available given her sufficiently low risk of loan default, and is her reasonable choice. Friedman-Savage evaluation of outcomes as if certain implies evaluating each act by the Friedman-Savage NM utilities in its far right and far left branches. This results in UR appearing to have the highest expected utility amongst the four acts and the choice. The Ramsey evaluation of outcomes independent of risk requires evaluating each act by its Ramsey NM utilities in its far left pair of branches. This results in act R appearing to have the highest expected utility.

Under act LR our investor has only a 10% risk of zero profits (analogous to only a 10% risk of defaulting on a loan repayment). This renders it attractive to her banker to offer both the small and the big loan. Both are attractive to her banker since, as can be seen from and (17), his cut-offs are just over a 16% risk of loan default on the small loan, equation (16) above, and just over an 11% risk of loan default for the big one, equation (18) above. Our investor's concave utils function renders both inputs attractive to her compared to not getting a loan at all, and the small loan more attractive to her than the big one. Thus the small loan is the one that she would accept under the less risky act LR. E[U(LR), her expected utils from this act are thus 9(58)+.1(20)=52.2+2=54.2. Under ultra risky act UR her risk of zero profits risk is too high for any sized loan so she anticipates none. E[U(UR), her expected utils from this act are thus .45(100)=45, and of her four acts, LR has the highest expected utils and is her choice.

Contrast this reasonable plausible choice with how EU with its NM utilities constraint would have our investor choose. For her less risky act LR, Friedman-Savage NM utilities, by falsely imputing no loan in the case of a zero net profit outcome, give it a *lower* value than is the case, putting that act's expectation as E[U(LR)=.9(58)=52.2. For her ultra risky act UR, Friedman-Savage NM utilities, by falsely imputing the big loan in the case of the 80€ net profit outcome, give it a *higher* value than is the case. Friedman-Savage NM utilities put the expectation of UR at E[U(UR)=.45(40+116)=70.2. But 70.2 is a higher expectation than under any of her three other acts, and thus under Friedman-Savage NM utilities, in the expanded choice set, UR is the act that she chooses.

For her ultra risky act UL, Ramsey NM utilities in ignoring any loan yield an accurate valuation, since no capital input is in fact available, and calculate that act's expectation as 45 utils. For her less risky act LR, Ramsey NM utilities give it a *lower* value than is the case, by ignoring the small loan (and the big one) available to her and that she accepts. Ramsey NM utilities put the expectation of LR at E[U(LR)=.9(38)=34.2. But 45 and 34.2 are both lower expectation than act R's expectation of 49, and thus under Ramsey NM utilities, in the expanded choice set, act R is chosen.

In summary, with the expanded choice set, our investor's reasonable choice is the less risky act LR. Her choice under Friedman-Savage NM utilities is the ultra risky act UR because of an illusory imputation of a loan under this act which in fact carries too high a default risk to enable her a loan. Her choice of the risky act R under Ramsey NM utilities differs from that of Friedman-Savage, and is similarly implausible and unreasonable because in evaluating act LR, Ramsey NM utilities ignore the loan and its attendant positive secondary satisfactions that our investor reaps as a consequence of LR having a low enough default risk for her banker to offer the small loan that she accepts.

The game tree then, when its payoffs (utilities) obey the constraints of NM utilities in how EU maps from outcomes into utilities involves at best an arbitrary implausible and unreasonable treatment of secondary satisfactions. EU excludes them entirely under the Ramsey way of imposing these constraints. Under the alternative Friedman-Savage way, EU sometimes excludes them when they are present, sometimes imputes them when they are absent.

15. Cause, Effect and Time under Risk

What has gone wrong is that under EU, standard game theory and other theories endorsing the dominance principle, there is a failure to discern the fundamental role of time in experiences of risk. As a consequence this class of theories employs an inherently static atemporal framework as regards stages of *knowledge ahead.* All its multiple periods, are in the terminology of this paper post-outcome periods, periods *after* all risk will be passed.

As regards the cause effect chains that a reasonable decision theory should take into account, there is in this class of theories a confusion of acts, which are the initiating causes, with outcomes that are the probabilistically anticipated proximate effects of acts. If there were a simple single linear transmission through the individual outcomes to satisfaction levels, utils in the terminology of this paper, as occurs under certainty, this class of theories might be adequate.

But for the cause effect chains distinctive to risk, this is not the case. These are the chains in which the degree of *knowledge ahead* of a relevant party matters for satisfactions. Satisfactions sensitive to *degree of knowledge ahead* may be termed risk attitude, or in the terminology of this paper, secondary satisfactions. Secondary satisfactions spring not from outcomes alone, but from *degrees of knowledge ahead* of the outcome. *Degree of knowledge ahead of* the outcome depends on which act embeds an outcome. The causal impact of the embedding act is therefore necessary information in attributing a satisfactions level to an outcome.

But information about the act underlying an outcome is excluded under the dominance principle constraint of a one-to-one correspondence between outcomes, sure acts and the chooser's satisfactions level (utility number) under which risky acts are probability mixes of sure acts. Breaking this one-to-one correspondence involves making the proper cause-effect distinction between acts and outcomes. Outcomes are probabilistic effects of causes, *ie* act*s*.For clear thinking, outcomes should be specified independently of *knowledge ahead.* Acts by contrast involve a *degree of knowledge ahead* of the outcome.

A sure act involves full, 100% *knowledge ahead* of the outcome. A risky act involves limited, merely probabilistic, *knowledge ahead* of the outcome. This contrasting degree of *knowledge ahead* should be included in how any reasonable decision theory specifies these two sorts of acts. It is not merely absent, but contradicted, when a risky act (which implies not knowing the outcome) is defined as a probability mix of two distinct sure acts (each of which implies that the outcome is known with certainty as a distinct outcome value, ie the outcome is known for certain to be two mutually exclusive values). Yet this is how EU defines risky acts. See *eg* Harsanyi (1986, pp22-23).

The EU specification of a risky act thus involves the inadvertent contradictions of 1) simultaneously assuming that the chooser knows and does not know the outcome, and 2) knowing that two mutually exclusive outcomes will occur. These contradictions are what thwarted von Neumann and Morgenstern in their quest to introduce secondary satisfactions and go beyond EU. These two scientists discerned that secondary satisfactions involve mutually exclusive outcomes interacting when more than one of them is a possibility. In three of the four risky acts that we considered in parts 10 to 13 of this paper, the possibility of a zero net profit outcome interacted with (prevented) player 1 from getting a desired capital input from player 2 under the possibility of a good net profit outcome. How, these two scientists asked, can mutually exclusive outcomes like good and zero net profits interact? Such interaction was, they deemed, a contradiction that they could not solve "on this level", and left to future researchers to resolve (1947, 1953 and 1972, pp628-32).

The higher level that eluded von Neumann and Morgenstern is to introduce the anticipated *change in knowledge ahead* distinctive of risk illustrated in this paper, Pope (1985). This involves dividing the future from the point of choice into two periods as regards the chooser's degree of knowledge ahead. EU includes the post-outcome period, the more distant part of the future when there will be *full knowledge ahead*, when the risk will be passed. What EU and all theories adhering to the dominance principle, omit is the earlier part of the future following choice of a risky act. This earlier part of the future is here termed the pre-outcome period. During the pre-outcome period, the mutually exclusive outcomes can — without contradiction — interact and generate sources of secondary satisfactions. If their interaction is favourable, there are positive secondary satisfactions during the pre-outcome period, *eg* through the distribution of outcomes being such that the risk of zero profits (loan default risk) is low enough that the chooser enjoys a capital input (a loan). If instead the interaction of these mutually exclusive outcomes is unfavourable, *eg* through the distribution of outcomes being such that the risk of zero profits (loan default risk) is too high for the chooser to be offered a desired capital input (loan), then the chooser misses out on the secondary satisfaction of additional cash in the pre-outcome period.

For reasonable choice, choosers anticipate events in both their pre-outcome period and their post-outcome period, and take both sets of events into account in putting a value on each possible outcome of an act. Doing so requires something excluded under EU and other theories imposing the dominance principle. It requires having some of the multiple periods of an outcomes space to begin before all risk is passed. In starting the outcomes flow earlier, we can still follow the clarity principle of specifying outcomes independent of *knowledge ahead* of any relevant party and hence of which act will be chosen. In starting the outcomes flow earlier, we avoid the endowments contrivance of assumptions 1-8 above, in which the outcomes are only defined as net profits in the post-outcome period 2, and in which the chooser is kept alive up to when all risk is passed via "endowments" not defined as outcomes and thus as outside the specification of acts.[26] Those endowments can be specified independent of *knowledge ahead*, yet with those occurring during the pre-outcome period included in the specification of the outcomes.

---

[26] This endowments contrivance amongst scientists seeking to grapple with positive and negative secondary satisfactions such as planning problems has a long history. It began in the 1960s as far as the author is aware, and continues up into the discerning analysis of this problem in Kreps and Porteus (1979?). But it is, to say the least, artificial to keep endowments outside the specification of acts, and severely restricts the generality of the problems decision theory can address!

16. Conclusions

This paper has argued that there are flaws in both the early and more recent lines of reasoning about the role of risk in NM utility, and that in fact this index is riskless. In turn, this implies that in its treatment of risk, EU and standard game theory are less general than many previously thought, and correspondingly less appealing as a normative decision model. EU's inclusion of risk considerations is limited to that discerned by Bernoulli and Cramer and illustrated in Friedman and Savage's famous 1948 diagram, namely to the indirect effect on risk taking arising from diminishing marginal utility when alternative outcomes are aggregated using probability weights to form an overall value of a risky act. That aggregation is an atemporal aspect of the process of valuing an act. It occurs after a utility number (satisfaction level) has been attributed to the experiences anticipated to occur temporally after that act is chosen.

In evaluating the experiences anticipated to occur temporally after that act is chosen, it has been shown that EU and all dominance preserving theories are restricted to experiences after all risk is passed. In turn this means that EU and this whole class of theories employ preference ordering and consistency requirements that are defined over an implausibly small sub-set of the sources of utility relevant to rational decision making and well-being. It excludes the entire class of secondary satisfactions, an emotional instance of which is satisfaction from wonder, and a material instance of which is satisfaction from being able to commit and obtain a loan.

Decision models designed to aid in rational decision making and in promoting well-being should have preference ordering and consistency requirements defined so as to include secondary satisfactions, that is satisfactions stemming from sources of utility based on relevant parties' degree of knowledge ahead, not just primary satisfactions, that is satisfactions from sources *independent of knowledge ahead*, independent of probabilities. The evolving stages of *knowledge ahead* framework required to consistently discern and include secondary satisfactions has been illustrated. For further details, see Pope (1983, 1995).

The paper has shown that such secondary satisfactions cannot be grafted onto EU by elaborating "outcomes" to overcome violations of the dominance principle and include the full set of sources of utility relevant to rational decision making and well-being. Such elaborations contradict the *knowledge ahead* independence features of EU and other theories obeying the dominance principle. Decision trees can be used to illustrate secondary satisfactions. Detailed modeling of the full decision situation via extensive form games can be used to show the contradictions between the use of commitment in game theory and its appeal to EU in employing analyzing mixed strategies.

References

Allais, M. and O. Hagen (eds), 1979, *Expected Utility Hypotheses and the Allais Paradox: Contemporary Discussions of Decisions under Uncertainty with Allais' Rejoinder*, Theory and Decision Library, **21**, Reidel, Dordrecht.

Allais, M., 1988, 'The General Theory of Random Choices in Relation to the Invariant Cardinal Utility Function and the Specific Probability Function: The (U, q) Model: A General Overview', in Bertrand Munier (ed), *Risk, Decision and Rationality*, Reidel, Dordrecht, 231-289.

Aumann, R.J., 1971, Letter from Robert Aumann to Leonard Savage, 8 January, in Drèze, Jacques H., 1987 Essays on Economic Decisions Under Uncertainty, (Cambridge University Press, Cambridge), 76-78, and in R.J. Aumann, 1997 Collected Papers 1, (Massachusetts Institute of Technology Press, Cambridge), 305-306.

Baumol, William J., 1951, 'The Neumann-Morgenstern Utility Index - An Ordinalist View', *Journal of Political Economy*, LIX, 61-66.

Baumol, William J., 1958, 'The Cardinal Utility which is Ordinal', *Economic Journal*, LXVIII(272), 665-672.

Bernard, Georges, 1984, 'On Utility Functions. The Present State', *Theory and Decision*, 17, 97-100.

Black, Max, 1986, 'Some Questions About Bayesian Decision Theory', in L. Daboni, A. Montesano and M. Lines (eds), *Recent Developments in the Foundations of Utility and Risk Theory*, D. Reidel, Dordrecht, 57-66.

Borch, Karl Henrik, 1969, 'A Note on Uncertainty and Indifference Curves', *Review of Economic Studies*, **36** (1), 1-4.

Camacho, A., 1979, 'Maximizing Expected Utility and the Rule of Long Run Success', in M. Allais and O. Hagen (eds), *Expected Utility Hypotheses and the Allais Paradox: Contemporary Discussions of Decisions under Uncertainty with Allais' Rejoinder*, D. Reidel, Dordrecht, 203-222.

Camacho, A., 1983, 'Cardinal Utility and Decision Making under Uncertainty', in B. Stigum and F. Wenstøp (eds), *Foundations of Utility and Risk Theory with Applications*, D. Reidel, Dordrecht, 347-370.

Canaan, Edwin, 1926, reprinted 1963, 'Profit', in Henry Higgs (ed), *Palgrave's Dictionary of Political Economy*, Augustus M. Kelley, New York, 222-224.

Caws, Peter, 1959, "Definition and Measurement in Physics", in C. West Churchman and Philburn Ratoosh, *Measurement: Definitions and Theories*, Wiley, New York.

Chechile, R.A., and A.D.J. Cooke, 1997, "An Experimental Test of a Generic Class of Utility Models: Evidence for Context Dependency.", Journal of Risk and Uncertainty 14, pp. 75-93.

Chechile, R.A., and R.D. Luce, 1999, "Reanalysis of the Chechile-Cooke Experiment: Correcting for Mismatched Gambles.", Journal of Risk and Uncertainty, 18, pp. 321-325.

Drummond, Michael F., Bernie J. O'Brien, Greg L. Stoddart and George W, Torrance, 1997, *Methods for the Economic Evaluation of Health Care Programmes*, 2nd edition, Oxford University Press, Oxford.

Dyer, James S. and Rakesh K. Sarin, 1979a, 'Measurable Multiattribute Value Functions', *Operations Research*, 27(4), 810-822.

Dyer, James S. and Rakesh K. Sarin, 1979b, 'Group Preference Aggregation Rules Based on Strength of Preference', *Management Science*, 25(9), 822-832.

Dyer, James S. and Rakesh K. Sarin, 1982, 'Relative Risk Aversion', *Management Science*, 28(8), 875-886.

Ellsberg, Daniel, 1954, "Classic and Current Notions of 'Measurable Utility'", *Economic Journal*, 64(Sept.), 528-556.

Feldstein, Martin S., 1969, 'Mean-Variance Analysis in the Theory of Liquidity Preference and Portfolio Selection', *Review of Economic Studies*, **36**, 5-12.

Fishburn, Peter C., 1970, *Utility Theory for Decision Making*, John Wiley & Sons, Inc., New York.

Fishburn, Peter C., 1976, 'Cardinal Utility: An Interpretive Essay', *Rivista internazionale di scienze economiche e commerciali. International review of economics and business*, 23, 1102-1114.
Fishburn, Peter C., 1988, *Nonlinear Preference and Utility Theory,* John Hopkins University Press, Baltimore.
Fishburn, Peter C., 1989, 'Retrospective on the Utility Theory of von Neumann and Morgenstern', *Journal of Risk and Uncertainty*, 2(2), 127-158.
Friedman, Milton and L. J. Savage, 1948, 'The Utility Analysis of Choices Involving Risk', *Journal of Political Economy*, LVI(4), 279-304.
Friedman, Milton and L. J. Savage, 1952, 'The Expected-Utility Hypothesis and the Measurability of Utility', *Journal of Political Economy*, LX(6), 463-474.
Harsanyi, John C., 1983, 'Use of Subjective Probabilities in Game Theory', in B. Stigum and F. Wenstøp (eds), *Foundations of Utility and Risk Theory with Applications*, Reidel, Dordrecht, 297-310.
Harsanyi, J., 1986, *Rational Behavior and Bargaining Equilibrium in Games and Social Situations*, Cambridge University Press, New York.
Hicks, J.R., 1956, *A Revision of Demand Theory,* Clarendon Press, Oxford.
Hicks, J.R. and R.D.G. Allen, 1934, "A Reconsideration of the Theory of Value", Parts I-II, *Economica*, **1**, Part I, 52-76 and Part II, 196-219.
Jeffrey, Richard C., 1983, *The Logic of Decision*, University of Chicago Press, Chicago.
Kreps, David M. and Evan L. Porteus, 1979, 'Temporal von Neumann-Morgenstern and Induced Preferences', *Journal of Economic Theory*, **20**, 81-109.
Krzysztofowicz, Roman and John B. Koch, 1989, 'Estimation of Cardinal Utility Based on a Nonlinear Theory', *Annals of Operations Research*, 19, 181-204.
Krzysztofowicz, Roman, 1983, 'Strength of Preference and Risk Attitude in Utility Measurement', *Organizational Behavior and Human Performance*, 31, 88-113.
Krzysztofowicz, Roman, 1987, 'Generic Utility and Theory : Explanatory Model Behavioral Hypotheses, Empirical Evidence', Part of this paper was presented to the *Third International Conference on the Foundations and Applications of Utility, Risk and Decision Theories*, Aix-en-Provence, June.
Krzysztofowicz, Roman, 1990, 'Comparative Validation of Six Utility Measurements', *Mimeograph.*
Machina, Mark J., 1981, 'Book Review' "Rational" Decision Making versus "Rational" Decision Modelling?', *Journal of Mathematical Psychology*, **24**, 163-175.
Machina, Mark, 1989, Dynamic Consistency and Non-Expected Utility Models of Choice Under Uncertainty, *Journal of Economic Literature*, XXVII, 1622-1668.
Markowitz, Harry M., 1959, *Portfolio Selection*, Wiley, New York.
Markowitz, Harry M., 1994, *Robin Pope's Findings on Elaborated Outcomes*, presentation to the *Seventh International Conference on the Foundations and Applications of Utility, Risk and Decision Theory,* Norwegian School of Business, Oslo, July 3.
Marschak, Jacob, 1950, 'Rational Behavior, Uncertain Prospects, and Measurable Utility', *Econometrica*, 18(2), 111-141.
Marschak, Jacob and Roy Radner, 1972, *Economic Theory of Teams*, Yale University Press, New Haven.
Marshall, Alfred, 1920 and 1956, *Principles of Economics*, Macmillan and Co., Ltd., London.
Pope, Robin, 1983, 'The Pre-Outcome Period and the Utility of Gambling', in B. Stigum and F. Wenstøp (eds), *Foundations of Utility and Risk Theory with Applications*, Reidel, Dordrecht, 137-177.
Pope, Robin, 1984, 'The Utility of Gambling and of Outcomes: Inconsistent First Approximations', in O. Hagen and F. Wenstøp (eds), *Progress in Utility and Risk Theory*, Reidel, Dordrecht, 251-273.
Pope, Robin, 1985, Timing Contradictions in von Neumann and Morgenstern's Axioms and in Savage's "Sure-Thing" 'Proof', *Theory and Decision*, 18, 229-261.

Pope, Robin, 1988, 'The Bayesian Approach : Irreconcilable With Expected Utility Theory?', in Bertrand R. Munier (ed.), *Risk, Decision and Rationality*, Reidel, Dordrecht, 221-230.

Pope, Robin, 1989, 'Additional Perspectives on Modelling Health Insurance Decisions', in C. Selby-Smith (ed.), *Economics and Health*, Public Sector Management Institute, Monash University, Melbourne, 189-205.

Pope, Robin, 1991a, 'The Delusion of Certainty in Savage's Sure-Thing Principle', *Journal of Economic Psychology*, 12(2), 209-241.

Pope, Robin, 1991b, 'Lowered Welfare under the Expected Utility Procedure', in A. Chikan (ed.), *Progress in Decision, Utility and Risk,* Kluwer, Dordrecht, 125-133.

Pope, Robin, 1992, 'The Elusive Utility of Gambling: A Formal Definition and Consistent Model', paper presented to the *Sixth International Conference on the Foundations and Applications of Utility, Risk and Decision Theory,* École Normale Supérieure de Cachan, Paris.

Pope, Robin, 1995, 'Towards a More Precise Decision Framework: a set of decision models which differentiate between the Disutility of Gambling, Diminishing Marginal Utility and the Keynes-Allais Preference for Safety', *Theory and Decision.*

Pope, R.E., 1996/7b, 'Debates on the Utility of Chance: A Look Back to Move Forward', *Journal for Science of Research (Zeitschrift für Wissenschaftsforschung)*, **11/12**, 43-92, reprinted in J. Götschl ed, 2001, *On the Dynamics of Modern, Complex and Democratic Systems*, Theory and Decision Library, Series A: Philosophy and Methodology of the Social Sciences, Kluwer, Dordrecht,
reprint of 18.

Pope, R.E., 2004, 'Biasses from Omitted Risk Effects in Standard Gamble Utilities', *Journal of Health Economics*, **23**, 695-735.

Ramsey, Frank Plumpton, 1926, 'Truth and Probability', reproduced in 1950, in R. B. Braithwaite (ed.), *The Foundations of Mathematics and other Logical Essays*, The Humanities Press, New York, 156-184.

Richardson, J., 2001, 'Rationalism, Theoretical Orthodoxy and Their Legacy in Cost Utility Analysis', *Centre for Health Program Evaluation Working Paper 93*, Business and Economics Faculty, Monash University, Melbourne.

Samuelson, Paul A., 1952, 'Probability, Utility, and the Independence Axiom', *Econometrica*, 20(4), 670-678.

Samuelson, Paul A., 1983, *Foundations of Economic Analysis*, Harvard Economic Studies, 80, Harvard University Press, Cambridge, Massachusetts, enlarged edition.

Sarin, Rakesh Kumar, 1982, 'Strength of Preference and Risky Choice', *Operations Research*, 30(5), 982-997.

Savage, Leonard J., 1954, *The Foundations of Statistics*, John Wiley & Sons, Inc., New York.

Schneeweiß, H., 1967, *Entscheidungskriterien bei Risiko*, Springer, Berlin.

Schneeweiß, H., 1968a, 'Die Unvertäglichkeit von (m, s))-prinzip und Dominanz-prinzip', *Unternehmensforschung (Operations research)* **12**, 180-184.

Schneeweiß, H., 1968b, 'Note on two dominance principles in decision theory, *Unternehmensforschung (Operations research)* **12**, 213-216.

Schneeweiß, H., 1973a, 'On the Consistency of classical Decision Criteria', *Inference and Decision* **1**,31-44.

Schneeweiß, H., 1973b, 'The (m, s) Decision criterion on the Class of Normal Distributions', *Inference and decision* **1**, 23-30.

Schoemaker, Paul J. H., 1982, 'The Expected Utility Model: Its Variants, Purposes, Evidence and Limitations', *Journal of Economic Literature*, 20(2), 529-563.

Selten, Reinhard, 2001, Konzeptionelle Grundlagen der Spieltheorie Einst und Jetzt (The Conceptual Basis of Game Theory Then and Now), in Dieter Gröske[Ed.], John von Neumanns und Oskar Morgensterns "theory of Games and Economic Behaviour (Verlag Wirtschaft und Finanzen, Berlin), 89-101.

Sen, Amartya, 1970, 1982, "The Impossibility of a Parietian Liberal", *Journal of Political Economy*, **78**, 152-207. Cited from Sen 1982, 285-290.

Sen, Amartya, 1982, *Choice, Welfare and Measurement.* MIT Press, Cambridge and Massachusetts, and Blackwell, Oxford.
Sen, Amartya, 1993, "Internal Consistency of Choice", *Econometrica*, **61**, 495-521.
Sen, Amartya, 2002, *Rationality and Freedom*, Harvard University Press, Cambridge.
Sonnenschein, H., 1973, "Do Walras' identity and continuity characterize the class of community excess demand functions?", *Journal of Economic Theory*, **6**, 345-354.
Stevens, S. S., 1946, 'On the Theory of Scales of Measurement', *Science*, 103 (2684), Friday June 7.
Strotz, Robert H., 1953, 'Recent Developments in Mathematical Economics and Econometrics: An Expository Session. Cardinal Utility', *American Economic Review*, XLIII, 384-397.
Traub, Stefan and C. Seidl, U. Schmidt, P. Groesche, 1999, "Knock-out for Descriptive Utility or Experimental Design Error", Journal of Economics, 70, pp. 109-126.
Von Neumann, John and Oskar Morgenstern, 1944, 1947, 1953 and 1972, *Theory of Games and Economic Behavior*, Princeton University Press, Princeton, New Jersey.
Walsh, V.C., 1996, *Rationality, Allocation and Reproduction*, Clarendon Press, Oxford.
Watson, Stephen R. and Dennis M. Buede, 1987, *Decision Syntheses : the principles and practice of decision analysis*, Cambridge University Press, Cambridge.

** Center European Integration Studies (ZEIb), Walter Flex Str 3, D-53113 Bonn, Germany Robin.Pope@uni-bonn.de, Telephones +49(228)731887, 739218, 9140361, Fax +49-228-731809 http://webserver.econ1.uni-bonn.de/, http://www.zei.de/

FSC
www.fsc.org
MIX
Papier | Fördert
gute Waldnutzung
FSC® C083411

Kolibri 360 GmbH
Ferdinand-Jühlke-Straße 7
99095 Erfurt, Deutschland
produktsicherheit@kolibri360.de